African American Actresses

African American

The Struggle for Visibility, 1900–1960

Actresses

Charlene Regester

INDIANA UNIVERSITY PRESS

Bloomington & Indianapolis

This book is a publication of

Indiana University Press
601 North Morton Street
Bloomington, IN 47404-3797 USA

www.iupress.indiana.edu

Telephone orders   800-842-6796
Fax orders   812-855-7931
Orders by e-mail   iuporder@indiana.edu

∞The paper used in this publication
meets the minimum requirements of the
American National Standard for Information Sciences—Permanence of Paper for
Printed Library Materials, ANSI Z39.48-
1992.

Manufactured in the United States of
America

Library of Congress Cataloging-in-
Publication Data

Regester, Charlene B., [date]
  African American actresses : the struggle
for visibility, 1900-1960 / Charlene
Regester.
    p. cm.
  Includes bibliographical references and
index.
  ISBN 978-0-253-35475-4 (cl : alk. paper)
  — ISBN 978-0-253-22192-6 (pb : alk. paper)
1. African American women in motion
pictures. 2. African American motion
picture actors and actresses—Biography.
3. Actors—United States—Biography.
I. Title.
  PN1995.9.N4R42 2010
  791.4302'8092396073—dc22
  [B]
                                    2009051159

1 2 3 4 5 15 14 13 12 11 10

FOR MY PARENTS

CONTENTS

ACKNOWLEDGMENTS

This project evolved out of my interest in and fascination with African Americans in the early period of cinema history. Reconstructing this experience and noting the contributions of those who were both responsible for the inception of the black screen image and who participated in shaping it is a tribute to and a testament of the struggles they endured, the obstacles they faced, and the barriers they confronted as artists attempting to cultivate their craft while making their mark on the cinema world. The research I conducted involved exhaustive reading of black newspapers, many of which have been preserved on microfilm, uncovering various collections that might reveal interesting material, exploring a number of internet sources, some of which became available after the project was started, collecting death certificates in those instances where such material was available, and locating visual records of the productions these women appeared in whenever possible. A project of this magnitude and that involves a paucity of resources could not have been completed without a number of persons who provided assistance at various stages. I would like to thank those who extended themselves and were instrumental, either directly or indirectly, in making this project possible.

First and foremost, I would like to thank J. Lee Greene, Jane Gaines, Mark Reid, Richard Dyer, and Peter Filene, all of whom read the manuscript at various stages and provided invaluable feedback. Greene, a brilliant scholar, mentor, and advisor who has known me since I was an undergraduate student, has had a tremendous influence on my work, and for his assistance I will always be indebted. Most of all, I hope I have met his expectations. Gaines and I worked together to coedit the *Oscar Micheaux Society Newsletter*, and because of our mutual interest in early black cinema, we joined forces to move black film history from the background to the foreground. I will be eternally grateful for her enthusiasm, support, and influence. It was Reid's valuable insight and thoughtful comments on an early draft of this work that helped shape its later development, for which I will always be indebted. Dyer's work on race and cinema played a major role in shaping my thinking about the black cinema experience, and his critique of a portion of this work proved invaluable. Finally, Filene read a draft of this work from a historian's perspective and provided incredibly useful comments; I cannot thank him enough.

Additionally, I would like to thank numerous colleagues who provided insights, leads, and support, who extended themselves in various ways, and who motivated me to remain encouraged about this project and about my research in general: Robert Allen, Blanche Arons, Nancy K. Bereano, Bernice Bergup, Pearl Bowser, Todd Boyd, Felicia Campbell, Teresa Church, Susan Courtney, Corey Creekmur, William Darity, Zeinabu Irene Davis, Anna Everett, Gloria Gibson, Ron Green, Ed Guerrero, Mae Henderson, Joanne Hershfield, Reginald Hildebrand, Kara Keeling, Arthur Knight, Elspeth Kydd, Julia Lesage, Antonio Lant, Mia Mask, Bishetta Merritt, Charles Musser, Elizabeth Nonas, Colin Palmer, Miriam Petty, Suzanne Regan, Ellen Scott, Beretta Shomade-Smith, Jacqueline Stewart, Precious Stone, Brian Taves, Robin Vander, Harold Woodard, and Michele Wallace.

This project could not have been executed without the staff of the Reference Division and Microforms at Davis Library, the Media Resources Center at the Robert B. House Undergraduate Library at the University of North Carolina–Chapel Hill, to whom I extend my thanks for assisting me in locating the various resources required to complete this project. In particular, Tommy Nixon, Scott Hamilton, Winifred Metz, and Chuck Sockell were instrumental in making sure I received adequate resources. Additional institutional support was provided by the Arts and Humanities Faculty Fellowship and a Research and Study Leave made possible by the Department of African and Afro-American Studies.

Numerous organizations were also instrumental in allowing me to present papers at their conferences that provided the basis for reshaping my thinking about black entertainers in the cinema industry. These include the Society for Cinema and Media Studies, University of Film and Video Association, Popular Culture/American Culture Association, Oscar Micheaux Film Festival, Far West Popular Culture and American Culture Association, and the Modernist Studies Association, among others.

Finally I would to thank editor Jane Behnken and others at Indiana University Press who expressed a genuine interest in this project and made themselves readily available throughout the entire process. Most of all, thanks should be extended to many of my students who may have participated in this project at its various stages by assisting in locating newspaper articles, verifying dates, raising questions, and providing feedback.

African American Actresses

INTRODUCTION

As black women during the first half of the twentieth century struggled to transgress the borders of Otherness and emerge as Hollywood actresses in their own right, the mainstream cinema industry erased, marginalized, and devalued them, denied them cinematic voice, and reduced them to the body. In addition, far too often black actresses' contributions to mainstream cinema have been either minimized or erased in the histories of Hollywood cinema. This examination of representative black actresses in this period seeks to reposition black actresses of the era, who frequently were positioned on screen as a shadow for leading white female screen stars, and to reclaim the space they have been denied in mainstream cinema history by foregrounding their contributions and reversing their invisibility.

Though there were several films written, produced, directed, and financed by blacks during the first half of the twentieth century which obviously included black actresses—notably the "more than forty feature-length films" between 1919 and 1948 by African American filmmaker Oscar Micheaux[1]—this study is concerned not with these black films but with ones by the mainstream film industry. This is not to ignore the contributions of Micheaux's leading black actress, Evelyn Preer, who was elevated to stardom by appearing in his films as well as on stage but whose untimely death interrupted her career as a dramatic actress and kept her from making the transition to Hollywood.[2] Neither is her omission from this study an attempt to disregard the fact that her roles ran the gamut from villain to heroine, an attribute that many black actresses who worked in the Hollywood cinema industry did not have the privilege or luxury to enjoy. Perhaps Preer was spared the subjugation they endured because she escaped the limited venues available to black actresses who did manage to penetrate the Hollywood industry. While she serves as an exemplar of those working outside of Hollywood, the present study is more centrally focused on those who worked within the industry.

Integral to and interconnected in this study are the concepts of shadow and Other. In both their noun and verb forms, shadow and Other have a variety of lexical and theoretical meanings, many of which are appropriate appellations for the form and function of black actresses in Hollywood cinema through the 1960s. As I use the term and concept in this study, a shadow self is a reflection of another subject, darker and less distinct in form and substance than the subject the shadow reflects. In its basic definition, Otherness refers to difference and usually carries an array of negative connotations. Self and Other typically are determined by the positions of the perceiver and the perceived. In the context of race relations in American society, past and present, a white subject is the self and a nonwhite subject is the Other. These subject positions are inscribed in mainstream films prior to the 1960s. From the purview of this study, however, a black subject (actress and character in this instance) is the perceiver and thus is the self, while a white subject (actress and character) is the perceived and therefore is the Other.

It is in mainstream or Hollywood films from before the 1960s that the form and function of the black actress can be seen as a shadow of the Other, with the Other in this regard referring to a leading white female actress/character. In many of these films, the black actress's principal function was—by contrast in language, costume, and behavior—to illuminate or aggrandize the virtue, beauty, morality, sexuality, sophistication, and other qualities embedded in the "whiteness" of the white female actress and character.

Even if she was a mulatto, which many were, the black actress was the "dark" self and usually a negative reflection of the white female Other. From a modified Jungian perspective[3] she was the shadow self of the white Other in that she embodied the negative for qualities such as race, gender, morality, and sexuality, while the white Other embodied the positive values for these qualities. As the white female's opposite, her other self, in some instances she reflected the Other's (conscious or subconscious) repressed emotions and desires and moral and ethical deficiencies, weaknesses, and instincts. Typically cast in a minor role and usually as a maid/subservient, mammy, matriarch, or hypersexualized woman, she remained an indistinct figure, a shadow, in a film's background. By contrast with the leading white character, she was form without substance. Even when moved to the foreground and assigned positive characteristics, as was Louise Beavers (the maid/subservient in *Imitation of Life*, 1934), Hattie McDaniel (the "mammy" in *Gone with the Wind*, 1939), and Ethel Waters (the matriarch in *The Member of the Wedding*, 1952), her form was still that of the "dark" side of the leading lady (visually conveyed in part through her darker complexion), though her function often was to reflect the positivity that the leading character should have and might have suppressed. In this regard, she frequently functioned as the leading character's moral conscience, as Mammy does for Scarlett in *Gone with the Wind*.

In the mid-1940s and later, prominent black actresses in Hollywood films (Lena Horne, Hazel Scott, and Dorothy Dandridge, for example) less often played a maid/subservient, "mammy," or matriarch, yet they still functioned as a shadow for the leading white actress/character. Even in cameo appearances as entertainers disconnected from a film's storyline, their hypersexualized nature shadowed the leading white female character and focused on her "normal" sexuality.

Projections and perceptions of the black actress, of the self and the Other, took an interesting and often inverse turn with the rise of Dorothy Dandridge's career in the early 1950s. Seldom paired on screen with a white leading actress (as were most other black actresses of the period), Dandridge, in her costarring and starring roles, became the Other, the shadow, for the male (usually white but sometimes black) self with whom she was paired. More important, though, she became a shadow of her own self in that the reel and the real, the self and the Other, merged. The line "Life is but a walking shadow, a poor player" (from Shakespeare's play *Macbeth*) seems an appropriate description for Dandridge's life and career. In theater arts, "a poor player" refers to a secondary actor, an understudy. As the reel and the real merged in Dandridge, she never became the lead player in her life (as she did on screen) but remained "a poor player." She did not want to transform into (to "pass" as) a white woman, yet her desire to become the lead player in her life, to have the power and privilege accorded a white female Other, expressed itself in her obsession to marry a white man, which during that time only a white woman could do. This conflation and confusion of the reel and the real, the self and the Other, was a futile desire that led to tragedy in her personal life and to the demise of her screen career.

The present study focuses on selected and representative African American actresses who were commodified both on and off screen. It investigates how they responded to on-screen depictions of their race, gender, and sexuality, interrogates how their on-screen representations intersected with their off-screen lives, and, finally, examines how they were appropriated by Hollywood's white-male-dominated cinema industry. Moreover, as this study examines how these women were constructed on screen and how these cinematic constructions intersected with their off-screen lives, particular attention is paid to the way the press, both black and mainstream, covered the African American actress and contributed to her public profile, which influenced the actresses' own internal struggles.

The cinema industry continually essentialized the black actress's race and gender, reducing her to what a white-male-dominated industry and society considered the essence of her being, from which she sought to escape and thus liberate herself. More specifically, rarely could the black actress expect to be viewed or judged on the basis of her acting talent; instead, the industry always identified her on the basis of her race and sexuality. While it is true that white actresses also were essentialized and endured their own struggles in the industry, black actresses endured struggles in the industry and in the society at large because of both their race and gender. The black actress's additional marginalization because of her race was an unbelievable hardship. This was, after all, a period in which racial segregation was not just accepted—it was expected. The black actress had to be prepared for segregated practices on the studio lot and for accommodations inferior to her white associates, as was documented when black cast members complained during the production of *Hallelujah* (1929).[4] Segregated seating in public transportation, public facilities, and restaurants, as well as pay inequities, complicated the black actress's experience working in the Hollywood industry.

Yet the alienation, ostracization, and marginalization of the black actress did not end with white Hollywood or with racist social practices in white society, but even extended to her press coverage. Black actresses varied in their responses to press criticism, particularly from the black press. Some internalized the criticism while others defended themselves against what they considered harsh and unfair criticism. Black journalists, primarily males, expressed their offense at the disturbing roles in which black actresses appeared, which often were of subservients and harlots to the exclusion of more diverse and redeeming roles and images. The black press and the black community considered such negative representations false and demeaning of blacks in general, and it was highly critical of black actresses for playing such roles. Because of the unique position the black actress was forced to assume in the industry, it is necessary to understand her struggles and to recognize the milieu within which she was forced to work.

The present investigation is guided by a critique of how the black actress was used to appropriate these two variables—race and gender—on screen. The discussions are foregrounded in some instances by drawing upon feminist critiques that evolve from the works of theorists that focus on race. While these theorists may not have written specifically with black women in mind, their ideas nonetheless are useful in the current investigation for deconstructing how the black woman was represented on screen.

Before the mid-1920s, black actresses appeared infrequently in Hollywood cinema. In the era of silent films, when white actresses such as Mary Pickford and Lillian and Dorothy Gish graced the screen, the best-known black actress to emerge was Madame Sul-Te-Wan. When the film industry transitioned to sound in 1927, a new set of white actresses debuted, including, among others, Greta Garbo, Norma Shearer, Colleen Moore, Gloria Swanson, Marie Dressler, Clara Bow, and Pola Negri. By the end of the 1920s, the best-known black actress working in Hollywood films was Nina Mae McKinney, one of the few to work for the major motion picture studios. The 1930s introduced many new white screen actresses, most notably Bette Davis, Joan Crawford, Shirley Temple, Marlene Dietrich, Ginger Rogers, Barbara Stanwyck, Katherine Hepburn, Jean Harlow, Vivien Leigh, Claudette Colbert, Mae West, and Loretta Young. In this decade, black actresses began to gain prominence as the screen companion to (the shadow of) these white actresses; among them were Louise Beavers, Hattie McDaniel, and Fredi Washington. With the beginning of the 1940s, white actresses such as Jane Russell, Lana Turner, Lauren Bacall, Rita Hayworth, Olivia de Havilland, Joan Bennett, Judy Garland, and Ingrid Bergman gained prominence. Only a few black actresses, in particular Lena Horne, Hazel Scott, and Ethel Waters, could be said to approximate this status in the industry. At the dawn of the 1950s, a decade that would be shrouded in the politics of the fear of communism, white actresses such as Elizabeth Taylor, Ava Gardner, Natalie Wood, Doris Day, Debbie Reynolds, and Marilyn Monroe dominated the screen. The black actresses during this decade who garnered comparable attention were Dorothy Dandridge and, perhaps, Eartha Kitt.

Prominent white actress of these decades received widespread popular attention and high critical accolades. Yet in mainstream film history and criticism, there was and is a paucity of critiques and raves for the black actresses who often worked with these actresses and may even be said to have provided the inspiration and support essential to their white counterparts' images.

There are many key investigative questions—with attendant answers—that guide this study. Who were these women prior to the 1960s who "took on" the Hollywood establishment and fought (with different degrees of success) for their place in the world of cinematic entertainment? How did the mainstream cinema industry utilize these women and how were they constructed on screen? How did these black actresses circumvent the racial politics that prevailed? How did they negotiate their dual roles as performers or entertainers who became screen actresses? How did they respond to their on-screen representations? How did they participate in constructing black stardom? How did their on-screen representations intersect with their off-screen lives? How were they constructed in the black press and in the mainstream press? In what ways did they appropriate themselves as black actresses attempting to penetrate the racial boundaries of white Hollywood? What did these black actresses contribute to the black screen image and to the public perceptions of their race? How did these black actresses accentuate the stardom often embodied by the white stars with whom they costarred? This study formulates answers to these questions through a combination of historical and critical examinations of selected black actresses from the cinematic era under consideration.

Prior to the 1960s, very few African American actresses in Hollywood had starring roles or even costarring roles, except in the all-black-cast films

Hollywood produced. The major exception was Dorothy Dandridge, who in the 1950s was assigned roles as leading lady (star and costar) in several films that were not all-black-cast films. In supporting (or costarring) roles, Louise Beavers and Hattie McDaniel are perhaps the most significant exceptions to white Hollywood's practices. In fact, the majority of African American actresses in Hollywood before the 1960s were assigned minor (some even very minor) roles as maids (Carolynne Snowden, Gertrude Howard, Hattie Noels, Libby Taylor, Marietta Canty, Theresa Harris, and Louise Beavers are examples), "primitives" (Laura Bowman, Catherine Curry, Madame Te. Outley), or characters inserted ostensibly for comic relief (such as Butterfly McQueen and Tommie Moore). Several actresses with name appeal as entertainers, such as Lena Horne and Hazel Scott, often were relegated to little more than cameo appearances, inserted in films as a drawing card for voyeuristic spectators.

For this study, I selected nine black actresses that I consider representative of black actresses in Hollywood for the pre-1960 period: Madame Sul-Te-Wan, Nina Mae McKinney, Louise Beavers, Fredi Washington, Hattie McDaniel, Lena Horne, Hazel Scott, Ethel Waters, and Dorothy Dandridge. I chose these actresses based on their popularity, prominence, number of screen roles, and invisibility in Hollywood film histories and critiques. Their popularity and prominence, especially in the black community, were determined by the extensive coverage they received in the press, particularly the black press. While the mainstream press often diminished and sometimes ignored these actresses' professional careers in the cinema industry, the African American press, particularly newspapers with national circulations, provided extensive information, both positive and negative, about their professional careers and personal lives. The black press of this era thus contains a wealth of information about these actresses and their reception in the black community, information noticeably absent from histories and critical studies of the mainstream cinema industry that cover this period. The kind and amount of coverage these women received in African American newspapers of the period allows for a reconstruction of their lives, careers, and public personas.

My selection of the nine actresses included in this study was also dictated by their emergence or appearance during pivotal moments in mainstream film history and at pivotal moments in their professional careers and private lives. Certainly it could be argued with validity that

Butterfly McQueen appeared at the same pivotal moment in mainstream film history as Hattie McDaniel—in *Gone with the Wind*—and that McQueen is as well-known among audiences now as is McDaniel. Though both played roles in this landmark film, and in other films that the black press and the black community castigated as demeaning to the race, Hattie McDaniel, I submit, is the more representative choice for the purposes of my study. McDaniel received an Academy Award for her performance, and press coverage of her as an actress (and thus her standing in the black community) is much fuller and more accessible than that of McQueen.[5]

With the exception of Eartha Kitt (whose career largely falls outside the period under study) and Butterfly McQueen (who landed a number of screen roles), black actresses of the period not included in this study were and are less well-known than the actresses I include as representative. From perspectives other than mine, the acting careers of Eartha Kitt, Jeni LeGon, Etta McDaniel (Hattie McDaniel's sister), Butterfly McQueen, Etta Moten, Hattie Noel, Lillian Randolph, Amanda Randolph, Valaida Snow, Carolynne Snowden, Maxine Sullivan, Libby Taylor, Edna Thomas, and Laura Bowman, among others, are also important and deserving of study. My study does not intend through its selection to further marginalize these women or to assert that the ones chosen for study were the most or the only important black actresses in mainstream cinema of this period.

Criteria such as those listed above, in addition to space limitations, guided my decision about which actresses to include and which to exclude. I hope that my choice of actresses will encourage and spawn inquiry into the professional and personal lives of African American actresses of the period who were and are less well-known than the ones I have chosen, and who are also deserving of study for their place in American mainstream cinema.

I devote chapter 1 to Madame Sul-Te-Wan, who was one of the first African American actresses to garner a motion picture contract with the mainstream cinema industry during the silent era and who appeared in the infamous landmark film *The Birth of a Nation* (1915). Sul-Te-Wan was one of the few African American actresses to make the transition from the silent to the sound era of filmmaking, and she was awarded screen roles as late as the 1950s, a time when most white actresses whose careers began with hers were no longer marketable in the industry. As a screen actress,

Sul-Te-Wan's early career is indicative of the "invisibility" imposed on black actresses in the industry and to which many black actresses who followed her in Hollywood were subjected. My use of "invisible" as a critical term refers not just to the erasure of a subject but also, and more importantly, to the reinscription or reconfiguration and projection of the subject as someone other than the authentic self. As Ralph Ellison uses the term in *Invisible Man* (1952), invisibility refers to the perceiver's tendency to recreate a black subject from the perceiver's own imagination. In my application of the term and concept to this study, the perceiver is the creator of a Hollywood film who projects the black actress (maid, mammy, sex object) as a figment of his (most were male) imagination. While such "creation" is inherent in the film industry, it takes on a heavily negative tone in reference to race and gender. It is the bedrock of black image control by the mainstream film industry that extended to the black community at large. This negativity extended from Sul-Te-Wan to the other black actresses included in this study. Sul-Te-Wan's vehement rejection of this invisibility, and of the typecasting (maids, exotics, wanton women) to which she and others of the era were subjected, established a pattern that some subsequent actresses followed and some failed to follow after the introduction of sound ("talkie") pictures.

Sul-Te-Wan epitomizes the image of Otherness that plagued most black actresses in mainstream cinema before the 1960s, most of whom were cast in roles (e.g., subservients, exotics, sex objects) that projected them as shadows to aggrandize a film's white leading lady. But, as Toni Morrison maintains, definitions belong to the perceivers and the definers, not to the perceived and the defined.[6] As such, many black actresses resisted on-screen and off-screen definitions of themselves as Other.

Sul-Te-Wan is at the beginning of a long line of African American actresses whose screen roles projected the concept of racial Otherness, both in a film's plot structure as well as for white spectators to indulge their self-concepts and their racial and sexual fantasies. What Sul-Te-Wan represented in terms of feeding white males' racial and sexual fantasies for the period under consideration reaches a pinnacle in the screen roles assigned to Dorothy Dandridge, the subject of this study's last chapter. Dandridge is also representative (almost singularly) of how the African American actress finally evolved on screen from a shadow for the leading white actress to a film's costar and star in her own right.

Chapter 2 is devoted to Nina Mae McKinney, whose life and screen career epitomize the reinvention of the (black) self as the (white) Other. For McKinney, as for some other black actresses of this period, the reel and the real merged and assumed different configurations as conceptions of the self and the Other, of on-screen and off-screen personae, became intertwined under the rubrics of race (McKinney and Fredi Washington), sexuality (Dandridge is a prime example), and class (McDaniel and Ethel Waters). In some instances, the intertwining became an inverse relationship as the actress (such as Sul-Te-Wan and Louise Beavers) resisted becoming or being defined as the type of film character she usually played.

While most black actresses before the 1960s functioned on screen as a shadow for the leading white actress, this is not to say that no black actress in Hollywood films before Dandridge landed a role as costar of a film. Indeed, Louise Beavers, the subject of chapter 3, rose to this level in *Imitation of Life,* a film that has been the subject of numerous investigations and has been vigorously interrogated in terms of race, class, and gender (manifestations of Otherness), subjects germane to studies of African American actresses in mainstream cinema prior to the 1960s (and after). *Imitation of Life*—and thus Louise Beavers—holds a significant place in film history, feminist theory and criticism, and racial representation. This film and Beavers's performance in it sparked extensive controversy and coverage in the black press and in the black community, with one controversy being Hollywood's failure to acknowledge the outstanding performances of black actresses by bestowing on them the industry's most prestigious award, a controversy that reignited when the industry did recognize Hattie McDaniel's outstanding performance in *Gone with the Wind.*

Imitation of Life was indeed another pivotal moment in Hollywood film history, and thus another black actress in this film, Fredi Washington, put the discussion of race and mainstream cinema on another trajectory. The discussion already had begun with Nina Mae McKinney, the subject of chapter 2, who was the first African American actress to assume a leading role in a Hollywood film, although an all-black-cast film, *Hallelujah* (1929). McKinney was a mulatto and was projected on screen as an object of primarily white male spectators' sexual desire. This was an on-screen role several subsequent black actresses played, a role that became as mired in controversy as that of the black maid. The new trajectory that the race-sex-cinema nexus took with Fredi Washington, to whom chapter 4 is devoted, was "passing." Washington's role as a black who passes for white contributed to a continuing fascination with this subject as well as heated and continuing discussion of the use of white actors and actresses in "black" roles to the neglect of black actors and actresses, a discussion that began as early as *The Birth of a Nation*. The concepts of mask and masquerade are integral to Fredi Washington's most notable screen role and to the psychological and social dilemmas she faced in her private life. Consistent with the idea of film as a fiction, the mask refers to a temporary camouflaging of the true self, and the masquerade refers to a sustained camouflaging of the true self. The chapter focuses on the concepts of masks and masquerades and interrogates the extent to which Washington, a white mulatto, did or did not internalize the role for which she is best known. The chapter also seeks to augment the relative paucity of information available on Washington in historical and critical venues.

The concepts of mask and masquerade, and of racial identity in its many manifestations, were issues germane to the black community of this era. Their significance in the black community and the black press was not limited to the issue of passing but also included issues of how a black actress's on-screen roles reflected on the entire black community. The self-mask controversy ranged from actresses such as Hattie McDaniel, who was accused of "being" the "mammy" figure she represented on screen, to Dorothy Dandridge, whom many (including this author) assumed internalized the typecast roles she played on screen.

I devote chapter 5 to Hattie McDaniel, one of the most recognizable African American names in Hollywood cinema of this era. McDaniel's role in *Gone with the Wind* and other films is at the heart of the controversy over how and why the mainstream film industry has used and continues to use black actors and actresses in roles the black community finds demeaning. It is at the heart of a controversy that is not limited to films of this era or to roles as maids and "mammies," but extends to post-1960s visual media to what is known as black exploitation films; to television shows; to the demeaning of black women as prostitutes and black men as thugs, criminals, and drug addicts—all to the relative neglect of more redeeming and diverse representations.

Louise Beavers played a maid in *Imitation of Life*; Hattie McDaniel played a "mammy" in *Gone with the Wind*. The two roles and actresses in them are representative of distinctions the black community and the black press made about the negativity of black female images on screen. Both were acclaimed for how well they played the roles assigned to them, yet both were criticized for playing such roles. Yet such roles were marketable to those white viewing audiences that perceived the black race as subservient and certainly as inferior to whites. One principal criticism leveled against McDaniel was that in her Oscar-winning performance she centered the black (female in particular) as Other. Her rejoinder was that she subverted the Otherness embedded in her character and that she moved this character type from the margins to the center. Also accused of commodifying Otherness (or blackness) through her role in *The Member of the Wedding*, Ethel Waters, to whom chapter 8 is devoted, made a counterargument similar to McDaniel's. Beavers, McDaniel, and Waters in several other ways represent, particularly physiologically, the antithesis of what the mainstream film industry (then and now) considered and treated as a commodification of the black female body. Perhaps the irony is that these three actresses were among the few allowed to "act" in major roles in Hollywood films before about 1950 and the advent of Dorothy Dandridge's acting career.

Lena Horne and Hazel Scott, the subjects of chapters 6 and 7 respectively, are representative of those black actresses during the pre-1960 period who negotiated lucrative contracts with major Hollywood studios that excluded them from playing roles (particularly maids and "mammies") that blacks considered demeaning of the race. They also are representative of Hollywood's accelerated commodification of the black body as a site for white males' sexual fantasies. In addition, these two actresses represent Hollywood's move to capitalize on black female entertainers of a certain physiological type (mulattoes—though Scott may not necessarily be categorized as such) who had a built-in box office appeal. Neither was given extensive acting roles, though Horne was given more than Scott in that she was featured prominently in all-black-cast films, and typically they had roles not directly related to the film's storyline. Such roles were and could be edited from the films when they were shown in the South. While southern filmgoers welcomed images of maids and "mammies," such as those played by Beavers and McDaniel, they were averse to images of blacks who did not fit this mold. Beautiful, talented, well-spoken, and with an air of confidence and pride, Horne and Scott certainly did not fit the image of blacks that southern whites (and many northern ones) relished.

Horne and Scott also represent the actualization of African American actresses' protest against how they were treated by Hollywood as well as by the society at large. Both resisted proscriptive measures leveled against them because of their race, but neither was successful in prompting Hollywood to significantly alter for the better its practice of representing black actresses on screen. Basically denied dramatic or even substantive acting parts—roles Hollywood reserved for those black actresses who physiologically fit Hollywood's notion of maid, "mammy," and matriarch—Horne and Scott and other mulatto entertainers-turned-actresses were assigned essentially cameo roles that showcased not only their singing and dancing talents but also, and especially, their sexual appeal. It was this kind of exploitation that largely motivated Horne to reject Hollywood and that largely motivated Hollywood to reject Scott.

Though several African American actresses of the period publicly criticized Hollywood and the white American public for its treatment of blacks, Hazel Scott took the criticism to unprecedented levels for a black actress. In fact, one might say that Scott's representative significance for this study is that she was more an activist than an actress, actualizing and bringing to the fore the dismay and disgust that her fellow black actresses felt. Chapter 7 gives concentrated attention to Scott's activism, in part to reveal the complexity and magnitude of issues that centered on black actresses (race and sex in particular), radiated to society at large, and that were debated in the black press, in the black community, in Hollywood, and in American society at large during this era.

Dorothy Dandridge is the subject of this study's final chapter. Dandridge—along with Lena Horne, Hazel Scott, and a few others—belonged to what Hattie McDaniel characterized as the "new Negro womanhood" in the Hollywood of the period: a new generation of actresses that gradually replaced the group to which McDaniel belonged. An interrogation of Dandridge's life and career is a fitting conclusion to this study. Dandridge is on the border between periods of change and lack of change for black actresses in Hollywood, just before the surge in civil rights and women rights movements of the 1960s. She represents change in that she becomes Hollywood's "dark" star, a leading lady in films, many of which were with white male costars. She represents the lack of change in that Hollywood commodifies her body for sale to voyeuristic gazers, especially white male ones. Like some of her predecessors with similar Eurocentric features, she is cast in many roles that erase her racial identity as a black and project her on screen as some other racial minority.

Dandridge perhaps represents the extreme of the debilitating toll Hollywood exacted from black actresses of the era. The related concepts of mask and masquerade that help configure this study's discussions of Fredi Washington and Hattie McDaniel are integral to its discussion of Dorothy Dandridge. Washington, McDaniel, and others, in response to accusations from the black press and the black community, proclaimed that they were merely wearing the masks of and masquerading as the characters they portrayed. For Dandridge, however, the mask fused with the person. Though she never attempted to masquerade as white (internally or externally), she nevertheless wore in her private life several of the various masks she assumed on screen.

In several ways, Dandridge's chapter is a culmination of issues explored in previous chapters. The black press accused several actresses and actors of this period of accepting demeaning roles in order to advance their careers. Some denied the accusation and a few admitted it, giving the excuse or reason that the duty of an actress or actor was to play the role assigned. Horne admitted marrying a white man in order to advance her career. Dandridge was obsessed with marrying a white man and admitted that she would relinquish her acting career if she could obtain this object of her unending desire. Ethel Waters infused her character Berenice (*The Member of the Wedding*) with aspects of her own biography, but the reverse was true for Dandridge, whose characters infused her off-screen life. Perhaps more than any other actress included in this study, Dandridge as actress and person warrants a psychological profile.

Though it is not the intent of this study, psychological profiles of these actresses perhaps would reveal deep-seated trauma induced during their early lives that impacted their adult lives and careers. One cannot help but notice that many of the actresses included in this study were children of parents who divorced, and most of them became divorcées. No doubt the pressures from careers and a spouse's competing career are partly to blame for these failed marriages, but other factors seem also to be at work, factors that other studies of these actresses might choose to pursue.

Most of the black actresses who preceded Dandridge and who were contemporaneous with her functioned as shadows for their white co-stars, particularly female costars. Once her acting career accelerated, Dandridge was not cast as a shadow for a leading white female star. She became a star in her own right, though a "dark" one, and she became a shadow for herself.

The African American press (specifically nationally circulated news-papers) is probably the most valuable source for contemporary informa-tion about the careers and lives of these actresses. I rely heavily on this source. Both its advantages and disadvantages as a major source are that it was current with the actresses' lives and careers without the mediation of historical and critical hindsight. The black press, however, cannot be absolved of commodifying these actresses. The careers and especially the lives of celebrities are grist for the media mill, and black newspapers of this era and later ones printed what they considered marketable to the public. As such, these papers contain a wealth of detailed information (some true, some not true) about the private lives of these actresses. Be-cause their format is different from newspapers, black magazines of the period provide more expansive coverage of aspects of the private lives of the actresses and thus are another valuable source of information on which I rely. For the pre-1960 period, one should not underestimate the power of the black press, not only to reveal information about the ac-tresses, but also to shape (make or break) their images within the black community and perhaps to have more than minimal influence on their public perception outside the black community.

One might wonder, given the issue within the black community of the ostensible preference for and privilege of those blacks, especially women, whose European ancestry was discernible, if the black press dem-onstrated any bias in the amount and content of its coverage. Evidence shows that the press was far less concerned with issues of intraracial privilege and preference than with issues of interracial privilege and pref-erence. The press was less concerned with the appearance of an actress's body than with how that actress represented the black race on screen and off screen, and this overriding concern dictated the amount and content of its coverage. The black press expressed dismay about Louise Beavers being excluded from Oscar nominations for supporting actress in *Imitation of Life* and about Dorothy Dandridge being excluded from

Oscar nominations for lead actress in *Porgy and Bess* (1959). The black press expressed elation about Hattie McDaniel's winning the Oscar for a supporting role in *Gone with the Wind* (though it was very critical of her for playing the role) and for Dorothy Dandridge's being nominated for the Golden Globe award for best actress in a musical (*Porgy and Bess*) and being nominated for an Oscar for best actress in a leading role in *Carmen Jones* (1954).

There are biographies or autobiographies or both for most of the actresses centered in this study, and this study is merely designed to add to the existing body of literature. Its intent is to fill a void that currently exists in cinema history because despite the existence of a number of biographies or autobiographies, few studies critically examine black actresses and how they were positioned both on screen and within the larger cinema industry. For example, recent works that have focused on black actresses frequently explore black women who performed on stage, as does Karen Sotiropoulos's *Staging Race: Black Performers in Turn of the Century America* (2006). In it she explores how black performers, such as Aida Overton Walker, manipulated the stage mask to create a dialogue that spoke to black audiences and that critiqued the racism implied in the performance. Jayna Brown's *Babylon Girls: Black Women Performers and the Shaping of the Modern* (2008) similarly explores the black woman on stage by examining performers such as Ida Forsyne, Valaida Snow, Josephine Baker, and Florence Mills, among others, to interrogate how the black body in motion coincided with ideas of the modern city space and politics of black cultural self-representation.

Other literature that explores the black female actress includes biographies such as Bennetta Jules-Rosette's examination of Josephine Baker in *Josephine Baker in Art and Life—The Icon and Image* (2007) that focus on the single black actress and that more broadly focus on her image beyond the screen. More recently, Karen Chilton's biography *Hazel Scott: The Pioneering Journey of a Jazz Pianist from Café Society to Hollywood to the HUAC* (2008) provides an examination of Scott's life and career in its entirety rather than focusing exclusively on her films. Jill Watts explored the complexity of Hattie McDaniel in *Hattie McDaniel: Black Ambition, White Hollywood* (2005). Donald Bogle's *Dorothy Dandridge: A Biography* (1997) attempts to provide a comprehensive critique of Dandridge and her life as well as interrogate her imperfections.

Kwakiutl L. Dreher, in *Dancing on the White Page: Black Women Entertainers Writing Autobiography* (2008), examines black female entertainers (Lena Horne, Dorothy Dandridge, Eartha Kitt, Diahann Carroll, Mary Wilson, and Whoopi Goldberg) who have written autobiographies and explores how these biographical works then become choreographed representations of their lives. Dreher's is more specifically focused on the storytelling process as unveiled in these biographical works and how these works inform who these women really are and how they see themselves.

Earlier works on black women and the cinema industry that assumed a more political position frequently explored black women as spectators, as did Jacqueline Bobo's *Black Women as Cultural Readers* (1995) and *Black Women Film and Video Artists* (1998), with the earlier work examining how black women as audiences or spectators responded to representations on screen and the later work examining the contributions of black women and video artists who have struggled to cultivate their own images of themselves. Similarly assuming a political stance, Kara Keeling's *The Witch's Flight* (2007) critiques the black femme in cinematic images as a means of exploring the possibilities for survival, identities, communities, etc., in more contemporary representations.

More recently, Mia Mask's *Divas on Screen* (2009) examines black actresses in cinema starting with Dandridge and examining actresses in the post-1960s era. Exploring black women in black exploitation films, Stephane Dunn's *"Baad Bitches" and Sassy Supermamas* (2008) is more narrowly focused on the role women played in these films and the implications of their representations.

Deviating from a study of black women specifically to a broader examination of the industry at large and its racial politics, Cedric J. Robinson in his *Forgeries of Memory and Meaning: Blacks and the Regimes of Race in American Theater & Film Before World Ward II* (2007) interweaves the contributions of black women to the black screen image in his discussion of how finance and capital at the center of American commerce in the late nineteenth and early twentieth centuries dictated the successive racial regimes popularized in motion pictures. Utilizing a similar approach, Anna Everett, in *Returning the Gaze: A Genealogy of Black Film Criticism, 1909–1949* (2001), explores the contributions of the black actress to the cinema industry in her larger discussion of black film criticism. Everett explores early film literature produced by black journalists and contends that these journalists returned the camera's gaze in their critique of how blacks were represented on screen. Her study is relevant to the present study only to the extent that it similarly exploits the black press to recapture the black cinematic experience.

This evolving body of literature would not be complete without noting those early scholars and historians who paved the way and similarly contributed to the study of the black screen actress, specifically Bogle's *Brown Sugar* (1980, expanded in 2007), *Bright Boulevards: The Story of Black Hollywood* (2005), and *Toms, Coon, Mulattoes, Mammies and Bucks* (2001 [1973]). Thomas Cripps's *Slow Fade to Black: The Negro in American Film, 1900–1942* (1993 [1977]) and *Making Movies Black: The Hollywood Message Movie From World War II to the Civil Rights Era* (1993) incorporated the black actress into his larger discussion of black cinema history, with the earlier work examining black survivors in the industry, the growing black protest to the industry, the underground film movement, and the struggle to reconcile film as art with the racial politics that prevailed. Henry Sampson's *Blacks in Black and White: A Source Book on Black Films* (1995) attempted to compile and synthesize the contributions of African Americans to all-black-cast films that frequently served as alternatives to those produced by the larger Hollywood cinema industry. The present study builds on this literature, but intends to foreground how selected black actresses were positioned on screen, how they commodified race, how they negotiated the industry in order to establish themselves as black actresses in an industry over which they had little control, and how their off-screen lives sometimes intersected with their on-screen image.

ONE

Madame Sul-Te-Wan

THE STRUGGLE FOR VISIBILITY

In the prologue to Ralph Ellison's classic American novel *Invisible Man* (1952), the nameless protagonist laments that he is "invisible . . . simply because people refuse to see me. . . . When they approach me they see only my surroundings, themselves, or figments of their imagination—indeed, everything and anything except me."[1] In the novel's last line he strongly suggests that his dilemma as an invisible African American applies not just to him but to most, if not all, American blacks.[2] The invisibility of which Ellison's protagonist speaks, and which he dramatizes through different episodes that reflect the chronological history of American blacks through the first half of the twentieth century, is an apt assessment of blacks in the American film industry, and particularly of the life (1873–1959) and career (1915–1959) of the black film actress Madame Sul-Te-Wan.

In the early years of American cinema, the mainstream (Hollywood) film industry frequently prohibited African American actors and actresses from depicting themselves on the screen. Such denial was a means the industry used to render African Americans invisible, as white actors often assumed black roles in blackface. This performative behavior was empowering to whites because it allowed them to vicariously experience blackness. At the same time, it was disempowering to blacks because whites ultimately controlled the black image.

Though generally forced to occupy a space of invisibility, some black actors were able to penetrate the boundaries of Otherness. Madame Sul-Te-Wan exemplifies an African American actress who, although deprivileged, emerged as a screen figure of note. While Hollywood made every attempt to render her invisible, she proved to be indomitable and established visibility for herself against all odds. This chapter examines Sul-Te-Wan's first screen role in *The Birth of a Nation* (1915); her subsequent screen roles as a subservient, multiracial, and evil character; and her exclusion from mainstream press film reviews to demonstrate how she attempted to render herself visible despite being made invisible.

Though the available facts of her birth and parentage are not definitive, it seems Madame Sul-Te-Wan was born Nellie Wan on March 7, 1873,[3] in Louisville, Kentucky. Reportedly, her father, Silas Crawford Wan, was a traveling Hindu minister and her mother, ostensibly an African American, was Mary Kennedy of Kentucky.[4] Some sources claim that her father was of "mixed race himself, he being one of the simmering millions from Mother India and from the land of romance, Hawaii,"[5] but Sul-Te-Wan usually is and was considered an African American.[6] She capitalized on her ambiguous background both by adopting her unusual name and by appropriating her mixed ancestry. She used her name to negotiate for "East Indian, American Indian, Spanish, African, and Negro character roles."[7] Sul-Te-Wan, regarded as a true cosmopolite, once [declared], "I carry no antagonism to anyone because of their skin and I don't get any from them."[8]

Sul-Te-Wan's association with the theatrical world began when she assisted her widowed mother in preparing laundry for white actresses, often delivering their laundry to the stage door.[9] Such exposure allowed her to observe their performances so that she could return to school and act out what she had witnessed on stage. Because her mother could not afford acting and dance lessons, Sul-Te-Wan gleaned inspiration and technique from white actresses such as Mary Anderson and Fanny Davenport. Given Sul-Te-Wan's natural talent, these actresses influenced the mayor of Louisville, James Whalen, to provide Sul-Te-Wan with an audition at the Buckingham Theater among some twenty-five buck and wing dance contestants. After Sul-Te-Wan emerged from the contest a winner, her mother agreed to allow her to work on stage intermittently, and later, impressed with her daughter's talent, she decided to move to Cincinnati, Ohio, to further her daughter's career.[10]

Sul-Te-Wan performed at a number of theaters as well as at the Dime Museum, where she was referred to as "the little dancing protégé of Mary Anderson and Fanny Davenport."[11] Promoting herself as "Creole Nell," she later joined the Three Black Cloaks Company. When Davenport recruited her to appear in a production in Cincinnati, Sul-Te-Wan accepted the offer. As Sul-Te-Wan gained some acting experience, she formed her own company, the Black Four Hundred, which consisted of sixteen performers and twelve musicians. Following her formation of this company, she organized a minstrel group that toured the East Coast.[12] It was during these tours that she married Robert Reed Conley, and they had three sons: Otto, Onest, and James (though some reports suggest that she bore eight children).[13] The couple relocated to Arcadia, California, but after residing in California for two years, Conley abandoned her when their youngest son was only three weeks old.[14]

As an abandoned wife and mother, Sul-Te-Wan sought help from J. W. Coleman, an employment agent who got assistance for her from the Forum Club, an organization devoted to cultural presentations and designed to assist those in need of food and shelter. Adamant that her family would not accept charity, Sul-Te-Wan agreed to her oldest son's proposal that the family sing for the attendees at the Forum Club in order to earn the benefits the family received. Later, she received assistance from the Associated Charities in Los Angeles, which moved her to Los Angeles, where she worked at the Pier Theater in the Venice region of California. Although money was scarce and acting opportunities were few, Sul-Te-Wan was uncomfortable receiving charity.[15]

Sul-Te-Wan's determination to work as an entertainer to provide for her family brought her into contact with white filmmaker D. W. Griffith. A circus affiliate, Dad Reddy, encouraged her to meet Griffith if she intended to work in motion pictures. Knowing that Griffith and Reddy were already acquaintances, she approached Griffith when he was filming *The Birth of a Nation* (1915).[16]

Reports vary about their first meeting. According to one report, when Sul-Te-Wan entered the studio she promoted herself as being "an African queen, East Indian Princess, or [member] of a circus side-show."[17] She wore a red satin turban, long straight braids that nearly reached her knees, and shiny gold earrings—a reflection of her aesthetic appeal, eccentricity, and affinity for dramatic flair.[18] Another version of this meeting contends that she pleaded with Griffith for employment, saying, "I know I ain't nothin' to look at, Mr. Griffith. Half what I'm wearin' is borrowed and the other half not paid for. But I got three little boys, and I need work—I need work bad. I'll do anythin'—anythin'—of course, nothin' that ain't decent and Christian."[19] Following her death, one report in the African American press presented a different version of Sul-Te-Wan's introduction to Griffith, claiming that she declared, "I know I'm no actress, but if I could only be your cook."[20] Perhaps the press was reflecting its own biases regarding Griffith, whom they disliked for his racially provocative *The Birth of a Nation* and for what they believed was his limited vision of African Americans as purely servile and dangerous.

Whichever version is accurate, Sul-Te-Wan's appearance, which was undoubtedly eccentric, was not offensive to Griffith. In response to her request for employment, he immediately hired her—at first as a maid to the white actresses employed with the Fine Arts studios, including Lillian and Dorothy Gish, Bessie Love, Mildred Harris, Pauline Starke, and Alma Rubens. In this capacity, Sul-Te-Wan performed a variety of services. She would "powder Bessie Love's back, hook up Mildred Harris, unhook Winnifred Westover and press a wrinkle out of Miss Gish's costume."[21] James Snead insightfully notes that both on and off screen "the dominant 'I' needs the coded 'other' to function: white female stars (themselves coded as subordinate to white males) employ black maids to make them seem more authoritatively womanly."[22] Therefore, it was in this capacity that Sul-Te-Wan worked for these white actresses and made her debut in the cinema industry. The personal nature of her relationship with these white actresses attests both to her indispensability to them and to her invisibility—she provided a service upon which they relied and she assumed a much less powerful position relative to these highly visible stars. Having first obtained only an entry-level position, she went on to obtain a seven-year contract with the studio as an actress,[23] becoming one of the first African Americans to land a contract with a major motion picture studio.[24] Not surprisingly for the times, she secured her first screen role in *The Birth of a Nation* as a maid, but despite the role's marginality, it enabled her to demonstrate her talent.

It seems that from the beginning of their acquaintance, an immediate and sustained affection between Sul-Te-Wan and Griffith developed, one of mutual and genuine admiration and affection. The affection Griffith had for her extended to her children, who on occasion referred to Griffith as "papa," an appellation this surrogate father welcomed.[25] Sul-Te-Wan was his bedside companion at his death, and she collapsed during the

Hollywood memorial service in his honor. Indeed, the beleaguered black actress and the "cock of the walk" white filmmaker had a strong and lasting relationship, and this may have enabled Sul-Te-Wan to sustain her long career in Hollywood. Yet the relationship between these two could not have prevented her from being rendered invisible—marginalized, devalued, and decentered. It was she, and she alone, who accomplished the feat of using her talent to establish her career. It is of note that Donald Bogle also hints as this paradoxical relationship between Sul-Te-Wan and Griffith.[26]

After establishing her acting career, at some point Sul-Te-Wan married for a second time, to a German, Count William Holt, who died shortly after their marriage.[27] In the later years of her career, reports revealed that she "mortgaged her Beverly Hills home to finance a stage failure, made her comeback as a chorus girl at 63, and married a Frenchman [an interior designer], Antone Ebenthur, at 70, only to divorce him three years later."[28]

In 1915, Sul-Te-Wan embarked on a long and illustrious screen career. Between 1915 and 1920, she appeared in several films, including *Up from the Depths* (1915), *Hoodoo Ann* (1916), *Intolerance* (1916), *The Children Pay* (1916), *The Marriage Market* (1917), *Stage Struck* (1917), and *Male and Female* (1919). In the 1920s, Sul-Te-Wan made her indelible mark in the cinema world, appearing in *Manslaughter* (1922), *The Narrow Street* (1924), *Lightning Rider* (1924), *Uncle Tom's Cabin* (1927), *Drums of Love* (1928), and *Queen Kelly* (1929), among others. Her work as an actress became even more prolific in the 1930s, and she often appeared in multiple films during a single year, including *Children of Pleasure* (1930), *The Thoroughbred* (1930), *Sarah and Son* (1930), *Heaven on Earth* (1931), *Women Go On Forever* (1931), *The Pagan Lady* (1931), *Employees' Entrance* (1932), *King Kong* (1933), *Ladies They Talk About* (1933), *The World Moves On* (1934), *Imitation of Life* (1934), *Black Moon* (1934), *So Red the Rose* (1935), *Maid of Salem* (1937), *In Old Chicago* (1938), and *Tell No Tales* (1939). Though she landed fewer film roles in the 1940s than in the previous two decades, she did appear in *Safari* (1940), *Maryland* (1940), *King of the Zombies* (1941), *Revenge of the Zombies* (1943), and *Mighty Joe Young* (1949).

By the 1950s, Sul-Te-Wan's screen career was on the decline, yet she still managed to be cast in films such as *Carmen Jones* (1954), *Something of Value* (1957), *Band of Angels* (1957), *The Buccaneer* (1958), *Tarzan and the Trappers* (1958), and *Porgy and Bess* (1959).[29] *Porgy and Bess* was her final screen role. She died February 1, 1959, at the Motion Picture Actors' Home in San Francisco Valley as a result of a paralytic stroke,[30] survived by her son Onest Conley.[31] In the aftermath of her death, more than two hundred people attended a Hollywood banquet to honor her, including Louise Beavers, Rex Ingram, Mae Marsh, Eugene Pallette, Jeff McDonell, and Maude Eburn.[32]

SUL-TE-WAN IN *THE BIRTH OF A NATION*

The film industry's disempowering of African American actors and actresses during the pre-1950 period has resulted in a partial erasure of its own history. Sul-Te-Wan, unfortunately, presents a prime example of this erasure. Even with her first film, *The Birth of a Nation,* it is only through rare and obscure reports that we know of her work in the film. For example, I am beholden to Delilah L. Beasley's *Negro Trailblazers of California* for reporting that in *The Birth of a Nation,* Sul-Te-Wan wore a fine gown to represent a colony of educated African Americans and she drove her own coach in a scene designed to reflect upon the "advancement" of African Americans during the postbellum period—a scene that was edited from the film's final version.[33] One synopsis of *The Birth of a Nation* reveals that Sul-Te-Wan played the role of a "Negro woman with Gypsy 'Shawl,'" and Fred Silva similarly notes that she did in fact have a role in the film. Melvyn Stokes reports that Sul-Te-Wan was visible in at least three shots in the film.[34] Raymond Lee provides a firsthand report of her performance during the production of the film:

> Madame tried to spit. No spit. She tried three times. Still no spit. Griffith's lids pinched his eyes. Madame tried again to spit. She whined that Miss Crowell was too nice a lady to spit at, besides she never thought working in pictures meant spitting at people. Griffith poked another hole in his straw hat. Madame thought her acting days were over before they started. Miss Crowell told her just to relax, it was only make-believe and she didn't mind it at all. Madame failed again. . . . When [Bert Sutch] came back, he handed Madame a piece of soap. . . . Madame got real mad then. . . . She got madder and madder and by the time the scene was shot, she nearly blinded Miss Crowell with her soaped up spit.[35]

Aside from these reports, there is barely any mention of Sul-Te-Wan with respect to this film.

The Birth of a Nation was one of the most disturbing films in American cinema because of the racial debate it provoked; surely her part as racial Other should be a significant part not only of her own story but also of the film's history.

According to Ed Guerrero,

> The insecurity and economic turmoil rampant throughout the postbellum South had undermined the white southern male's role as provider for his family; thus he sought to inflate his depreciated sense of manhood by taking up the honorific task of protecting White Womanhood against the newly constructed specter of the "brute Negro." The historian Joel Williamson notes that Thomas Dixon's novels [upon which the film was based] and lectures translated this political, psychological background, as well as his own racial pathology, into a fanatical campaign to save White Womanhood by punishing the black incipient rapist.[36]

Thus, *The Birth of a Nation* was born—a film that according to Guerrero became "a focal point of black intellectual and social energies organized to protest the codified racism of a powerful, nascent film technology and industry. African Americans and an array of concerned citizens were challenged to answer these new expressions of racism with new discourses, critiques, and political strategies."[37]

Following its release, the film met with strong resistance in Los Angeles from African Americans who objected to its racist representations. Outraged, they saw it as an attack on their public profile. They targeted their criticisms toward specific scenes they found objectionable—including the Ku Klux Klan's ride to rescue the white South in the aftermath of the Civil War; African Americans stuffing ballot boxes to alter political elections; a white female who escapes a black rapist and decides to leap to her death rather than confront her black attacker; and black legislators who drink alcohol, eat fried chicken, and prop their bare feet on desktops during legislative sessions, indicative of their disrespect for the political system. Concerned that there might be a displacement of such representations onto them in the real world, African Americans lobbied for censorship of Griffith's picture.[38]

Such extreme measures to silence his racially inciting film greatly disturbed Griffith, and he responded by targeting the one black actress in his employ, Sul-Te-Wan. Through her association with the film, Sul-Te-Wan automatically became the one he considered guilty of instigating the African American resistance. The implication seemed to be that most African Americans would not have the insight to recognize these defamations and that only Sul-Te-Wan could have inspired such reaction from the black community. These accusations and her alleged involvement caused her subsequent discharge from the studios.[39] In defense of her career, name, and public image, Sul-Te-Wan challenged her dismissal. Studio officials then provided an unrelated explanation for dismissing her, claiming that a white actress had accused Sul-Te-Wan of thievery when her book disappeared. This allegation, combined with the assertion that she was responsible for the public resistance to *The Birth of a Nation*, provided all the ammunition officials needed to dismiss her from the studios. But Sul-Te-Wan refused to accept such treatment, and in an attempt to clear her name, she hired a lawyer and threatened legal action against Griffith in a letter she sent to refute the allegations.[40]

Griffith's defensive response to the racist label attached to him and his film continued well past the film's immediate aftermath. As Donald Bogle reports,

> Throughout the years, D. W. Griffith defended himself as a mere film-maker with no political or ideological view in mind. Surprised and apparently genuinely hurt when called a racist, Griffith made speeches across the country, wrote letters to the press, accused the NAACP and its supporters of trying to bring about screen censorship, and even went so far as to issue a pamphlet entitled "The Rise and Fall of Free Speech in America," all in an effort to squelch the controversy. As late as 1947, one year before his death and some thirty-two years after the movie's release, D. W. Griffith still maintained that this film was not an attack on the American Negro.[41]

Shortly after Sul-Te-Wan submitted the letter to Griffith, the studios rescinded the charges and reinstated her—and this time her employment title was that of exclusively an actress, not a maid.[42] Yet the controversy, which would seem like a press-worthy item, did not result in a mention of her connection with the film. This exclusion demonstrates just how invisible she was. Of course, in the case of *The Birth of a Nation* this may have been a blessing rather than a curse, since not having her name connected with the film allowed her to dissociate herself from one of the most racially inflammatory films in American cinema history.

SUL-TE-WAN IN ROLES OF THE OTHER

Though her employment title changed from maid to actress, Sul-Te-Wan subsequently still was cast in various roles as subservient, multiracial, and evil characters. Despite the insignificance of her screen roles and the mainstream press's failure to cover her performances, Sul-Te-Wan frequently transformed these minimal roles into notable performances. For example, in *The Children Pay* (1916), Sul-Te-Wan appears on screen with Lillian Gish, a signifier of white womanhood,[43] and in *Stage Struck* (1917), she appears with Lillian's sister, Dorothy Gish, herself a signifier of white femininity and chastity.[44] The details of her specific roles in these films remain unknown, but it can be inferred that because of her blackness she was likely used to imply racial codes that positioned her in direct opposition to these white stars. Such positioning, according to Lola Young, enabled "Black people . . . to embody the threat to the illusion of order and control and represent the polar opposite to the white group."[45] Therefore, Sul-Te-Wan's roles were deliberately designed to position her as the shadow of (that is, the negative to) these white stars and what they represented.

In the screen roles for which she is best known, Sul-Te-Wan personified the quintessential subservient when she was paired with—or was a shadow for—white actresses on screen. For example, in *The Narrow Street* (1925) she is "a housekeeper and a servant"[46] who shadows the white actress Dorothy Devore, a representative of whiteness. *In Old Chicago* (1938), a film that reconstructs the crime, corruption, and political dynamics that proliferated in Chicago in the 1870s, Sul-Te-Wan is cast as a maid, Hattie, and functions on screen as a shadow for white actress Alice Faye.[47] Assuming a similar role in *Kentucky* (1938), a film that centers on the Kentucky Derby, Sul-Te-Wan is cast as Lily, ostensibly the subservient to and shadow for white actress Loretta Young.[48] In *Maryland* (1940), regarded as a companion to *Kentucky* (both were produced by Darryl Zanuck and reflected his affinity for horses), Sul-Te-Wan plays the part of Naomi, a black subservient to the white actress Fay Bainter.[49] In these and in similar films, it seems obvious that her respective characters' principal function is to bolster the myth of superiority, privilege, status, and power assigned to whiteness.

Sul-Te-Wan's screen image was not limited to subservient characters, but extended to roles that allowed her to capitalize on her multiracial identity. For example, her vaunted multiracial identity enabled her to obtain a role in *Gunga Din* (1939), a film that explored British rule in India. Although she is unrecognizable in this film, she probably appeared in the crowd scenes as an East Indian.[50] Because of her unusual coloration, the African American press characterized her as a "strange Oriental-colored Ethiopian woman whose life is as mystic as the blood which flows through her veins."[51] Like a number of other African American actresses, she exploited her racial identity to play a wide range of ethnicities. This report revealed that "she is very dark [yet] through the art of make-up she may pass as octoroon, or even . . . Caucasian."[52] Despite such racial exploitation, she was viewed as an "Ethiopian-Oriental who is a worthy representative of her American brothers and sisters," which also made her the subject of subjugation in white Hollywood.[53]

Not confined exclusively to subservient roles or roles that allowed her to project her multiracial identity, Sul-Te-Wan also personified "shadowy" characters that are associated with evil. In particular, she was cast in *Hoodoo Ann* (1916) in the role of "Black Cindy," an orphanage cook.[54] The character's subservient position and her blackness (itself often associated with evil) mark her as a signifier of evil. The "foreboding pronouncements of Black Cindy" are alleged to influence Ann's perception that she has been "hoodooed."[55] As a subservient in the film, Sul-Te-Wan is directly contrasted to the white actress Mae Marsh (who plays the white protagonist, Ann). Because of Sul-Te-Wan's subjective positioning, she is strategically inserted to embellish the characterizations of the white stars—an affirmation of her and her character's devaluation. Black Cindy is assumed to exert an evil influence over the pure and white Ann. Ann's whiteness is equated with purity and goodness; Cindy's blackness is equated with subservience and evil. Toni Morrison expounds on the juxtaposition of whiteness to blackness that is reified in the relationship between Cindy and Ann and suggests that

> Images of impenetrable whiteness need contextualizing to explain their
> extraordinary power, pattern, and consistency. Because they appear al-
> most always in conjunction with representations of black or Africanist
> people who are dead, impotent, or under complete control, these images

of blinding whiteness seem to function as both antidote for and medita-
tion on the shadow that is companion to this whiteness.[56]

In *Heaven on Earth* (1931), Sul-Te-Wan landed the role of "Voodoo
Sue"—a role that allowed her to capitalize on her unique name, ancestry,
physical construction, style, and "eccentric dress . . . (flowery hats, turbans, flowing beaded necklaces, and an array of cotton/silk color combi-
nations)."[57] The film was based on a novel by Ben Lucien Burman, titled
Mississippi.[58] Cast in this film as a "voodoo doctor," Sul-Te-Wan heightens
her appeal and increases her marketability by catering to white Hollywood's preconception that blackness is inseparable from the occult, since
"black . . . people and symbolic figurations of blackness are markers for the
[malevolent] and the wicked."[59] *Heaven on Earth* focused on "poor whites
of the lower Mississippi, who believe in spirits, sing their dirges and dwell
on floating shanties."[60] Sul-Te-Wan plays opposite white actress Anita
Louise, whose character (Towhead) consults the spirits for assistance in
an ill-fated romance. Sul-Te-Wan's role associates her with evil spirits and
"weird superstitions,"[61] in contrast to Anita Louise's role, which projects
her as the embodiment of white womanhood. In this role, Louise is the
"blonde ingenue who looks fresh and young, with the type of facial beauty
that makes her performing secondary."[62] Although Sul-Te-Wan sought to
broaden her screen roles by making the transition from subservient and
multiracial to voodoo woman, she still remained inextricably linked to
the trope of darkness and its inscribed implications.

Because of Sul-Te-Wan's on-screen appeal as a voodoo woman, she
established a niche for herself in white Hollywood. In 1933, she became
a handmaiden in *King Kong.*[63] The film focuses on native islanders who
are visited by Europeans, primarily white male explorers, accompanied
by one lone white female named Ann (Fay Wray)—blonde, beautiful,
and a signifier of desire. Ann is to become the official bride of the giant
gorilla, Kong. Negotiations between the Europeans and the islanders
ensue (including an offer of six black women for the one white woman),
but they fail. However, Ann's beauty overwhelms Kong, and he feels compelled to protect her. Transported to New York for exhibition purposes,
Kong demonstrates his unrequited love for Ann. Attacked by military
airplanes, he hangs from the top of the Empire State Building before falling to his death. Yet the film asserts that it is not the physical attack that

ultimately subdued Kong, but rather his emotional attachment to Ann: "It was beauty that killed the beast."

Although *King Kong* was regarded as a kind of horror film, it has much in common with the social politics of *The Birth of a Nation*.[64] For instance, Thomas Wartenberg argues that while *"Birth of a Nation* represented Black males as sexual monsters in order to justify a narrative in which Black males were subdued by White males [it is] the Skull Island sequence of *King Kong* [that] replicates this narrative structure, although it does so within the context of a standard 1930s jungle film."[65] Wartenberg adds, "This association of Kong with the stereotype of the sexually threatening Black male established by *Birth of a Nation* is effected not merely by the film's representation of Kong, but also by the way that it represents the White beauty's response to him."[66]

King Kong plays upon a variety of sexual and racial codes that are not restricted exclusively to black male sexuality but extend to black female sexuality. Ann is symbolic of white innocence, beauty, desirability, and vulnerability, while Kong signifies the beastly excesses inscribed in black maleness. James Snead asserts that "the figure of King Kong would allow the white male to vent a variety of repressed sexual fantasies: the hidden desire of seeing himself as an omnipotent, phallic black male; the desire to abduct the white woman; or the combined fantasy: to abduct a white woman in the disguise of a phallic black male."[67] Wartenberg further notes that "[t]he film uses its huge black ape as a stand-in for Black males so that it can criticize Hollywood's demonization of this group. Because Kong is not in point of fact a Black man, the film is able to articulate its social criticism in a veiled form that can escape both the anxious eyes of the censor and the conscious racist attitudes of (some members of) its audience."[68] As the film develops these racial and sexual complexities, it associates the handmaiden (played by Sul-Te-Wan) with the natives' sacrificial ceremonies, rendering them as Other and referring to them as "queer" and thus demonstrating the handmaiden's linkage with the world of the occult.

The film designates the white woman as victim and the black woman (handmaiden) as a principal agent through which the white woman's victimization occurs. The handmaiden signifies evil—a signifier that both the presence of the monster and the film's narrative reifies. Most notably, Ann's being taken to the altar and tied between two stone columns symbolizes the splitting of the self and the Other; as they split, Ann undergoes a transformation as the self, while the Other undergoes a displacement onto the natives, the handmaiden, and Kong. Ann's positioning also simulates the classic rape position, an exposure of her body while she hangs between these columns. The implied rape of Ann—a white female by a black male figure—serves to justify the historical rape of black females by white males. From this purview, the handmaiden functions as a representative black female. The juxtaposition of the black woman with the white woman, though reducing both to their bodies, negates the rape of the black woman through the symbolic rape of the white woman. Because of the association of the black woman with evil and the occult, there is a virtual erasure of her rape, presaging and deeming more important the violation of white women's bodies. This is another way in which Sul-Te-Wan's character remains invisible.

Later in the film, Kong's capture becomes symbolic of the lynching of a black man accused of raping a white woman. As Kong hangs from the Empire State Building, his positioning simulates that of a lynching victim in that "the ghostly post . . . with one noose cut and the other still dangling" visually conveys that the lynching has occurred.[69] Though Kong symbolically represents the threat of black male sexuality, Wartenberg writes that "rather than maintain this view of Kong, the film employs a romantic narrative in which Kong figures as a tragic hero. Because Kong can feel romantic love for Ann Darrow, he becomes an object of the viewer's admiration and empathy, not their fear and hatred. This allows the film to criticize the stereotype of the Black male as a savage beast."[70]

In part because of her role in *King Kong* that associated her with the occult, evil, witchcraft, and voodoo, Sul-Te-Wan became typecast. In 1934 she played the role of Ruva in *Black Moon*, a film that explores voodoo in the West Indies. Describing the film, the *New York Times* wrote:

> A hasty and deplorably incomplete inventory would show two blood sacrifices, two ordinary murders, incantations in three languages, a lunatic witch doctor, a white woman with a bad case of heebie-jeebies and a patriotic effort on the part of 2,000 crazed natives to exterminate all the white folk on the island, not counting the white goddess.[71]

The film focuses on a white woman, Juanita Lane (Dorothy Burgess) who, because of her possession by evil spirits, attempts to murder her own child, but in the process her husband murders her. The husband then leaves the West Indies and returns to the United States with his new love interest, his secretary Gail (Fay Wray).[72] As in *King Kong,* there is a juxtaposition of white to black femininity and an equation of the black female (Ruva) with sorcery and voodoo. But this picture also depicts the white woman as possessed by evil, an association that ultimately results in her death. Following her exit from the picture, another white woman takes her place as a signifier of white femaleness, which effectively erases the white woman's being signified as evil and leaves the association of evil related to the occult to rest only with her black companion, Ruva.

In *Maid of Salem* (1937), Sul-Te-Wan assumed yet another role associated with the occult, this time as Tituba, a voodoo practitioner. The film elicited scathing criticism from the African American press, which took offense at the implication that a black slave, Tituba, had initiated witchcraft at Salem. Bishop Walls of the *New York Amsterdam News* contended that the film's distortion of historical fact in its so-called exploration of witchcraft resulted in a gross misrepresentation of African Americans. According to Walls, Tituba "is pictured in weird and disgusting superstition, conjuring the minds of groups of old and young with blood-curdling stories, telling fortunes by palmistry and giving herb drinks to intoxicate the brain." Walls asserted that an Irish woman servant who was arrested for initiating a frenzy that caused deaths, rather than the black female slave, was the so-called culprit in this historical event. While he did not deny that a black slave girl figured in the story, Walls minimized her involvement by asserting that she was among a group of girls, two of whom were white, when the three were arrested for "palmistry and hysterical acts."[73] Although the white girls denied these accusations, the black slave girl revealed the truth.

Challenging the film's racial polemics, Walls declared, "Mark you, the picture makes the mobbish officers arrest only the colored slave and connects her with the 1688 Boston incident, in place of the Irish woman servant."[74] Claudette Colbert is cast in the leading role as Barbara Clarke, who stands accused of practicing witchcraft. But because she is a signifier of white femaleness, she receives vindication.[75] Tituba's blackness becomes a link to evil and because of the black female's inescapable association with evil, Tituba, when juxtaposed to (that is, used as a shadow for) Clarke, becomes all the more symbolic of the occult.

While the film's alleged misrepresentation of history may have disturbed the African American press, the press nevertheless applauded Sul-Te-Wan's performance. In the opinion of the *Baltimore Afro-American,* "she came forward as a guest artist, and rendered a dramatic bit from the screen play . . . in which she had almost stolen a scene from Claudette Colbert, the star."[76] In effect, the visibility of her acting negated the invisibility of her role in this picture.

Attempting to broaden her range as an actress, Sul-Te-Wan on a few occasions assumed more diverse roles, but these roles were not necessarily any more redeeming because they continued her on-screen association with the immoral or illicit. For example, in *Queen Kelly* (1929) she played a prostitute in a drama that focused on a queen's fiancé whose love interest is other than the queen. Developing an attraction for Patricia "Kitty" Kelly (Gloria Swanson), an orphaned girl residing in a convent, the fiancé sets fire to the convent and facilitates her escape. He then provides refuge for her in the queen's palace. The queen, however, soon becomes aware of her fiancé's exploits and warns him that unless he dissolves his relationship with Kitty, she will prevent Kitty's leaving the palace. The queen proceeds to brutally punish her fiancé for his actions, while Kitty attempts to commit suicide by drowning. Following Kitty's suicide attempt and rescue by the guards, she becomes a madam in an African bordello that employs a prostitute named Kali, the character Sul-Te-Wan plays. Although Sul-Te-Wan does not appear on screen in the available film version that I screened, Richard Koszarski affirms her role: "the black prostitute in the African sequences [is] played by Madame Sul-Te-Wan."[77] Koszarski further suggests that her landing this role may have been the result of her appearance in *The Birth of a Nation,* asserting that Erich Von Stroheim may have remembered her from *The Birth of a Nation* and *Intolerance.*[78] Sul-Te-Wan's role as a prostitute in *Queen Kelly* constructs this character as a racial, sexual, immoral, and illicit Other.

Appropriated as a signifier of immorality because of her blackness, Sul-Te-Wan was also linked to prison life in *Ladies They Talk About* (1933), a reconstruction of a real-life drama of a woman incarcerated for robbing a bank, featuring Barbara Stanwyck as Nan Taylor. Peter Stanfield notes, "While serving her sentence, [Stanwyck as Taylor] plays an instrumental version of 'St. Louis Blues' on a phonograph to cover the sound of prisoners trying to dig their way out. The choice of the song fits neatly alongside the film's exploitation of abject and vulgar femininity, as displayed by Stanwyck's character and the other inmates. The song also underscores the essential loneliness of the emotionally abused heroine—the woman who has lost her man."[79] According to one critic,

> *Ladies They Talk About* is effective when it is describing the behavior of the prisoners, the variety of their misdemeanors, their positions in the social whirl outside, their ingenuity in giving an intimate domestic touch to the prison, and their frequently picturesque way of exhibiting pride, jealousy, vanity and other untrammeled feminine emotions.[80]

Consistent with Hollywood's sexualization (and occasional masculinization) of all women, Sul-Te-Wan receives both treatments in the role of Mustard, a prison inmate. This is particularly apparent in the description of her as lending to "this part of the picture a diversity of mood and character."[81] In a similar vein, Thomas Cripps characterizes the film as a "socially precise vehicle"[82] for Barbara Stanwyck, but he acknowledges the strategic positioning of blacks to accentuate the prison landscape, a landscape that included "a darkly ominous Sul-Te-Wan."[83]

Sul-Te-Wan is again associated with prison life in *Sullivan's Travels* (1941), a film that foregrounds class through its focus on a wealthy film director who decides to make a documentary about poverty. In order to do so, he poses as homeless and has several adventures, culminating in his being falsely convicted of murder. While he is in prison, his absence leads his colleagues to believe he is dead. In a church scene within the prison, Sul-Te-Wan's character is the organist who plays while the preacher sings "Let My People Go."[84] It is then that Sullivan decides that in order to escape his predicament he must confess to a murder that he did not commit. He correctly assumes that his confession will result in his picture being printed in the newspaper and his friends will see it and know that he is still alive. His friends do recognize him and he is rescued from the labor camp. Although in this film Sul-Te-Wan's character's association with prison life is not a direct one, it is still enough to perpetuate a link between the black actress and the immoral.

INVISIBILITY IN THE MAINSTREAM PRINT MEDIA

Ralph Ellison sees African Americans as decentered and marginalized by virtue of their relegation to the invisible.[85] Ellison affirms that in constructing a racial Other there is a deliberate attempt to render that Other invisible (to those who do not want to see), perhaps because the Other reflects the darker side of the self.[86] Thus Sul-Te-Wan, constructed in film roles as the Other, was relegated as an actress and as a person to the position of the invisible, not only on screen but also in the mainstream press's coverage of her screen career.

Building on Ellison's views, James Snead posits that the creation of invisibility occurs through the process of omission or exclusion, rendering the racial Other insignificant and unimportant.[87] From this perspective, the mainstream media worked in tandem with Hollywood to render Sul-Te-Wan invisible. Victimized by the then-prevailing Hollywood racial politics—and the politics that reverberated in the racially divided America in that period—Sul-Te-Wan automatically was positioned as invisible in that she was omitted from film credits and reviews. While her roles were often minimal and secondary and therefore might not have warranted inclusion, it was her race and sexuality that also caused her to be unmentioned in mainstream press reviews.

This pioneering actress remains unrecognized for her contributions to *Up From the Depths* and *Intolerance,* films that appeared respectively in 1915 and 1916, the latter a film Griffith made in response to the earlier widespread criticism he received for *The Birth of a Nation.*[88] Although few remember or know of Sul-Te-Wan's contributions to these films, she did appear in *Intolerance* as the female figure in the marriage market scene of the Babylonian story.[89] In its review of *Intolerance, Variety* does not mention Sul-Te-Wan or other secondary actors in the cast; perhaps the most public acknowledgment of her role in this film came only at the time of her death.[90] She is posthumously noted for her appearance in *Hoodoo Ann* by the *American Film Institute Catalog: Feature Films 1911–1920* and Internet Movie Database, even though she remained unnamed in a *Variety* review of the picture at the time of its opening. Sul-Te-Wan's invisibility extended beyond this early period into later decades of her career.

In the 1920s, while her name appears more frequently in film reviews because of her increasing involvement in the industry, she is still relegated to minimal reports. For example, the *New York Times* was among the few mainstream publications to identify Sul-Te-Wan as a cast member who appeared in *The Narrow Street* (1925), which focuses on a bachelor who discovers an attractive young woman hiding in his home, located on a narrow street; in this film, Sul-Te-Wan plays the role of Easter.[91] This notice by the *New York Times* makes Sul-Te-Wan one of the first African American actresses to receive mention in a film review by a mainstream publication. The African American press, though, covered black actors extensively during this period, despite their insignificant roles, and frequently mentioned Sul-Te-Wan's screen performances and gave notice to her work in the industry regardless of its prominence. In comparison, the mainstream press was more preoccupied with covering the actors in primary or starring roles, who more often than not were white actors in this early period of the cinema industry.

Despite rare occasions when the mainstream press recognized Sul-Te-Wan for her minimal contributions to films, as was the case with *The Narrow Street,* her continued exclusion from such reports persisted. One case in point is her appearance in *Uncle Tom's Cabin* (1927), which featured African American actor James B. Lowe.[92] Though there was little or no mention of her in the mainstream press, the African American press noted her contribution to the picture. The mainstream press also did not mention her appearance in *Drums of Love;* the *New York Times* and *Variety* in particular ignored her. The African American press not only verified her contributions to this 1928 film, it also castigated studio officials for editing her role from the film: "None other than D. W. Griffith himself called for her to act in *Drums of Love,* and she responded only to have the editor of the film ... clip her dancing. But they, the power[s] that be, know of her anyway, so what does it matter!"[93] In the year following *Drums of Love,* Sul-Te-Wan graced the screen in *Thunderbolt* (1929), a gangster drama involving the police who hunt and capture a leading criminal, a capture that is achieved through the assistance of a dog. *Variety*'s review of this film does not mention Sul-Te-Wan. To add insult to injury, it does mention the dog, King Tut, among other cast members.

In the 1930s, some major mainstream publications continued to ignore Sul-Te-Wan, while a few others mentioned her. For example, the *New York Times* mentioned her in its reviews of *Heaven on Earth, Ladies They Talk About, Black Moon, Maid of Salem, In Old Chicago,* and *Kentucky,* while publications such as *Variety,* which reviewed many of these films, failed to mention her at all. Several of the minor publications did cite her work, perhaps because she had established a reputation as an actress and received more prominent screen roles. It was not until 1938, when she was cast in *In Old Chicago* and *Kentucky,* that *Variety* would cite her contributions.

Despite such marginalization, with each decade Sul-Te-Wan gained increasing visibility, and by the 1940s, a decade that witnessed a growing acceptance of African Americans in Hollywood and in society in general, she was more often mentioned in the mainstream press's film reviews. Nevertheless, she still could not escape a significant amount of continuing invisibility. Both the *New York Times* and *Variety* mentioned her in reviews of *Maryland,* but *Variety* failed to mention her in less popular films such as *Mighty Joe Young.* And by the 1950s, the *New York Times* and *Variety* rarely mentioned her again for her screen work.

In view of Sul-Te-Wan's contributions to the screen, and to draw upon Michele Wallace's views, "Could it be that most critiques of racism, which aim for an impossible ideal of colorblindness, continue to render the social and cultural histories of bodies of color (e.g., black women) invisible?"[94] Because of this kind of racial exclusion with respect to Sul-Te-Wan, it is incredibly difficult to compile a definitive filmography for this African American actress, even though her screen appearances conceivably approach some one hundred films, with at least fifty identified roles, in a career that extended from 1915 to 1959.

MAKING THE INVISIBLE VISIBLE

To cite again Ralph Ellison's definition of invisibility in the prologue to *Invisible Man,* to render a subject invisible is not only to refuse to see the subject but also to transform the true nature of the subject—to project the subject as a figment of the perceiver's imagination.[95] The film industry gave Sul-Te-Wan numerous yet minor or insignificant roles. Despite her talent and lengthy screen career, mainstream film reviews and screen credits more often than not ignored her, which was part of a general pattern by the cinema industry to minimize the contributions of African Americans. Morrison notes that "in matters of race, silence and evasion have historically ruled."[96] Sul-Te-Wan and other African American actresses could not escape the racist and sexist perceptions characteristic of the period. When black actresses were mentioned, reference was often made to their skin color. In particular, critics often referred to Sul-Te-Wan, because of the character she played, as "dark" or "ominous."

In addition, the screen roles Sul-Te-Wan assumed often were designed primarily to embellish the whiteness of her white costars. As a signifier of the racial Other, she recreated a variety of subservients whose very names became indicative of her marginalization. It is conceivable that in her struggle for visibility, she set out to preemptively contrast this image by adopting for herself a name that implied royalty. In the end, however, she acceded to the rules of the Hollywood game, which meant that because of her blackness she had to accept roles associated with the occult, voodoo, evil, immorality, and sexual promiscuity in order to remain employed as an actress. She accepted the marginalization that equated her with invisibility. As Hortense Spillers argues, "'femaleness' itself [became] the site of absence."[97] However, while seemingly accepting this multiply coded position of invisibility, Sul-Te-Wan managed to establish her space as the racial Other and to turn invisibility into visibility, through the power of her acting in minimal roles and through the eccentricity of her personal appearance.

For Sul-Te-Wan, it is in this very space of disengagement, dissociation, and disenfranchisement that she constructed visibility for herself. Morrison writes, "To enforce its invisibility through silence is to allow the black body a shadowless participation in the dominant cultural body."[98] Sul-Te-Wan gave meaning and importance to the visible, using the power of invisibility itself.[99] Trinh T. Minh-Ha alludes to the problems associated with the invisible in its attempt to claim its visibility:

> A space is created and offered, but it would have to remain unoccupied. Accepting negativity (otherness as defined by the master) has led to a new positivity (identity as reclaimed by the other), which in turn opens to a new set of negativities and positivities (the questioning and renaming of otherness, through the unnaming of both the master and his other). She can only build from the invisible as she unbuilds the invisible, and vice versa.[100]

While Sul-Te-Wan may have had to wrestle with such dynamics, she developed her own unique response to her invisibility through this construction of the invisible, thus rendering herself visible. "She [in this instance, Sul-Te-Wan] had not drawn something out of nothing (a meaningless act), but given to nothing, in its form of nothing, the form of something. The act of not seeing had now its integral eye. The silence, the real silence, the one which is not composed of silenced words, of possible thoughts, had a voice."[101] Jane Gaines affirms that "the eloquence missing in the spoken word is thus given to the body in silent cinema. Perhaps, then, in the shimmering quality of silent cinema, we are seeing the image that exudes speech—all of which is to say once again that the silent image was never truly silent and that it never seems exactly mute."[102]

In responding to her invisibility, Sul-Te-Wan managed to sustain a career in white-dominated Hollywood during a period when few African American actresses could even dream of doing so. Furthermore, she maintained this career in cinema for nearly half a century (1915–1959), despite her declining physical appeal with the onset of old age, the fluctuating economic whims of the cinema industry, and competition from emerging actresses. In film history, she is one of the few black actresses to sustain such a long career. Although relegated to the space of the invisible, she used her invisibility to render herself visible. Donald Bogle surmised that "Madame Sul-Te-Wan, however, remained a grizzled, tough Hollywood fighter to the bitter end. Colorful as ever, dressing exotically with her scarves and bold costume jewelry, her fanciful hats, and her stylish dresses, she refused to let the town forget her."[103]

TWO

Nina Mae McKinney

EARLY SUCCESS AND TUMULTUOUS CAREER

One can say with justification that Sul-Te-Wan was the first significant African American actress, even though her earliest roles were minor ones and in silent films. Justifiably, one can also say that Nina Mae McKinney was the first African American actress to have a leading role in a mainstream film, even though the film, a "talkie," *Hallelujah* (1929), had an all-black cast. McKinney's physical features and the role she played in this film were precursors for subsequent African American actresses with similar physical features (mulattoes), who typically were cast in roles, either major or minor, that projected them as objects of male desire.

In one of the first attempts by a major motion picture studio to produce an all-black-cast film, McKinney, at age sixteen, played her most popular role, that of a sassy young dancer and conniving suitor called Chick. McKinney, like many African American actresses during the second quarter of the twentieth century, found it difficult to escape the role she popularized. *Hallelujah* elevated her to stardom within the African American community and made her newsworthy in the African American press, but her on-screen roles increasingly crossed over into her off-screen private life as the reel and the real began to merge. In her effort to capitalize on her stardom and maintain the fleeting and illusory image of a star, she helped make herself the object of admiration, gossip, and vilification. Toward the end of her acting and stage career, she was reduced to working as a domestic—the very role that she escaped in her early off-screen life and that she sought to escape as an actress on-screen.

The reports about McKinney's early life, like those of her later years, are often conflicting, but a clear overall picture emerges of a black woman who aspired to be an actress and who aspired to promote her image as well as her talent to the public. McKinney, the only child of Hal N. McKinney and Nannie Crawford (also referred to as Georgia), was born on June 12, 1912, in Lancaster, South Carolina. Taking her mother's first name, she was christened Nannie Mayme but later changed her name to Nina Mae. Her parents left the South and moved to New York City, leaving McKinney to be reared by her great-aunt. Other reports suggest that she may have been reared by her grandmother (her grandparents were former slaves). However, in these early years, it was McKinney's aunt, Mrs. Kelly Sanders, also known as Carrie and employed by the white southern aristocrat Col. LeRoy Springs of Lancaster, who reared McKinney. Several generations of the McKinney family apparently had worked for the Springs family, and Nina Mae, along with her aunt, provided them with domestic services. As a child, McKinney attended the Lancaster Training School (sometimes called Lancaster Industrial School) until about sixth grade. When she was twelve or thirteen years old, she moved to New York and joined her parents, attending Public School Number 126 in New York. Apparently, after her parents' separation, McKinney's mother remarried—this time to a New York postal clerk; she became Mrs. Georgia Maynard. Another report claims that it was McKinney's father who was a postal clerk.

In 1928, McKinney joined Lew Leslie's *Blackbirds* stage show in which she performed as a chorus line dancer. Then, at the age of sixteen, she landed a role in *Hallelujah,* the film that launched her acting career. Although McKinney continued to work as an actress in several films following *Hallelujah,* she never became a major screen star and never really achieved the same screen success she garnered with this film and that she desired. Nonetheless, many of her early roles allowed her to make the transition from screen to television; in the 1930s, she was credited as the first black person to appear on British television. In the 1950s and 1960s, she reportedly lived in Athens, Greece, where she was billed as the "Queen of Night Life." It is possible, though, that this report is in error and refers only to some performances abroad, since her death certificate indicates that she remained a resident of New York City for some forty years prior to her death. Of course, McKinney could have maintained her residency in New York even though she resided outside of the United States. That she was living in New York in the late 1960s is not disputed, nor is the fact that she suffered from heart disease. McKinney died May 3, 1967, in Manhattan. Several years later she was inducted into the Black Filmmakers Hall of Fame, where she was heralded as the first black actress to perform in a sound motion picture. Since that time McKinney's portrait has been displayed on the county courthouse wall in Lancaster, South Carolina, with other notables of the city, including President Andrew Jackson, Dr. J. Marion Sims (physician/gynecologist), Col. Elliott White Springs, and Gen. Charles Duke (astronaut).[1]

STARTING AT THE TOP: MCKINNEY LANDS *HALLELUJAH* ROLE

The role for which McKinney became famous and that catapulted her to stardom was one she did not secure instantly. King Vidor directed *Hallelujah,* MGM (Metro-Goldwyn-Mayer Corporation) produced it, and Irving Berlin contributed the songs "Waiting at the End of the Road" and "Swanee Shuffle."[2] Early reports indicate that in 1928, when Vidor began recruiting actors for his all-black-cast film, Josephine Hall (a singer at the Cotton Club in New York), Honey Brown (a toe dancer at the Club Harlem), and Langdon Gray (an eighty-six-year-old non-professional) were selected from among some five hundred applicants vying for a part in the film.[3] To find black actors to appear in the film, Vidor launched a search in Hollywood and Chicago, but he was unable to secure appropriate actors for the roles desired until he ventured to New York.[4] Singer and actress Ethel Waters claims that she was among those considered for a role, but that her recruitment was halted by Vidor's casting assistant. According to reports, blacks in the New York theater world who viewed Waters unfavorably thwarted Vidor's assistant's efforts to recruit her, and the assistant's explanation was that he could not locate Waters upon his arrival on the East Coast.[5]

Despite his inability to recruit Waters, Vidor was impressed with other New York talent and selected Honey Brown, who was in competition with Josephine Hall, for the lead role. After selecting Brown, Vidor proceeded to shoot several scenes using his newly recruited actress, but he later decided to replace her. According to reports, "Miss Brown worked too fast for the picture photographers. Of a naturally nervous disposition, she could not keep still for long periods at the time."[6] Honey Brown also allegedly developed pneumonia while Vidor was shooting the film, which caused him to search for another leading actress. Meanwhile, rumors circulated in the black press that due to Brown's illness (she was supposedly near death), "her husband, Buck Taylor, grief stricken attempted to kill Vidor in a fit of rage, during which he accused the director of having mistreated Miss Brown. It was a pathetic case and those who knew the sunny-smiled girl and her genial husband were heart-broken."[7] Of course, these rumors were dispelled when it was revealed that Brown was dancing at the Lafayette Theater in New York and therefore was not near death as previously implied, and that her husband, a waiter at the Lenox Club, did not recall meeting Vidor and therefore could not have issued a death threat.[8] Such rumors printed in the black press were bound to attract attention for the upcoming film.

Initially, Vidor considered both Brown and McKinney for the leading role in *Hallelujah*. Both were former chorus girls with Lew Leslie's *Blackbirds*. Vidor tentatively selected Brown and sent her along with other cast members to Memphis, where some of the film's scenes were being shot. It was two weeks after shooting started that McKinney was invited to join the preselected actors, and when she arrived in Memphis with her mother, Brown informed her that *she* was being considered for the leading role. According to the *New York Amsterdam News*, though, "The decision as to who, Honey or Nina May, would win the part hung . . . until the day of the making of the big baptism scene. . . . Vidor favored Honey, but he took along Nina May anyway. A last-minute phone call to the studio convinced him of the wisdom . . . [that] Nina May [had] been chosen by the powers-that-be."[9]

Perhaps it was the undeniable sexuality McKinney exuded that influenced Vidor to finally select her for the leading role. A reviewer for the *Pittsburgh Courier* certainly suggested such when he described the New York performance in which Vidor observed McKinney as a stage actress: "Rhythmically bowing and dipping, swaying, and turning with a troupe of seasoned chorus girls, she was unconscious of the critical eyes of the great director, King Vidor. She did not know that the pendulum had swung from mediocrity to stardom when he viewed her with unusual interest."[10] Although the reviewer implies that McKinney was unaware of

Vidor's gaze, it seems that she was in fact quite aware of it and was using her body to fascinate onlookers. That McKinney presented herself in this manner is confirmed by Ruby Berkeley Goodwin, a newspaper critic and black[11] Hollywood reporter who described McKinney as "the seductive little cabaret dancer," "the vampire," "the true daughter of Eve," "beautiful and irresistible"[12]—descriptions that emphasize her as sexy and with more than a touch of naughtiness. While these descriptions characterize her screen persona in *Hallelujah,* they also apply to her off-screen personality. Given the sexually alluring role she played, McKinney's character was regarded as "a child who wants the admiration of the world,"[13] but McKinney the actress became indistinguishable from McKinney the off-screen person.

Hallelujah focuses on a black cotton picker in South Carolina, Zeke (Daniel Haynes), who ventures to the city to sell cotton that his family grows on their cotton farm. Eagerly awaiting his return, his family expects that their efforts will translate into cash, goods, and gifts. Having received cash for the cotton, Zeke is distracted by the city-wise and sexually alluring Chick (McKinney). Initially unimpressed with Zeke's rural appearance (he is dressed in overalls), Chick sees him as just a poor country farmer, but when she sees the roll of bills he proudly displays, she reconsiders. Mesmerizing Zeke with her languorous body movements while dancing, Chick tells Zeke she knows how to double his money. She lures him into shooting craps with her partner, Hot Shot (William Fountaine), who uses loaded dice to cheat Zeke out of his money. Enraged, Zeke retaliates with gunfire, and the game ultimately results in Zeke's brother (Spunk) being killed.

Zeke thereafter becomes a roving preacher and again encounters Chick and Hot Shot standing among the onlookers. Although Chick initially questions Zeke's religious metamorphosis, later she becomes consumed by his religious zeal. After she attends one of his revival meetings, she is so overwhelmed by the spiritual experience that she decides to join the converts.

Abandoning his role as preacher, Zeke flees with Chick, marries her, and becomes a sawmill worker. But Chick is unable to overcome her passion for excitement and is unable to adjust to domestic life with Zeke. Chick tries to run off with Hot Shot, but Zeke blocks their escape, wields a gun, and shoots Chick, who dies in his arms. At the film's end, Zeke is imprisoned for the murders of Chick and Hot Shot, and following his release from prison, he returns home to be reunited with his family and his former love, Missy Rose.

We have to wonder if Chick's conversion occurs out of embarrassment, out of her desire to again attract the attentions of Zeke, or out of a genuine change, even if only temporary, in her moral beliefs. As film scholars Raymond Durgnat and Scott Simmon note, "Her conversion involves something that isn't quite bad faith at all. An important element in Chick's capitulation is the fact that she who came to mock the pious ('Betcha ten-to-one you can't save me, Brother Zekial!') is suddenly the only 'sinner' who hasn't repented, which puts her in a position of acute social embarrassment."[14] Whatever her motivations, her transformation is short-lived, and once again she exerts her control over Zeke, forcing him to leave his family and church.

While placating black spectators' craving for black images on the screen, Vidor was also catering to the interests and appetites of white spectators. The film became a window through which whites could explore black life from a disengaged perspective and construct their fantasies of black male and female sexuality. Whether or not the filmmakers' tactics were intentionally racist is debatable, but racist assumptions certainly seem to have provided an underpinning for this film. In reviewing the film, *Variety* stated, "*Hallelujah* to the whites is a big, entertaining picture. To the negroes it will either be a gigantic sensation or revelation or looked upon as holding up some of their ancient sacred rites of the race to ridicule."[15] The racism in *Hallelujah*, I will show, is not an independent characteristic, but rather a by-product, the first and most blatant configuration being sexualization.

While *Hallelujah* attempts to foreground the weakness of the black male, it really becomes an exploration of the allure of black female sexuality. Chick is clearly the object of the male gaze. She is dressed in a short tight black dress when she is introduced in the film. A pair of white dice (with black "eyes") are positioned on the shoulder, simulating the gaze she both elicits and projects, implying that she is a woman associated with gambling and the underworld.

Affirming her sexualization, Donald Bogle observes, "Executing sensuous bumps and grinds in the famous cabaret scene in *Hallelujah*, Nina Mae McKinney was the movies' first black whore."[16] Although harsh in his assessment, he does point out her undeniable sexuality. To complement her character's dress, McKinney wears black shoes, fastened with bows—subtly connecting her adult body with her childlike status. (McKinney was only sixteen when she was cast in this role.) That Chick embodies adultlike characteristics even though she assumes childlike status coincides with the adult/childlike positioning of the woman who, according to Julia Lesage, is deliberately designed to play upon the woman's sexuality and mark her vulnerability for the exploitation of her sexuality by males. Lesage notes that the "awakening to her childhood, sexuality and maternal emotion all at once, [plays into] . . . the other drama, that of masculinity and of men's need [to exploit her sexuality]."[17]

Adding to her sexualization is her dancing style. When Chick dances, she lifts her legs high and wide in order to elicit the voyeuristic gaze of male spectators; "the exotic and erotic . . . welded together, situating the African woman as the signifier of an excessive, incommensurable sexuality."[18] Of course, males are led to believe that it is her sexuality that invites and gives license to the victimization they are likely to inflict. When Chick dances, she is surrounded by a crowd of males who shout, "Shake those hips," "Boy, open that door and let me in," "Boy, she's chocolate to the bone," and "Heaven's angels [are] walking on earth." Their references to her hips, eyes, and bones reduce her to her body, and she becomes a site on which males can fantasize. Conversely, the male body per se is not a primary site of attraction and fantasy for Chick. While she attracts the attentions of Zeke through her body, she is drawn to Zeke primarily because of his money. Her reference to him as "Big Boy" is clearly a play upon his sexuality but also a sign of her attraction to his perceived financial and social status.

In addition to the film's use of blatant devices to depict black female (and black male) sexuality, there are also more subtle devices at work. The film uses Chick's dancing to inscribe her sexualization, but it also uses music and other characters. For example, when Chick persuades Zeke to join her at a nightclub, the atmosphere is seductive, with a jazz band playing in the background, dancing waiters, smoke spiraling to the ceiling, and bodies clinging to each other on the crowded dance floor. The music serves as a narrative device to accentuate the sexuality embodied in the black characters. As the music increases in intensity and the pace of the dancing accelerates, the scene almost simulates an orgasmic experience: the music, the movement, the emotional fervor all reach a crescendo, achieve a climax, and then begin to subside. Significantly, Chick's dances are doubly seductive, simulating both a feminine and a masculine position. At times she appears to imitate clownish behavior that is preceded by a march; then this dissolves into a wiggling of her hips. She occasionally widens her eyes, as if to play upon the typical parodic constructions of the African American screen image.[19] McKinney's sexualization in the nightclub scene is reinforced through the provocative dancing of the other women. Wearing a plaid skirt that tightly hugs her body to accentuate her wide hips, one unnamed woman rotates her hips to attract attention to her sexuality. Her partner is a much shorter male, which reinforces the impression of the black male's subordination and the black female's dominance.[20]

The sexualization of Chick is further marked by her association with immorality—automatically implied because of her gender and race. For example, in the first scene, the film introduces a couple attempting to marry after having produced eleven children. When the couple announces to "Pappy" (Zeke's father) that they intend to marry, he remarks, "the damage is already done." While the remark is rendered as a joke, the harsh reality is that it intends to point to a lack of moral behavior associated with blackness.[21] Zeke's father's assertion also may serve to define black sexuality, and thus Chick's uncontrollable sexuality, even before she appears in the film. Chick's association with the immoral is further apparent when she is contrasted with other black women in the film, who are desexualized and have thus become symbolic of morality; most of the primary female characters are fully covered in long dresses and staid head wraps (or wear unkempt hairstyles).[22]

Chick's sexuality is not only portrayed through her association with immorality and her body language, dress, and dancing style: it is also developed through the black male body. For example, when Zeke conducts a baptism and immerses Chick, in addition to a number of other converts, in the river, Chick is so overcome by the experience that she has to be carried away to an isolated tent. It is apparent that Zeke's attraction for Chick overwhelms him and his lust becomes uncontrollable. Bogle contends that Chick's baptism becomes symbolic of the fact that "McKinney's been such a hot little number that we know she's being dunked in the water not so much to purify her as to cool her down."[23] Zeke, however, is so drawn by her magnetism in the tent that he falls into her arms. In this moment, Zeke allows his spiritual beliefs to be momentarily supplanted by sexual fantasies. While embracing Chick, however, he is halted by his mother, who pulls Zeke away from Chick and interrupts their embrace. Zeke, extending his shaking hands (an indication of his uncontrollable sexuality)[24] asks for the Lord's forgiveness. In this scene, the sex act never occurs, but it is implied as Zeke becomes symbolic of black (and thus also Chick's) sexuality. According to Durgnat and Simmon, "The baptismal cries called forth by her feigned (or sincere, or naturally overdetermined) sensations of regeneration by grace in Zeke's arms become ecstatic wails of love, of surrender, and—by no very great stretch of the imagination—orgasm. For sensuality lurks in the very temple of religion, perhaps because each plunges its roots so deep into human nature as to draw half its strength from the other."[25]

Chick's sexualization is further heightened by her mulatto appearance. According to Lola Young, the belief that "light skinned black women—especially those who can 'pass' for white—are often sexually troublesome"[26] raises associations with the black slave experience. Chick's mulatto appearance, therefore, automatically codes her as a product of miscegenation who, because of her mixed-race ancestry, is destined to be both problematized and, more specifically in this instance, sexualized. bell hooks professes that "As sexist/racist sexual mythology would have it, she [the mulatto] is the embodiment of the best of the black female savage tempered by those elements of whiteness that soften this image, giving it an aura of virtue and innocence. . . . She is the perfect combination of virgin and whore, the ultimate vamp."[27] That Chick assumes the mulatto role and becomes a tragic figure is apparent at the film's end when she dies tragically at the hands of Zeke, who shoots her, perhaps deliberately.[28]

Chick's sexualization is further evidence that not only is she objectified by the black male on screen and by white spectators who identify with the black male protagonist, but that she also thwarts the gaze projected by the black male, inverts the traditional male-female roles, and objectifies him. The black male assumes a passive (feminine) position, while she assumes an active (masculine) position. The "masculinization" of Chick and "feminization" of Zeke are played out in other ways in *Hallelujah*. For example, when Chick confronts Hot Shot regarding his inability to pay her the money he owes her, she displays fearlessness and a willingness to challenge the accustomed social status of the dominant male figure. Even being involved in a money scheme at all (a traditionally masculine pursuit) reflects this switch in roles. When Hot Shot attempts to keep Chick from attending the revival meeting led by Brother Zeke, Chick assaults Hot Shot with a fireplace poker (a phallic symbol); she is clearly assuming a masculine position, as she exclaims, "That's what I do to anybody [who] stands in my path to glory!" Durgnat and Simmon, in a critique of this scene, note, "That violence in her sexuality, which Nina Mae McKinney carries off with ebullient spasms, has Zeke in open-nostriled, slack-jawed awe."[29]

After Chick and Zeke marry, she becomes bored both with him and the mundane life of a sawmill worker and is lured away by Hot Shot, who intends to re-introduce her to city life and her city ways. Bags in hand, Chick escapes through the bedroom window and rushes to reach Hot Shot. "As Chick and Hot Shot, eloping, speed off into the forest in their horse-drawn carriage, Zeke blasts away with his shotgun, ready to risk killing the girl, whom he might have wanted to rescue."[30] When Zeke reaches the screaming Chick, he holds her in his arms, recognizing that she is nearing her death, and reassures her that she should not fear the devil—nearly an affirmation of her final metamorphosis from evil to good. Facing death, she is forgiven for her sins. With an animal-like magnetism as a predator stalks his prey, Zeke next chases Hot Shot through the dense and foggy swamp. These scenes are dark and dimly lit to reverberate the film's tragic ending and to reflect on Zeke's dark side. Zeke captures Hot Shot, they wrestle in the murky waters of the swamp, and Hot Shot succumbs to strangulation—a strangulation that is not visible on screen. According to Durgnat and Simmon, "The strangulation of Hot Shot is left to our imagination (except in publicity stills . . .). Thus the moments of highest ecstasy, violent or erotic, are denied us. It's possible to see this tantalizing avoidance as catering to an audience embarrassment at passion. . . . One might even see it as a way of restraining the too-soulful frenzy of black folk."[31] That Chick is punished by Zeke's violent shooting of her speaks to how women are victimized and rendered as tragic figures. bell hooks suggests that the black female as a wild sexual savage can only be tamed through the violent and sexually dominating machinations of the black male indoctrinated by the patriarchal culture.[32] Therefore, Chick's violent death is viewed as warranted in view of the deception she inflicted on Zeke as well as the sexualization that she appropriated to lure him from his path of righteousness.

Apparently, Nina Mae McKinney played the part of Chick so convincingly that some wondered exactly when she was playing Chick and when she was playing herself. Whatever the case, McKinney's successful appearance in this leading role had a strong effect on blacks inside and outside the industry. The period following *Hallelujah's* 1929 debut gave false hope to black audiences, who assumed that with the production of this film they could expect Hollywood to take a serious interest in blacks and black life. According to Thomas Cripps, black spectators were even willing to ignore the racial discrimination endured during the production of this picture. Cripps revealed that according to "the gossip of the movie lots—Nina Mae McKinney . . . had almost quit after a grip called her 'nigger'"[33] Eva Jessye, black musical director for *Hallelujah,* reconstructed the gross inequities that existed between white actors and black actors in this film and the discrimination endured by the film crew. For example, according to Jessye, "she [Jessye] was paid but $100 per week for her very exacting work whereas a white person doing the same work would have received three or four times as much. . . . Miss Jessye also [reported that on] location in the South, the company issued each day two sets of lunches, one for the Negroes and another for the whites."[34] While these discriminatory practices occurred during the picture's production, off-screen whites in Hollywood were more inclined to interact with blacks on a social level.[35]

When *Hallelujah* was completed, and prior to its release, the film created controversy with the announcement that there would be a double premiere in New York: one for black audiences at the Lafayette Theater and one for white audiences at the Embassy on Broadway, a downtown theater.[36] The *Chicago Defender* reported that "Arrangements for the dual presentation of Mr. Vidor's long awaited dramatic study of the Negro, his life and his spirituals, were made to meet the thousands of requests for a showing in Harlem."[37] When blacks attempted to gain entrance to the film's premiere at the Embassy Theater, they were denied admission and subsequently filed discrimination lawsuits.[38] The *New York Amsterdam News* reported that "When announcement of the opening, said to be the first of its kind in theatre history, was made, immediately the cry went up in Harlem that the Lafayette secured the photoplay because Negroes were not desired at the downtown playhouse."[39] In addition to filing lawsuits against the Embassy Theater, blacks in Harlem similarly protested the dual exhibition of the picture.[40]

GOOD PRESS, BAD PRESS

Long-standing adages in the film industry assert that bad press is better than no press and that controversy (i.e., bad press) often is potentially good for all concerned. It is said to attract audiences to films and popularize actors and actresses, who hope that their popularization will lead to additional film roles. The latter applied to Nina Mae McKinney. When the controversy over *Hallelujah* became public, McKinney was escalated to stardom, and during the same month of the film's controversial premiere, August 1929, she reportedly wed Jimmie Marshall, manager of the Lafayette Theater, where *Hallelujah* premiered for black audiences.[41] McKinney, however, denied the story:[42] "In an interview with a representative of the *Amsterdam News* on Monday night, little Nina Mae McKinney . . . emphatically denied that she was ever married as reported by a number of newspapers many months ago after she had left New York for Hollywood."[43] The report is typical of the way details of her private life were devoured and distorted by the black press.

Off screen, McKinney was always an object to be viewed "with unusual interest." Attending *Hallelujah*'s premiere in Hollywood, she was described as "the beautiful Nina Mae McKinney . . . gorgeous in her pink tulle frock with pink taffeta shirred evening wrap, bearing a mammoth cape collar and wearing the pink tulle turban."[44] Her appeal was often exaggerated, as for example when it was reported that the Maharajah of Kapurthala was so impressed with her that he extended an invitation for her to tour Europe and then travel to India.[45] Her hyped appeal was complemented by her continuing self-promotion as a sex symbol. One year after the premiere of *Hallelujah,* to cite just one example, she struck a sexually alluring pose for photographers on the announcement of a new movie contract for a part as "queen of the night club" in *Taking It Big* (1930—a film that may never have materialized).[46]

But despite her talent and proven ability, McKinney received few additional film offers. Hollywood, apparently, did not intend to create additional roles for its "dark star." Although she did land a role in the

MGM production *They Learned about Woman* (1930)—playing the part of a "Harlem Madness" singer—she soon found it necessary to return to the legitimate stage to continue her career as a performer.[47]

There were also reports suggesting that she was in conflict with other actresses, such as white actress Clara Bow. McKinney resented a comparison made between the white actress and the black actress, and she publicly stated that she had no intention of profiting from such a comparison. Yet the "press continued to eulogize her as the 'it' girl, much to Miss Bow's discomfiture."[48] The black press exacerbated such conflicts to both manufacture news and elevate the black actress.

There, too, the emphasis was often on her person and the psychological effect of her performance. In 1930, William Smith, a *Chicago Defender* columnist, reviewed one of her stage performances in Chicago and assured his readers that she was more attractive in person than on screen: "She is much prettier, folks, very much prettier. Her skin is golden, and her eyes fascinating. Her voice is low and mellow, and to see her in the flesh is a delightful experience."[49] Other *Chicago Defender* news reports described her as "vibrant with the mysterious, fetching quality called 'it,'" and noted that "the feminine portion of her audiences seem to like her as well as the men."[50] A performance in Pittsburgh was covered extensively by the *Pittsburgh Courier*; its reports, too, concentrated on her body as commodity: "Being small and daintily curved, she wears present-day fitted garments with a decided air."[51]

As new accolades were heaped upon her, there seemed to be a concomitant increase in reports regarding her sexuality. For example, an African American newspaper critic, Floyd Snelson, described McKinney by stating that her "vamping role in *Hallelujah* was as natural to Nina as though it was written and staged exclusively for her benefit. She has plenty of that so-called rhythm in her bones and it takes but little syncopation to put her in action—for she can shake a wicked hip as well as a 'mean' Charleston. . . . [She] wears only a vest, bloomers, and slip under her dresses."[52] Even some publications affiliated with the mainstream press rendered McKinney as little more than a black sex symbol, diverting interest away from her acting talent. From such innuendo, it was a short step to declaring her immoral, since black femaleness was associated with uncontrolled sexuality.

The April 1930 issue of *Motion Picture Classic* magazine contained one of these hostile articles. Written by white columnist Elizabeth Goldberg (whose name was later misspelled by the black press as Elisabeth Gold-beck, perhaps as a kind of insult to Goldberg in response to her denigrating comments about McKinney), the article was entitled "Black—and Potentially Blue."[53] The *Baltimore Afro-American* excerpted the article to demonstrate how McKinney was being defamed in the mainstream press. Goldberg had asserted that "Nina Mae imagines she has made the big jump from the black world to the white. Poor little Nina. Colored people no longer appeal to her fastidious taste. . . . In her illusory success, she has drawn away from her own race." Goldberg quoted McKinney's public statement that she found it necessary to distance herself from the masses: "If you start going out with them, pretty soon they think they're just as big as you are." The newspaper, speaking for the African American community, was disturbed that Goldberg was exposing McKinney's dubious racial politics, but was even more outraged at Goldberg's attempt at the end of the article to undermine their star's sexual power: "Nina is a Cleopatra for sure. She wants to be a siren and a heart-breaker. Crazy for men. Crazy for money. Crazy for admiration. No wonder she has accepted the illusion of Hollywood's friendliness."[54] Offended by this attempt to undermine her and in an effort to repair any damage done to her image, McKinney reportedly filed a lawsuit for damages against both Goldberg and the *Motion Picture Classic*. The *Pittsburgh Courier,* perhaps to muster support for McKinney, reported that Goldberg's article was so upsetting to McKinney that it brought her to tears.[55]

To restore luster to her damaged public image, McKinney again turned her attention to her screen career. Though some in the press had begun hinting it would be short-lived,[56] other reports attested to her viability in the industry, declaring that she had signed several long-term contracts. The *Chicago Defender* reported that "M-G-M has no intention of letting Nina Mae go. Warner Brothers Studios and Fox have both been negotiating for the bronze siren of *Hallelujah,* but Metro-Goldwyn-Mayer will not even lend the star out to other studios."[57] Meanwhile, to sustain her career between screen roles, McKinney performed on stage in New York, Pittsburgh, and Chicago (where she was met by a delegation of city officials and a parade), singing songs that she had popularized on screen in *Hallelujah*.[58] But McKinney was seen again on the screen in only one all-black-cast musical short, *Manhattan Serenade* (1930).[59]

When McKinney's screen career stalled and the black press had little to report on her career, they shifted their focus to her personal life. For example, McKinney again became a subject of controversy in the black press when, in August 1930, the *Baltimore Afro-American* reported that she had married the prizefighter Willie (Gorilla) Jones; again she denied the press report.[60] McKinney's purported marriage to Jones also was reported in the *Chicago Defender,* which denied the rumor: "Rumors have it that Nina Mae McKinney isn't married to Gorilla Jones, the Ohio prizefighter, as reported from San Francisco. Jones is alleged to have called Nina Mae over long distance when the news of his supposed tie-up reached him and informed the former movie star that that kind of publicity wasn't desired by him. It is also alleged that the star of *Hallelujah* is out of the talkies and without one single bid from producers."[61] These rumors persisted and it seems they were intended to rekindle her languishing screen career by keeping her name before the public—coverage the black press was eager to provide. In fact, the *Baltimore Afro-American* reported that this was a strategy McKinney employed to sustain her career as an actress even when Hollywood provided few roles.

> After her marriage to Douglas "Master" Daniels, she declared that the Gorilla Jones stuff was the bunk, just a sort of nice way of keeping her name before the public. Others now say that the publicity at that time served skillfully to cover-up her failure to get more work to do at Hollywood—that she would rather have had the public to believe that she had been overcome by love and had thus deserted the glare of the movies for the quiet pleasures of domestic life, than for the story to get out that she was no longer useful.[62]

Other black newspapers printed similar stories, and some made her age an issue. The *Chicago Defender* reported that McKinney had married Douglas Daniels, a vaudeville performer.[63] The *Baltimore Afro-American* noted that the "nineteen-year-old star of the film *Hallelujah* ... took unto herself a seventeen [or sixteen]-year-old cabaret dancer husband, last week in Chicago; and instead of a honeymoon—[she] faces the court on the charge of having had too violent a love affair with a sixteen-year-old child."[64] Sensationalizing the report on McKinney's marriage, the *Philadelphia Tribune* claimed that she allegedly invited Daniels out to lunch and "cast some sort of spell over him,"[65] after which they drove to Crown Point, Indiana, to be married by the justice of the peace. The *Baltimore Afro-American*, a few weeks later, reported that McKinney was seeking to have the marriage annulled and admitted that Daniels stayed away from home for nearly a week after their marriage.[66] Printing Daniels's attempt to defend himself, the press reported that "The boy husband also charges Nina Mae also stayed out nights and said he feared she would take up with a count or prince when she sets sail for Paris soon."[67] Though press reports such as the ones noted above kept McKinney in the public's eye, they did little or nothing to vitalize her screen career.

McKinney seems to have tried other ways to give the public the impression that she was still sought after and to revive her screen and stage career. She had tried to promote the idea that her domestic life was more important than a career, but when this theme failed to sustain her popularity, she may have begun to believe that not only was she failing herself but she was also failing the African American community. In another attempt to escape Hollywood's neglect, McKinney turned to Europe in an effort to revive her career. In December 1930, amid public scrutiny and controversy, she traveled to Europe, like other black stars before her, determined to revive her career as an actress. Newspaper critic Bessye Bearden of the *Chicago Defender* announced the trip: "Sailing with little Nina are the thoughts and good wishes of her stage and screen[-]loving public. They are hoping and wishing that her name may become as shining and as bright as it has in her own land, and that she will return the wearer of the laurels of fame and success."[68] McKinney had reportedly negotiated offers of $1,000 per week, which attests to her talent and international appeal.[69]

McKinney's departure elicited a forced farewell from director Ben Thau, who lauded her talent:

> I understand that you are leaving for Europe shortly, so here's best wishes. It was a pleasure to have you at our studio. The whole world knows you gave an outstanding performance in our *Hallelujah* and I am sure that anything you do on the stage or screen must be outstanding, as you are a great artist.[70]

The press covered her departure extensively, and one newspaper reported that "Nina Mae boarded the S.S. Bremen wearing a black satin and black velvet coat trimmed with fox, and carried a huge bouquet of chrysanthemums."[71] The countries McKinney visited on her European tour as well as the length of her stay abroad remain confusing because of conflicting reports that appeared in the black press. Reports suggested that she was scheduled to perform in Europe for one year and tour Berlin, Paris, Cannes, Deauville, Monte Carlo, Vienna, and London.[72]

Continuing to report on McKinney's success abroad, the African American press announced that she was scheduled to appear in an unnamed European production to be filmed in Africa.[73] McKinney may have been invisible in the mainstream press and in Hollywood, but she was still revered in the black press. According to Bogle, while performing in Europe, McKinney was billed as the "Black Garbo," indicating how black stars sought validation by identifying with popular and widely acclaimed white screen stars.[74]

The black press also reported incidents in her private life while she was in Europe, such as the January 1931 article titled "Does Vivacious Motion Picture Queen Hold Important Angle in Backstage Romance? What Will Happen When Franc [McLennon] Meets Nina Mae in Paris?"[75] The reporter claimed that Nina Mae had been involved with Franc McLennon, who had been a friend of Douglas Daniels (McKinney's former husband) when both men worked with a theatrical group known as the Whitman Sisters Company. According to the story, McKinney had ended her friendship with McLennon to become involved with Daniels, and that after his relationship with McKinney failed, McLennon became engaged to another woman but their engagement ended and he was hospitalized for a bout with pneumonia. Exploiting these rumors, the paper reported that prior to McKinney's departure to Europe she paid McLennon's hospital bill.[76] Whether this report was fact or fiction, it demonstrates the press's insatiable appetite for information on its black star, even though McKinney was in Europe by this time.[77]

According to a report in March 1931, McKinney returned to the United States after three months abroad either because she developed appendicitis or desired to visit her ailing father.[78] This source added that McKinney's Hollywood hit *Hallelujah* had not been well received in Berlin "due to the fact the citizens were unable to understand the meaning and particular psychology of the American black people."[79] By this time, McKinney had become disillusioned with Europe and missed her friends and relatives.[80] On her return to the United States, she resumed her American stage career. This brought the renewed attention of the African American press, although she was becoming disenchanted with the scandalous reporting that appeared in their pages, especially regarding her private life. The *Baltimore Afro-American* claimed, "Miss McKinney was greatly aggravated when she read newspaper reports of her supposed marriage, and is disgusted with many of the papers that seem, she says, 'to be so interested in my affairs.'"[81] The *Chicago Defender* reported that McKinney's photo had appeared on a motion picture magazine, *El Cine,* published in Barcelona, Spain,[82] an attempt to elevate their black star rather than report on her private affairs. And when McKinney performed on stage at the Regal Theater in Chicago following her return from Europe, the *Chicago Defender* declared that the "dainty little star of *Hallelujah* [is] back from Europe and [is] more beautiful than ever."[83] But McKinney's return to the stage did not create the excitement she had known in the past. One reviewer wrote that when McKinney performed in Chicago, she "failed to conquer despite the intensive support one Earl Hines gave her."[84] She faced a similar reception in Washington, D.C., where, in her words, audiences were "stingy with their applause."[85]

To revive her career, McKinney once again began to circulate personal rumors, the same strategy she had used earlier to keep her name in the public eye. This time it was announced that she would marry Jimmy Monroe, the man who had served as her manager and had frequently accompanied McKinney on her European tours.[86] Monroe later became Billie Holiday's spouse, but it is of note that without marriage certificates it is often difficult to determine if these entertainers actually did get legally married.

In 1931, McKinney, back in the United States, appeared in a film, *Safe in Hell,* with white actress Dorothy Mackaill. This film provided an opportunity for the press to pay attention to McKinney's screen career rather than concentrating on her private life. In the film, McKinney was cast in the role of Leonie, the hotel manager, and according to one source, "At a time when most African Americans were stereotyped, both Nina Mae McKinney and Clarence Muse were the two most reputable characters in the movie."[87] Thomas Cripps's review of the film describes McKinney as a "slim brown waitress." Cripps writes, the whites live off their past; the blacks off their carefully cultivated principles, hidden under their cool manners. They rise above the script. "I'm a New Orleans lady too," says Leonie when the writers ask her to say, "I's from N'Orleans myself." . . . Leonie sets a cocky example by waiting tables, sings, holding to her faith, and fending off the whites. In a contrived ending and a sham trial the white woman [protagonist] is convicted and chooses death rather than a life in the hands of Bruno. In the last sequence the blacks help her die in peace by steering her sailor away, Leonie embraces her in tears.[88]

A reviewer for the *Chicago Defender* similarly commended McKinney's role, stating, "Nina Mae McKinney does some fine acting and singing in this picture. She is keeper of a house where murder is committed and where gangland [hides] out."[89] But while McKinney longed for a screen career, the black press was becoming disillusioned with her relationship with Hollywood. Its writers questioned her role in *Safe in Hell*, asking "[w]hy Nina wasn't permitted to appear in the picture more."[90]

It seems that McKinney also felt it necessary to engage in advertising campaigns, both as a means of enhancing her income and as a means of remaining in the public eye. She appeared in an exploitive newspaper ad for Golden Brown skin ointment that claimed that by using this product, one could have "skin glorified with that Creole-like charm typical of successful Race men and women."[91] For McKinney, this was a form of compromising herself as well as a not-so-subtle endorsement of the idea that success depended solely on one's physical appearance. Actually, it was commonplace for black actors and entertainers of that period to endorse such products. Anna Everett contends that the press used the star power of these black actresses to sell products.[92] Such advertisements allowed McKinney to remain on the pages of the black press and thereby in the public eye.

McKinney continued to perform successfully on stage with her own company that consisted of a pianist and a partner, both of whom contributed to her act. One reviewer commented, "The little girl, who just a few months ago was blundering about on the stage trying to get herself the praise that was already handed over in pictures, is now worth reviewing. We thought her particularly good in a trio of songs at the Michigan [Theater] last Sunday night."[93] These performances were often complemented by brief appearances in movie shorts, such as when McKinney appeared in *Pie, Pie Blackbird* (1932) with Noble Sissle, Eubie Blake, and the Nicholas brothers, Harold and Fayard.[94] In its review of this film, the *Motion Picture Herald* stated, "Fairly entertaining, moderately enjoyable if the patron likes the negro band, with its own peculiar type of melody, and the singing negress, Nina Mae McKinney, with her crooning but quite melodious voice."[95] The *Film Daily* reported, "Miss McKinney does several typical song numbers with a lot of class, and she is a good looker too."[96]

The African American press, observing her limited screen roles and believing she deserved a better career, continued to promote her as a star, sometimes even circulating rumors that additional screen roles were imminent.[97] Resorting again to references to her alluring sexuality, the *Pittsburgh Courier* released a photo of McKinney titled "Nina, Be Good" and captioned "This bewitching pose is very trying to the male of the species."[98] By being reduced to her sexuality, McKinney was newsworthy in the black press.

ACT TWO

A fading star's attempt to revive her or his career is a kind of second act. Indeed, this second act, whether successful or unsuccessful, has been the focus of more than a few Hollywood films. Act-two plots such as these often draw attention to problems in the fading star's personal life and how the problems affect the star's career. The act-two metaphor certainly applies to Nina Mae McKinney's attempts to revive her declining screen and stage career. In 1933, frustrated by Hollywood's lack of appropriate roles for her, McKinney returned to Europe, where she appeared in Paris and London and was billed as "The Fascinating Creole Film Star and Cabaret Artiste."[99] While performing in London at the Leicester Square Theater, McKinney appeared in a stage show titled "Chocolate and Cream."[100] A review of her performance in the show noted that

> The colored section of the show is laid in a plantation scene in Mississippi. The attraction is Nina Mae McKinney, the *Hallelujah* girl, who has received so much pre-publicity that she is apt to be disappointing. Girl undoubtedly has best personality since Florence Mills, but is a long way behind in her talent, although she can put over a song. Miss McKinney is causing a lot of controversy and keeping the box office busy, which is what matters most.[101]

Even during her absence from the United States, the black press paid homage to its "dark star," continuing to provide coverage of her European triumphs. McKinney professed that she saw "no reason for returning to the States and its prejudices" until she faced some of the same racist practices in Europe that she had experienced in America.[102] On one occasion, a European woman refused to patronize a well-known restaurant in London because it had accommodated McKinney. While the woman was confronting the restaurant's management and expressing her distaste for any establishment that catered to blacks, McKinney was enjoying dining in the restaurant, whereas the objector was not.[103]

McKinney's European tour to London and Athens, with a side trip to Cairo, was interrupted in May 1934; this time she returned home because her mother was ill.[104] Back in the United States, she performed on stage and worked with Eubie Blake's orchestra at the Granada Theater in Pittsburgh.[105] At that time, the African American press announced that McKinney would again be visible on screen in the British film *Sanders of the River* (1935, alternately titled *Congo Raid*). McKinney would play the wife of an African chieftain, played by Paul Robeson. This film was scheduled to begin production in August of 1934,[106] and apparently McKinney remained in London while the film was in production. During this time, she received harsh criticism from the British press for arriving late to a Royal party and for not staying long enough. According to the *Chicago Defender*, "Nina Mae McKinney will have plenty to explain before she is able to return to favor with producers and scribes over here as a result of ... walking out on a 'Royal' party last month.... Invited to ... the party that was to have been attended by Royalty, not only was [McKinney] late, but [also, she] remained less than fifteen minutes.... One paper was bitter in its attack on the famous movie stage star."[107] A month later, the *Defender* revealed that McKinney was scheduled to appear with Will Rogers in the film *Steamboat Round the Bend* (released 1935), but McKinney is not mentioned among those credited for appearing in the film.[108] Such reports could have been attempts by McKinney or the press to keep her name before the public, to remind Hollywood producers of this talented black actress. McKinney did, however, appear in the British film *Life Is Real* (1934)—a film about which little is known, although it did premiere in Los Angeles some two years later.[109]

By the end of 1934, McKinney had returned to the United States and organized her own swing band; she was touring between screen roles and performing in a variety of nightclubs. She was still described by the African American press as the "vivacious star of stage and screen."[110] McKinney's sexual appeal on screen continued to permeate her stage image, as one report revealed that McKinney "to the world at large is known as exotic. The whole [flair] for eccentric, gay apparel and a gaudy hair dress is no doubt, what will make her a sensation before an orchestra. That [flair] is doubtless just protective coloration for a timidity of spirit which would have thwarted her ambition to be a femme band leader is revealed in full."[111]

By the beginning of 1935, McKinney's British picture, *Sanders of the River,* was completed, and its American premiere received extensive coverage by African American newspapers.[112] *Sanders of the River* focuses on a tribal chief of colonial Nigeria and stars Paul Robeson as Bosambo and McKinney as Lilongo, wife of Bosambo. Chieftan Bosambo, acting on behalf of the British government, attempts to establish himself as the ruler over other African leaders. Bosambo first meets Lilongo among a group of natives and is much taken by her. Marked as an object of the gaze, Lilongo wears an off-the-shoulder wrap; she is light-complected and her arched eyebrows, lipstick makeup, and short straight hair clearly separate her from the rest of the natives. The other African women are darker in complexion, are without makeup, and wear natural hairstyles—they are marked as natives, different from Lilongo. Lilongo's physical difference coincides with Bosambo's symbolic difference, as he sides with the British government and assumes the ways of the Western world.

Interestingly, later in the film when Lilongo appears again, it is clear that the native women all have a desire to become one of Bosambo's wives. Lord Sandy (Bosambo's superior, played by Leslie Banks) reveals that Bosambo already has five wives.[113] Despite having been taken captive as slaves, these native women prefer serving as wives to Bosambo rather than returning home to their mothers and fathers. Lilongo also expresses a special interest in marrying Bosambo, but she declares that she knows that Bosambo, strictly speaking, has no other wives, because he always is seeking the wives of others. When Lord Sandy tries to discourage Lilongo from marrying Bosambo, she insists, proclaiming that she will marry him if he agrees not to have any other wives. With the blessing of Lord Sandy, the two marry, and a tribal ceremony is performed to celebrate their marriage.

Dancing plays an important part in the marriage ceremony. While Lilongo dances in a grass skirt and short top, the native women dance bare-chested. Dancing becomes important again at the film's end when Bosambo teaches his son the warrior dance, though Lilongo opposes this indoctrination for fear of his endangerment. By this point in the film two issues are established: first that Lilongo has strength of character and second that Lilongo is physically attractive. Yet, the downside of her attractiveness and sexualization is that she is taken captive by an opposing African leader in pursuit of Bosambo; recognizing that he can lure Bosambo into his trap, he captures Lilongo and prepares for her death.

Reviews focus on McKinney's performance as performance: the *New York Times* critically wrote, "The talented Nina Mae McKinney is likely to impress you more as a Harlem night-club entertainer than a savage jungle beauty."[114] The *Chicago Defender,* more laudatory of McKinney and Robeson, stated, "In the thrilling cinema, both Nina Mae McKinney and Paul Robeson are heard to great advantage, singing several haunting native chants, arranged for European orchestration. This picture gave both Miss McKinney and Mr. Robeson a chance to display acting ability never yet allowed in America."[115]

Despite the film's exploitation of African American talent in these racialized roles and its perpetuation of colonialism, the Institute of Amateur Cinematographers regarded the film as the most significant talking picture of 1935 and awarded Robeson and McKinney the annual gold medal.[116] According to the *Baltimore Afro-American,* "The Institute's gold medal is comparable to that of Hollywood's Academy of Motion Picture Arts and Sciences and is the most coveted trophy of English producers. It was awarded last year to Alfred Hitchcock, British director, for his melodrama *The Man Who Knew Too Much* (1934)."[117]

Despite the continued paucity of roles for black actresses, particularly in American films, in 1935 McKinney landed a role (as a singer in the "Reckless" number) in *Reckless* (1935), an MGM production that featured white actress Jean Harlow, although Bogle claims that McKinney's scenes were eliminated from the final version of the film.[118] However, the *Pittsburgh Courier* was complimentary of McKinney despite her limited success in the cinema world: "Electrifying filmdom with her intoxicating rhythm, the glamorous Nina Mae McKinney, gorgeous golden star of the cinema, is on her way home to Hollywood."[119] These reports, however enthusiastic, were frequently interspersed with reports of McKinney's return to the stage. For example, in April of 1935, it was announced that McKinney was scheduled to appear at the Harlem Opera House. This time, she was promoted as the "exotic cinema player."[120] McKinney also appeared on stage at the Cotton Club in New York, where she "came through according to expectations, scoring a tremendous triumph with a big dramatic number about 'Good for Nothin' Joe' (He done her wrong), and especially suited to the temperament of the exotic young lady whom we first saw in *Hallelujah*."[121] Bogle professes that during this period she also performed with Curtis Mosby's band in clubs on the West Coast.[122]

Attempting to extricate herself from the narrow characterizations by the African American press of both her stage and screen roles, McKinney publicly declared that she was seeking more positive screen roles. According to the *Baltimore Afro-American*, "Miss McKinney was sought by Hollywood directors who were anxious to portray her as the flaming Latin Lupe Valez type. Having given 'thumbs down' orders, her manager negotiated with film magnates for much finer roles for the talented star.... She was anxious for the opportunity to get away from the 'Katie Red' and 'Chick' roles."[123] In defense of McKinney, this report claimed, "Because of her use of cuss words on the screen few people liked her. It is written in the script, of course, but the average theatre-goer doesn't realize that. Therefore, Nina Mae in the public's opinion is the rough type. This is not true."[124]

As McKinney's screen roles became fewer, the press frequently reported on her stage performances as well as her physical appearance. For example, one source noted that "One thing that makes Miss McKinney stand out is the clothes she wears. While in Paris she had several gowns designed for her work and today she leads the country in dress both on stage and off. Broadway as well as Harlem [have] been turning out to see just what Nina Mae McKinney is wearing and why."[125] When she performed on stage with black comedian Johnny Hudgins in Newark, the press noted that "each time [she appeared] dressed in a different and expensive gown."[126]

In 1936, after working for several months at the Cotton Club, McKinney again returned to Europe. Dominating the press coverage was McKinney's European tour to Edinburgh, Scotland, and her failing health. Reports circulated that she had suffered from throat problems for some five years but had delayed undergoing an operation.[127] Refusing to have the surgical procedure performed, McKinney continued her European tour and arrived in Edinburgh, where she was well-received by the press. Regarding her performance in Scotland, the press reported, "She gives a brilliant display of rhythm-style singing, clever dancing and vivid impersonation. She is an artist in everything she does and well deserves to be leading a program of exceptional merit."[128] It was also during this year that McKinney appeared in Vitaphones's *The Black Network* (1936)—a jazz movie short that featured the Nicholas Brothers dancing team, the Washboard Serenaders, Amanda Randolph, and Bill "Basement" Brown.[129] According to Henry Sampson, others who appeared in this production included Eddie Green, Emmett "Babe" Wallace, and Thomas Chappelle.[130] The *Film Daily*'s review of this movie short noted that "A troupe of colored stars, headed by Nina Mae McKinney and the Nicholas Brothers, turn in highly entertaining performances in an unoriginal story of a colored radio sponsor with an ambitious wife who wants to be the whole show. . . . Nina Mae McKinney sings in the new fashion of 'swing.'"[131] This movie short, however, was probably made before her departure to Europe.

One year later, while performing in Sydney and Melbourne, Australia, McKinney's health problems resurfaced. She became ill from tonsillitis and appendicitis and was forced to undergo surgery, which again thrust her into the pages of the African American press.[132] McKinney's illnesses may have caused her to lose a role in the all-black-cast film *The Duke Is Tops* (1938), directed by Ralph Cooper; Lena Horne took the role.[133] Although McKinney had to compete with Horne and other new and younger actresses, she was still commanding press attention. McKinney's health problems were compounded by press reports such as, "Her stormy marriage to Jimmy Monroe [his name is spelled differently by different sources] ended in divorce."[134] The *Chicago Defender* certainly did not reserve its editorial remarks about the deteriorating marriage when it revealed that these reports had surfaced "as a result of hubby's recent elopement to Paris with his Nordic love and 2,000 pounds of the star's cash."[135] The dissolution of her marriage was played out in the black press when Monroe submitted a letter to the *Chicago Defender* in defense of his own role in their marriage. Writing from Paris, France, Monroe stated:

> It appears that my wife, Nina Mae McKinney, made an unfair stab in the back in attempting to bring me into contempt; to expose me to public ha- tred and derision. This effort to lower my reputation; to defame my char- acter, is not a surprise to me, for after six years of experience as my wife's manager I am quite well acquainted with her peculiar psychology. She has been guilty many times previously of scandal, but now she is trying libel for a change. Since your paper has been chosen as the medium for her un- fair and unethical attack, I trust you will be fair enough to state both sides of the case without prejudice.
>
> First, I wish to deny most emphatically and categorically that there is any truth in the enclosed article re[garding] myself. She left me; I did NOT leave her. I did NOT flee England with any woman, and as regards $10,000 I haven't handled over $1,000 of her money since she was a popu- lar movie player. I have never taken any of her possessions or cash without her consent, and be it known that I intend to begin divorce proceedings at the earliest possible time, as her behavior in London is not and has not been in accordance with accepted standards. Yours very truly, James Monroe[136]

Clearly, this controversial marriage that was nearing an end became excellent copy for black newspapers to both sell papers as well as appro- priate their black actress.

McKinney apparently longed to overcome these obstacles and return to the motion picture screen. By 1938, she vowed she would not return to roles that did not present African Americans in an appropriate man- ner. McKinney's diminishing professional appeal was described by the *Pittsburgh Courier* as "shedding glamour."[137] Playing upon this character slur, McKinney lashed out at Hollywood, shifting the controversy to the racial issue and declaring, "I will not act in another Hollywood picture until the prejudice is removed against colored actors in dramatic roles. Personally, I will not accept any maid parts. I am not a maid and will not act [like] one."[138] According to the *Chicago Defender,* which restated McKinney's strong views, she insisted that, "I will definitely not play maid-role[s] any longer. I would like to do a drama or such roles as will benefit the Race."[139]

As McKinney attempted to revitalize her screen career, she was often the subject of denigrating reports on her private life. For example, notice that she intended to marry her manager, Jack Evans, was coupled with reports about her public appearances with a prosperous physician, Dr. Roscoe Buckner of New Jersey.[140] But these personal reports were short-lived, as the press eagerly returned to her acting career. Rumors had it that she was scheduled to appear in several all-black-cast films, *St. Louis Gal* and *Beale Street* (Creative Cinema Corporation productions), when actually these films were proposed but never completed.[141] By September of 1938, McKinney was again reported to be performing on stage at the Club 65 in Chicago,[142] although such performances were often interrupted by reports on her return to the screen, if not in Hollywood productions then certainly in independently produced films.

END OF ACT TWO

As an example of her checkered career, in 1938 McKinney managed to land a starring role in an all-black-cast film, *Gang Smashers* (1938), produced by Ralph Cooper of Million Dollar Productions. But in this film McKinney encountered another kind of trouble. Reports circulated that during the production of *Gang Smashers,* Cooper physically assaulted her when she refused to sing. According to reports,

> Nina Mae McKinney, petite cinemactress and artist of international note, was the reported victim of the assault. To her friends that included Gladys Bentley and Evelyn "Hot Shot" Burwell who arrived at the home of the actress shortly after the alleged beating, Miss McKinney related her horrible experience supposedly at the hands of Ralph Cooper, veteran actor and an executive of the Million Dollar studios where the actress is under contract. Miss McKinney told friends that an argument developed between her and Mr. Cooper at the studio over a song she was slated to sing in a forthcoming film story. The actress is said to have refused to sing the number because she thought her voice was not capable of matching her acting and might hurt her reputation at the box office.[143]

McKinney denied the report.[144] But if the assault did take place, perhaps she was just using the report to try to salvage her fading screen career by insisting that she had not been victimized.

In addition, McKinney had to have bodyguards to protect her when it was revealed that she knew too much about underworld characters

NINA MAE MCKINNEY · 67

and their methods, information she had learned when she worked as a nightclub entertainer. She was reportedly escorted to and from the studio during the production of *Gang Smashers* for fear of her being accosted by New York gangsters. It is conceivable that such reports were designed to draw attention to the film and titillate the imagination of audiences, thus increasing box-office proceeds.[145] In *Gang Smashers,* McKinney plays the role of an undercover policewoman (Laura Jackson) who disguises herself as a nightclub entertainer to capture gangsters. A contemporary reviewer stated, "This is one of Nina Mae McKinney's best movies. . . . McKinney steals this movie, she shows her singing talents, comedy and sense of humor, and all in all, her great acting that won our hearts when she was in *Hallelujah.* . . . McKinney surely has the acting talents of Clara Bow, Greta Garbo, and Ann Sheridan. But she's in a class of her own for sure."[146]

By the end of the 1930s, McKinney revived her swing band under the banner of the Paramount Orchestra Bureau.[147] Returning to the stage with her orchestra, McKinney again began touring the United States, including a southern tour where she performed in Atlanta, Georgia; Columbia, South Carolina; New Orleans, Louisiana; Mississippi; North Carolina; Virginia; and West Virginia.[148] Predictably, it was in the South that she encountered difficulties. In Lake City, Florida, she was "brutally assaulted" while being refused a cup of coffee by a white soda fountain attendant, and "a near race riot ensued when Dick Boone, her white manager, and other members of the band interfered."[149] Although now a seasoned screen star, she could not escape the marginalization all blacks endured under the Jim Crow laws of the South. The incident was covered extensively by the African American press to warn other black artists to anticipate similar exploitation.

The late 1930s witnessed McKinney's return to the screen in another Million Dollar Production titled *Straight to Heaven* (1939), an all-black-cast film that similarly explored racketeering associated with the underworld. One source noted that "Nina Mae McKinney has a part that critics have called the outstanding role of her career."[150] McKinney, cast in the role of Ida Williams, acts as well as sings "When the Dark Became Dawn." The *New York Amsterdam News* observed that "Nina Mae McKinney, as the wife of Joe Williams (Lionel Monagas), plays a big part in clearing her husband of murder charges engineered by Lucky John [Percy

Verwayen]."[151] When she performed on stage in *Good Neighbor*[152] and *Tan Manhattan*, newspaper critic Ralph Matthews commended her performance in the stage production of *Tan Manhattan*. He wrote, "Miss McKinney topped anything she had previously done here in her revue appearances and displayed rare dramatic ability."[153]

McKinney's stage performances allowed her to continue to act when her screen roles were few and far between. In 1939, she was again cast in an independently produced all-black-cast film, *The Devil's Daughter* (1939, Sack Amusement Enterprises). *The Devil's Daughter* depicts two sisters whose relationship is strained because one sister, Sylvia Walton (Ida James), is moral and has received the family inheritance of a Jamaican banana plantation, while the other sister (a half-sister), Isabelle Walton (Nina Mae McKinney), is immoral and is denied the family inheritance. To receive the inheritance she believes is rightfully hers, Isabelle plots a scheme involving voodoo to intimidate her "good" sister, Sylvia. As Isabelle, McKinney is reconstructed as a "dark" character who practices voodoo, intoxicates her sister and plots to have her killed, and desires her sister's lover, John Lowden (Emmett Wallace). Isabelle epitomizes evil; there is no limit to the extreme lengths she will go to try to take the family plantation from her own sister. At the film's end, the two sisters are reunited, and Isabelle is forgiven for her evil acts; ultimately, she even receives the family plantation. Of note is the film's promotion. It was advertised as "A She Devil So Wicked All Hell Pitied Her!"; "A Two-Faced Woman So Mean All Men Hated Her!"; "A Harlem Hell-Cat So Jealous All Women Feared Her!"[154]

The *Chicago Defender's* review of *The Devil's Daughter* states, "Miss McKinney's superb acting makes *The Devil's Daughter* one of the most perfect colored pictures ever shown on the screen. She is seen as an island girl [who is] anxious to become a queen among her people—who willingly sacrifices her own sister on the burning altar."[155] Another reviewer noted that "Miss McKinney's work as an actress was flawless. She received able support from the rest of the cast. But excellent acting is not enough to make a great play out of a poor story, and *The Devil's Daughter* is lacking."[156] As Isabelle, McKinney is again both sexualized and victimized (in that she is marked as an evil character): not only does she attempt to murder her own sister, she is also desirous of her sister's lover. It seems that McKinney could not escape the image that she and the press popularized in her role as Chick of *Hallelujah* and now as Isabelle of *The Devil's Daughter.*

THE FINALE

McKinney's attempts to revive her stage and screen career in the 1930s were far less than successful. Her sustained attempts to do so in the 1940s only continued her downward turn. Throughout the 1940s, she was still promoted as a screen actress with great sexual allure. Once again, a marriage was announced—this time to Melvin C. Woolfork of New York.[157] Despite McKinney's past public declarations that she would not submit to Hollywood's parodic constructions of African Americans on screen, she did assume maid roles both in *Dark Waters* (1944, playing the part of Florella) and in *Together Again* (1944, playing the part of an unnamed maid).[158] Nevertheless, this did not lose her the support of the black press: "Hardly recognizable after all those years absent from the Hollywood scene and motion pictures is the above sparkling likeness of the 'new' Nina Mae,"[159] wrote the *Baltimore Afro-American.* In a similar vein, the *Chicago Defender* reported the following:

> The former star of the All-Sepia cast film *Hallelujah,* proved photogenically to be one of the best looking women of her race yet to appear before the cameras. The beautiful brownskin actress . . . was most strikingly beautiful in the scenes she appeared in [in] the Ben Bogeaus production, *Dark Waters* and her voice registered perfectly. The same was noted in the lengthy scene she appeared in [in] the Columbia Film studio production, *Together Again.* In both pictures, Miss McKinney essays the role of a maid. . . . She is actually refreshing in the minor roles making them stand out. Her diction should forever convince Hollywood, that it is not necessary to make Negro characters use southern dialect in order to establish their racial identity.[160]

Although McKinney's role in *Dark Waters* was lengthened to display her range of acting talent,[161] such efforts by the industry could not erase the humiliation she endured as a leading actress who had been reduced to playing a black subservient on screen.

In 1949, McKinney appeared in the Hollywood-produced motion picture *Pinky.* Cast as Rozelia—a woman associated with a character from the underworld and reminiscent of her role in *Hallelujah*—she was not acting as a maid. But she could not escape being cast as a sinister, money-grubbing partner in crime with an extortionist. This role infuriated some black critics. *Ebony* magazine described her role a "razor toting hussy," a label that caused McKinney to threaten a libel lawsuit against the publishers.[162] In this minimal role as Rozelia, McKinney signifies how the black female is reduced to violence and sexuality. The film focuses on a black woman, Pinky (played by white actress Jeanne Crain), who passes as white in the North but decides to return to the South and assist her grandmother (Ethel Waters). McKinney, as Rozelia, is associated with a deceptive black male, Jake (Frederick O'Neal), who extorts money from Pinky's grandmother. In one scene, Rozelia is accosting Pinky, whom the police believe to be a white female, and is searched by police. She hides a knife in her thigh-high hose, an act which characterizes her as unruly and willing to resort to violence. The police officers' raising her skirt to retrieve the knife is an obvious hint at Rozelia's sexuality, and when she is slapped by the police for being outspoken and insolent, the film suggests that because of her race and gender she deserves to be victimized.

Unfortunately, there is a parallel between McKinney's on-screen sexualization and her off-screen life. It was perhaps out of frustration with the black press's attempt to marginalize her that in 1949 McKinney eloped to Tijuana, Mexico, with Frank Mickey.[163]

The decade of the 1940s ended with reports that McKinney would return to the screen in *Copper Canyon* (1950), playing the part of a maid, Theresa, who served as the subservient and confidante to white actress Hedy Lamarr.[164] Although such roles were certainly not what McKinney desired, they at least sustained her career as an actress and helped her return to the stage. Even as an aging actress, she was still lured by the entertainment world, and in 1951 she was cast in the stage production of W. Somerset Maugham's *Rain*. As Sadie Thompson, McKinney was again cast in the type she had been trying to escape, playing a character described as "a fugitive practicing 'the world's oldest profession.'"[165]

After 1951, McKinney rarely appeared in the black press, and when she did, the reports more often than not referred to her most famous role in *Hallelujah*. For example, in 1958, a report that focused on the all-black-cast film *Porgy and Bess* (1959) noted that McKinney's struggles to land the leading role in *Hallelujah* were similar to the casting struggles endured by black actors for this film. During this decade, McKinney's acting career seemingly came to a halt as she virtually disappeared from the pages of the black press. As previously noted, she may have lived outside of the United States during this time, but this remains unclear.[166]

The *New York Amsterdam News* reported McKinney's death (May 3, 1967) at the age of fifty-four.[167] According to her death certificate, McKinney was widowed; her occupation was classified as domestic, and the business or industry in which she worked was listed as "private families."[168] There was no mention that she had been an actress in Hollywood. Most disturbing is that in spite of her talent and her desire to become a prominent screen actress, in death she was reduced to the very role that she had attempted to escape, that of domestic servant. According to Bogle, a former technician who worked on the production of *Hallelujah* had actually recognized McKinney serving a dinner party in New York during her later years.[169]

That McKinney had descended from screen actress and sex symbol to maidservant was not so unusual for black actresses. These women, regardless of their talents, had extremely limited opportunities, and if black actresses desired screen careers badly enough, they were forced to take what they could get, regardless of how degrading the roles were. However, McKinney did become the screen's first prominent black actress to assume a leading role in a Hollywood production and will be recognized in cinema histories for her contribution.

Although McKinney's Hollywood career was relatively short-lived, she had paved the way for another generation of black actresses by demonstrating that they could be convincing in leading roles and that they had to persevere despite the limited roles available. In spite of the inequities and personal acts of racial discrimination practiced by filmmakers, black spectators remained optimistic, clinging to the hope that Hollywood would provide improved on-screen images of blacks. But as time progressed, the issue of the black screen representation became more complicated.

THREE

Louise Beavers

NEGOTIATING RACIAL DIFFERENCE

Sul-Te-Wan and Nina Mae McKinney were among numerous African American actresses and entertainers during the first half of the twentieth century whose physical (Eurocentric) features garnered them privilege in the entertainment industry over other African American actresses and entertainers with equal or superior talent, but whose physical features were considered more Afrocentric than Eurocentric. On stage and on screen, mulatto women often were objects, and sometimes victims, of the desiring male gaze. Nevertheless, the mainstream film industry considered and treated them as Other, just as it did those African American actresses whose physical features were decidedly Afrocentric—neither group was white. One African American actress in this latter group who rose to a level of stardom within Hollywood's proscriptive racial practices during the 1930s and 1940s was Louise Beavers. Beavers responded to her marginalization by negotiating her screen representations. Recognizing that screen roles available to African American women (mulatto or not) were limited, she used her histrionic talent to elevate her roles to a level of unquestionable dignity. Although she represented the quintessential "mammy" on screen, in her private life she was not the subservient figure that her screen roles signified.

Louise Ellen Beavers was born March 8, 1902, in Cincinnati, Ohio, to Ernestine Monroe Beavers of Ohio and William M. Beavers, originally from Georgia.[1] Beavers may have been a descendant of a powerful white patriarchy, for she often stated that her grandfather, James Monroe, was a descendant of the former president of the same name. In 1912, when

Beavers's mother, a schoolmarm in the Cincinnati public schools, began to have health problems, the family moved to Pasadena, California. While attending public school in Pasadena, Beavers reportedly played on the girl's baseball team,[2] but one source notes that her early training for the theater was fostered by her singing in her church's choir. By June of 1920, she graduated from Pasadena High School[3] and later worked as a dressing room attendant for a photographer and served as a personal maid to white film star Leatrice Joy.[4] Later, Beavers performed with the Lady Minstrels, a group of young women who staged amateur productions and appeared on stage at the Loews State Theatre. These appearances may have showcased Beavers's talent and attracted the attention of studio executives. Her entrance into the mainstream cinema industry, however, is clouded by two differing versions of her discovery.

According to the *Baltimore Afro-American*, after Beavers appeared with the Lady Minstrels, she was recruited by an agent to audition for a role with Universal Studios.[5] Yet according to *Negro Digest* in 1949, she was recruited after participating in an amateur contest held at the Philharmonic Auditorium in Los Angeles. Beavers, commenting on her amateur contest appearance, is quoted as saying:

> I sang. I don't know how good I was or how I even managed to get through the song. But I kept telling myself—"You've got to do it—you've got to!" I sang a song called *Pal of My Old Cradle Days.*
>
> When the song ended, I didn't even wait for the applause but then I stopped and turned to the audience again and bowed to my mother on the side of the auditorium. I blew her a kiss and left the stage.[6]

A few days after her performance, she received a call from Charles Butler of the Central Casting Bureau, who recruited black actors to appear in Hollywood productions. Butler allegedly "discovered" Beavers after hearing her sing in this amateur contest and was responsible for her transition from the stage to the screen.[7] On Butler's recommendation, Beavers landed one of her first Hollywood roles, in *Uncle Tom's Cabin* (1927).[8] According to one account, Universal studios called Beavers three times before she responded to their offers; she contended that she resisted "because of the African roles given to colored people."[9] Another version of the story is that Butler simply invited her to audition for a role in *Uncle Tom's Cabin,* and she auditioned and received the part, thus launching her acting career in the cinema industry.[10] Other sources suggest that she was not given the part because she was deemed too young for the role, yet she does appear in the film.[11]

Beavers had been reluctant to pursue an acting career, primarily because of the demeaning and parodic constructions of African Americans that dominated the black screen image. Articulating her objection, she asserted, "In all the pictures I had seen . . . they never used colored people for anything except savages—and I had no ambition to appear before the public in a G-String and an African smile. The costume seemed a little bit to[o] sketchy for general use."[12] Although the exact number of her screen appearances remains in dispute, by the late 1930s she apparently had worked in more than 260 films.[13] These are a testament to her talent and prolific career, and Beavers, while acknowledging that her screen roles were as subservients, at least could say, "I have never been called on to impersonate a savage!"[14]

Beavers's best-known role was that of Delilah in *Imitation of Life* (1934). Following her appearance in this film, in 1936 she married Robert Clark, a native of New York. Clark served as Beavers's manager by arranging her twenty-week tours of theaters that she conducted annually, and that supplemented her income from her screen career.[15] After this marriage ended in divorce, Clark married a dancer, Anise Boyer,[16] and Beavers later married Leroy Moore, an interior decorator from Dallas, Texas; their marriage lasted until her death in 1962.[17] It is ironic that although Beavers (herself an only child) never had children, she played the black matriarch on screen.

Beavers appeared in several screen roles with white actress Mae West, and the two became close friends—a friendship that continued into the 1950s, when they appeared together on stage in Las Vegas. Also during this period (1952–1953), Beavers replaced Hattie McDaniel on the television series *The Beulah Show,* based on the radio show of the same name. Beavers was one of the few actresses who made the transition from film to television, appearing in television shows such as *Cleopatra Collins* (1956), *The Hostess With the Mostest* (1957, Playhouse 90), *The Swamp Fox* (1959, World of Disney), and *You Bet Your Life* (1959, a Groucho Marx Production).[18]

In 1945 Beavers received the honor of becoming a board member of the Screen Actors Guild.[19] During the 1950s Beavers was also interested in the political arena, evident in her public support for Richard Nixon, who later became a U.S. president.[20]

During the early 1960s, she began to experience health problems due to the onset of diabetes. She died of a heart attack on October 26, 1962, at the Cedars of Lebanon Hospital in Los Angeles.[21] Beavers was inducted into the Black Filmmakers Hall of Fame in 1976.

EARLY SCREEN ROLES

Louise Beavers entered the Hollywood film industry in the late 1920s, and her most visible role of the decade was in *Coquette* (1929), with white actress Mary Pickford.[22] This film established Beavers as a prominent African American actress within the mainstream industry, even though she was cast in a subservient role. Her stereotypical role as Julia in this film solidified her screen persona forever and reinforced pre-existing notions about race, but perhaps she rationalized that this was less disturbing than playing a "jungle savage." As Julia, Beavers popularized an on-screen image of black women that conformed to what Homi K. Bhabha characterizes as the "colonial stereotype." According to Bhabha, "it is the force of ambivalence that gives the colonial stereotype its currency: ensures its repeatability in changing historical and discursive conjunctures; informs its strategies of individuation and marginalization; produces that effect of probabilistic truth and predictability which, for the stereotype, must always be in excess of what can be empirically proved or logically construed."[23] Unfortunately, African American spectators witnessed with dismay a virtually endless parade of such representations on screen, particularly mammies, maids, and matriarchal figures, and Beavers's role as Julia in *Coquette* was a harbinger of what was to come for her and for many other black actresses in Hollywood.

Donald Bogle points to Beavers's size as a way by which she commodified the quintessential mammy for white audiences and contends that Beavers "came to prominence portraying overweight mammy figures ready to take on the troubles of the world. Beavers was a big-boned woman, dark, full-faced, wide hipped. She perfected the optimistic, sentimental black woman whose sweet, sunny disposition and kindheartedness almost always saved the day."[24] In *Coquette* and in later films, Beavers, as a subservient racial Other, was multiply positioned—matriarch, maid, and mammy, among a few other images.

Although ostensibly a romance, *Coquette* actually foregrounds class differences and attempts to reduce them to binary opposites—upper and lower. In *Coquette,* Beavers portrays the matriarchal figure for Norma Besant (Pickford), an upper-class, tragic figure who is in love with a man from the lower classes. Norma's father, Dr. John Besant (John St. Polis), objects to the relationship because of the class difference. As tensions mount, her father and her fiancé engage in a duel, resulting in her fiancé's death and the incarceration of her father on murder charges. At the trial, Norma testifies on behalf of her father, despite her ambivalence toward him. But there is a curious twist: At the trial's end, having witnessed his daughter on the stand fabricating a story to secure his liberation, the father is so overwhelmed with guilt that he commits suicide in the courtroom by shooting himself.

As the film's narrative unfolds, we learn that Norma is motherless. Julia automatically becomes a surrogate mother to Norma. In fact, Julia serves as Norma's black racial Other as well as her servant—the latter position reinforced not only by Julia's uniform, but also by her association with the kitchen (she appears wearing a handkerchief on her head and an apron around her waist). The film establishes the kitchen as Julia's territory; it is in this space that she exerts control, power, and authority as a matriarch. This is evident when Norma's brother, Jimmy (William Janney), an excited and impatient adolescent, rushes in to hurry Julia and demands with his command "to shake a leg" that she increase her pace. Responding to his demands and demonstrating that she is in power there, she retorts emphatically that she does not intend to "shake a leg for anyone."

If Julia's size accentuates the emotional effect that she arouses, then she similarly signifies emotionalism by exerting a calming effect in times of emotional intensity. As Julia is urged by Jimmy to hurry, she serves as a device to alter the emotional intensity of the film and becomes an agent for transmitting that intensity. Richard Dyer argues that "whiteness is related to blackness, materially and emotionally dependent on it yet still holding sway over it."[25] In several scenes in the film, Julia's blackness, her dialogue, and her actions encode at the same time the functions of matriarch, maid, and mammy; she is the racial Other in a variety of meanings and applications.

This "shake-a-leg" dialogue is also a not-so-subtle attempt to reduce the black subservient to her body. Bhabha contends that "the construction of the colonial subject in discourse, and the exercise of colonial power through discourse, demands an articulation of forms of difference—racial and sexual. Such an articulation becomes crucial if it is held that the body is always simultaneously inscribed in both the economy of pleasure and desire and the economy of discourse, domination and power."[26] The "shake a leg" remark suggests how the black woman—Julia, in this instance—is reduced to her body and to sexuality. Though Julia is deliberately constructed as unattractive when contrasted with Norma, she at the same time becomes symbolic of the hypersexuality denied to white women in that she is allowed to make sexually explicit remarks that white actresses would not dare articulate.

A more subtle example of how Julia is multiply positioned as the maternal figure and the black racial Other is her role as a surrogate male for the male figure denied to Norma. This is not to argue that Julia is masculinized, but if we consider Freud's position that the woman is predetermined by her lack, then Julia is a surrogate male figure in the absence of a male figure for Norma. This position is further supported by Laura Mulvey's suggestion that "it is her lack that produces the phallus as a symbolic presence, it is her desire to make good the lack that the phallus signifies."[27] It is conceivable that Norma is preoccupied with her lack, which in this instance refers to the male character she desires but is denied. Thus the black maid often serves to fill this void caused by the absence of a male figure for her white female employer. Yet when the male figure enters the picture, the black maid usually disappears or remains in the background.

Michael (Johnny Mack Brown), Norma's fiancé, is characterized as wild, unstable, and unemployable; he is also rendered as an Other, albeit not a racial one. His Otherness is palpable in his speech, style, and dress; he is counterposed to the other white males in the film, and their class differences are heightened. But what is particularly interesting is that Michael's speech closely resembles black dialect—raising the question of whether his voice was dubbed by an African American. That white characters have been constructed to personify blackness is certainly tenable in view of Joel Williamson's position on Rhett Butler (Clark Gable) in *Gone with the Wind* (1939), Linda Williams's subtle suggestions regarding the character of Scarlett in the same film, and Richard Dyer's indirect interpretation of Bette Davis as the protagonist of *Jezebel* (1939).[28] Black, with its various connotations and associations, seems to be the sign the filmmakers use to render Michael different, as the Other. Moreover, he is tall, dark in complexion, and dressed in dark clothing. Michael's positioning (blackness being a signifier of the underprivileged class) makes him a threat to whiteness (which signifies privilege). Although race is not a primary theme in *Coquette,* if spectators are made to perceive Michael as approximating blackness, this intensifies the conflict caused by his desire for the white beauty. Norma overtly signifies whiteness: a blonde, she is dressed only in white or light colors. A signifier of beauty and sexuality, she wears low-cut, sleeveless dresses, parades in pearls, and flounces about in frills and lace. If Michael approximates blackness, then he is equated on some level with the only black character in the film, Julia. And if Michael is equated with Julia, then it is arguable that Julia comes to symbolize the male figure denied to Norma.

As Julia, Beavers often assumes her myriad positions simultaneously. This is evident in a climactic scene in which Michael returns to visit Norma after being absent for several months trying to earn money for marriage and to prove his worth to her father. Michael secretly enters a party that Norma is attending so that the two can be reunited. Norma cannot publicly admit to her affair with Michael, so she leaves the party with him and they seek refuge in a cabin his mother owns. As the two leave the cabin in the early morning hours, however, they are watched. Michael proposes to silence rumors of an illicit affair by suggesting to Norma's father that he grant permission for them to marry. The proposition enrages Dr. Besant, who vows to bring a resolution to Michael's pursuit of his daughter even though Michael insists on marriage to protect her name. Michael leaves, declaring that he will return to retrieve Norma so that he can marry her and clear her name, but Dr. Besant grabs his gun and follows Michael to his cabin.

Fearing for the life of her lover, Norma succumbs to despair, and Julia has to comfort her. Julia embraces Norma and reassures her that "your mammy understands." Norma even sits on Julia's lap, simulating the mother-child position, while pouring out her grief and declaring that she is no longer a "coquette"—as beauty, purity, chastity, and virginity are all inscribed onto whiteness in this scene. Julia's comforting of Norma invokes the mother-child positioning to which Julia Lesage alludes in her critique of *Broken Blossoms* (1916). Lesage suggests that if the female is constructed in the liminal position between childhood and adulthood, her sexual exploitation becomes more understandable and problematized.[29] Therefore, when Norma sits on Julia's lap, she simulates the half-child/half-adult position; by doing so, she reflects her vulnerability and innocence, which explains why she is likely to be the victim of a sexual assault. Perhaps Julia is strategically inserted at this point to diffuse the increasing emotional intensity leading up to Michael's death. Her embrace of Norma becomes a substitute both for the dead mother's embrace and for Michael's embrace, an embrace that presumably took place in the cabin, off screen. Norma could not be shown in that scene—a scene in which she is depicted as tainting the purity of white womanhood.

Wounded by Norma's father from a gunshot, Michael later dies in Norma's arms as she attempts to rescue him on his deathbed. Julia witnesses Michael's death in the presence of Jimmy (Norma's brother) and Stanley (Matt Moore), a suitor who is acceptable to her father's class interests but whose advances she has spurned, and again Norma seeks refuge and comfort in Julia's arms. The scenes cited above and several others demonstrate Julia's multiple positioning: simultaneously representing blackness, shadowing the leading white character by signifying the sexuality denied to white women, serving as a surrogate mother to Norma, and functioning as a symbolic male figure. By providing emotional support during Norma's distress, Julia, as the racial Other, enables Norma to come to terms with the emotional void that the deaths of her mother, her father, and Michael have created.

In *Coquette,* her first major film, Beavers established a pattern of multiple positioning that she replicated in most of her subsequent screen roles. According to Bogle, Beavers assumed the roles of "cheerful, naïve maids and companions [who] were always there to soothe, never to rock the boat. Perhaps it is the unyielding gentleness and submissiveness of her heroines that make them seem less complex and invigorating."[30] The traits to which Bogle alludes may have been borrowed from Beavers's own personality. Newspaper columnist Lillian Johnson suggests such:

Personally Miss Beavers is just splendid, just as fine as she appears on screen, but she also has a charm all her own, which needs no screen role for recognition. She has a very pleasing personality, one that draws people to her instantly and makes them feel that they are meeting a friend instead of a Hollywood star.[31]

As an actress and as a person, Beavers provided the vehicle by which Hollywood could experiment with blackness. She was cast as the companion (Pearl) to the white protagonist Lady Lou in *She Done Him Wrong* (1933). Mae West plays the protagonist, who challenges the white patriarchy through her assertiveness and alluring sexuality. Lady Lou is a nightclub performer who moves between two worlds—the world of legality and morality and the world of illegality and immorality. Although this is a woman's picture and men are objectified as part of the landscape of Lou's world, Lou is nonetheless also rendered as an object of the gaze. She becomes a signifier of male desire and a symbol of female sexuality.

The plot of *She Done Him Wrong* revolves around Lady Lou's manipulation of men in order to claim her space and territory. During her ex-lover's imprisonment, Lady Lou reconstructs a life for herself by establishing new relationships with other men through her connections with the underworld and by elevating her career as a nightclub performer. When her imprisoned ex-lover, professing his love for Lou, escapes from prison to reclaim her, he kills one of Lou's suitors. Even Lou herself is reduced to committing murder when she accidentally kills a jealous female competitor in a dispute that erupts when the other woman's lover succumbs to Lou's overwhelming appeal. As police raid the nightclub seeking Lou's ex-lover, an escaped murderer, they discover an illegal counterfeit operation. The police proceed to arrest all the club patrons except Lady Lou, who manages to elude the authorities because she is rescued by an infatuated policeman (Cary Grant). The film ends with the club patrons heading for jail while Lou and her policeman head for marriage.

In order to examine Beavers's role as Pearl, Lady Lou's shadow and racial Other, it is necessary to first examine Lady Lou as a signifier of white femaleness. Laura Mulvey contends that "the free and easy approach to sex epitomised by the 'new woman' reached its zenith in the pre-Code raciness and sexual self-sufficiency of screen heroines. . . . Mae West has now become emblematic of this period. . . ."[32] West signified the newly liberated woman in that she was sexualized, she exerted power and control over males, she represented independence, assertiveness, and aggressiveness, and, most of all, she appeared invincible. Moreover, she was white and blonde and therefore epitomized Eurocentric standards of beauty. She was somewhat stout, exhibiting what Dyer refers to as "undulating contours,"[33] and her tight gowns accentuated her large bust and wide hips. It is interesting that in *She Done Him Wrong,* West's black servant, Pearl, is similarly stout; codes associated with black female sexuality (large hips, etc.) could then be displaced onto Lady Lou, rendering her even more sexually alluring, even hypersexualized. Lou's sexuality in *She Done Him Wrong* is accentuated by her deep voice. Speaking with her mouth partially closed, she provocatively asks, "Why don't you come up and see me sometime?" This question, which became Mae West's trademark, is followed in the film with "and I'll read our fortune." Proud of her exploits and skill, Lou even declares, "Once I get them, they're branded." That Lady Lou is paired with her black maid speaks to the fact that "West [as Lou] also participates in complicated cross-racial identifications with blackness that are key to her transgressive image."[34]

Lou is always elegantly dressed, suggesting power and authority without denying sexuality, but her grandeur is excessive, and this undermines her representation of the new liberality. Perhaps this was a deliberate device by the filmmakers to undermine the female liberality expressed while ostensibly portraying its screen icon. As Lou flaunts long, tight-fitting gowns, feathered hats, gloves, and jewels and strategically positions her hands on her hips to draw attention to her sexuality, she is perhaps too successful. But even more important are the symbols of white male authority and power that she wields—a jeweled walking cane and cigarettes, subtly suggesting masculinity. It has been argued that Lou appears more like a male in drag than like a liberated woman, unless liberation means assuming male characteristics. Mary Ann Doane has observed that Lou appears to be "masquerading" her femininity.[35] But if her femininity is a masquerade, then so too is her masculinity. Molly Haskell notes of West that

> In her size, her voice, her boisterous one-liners, and her swagger, there was something decidedly, if parodistically, masculine. But she was a woman, and she thus stretched the definition of her sex. Those who object that in her masculinity (and her maternalism) she reinforced the myth of male

supremacy (phallic, imperialist, sexist) in the cinema fail to see that it is the valuation of the sex itself, male over female, rather than their inherent qualities, which is the basis of structural inequality.[36]

Adding to these views, Tania Modleski argues that such masculinization of women supports Judith Butler's prediction of gender trouble "in which gender, anatomy, and performance are at odds with one another [and which] does not necessarily result in the subversive effects often claimed for it."[37] Thus Lou demonstrates how issues of gender and performance become confused. When gender is complicated by race, Modleski continues, "the black woman is seen either as too literally a woman (reduced to her biology and her biological functions) or in crucial ways not really a woman at all."[38] As for Lou, she is reduced to her body, implying that she is "too literally" a woman. At the same time, she is constructed as "not really a woman at all" because of her masculinization and her association with her black screen foil. Therefore, the white woman's liberation as Lou embodies it is ultimately claimed by males, and if Lou becomes associated with blackness through her black racial Other, then she also signifies the ambiguity reflected in the black woman's image.

Indeed, Lou's persona is complemented by her on-screen shadow, her black maidservant, Pearl, who also is well-dressed in her maid's white pinafore and ruffled headpiece. Pearl expresses delight in the fact that she works for Lady Lou, a woman of stature and wealth who has men falling at her feet. Of course, Pearl also is delighted by the diamonds Lou parades. Making herself indispensable, Pearl unzips Lou's dress, carries her packages, and straightens the ruffles of her long gown. It is noteworthy that in attending to Lou's most personal needs—unzipping her dress, preparing her bath, removing her shoes, undressing her behind a screen—Pearl reinforces how sexuality is linked with blackness.[39] Pamela Robertson observes that "West is clearly the boss and center of attention. The maids frame her and set off her whiteness as well as the whiteness of the room. ... West's conversation with her black maids, however, masks racial difference by focusing on gender [and] simultaneously foregrounds her racial difference from the maids and her gendered identification with them."[40]

When Lou remarks to Pearl that "the wolf is at her door," Pearl responds that while this may be the case, this wolf is certainly unlike the wolf (economic hardship) that frequents her own door. The self and Other share in their sameness and their difference: Lou and Pearl at times mirror each other; at other times they are in direct contrast, revealing two functions of the shadow. Black maidservants also signify the intellectual incompetence men attribute to women. The white woman is allowed to displace her lack of intellect onto her black racial Other. For example, Pearl is slow to respond and lacks the skill to manipulate men the way Lou does. When Lou summons her maid, Pearl responds that she has been asleep—the slow response is designed to play upon the stereotype of the African American's perceived mental inferiority, while suggesting the white screen star's mental superiority.

While allowing the white female to seek refuge intellectually through her black Other, Pearl similarly becomes a foil to the white protagonist in that like Lady Lou she is somewhat masculinized. According to the Freudian view of the female as troubled by the lack of a phallus (which in this film could be read as the lack of a *stable* male figure), Pearl stands as a surrogate for the stable male figure denied to Lou. Pearl appears to have been masculinized for the film as is apparent in a close-up: a light mustache has been applied to her upper lip. While the film masculinizes both the black woman (perhaps subconsciously) and the white woman (consciously), it continues to position them to elicit the male gaze. At the film's conclusion, Lou is finally united with a stable male figure, the policeman referred to earlier in the film as "talk, dark, and handsome." Pearl, on the other hand, curiously disappears from the film. Now that Lou has a stable male figure in her life, she no longer needs her surrogate male (Pearl). But even this refeminizing of Lou suggests that the liberation of women depends on males.

In *Forty-Second Street* (1933), Beavers's character is again multiply positioned and made vital to the development of the white female protagonist with whom she is paired—in this case Dorothy (Bebe Daniels). This film uses Beavers's character less to embody or mirror the hypersexualization of the white protagonist and more to regulate the film's emotional intensity, but again Beavers's character serves as a surrogate maternal figure.

Forty-Second Street centers on the perennial tragic white female, this time a stage performer, Dorothy Brye, who launches an ill-fated romance with the show's elderly producer, Abner (Guy Kibbee), while maintaining her affection for a younger male. The romantic conflict develops within the larger context of the film's narrative, which focuses on a stage director's ability to match his previous success despite suffering emotional and psychological stress. Dorothy, the director's leading actress, suffers an ankle injury while performing on stage and is replaced by a less-well-known actress, which jeopardizes the show's success. Dorothy's absence from the production reunites her with her young lover and allows her to dissolve her relationship with the elderly producer, who had planned to replace her when he learned of her affair.

The play within the film is called "Pretty Lady," a title designed to valorize Dorothy's star status and to signify the desirability and sexuality embodied by this white Hollywood actress. Dorothy is elegantly dressed, usually adorned in jewels, a mink wrap, a veiled hat, and gloves. Her elegance is accentuated by the film's choreographer, Busby Berkeley, who utilizes chorus girls instead of the black maidservant to signify the hypersexualization associated with (but ultimately denied) the white screen star. For example, the chorus girls auditioning for the stage show are instructed to elevate their skirts to display their legs; the camera then pans an endless display of legs, clearly sexualizing these women and reducing them to their bodies. Their commodification as sex objects and their reduction to the body is again apparent when one of the stage producers remarks, "We need a girl who can count to forty without a pad or pencil." The implication of course is that because these women lack intellect their only useful assets are their bodies.

Beavers's first appearance as the black maidservant does not come until the second half of the picture, which was consistent with the Hollywood practice of featuring black actors only in cameo appearances or appearances late in a film. Beavers first appears in a scene in which the producer announces—the day before the play's opening—that the show must be moved to another city. Taken by surprise, Dorothy exits the stage, still holding her coffee cup, but the maidservant, dressed in a black uniform with white collar, cuffs, and apron, takes the cup from her. The insertion of Beavers's character at this point in the film suggests that she has been introduced to alter the emotional intensity of the film, since Dorothy's resistance to traveling to another city could threaten the survival of the show. In fact, the maidservant always appears at climactic points in this film, though, interestingly, she remains unnamed throughout the picture.

As the racial Other, this black maidservant is deemed vital and central to Dorothy's development, in spite of her subservience. When Dorothy sings on stage and her performance is interrupted because she has forgotten a handkerchief that is part of her costume, it is the maidservant who provides the handkerchief, which suggests that Dorothy's performance would be incomplete without her. Beavers's character is again used as a calming element prior to the film's emotional apogee when Dorothy sings on stage surrounded by an entourage of men strategically positioned to heighten her sexuality. After Dorothy's performance, the maidservant greets her and remarks, "You nearly was elegant Miss Brye." The unnamed maidservant's presence yet again signals a shift in the film's emotional intensity when Dorothy, distraught that she has not received the phone calls she desired from her lover, begins a tirade. When Abner, the show's producer, attempts to enter Dorothy's dressing room, it is the maidservant who halts him. This is symbolic of Dorothy's romantic rejection of Abner. Thus the maidservant becomes a stand-in for Dorothy, converting her mistress's intent into action. In these and other scenes, Beavers's character basically serves as a prop to motivate action.

Beavers's character also serves as a surrogate male figure denied to the female protagonist. Because of Dorothy's relationship with Abner—a relationship she had launched to advance her career—she is without the male figure she truly desires. When Dorothy rejoins her lover, the black maidservant disappears from the film. As *Forty-Second Street* ends, the elegantly dressed chorus girls dance on a rotating stage and the camera gazes through a pyramid of legs. This scene is designed to objectify women and to hint at Dorothy's hypersexualization now that she is reunited with the male of her desire.

Throughout her film career, Beavers often played characters who were paired with (that is, functioned as a shadow for) white tragic characters—a linking that is both figurative, as blackness is associated with darkness or tragedy, and literal, in that Beavers herself could be viewed as tragic because she portrayed the quintessential matriarchal figure. By extension, because of her blackness, she is an agent for transforming white womanhood on screen.

In *What Price Hollywood* (1932) she was the shadow for Constance Bennett, who starred as Mary Evans, an aspiring actress who is working as a waitress when she captures the attention of an alcoholic Hollywood producer. In several ways, the plot structure of this film in similar to that of *Forty-Second Street*. The leading character and her black maidservant are essentially duplicates of those in *Forty-Second Street*. Mary Evans, formed as an icon of Eurocentric beauty, exudes sexuality, which the film's technical aspects (costumes, lighting, camera work, makeup, script, and so forth) highlight. The press promotes her as a "devastating blonde beauty."[41]

Prior to Beavers's appearance in the film, African American actor Eddie "Rochester" Anderson appears as Max's (the leading male character's) valet. He functions on screen as an Other, strategically inserted to provide comic relief and serve as a signifier of black maleness. His introduction nearly prepares us for Beavers's entrance in the part of the maidservant, Bonita. As the subservient, Bonita is a foil for her employer, the blonde and beautiful Mary, who is already a star. With a million-dollar, seven-year contract, Mary has been cast as the "typical American girl." In character, Bonita is the embodiment of maternalism, subservience, and the sexuality denied to white women. Moreover, Bonita is the agent for transmitting the film's emotional intensity. Her entrances and exits signal changes in the plot, and she especially functions as a harbinger of impending tragic moments within the script. She also functions as surrogate mother and surrogate male for her employer, Mary Evans.

As in other films, Beavers's character in this film assumes a multiplicity of positions simultaneously. Bonita appears on screen dressed in a black uniform with white pinafore, cuffs, and ruffled headpiece. Her costume and actions demonstrate that she is indispensable to Mary. While Bonita signifies subservience to validate Mary's star status, she also functions as a shadow to accentuate Mary's whiteness and beauty. For instance, one scene foregrounds Bonita holding a cosmetic case into which Mary peers to perfect her makeup. The scene contrasts the two women as a way to highlight Mary's beauty.

Bonita, however, plays a more interesting role in this film than mere stereotype or motivational prop. It is through her visual gestures that spectators receive clues about what is most important. Her gaze merges with the gaze of the spectator and controls it in much the same way that Hattie McDaniel controls the gaze of spectators in *Gone with the Wind* (1939). Yet in this instance, Bonita's gaze is the scopophilic gaze—one that observes and documents. In light of bell hooks's argument regarding the "oppositional gaze" and her contention that it emerged out of a historical terrorization in which blacks were denied the right to look, it is interesting that it is Bonita who is strategically positioned to dictate the gaze of spectators.[42] But there is an irony here, for the gaze in this instance is still ultimately claimed by whites. When Bonita delivers the note from Mary declining Lonny's (her suitor's) dinner invitation, she peers past Lonny to direct our attention to the lavish dinner arrangements. It is as if Mary has played a joke and used her Other to carry it out. Lonny, having gone to such extremes to prepare for the elaborate evening, retaliates by crashing through a glass door to invade Mary's home. He physically carries her back to the dinner, dressed only in her nightgown. (Resorting to physical force is of course one way white masculinity is represented on screen and is directly contrasted with femininity.) The romance ultimately results in marriage, in true Hollywood fashion.

Bombshell (1933, alternately titled *Blonde Bombshell*) is another film in which Beavers's role and functions differ little from those assigned to her in other films of this early period, and the film's storyline in many ways resembles the storylines in *Forty-Second Street* and *What Price Hollywood*. The film foregrounds a white female protagonist who is thrust into the turbulent world of Hollywood. Beavers plays Loretta, the maid and black Other to Lola (Jean Harlow). The similarity in their names hints at their sameness and at their interwoven identities. Loretta is a shadow for Lola, and Beavers is a shadow for Harlow. To be sure, Loretta is a maid whose servile position is indispensable to her employer, Lola, a white film star, even to the point of helping Lola learn her lines. Loretta's sexuality is displaced onto her white employer to render her (Lola) desirable but not too sexually explicit. She functions as the surrogate male figure for the white female lead. She is assigned self-berating actions (verbal and physical) ostensibly designed for comic relief but which are demeaning and which exploit black stereotypes.

One thing different about Beaver's role in this film is that her character is more assertive (in relation to whites other than her employer) than the ones she played in her previous screen roles. For example, Loretta refuses to succumb to a scolding by Lola's white secretary. Perhaps her assertiveness, like her sexuality, is strategically designed to be displaced onto the white screen star.[43]

Although she is Lola's caretaker, Loretta is more often the caretaker for Lola's sheepdogs. Indeed, this film's most disturbing assertion is that

Loretta is not only undeniably associated with animalism, but is also subordinate to the dogs. To some extent the dogs become an extension of Loretta's physical size and psyche. The three leashed dogs are always shown leading the way, with Loretta struggling either to keep pace behind them or to maintain order as they proceed in three different directions simultaneously. It becomes clear that it is not Loretta who leads the dogs but the dogs who lead Loretta. It is as if Loretta has become an Other to the three dogs, who are referred to as Trio.

Beavers was inextricably linked to animalism in another film, *Reap the Wild Wind* (1942). The African American press reported that while cast in her customary role as a maid, "Beavers tries to reason with an obstreperous monkey."[44] When the monkey raids the star's dresser to find her undergarments, he becomes entangled in the lingerie. John Wayne, as the white male protagonist, comments on the monkey's behavior and declares that he's "quite a ladies' man." Thus Beavers, who is tussling with the monkey, is implicitly linked to both animalism and sexuality in this scene—an association that permeated some of her other screen roles, such as the one in *Bombshell*.

Beavers's multiple positioning in *Bombshell* is similar to that in many of her earlier films. As the racial Other, she differs only in name as she portrays the characters Julia, Pearl, Bonita, and Loretta—and sometimes she even remains unnamed. After many years of being assigned only minor roles, Beavers emerged as a screen star in her own right playing the part of Delilah in *Imitation of Life* (1934). Still signifying the stereotypical matriarch and still multiply positioned, in this film she also continues to embody sexuality, to serve as both a surrogate maternal figure and a surrogate male figure, and to function as a device to alter the emotional intensity of the film. Seemingly, little has changed, but one major difference can be noted: though she is not the film's star, her performance as the negative Other steals the show.

THE SHADOW AS THE "STAR": *IMITATION OF LIFE*

It was relatively early in Louise Beavers's Hollywood career when she landed her most memorable role, one that transformed her from the shadow for the leading white actress to the film's "star." Though her supporting role in this film, *Imitation of Life,* was that of the racial Other—

perhaps even an exaggerated form of the stereotype—in the opinion of several film critics her performance eclipsed that of the film's star, Claudette Colbert. Delilah (Beavers's character) struggles to escape from the ownership claimed by her white mistress, Miss Bea (Colbert). Moreover, she attempts to establish her independence through her daughter, Peola (Fredi Washington), who becomes the agent by which Delilah liberates herself, albeit a liberation through death. Thus *Imitation of Life*—a film that canonizes black subservience and subordination—can also be read as a film that represents the politicization of the black female as she attempts to liberate herself from her dominant white employer. Deconstructing the film from this perspective casts it and Beavers's performance in a new light.[45]

Imitation of Life strategically defines what it meant to be black in America in the 1930s. It depicts white female liberation at the expense of the exploitation of black labor through the pairing of a white female entrepreneur, Miss Bea, and her black maid, Delilah. Thus, rather than functioning as merely a shadow for the white leading character, Delilah has a story that is basically coequal to Bea's. The two women are drawn together, almost interwoven, as mistress and maid. They combine their efforts to conquer the world's perils and elevate themselves socioeconomically. Yet they are dually positioned in that each is a single mother, each is a woman without a man, and each has a daughter with her own aspirations. Miss Bea's daughter, Jessie, desires Bea's fiancé, while Delilah's daughter, Peola, desires whiteness. On first examination, the film appears straightforward, with no need for examination beyond the obvious. Yet it is the film's racial politics that call for re-examination. Although a number of scholars have explored the film's racial and sexual politics, there is still a need for a return to the film's disturbing subtext: Delilah's indomitable subservience. This is the film's most offensive element, suggesting that to be black implies unwavering compliance, passivity, and resignation. I argue that Delilah's subservience camouflages her desire to escape Miss Bea's ownership of her (Delilah's) personhood.

If we view Delilah as a character who lacks a phallus because she is a woman, then she becomes a woman in search of that which she has been denied. Moreover, if the phallus can be viewed as a weapon or political instrument that she desires, then through her desire for the phallus she automatically becomes associated with a political weapon. By association with a political weapon, Delilah then can be viewed as a political agent. Delilah's empowerment and political agency are evident if we view her daughter, Peola, as the vehicle for her liberation. To develop this argument, this critique will reconstruct the politicization of Delilah and re-examine Peola's role in Delilah's liberation, which her death symbolizes.

Germane to this argument is an assessment of Delilah's unrelenting subservience and an understanding of how morally offensive and unacceptable her behavior is. Her seeming lack of desire to achieve liberation for herself epitomizes, on one level, the struggle between the conscious and the unconscious. While she longs to provide for her daughter, at the same time she must come to terms with her blackness and the lack of opportunities afforded to black women in this period. Absurd as it may seem, Delilah has an unrelenting desire to placate her white employer, so much so that we begin to wonder if her subservience is not an expression of considerable radicalism. Her submissiveness, obeisance, and self-denial are practiced to such an extent as to be offensive even for 1930s America. Could she perhaps have been expressing the opposite of what she projects? The extremity of her behavior calls into question the reason for such a degree of servility. Is it perhaps a hidden form of radicalism? Is it conceivable that through Delilah's subservience she is actually camouflaging the resistance or radicalism that she possesses in her attempt to liberate herself from the oppression and exploitation that her life as a subservient ascribes? I assert that the answer to these questions is yes.

The conventional costuming of the period does not define Delilah's first on-screen appearance; she does not first appear in a maid's uniform, which is perhaps a sign that her role will be different from that of the conventional black maid in mainstream cinema of the period. Delilah establishes herself in the beginning of the film as a self-sacrificing and self-negating character. She arrives at Miss Bea's door nearing desperation and seeking employment. She smiles incessantly, and leaves her daughter standing outside, baggage in hand, as though her daughter's presence might interfere with her ability to obtain employment. Delilah immediately demonstrates her skill at housekeeping by taking charge of a boiling coffeepot. Though the two women have much in common, their vast difference is made evident: Delilah's darkness is contrasted with Bea's whiteness, her frame is exceptionally large when positioned next to Bea's small stature, and her domestic attire is contrasted with Bea's middle-class working attire. Their differences are reified even in their naming: Delilah is always referred to only by her first name, while Bea is always referred to as "Miss Bea." This is a practice, common for the period, to mark social, racial, and status distinctions between blacks and whites. Blacks were to be reminded that they were subordinates, and the Miss or Mister that preceded the first name of the whites were meant to denote respect "due" the "superior" race.

Particularly offensive is the self-denigrating diatribe that Delilah delivers to Miss Bea, attempting to convince her to hire her by affirming that she will not be an expense, since "I don't eat like I look." Then, further insulting herself, Delilah feels it necessary to correct Miss Bea's claim that Delilah is "200 pounds of mother" trying to take care of her child; Delilah emphatically proclaims that she weighs 240 pounds. These remarks are coupled with a dialect that Sterling Brown observes is a white fabrication of black dialect. Brown identifies black dialect as that which evolved from a black slave tradition and that becomes indicative of their transcendence into American life and culture. He suggests that in this film, whites attempt to fabricate black dialect but their efforts distort the dialect. Brown states of Delilah, "Her idiom is good only in spots; I have heard dialect all my life, but I have yet to hear such a line as 'She am an angel.'"[46] This opening scene is so offensive as to make the spectator nearly dismissive of Delilah's dire need to earn a living for herself. It demonstrates, in the decade of the 1930s, in the words of Houston Baker, "black domestic labor mak[ing] a narrow circuit from kitchenettes to white folk's kitchen."[47]

Compounding Delilah's construction as the quintessential subservient, her complicit behavior throughout the film seems inexplicable and inspires resistance in many spectators. Delilah's complicit behavior is especially evident when (a) she refuses to leave the white family even though she is offered the opportunity to become a partner in a business that she helped to build, (b) she rubs Miss Bea's tired feet in a negation of her own exhaustion as a domestic, (c) she is more committed to Jessie (Miss Bea's daughter) than to her own child, and (d) she otherwise incessantly desires to fulfill Miss Bea's needs while neglecting her own. Affirming this position, Jeremy Butler asserts that "Delilah fits comfortably into the 'mammy' type: large framed, self-effacing, religious to the point of superstition, uneducated but 'wise' in matters of the heart, and above all else totally committed to nurturing not just her own daughter but Bea's daughter and Bea herself."[48] Delilah's behavior is reminiscent of the slave retainer who exhibits an unwavering fidelity to her mistress, but whose behavior is actually subterfuge. Delilah is so convincing in her subservience and dedication to her white employer, and in denying her own needs, that it is left to the spectator to beg for Delilah's liberation, self-reliance, and autonomy.

While on the surface of the film such an assertion of the black self is visibly absent, it is present in Peola. Delilah's subservience is transformed in Peola's resistance, which is indicative of Delilah's desire for liberation. Could she publicly express such a desire? In the sociopolitical climate of that time, the answer is absolutely no. Therein lies a way for the behavior of both characters—a resistant Peola and a subservient Delilah—to be better explained and understood.

That Delilah's conscious subservience is displaced onto Peola in the form of her unconscious resistance is apparent in nearly every scene in which Peola appears. Affirming Peola's resistant behavior, Sandy Flitterman-Lewis characterizes it as indicative of her "violent refusal of her mother's culture."[49] When Peola is introduced in the film, she stands outside a door, peering through the screened wire mesh as though she is an Other. Peola remains silent until her mother instructs her to speak to Miss Bea and Jessie. Her silence becomes predictive of the defiance that she soon comes to represent. In denying her voice, she disavows herself from being allowed to speak. Conceding the difficulty of obtaining employment when a prospective employer discovers she has a child, Delilah acknowledges, "Folks just don't want Peola." Thus Peola is constructed as an outsider, an Other. Her silence early on prepares us for her later outbursts of anger, frustration, and continual resistance.

Throughout the film, Peola gives the impression of resenting and resisting her blackness, but perhaps it is really Delilah, living vicariously through Peola, who is really resenting and resisting whiteness. Moreover, in one scene, in which Peola stands outside the door, with Miss Bea, Jessie, and Delilah positioned on the inside, the door becomes a metaphor for Peola's exit from blackness and entrance to whiteness. Or, more importantly, the door becomes a metaphor for Delilah's exiting whiteness to achieve her liberation in blackness.

Peola desires the very whiteness that Delilah seeks to escape. This is made clear when Jessie and Peola are shown leaving together for school,

reciting world capitals. At that moment, Miss Bea and Delilah acknowledge to each other the affinity the two children have developed for each
other. But when Miss Bea admits that Peola is smarter than Jessie, Delilah
quips, "We all start out that way—we don't get dumb until later." The
implication is that blacks are intelligent but are forced to compromise
themselves when their knowledge becomes threatening to whites. Even
more poignant, Delilah is talking about herself while hiding that fact in
her groveling, subservient manner. Again, her behavior is reminiscent of
the faithful slave retainer.

While Delilah's secret recipe for a pancake mix propels Miss Bea into
becoming a wealthy entrepreneur, Delilah continues to act out the part of
the black maid. This is reified in the secret Peola engages in when she attempts to masquerade as white, and it further signifies Delilah's secret in
that while she poses as a black subservient, she really is quite rebellious.

The more subservient Delilah becomes, the more rebelliously Peola
behaves. It is as though the two dispositions coexist and coincide with
one another, ultimately reaching a crescendo upon Delilah's death. For
example, in the first scene where Peola begins to display her resistance
to her blackness (a term that supposedly defines her being and not her
skin color), she returns from school and reveals that Jessie called her
"black." Peola is distraught: "I'm not black, I won't be black," she cries
out, and then she turns on Delilah and proclaims, "It's because of you
that I am black! You make me black." Such a declaration raises the question as to whether Peola means that genetically Delilah is responsible
for her blackness (her social being), or whether she is suggesting that if
Delilah did not look so identifiably black then Peola could live in denial
of her socially imposed blackness and exist as white. The tension here, as
in several of the film's scenes that include Peola, is between social being
and social body.

Such implications invoke the debate surrounding racial purity, racial
origin, "black blood," and the "one-drop rule." Jane Gaines addresses
such issues when she argues that "all of these glaring inconsistencies—
the child who looks white but is classified black, the mother who is [the]
producer of slave labor, the father who is but is not a father—are indicative of the trouble the social imperative encounters in its attempt to manage the incontrovertible evidence of the human body."[50] Affirming the
conflicting positions and complexity related to miscegenation, Gaines

further contends, "Biologically, white bodies can produce black bodies just as easily as black bodies can produce white ones."[51] Susan Courtney examines how the film confused miscegenation for the Production Code Administration and contends that the film "not only confounded the PCA's ability to discern racial identity, but perpetually threatened to unmask 'race' as itself an imitation through and through—a cultural fiction in which we are asked to believe which has no natural life of its own."[52] Courtney adds that "what is at issue here is precisely the psychic dimension of racial ideology: not only how subjects are culturally identified as raced subjects ('black,' 'white,' etc.), but how subjects psychically identify with such interpellations."[53] Thus, in an early scene, when Peola exhibits resistance to her blackness, it is almost simultaneous with our seeing Delilah washing windows for Miss Bea's new business. It is as though Peola's resistance coincides with the exploitation of Delilah's labor.

Peola's resistance—the psychic tensions between her social being and her social body—becomes ever more pronounced as the film's narrative unfolds, as does Delilah's subservience. The next scene in which we witness Peola's rebelliousness is the one in which there is a heavy rainstorm and Delilah has gone to Peola's school to provide her with rubbers and a raincoat. Delilah doesn't know which room Peola is in, so she approaches the teacher to find out, but the teacher proclaims emphatically that there are no "colored children" in her room. Again, the door becomes a metaphor for Delilah and Peola's racial positioning. Standing behind the door, Delilah peers into the class and finds her daughter. Peola is embarrassed and furious that her black mother has uncovered her masquerade and that her classmates now know she is black. She flees the classroom in a rage and exclaims to her mother, "I hate you, I hate you!" Returning home, drenched from the rain, Peola refuses Delilah's assistance.

At this point, Miss Bea intervenes, and Peola becomes receptive to instruction from Delilah. Peola's responsiveness to Miss Bea and dismissal of her own mother signifies her desire for whiteness and canonizes her displeasure with blackness. Yet Peola's rebelliousness could also be interpreted as Delilah's resistance to her white employer and to the segregated education system that denied blacks access to institutions like those Peola attended when passing for white.

Peola's resistance to her blackness coincides with Delilah's lost opportunity to own 20 percent of a pancake company she had helped to establish—an offer that was unusual even though it no doubt was less than she deserved. Delilah's subservience reaches a pinnacle when she declines this offer, finding it more important to continue to fulfill the needs of the white family for whom she works, while denying her own and her family's needs. Delilah's declaration implies that rather than enjoying a life of self-sufficiency and autonomy, she chooses to continue in self-imposed bondage. She seems to be saying that her self-worth is so dependent on this white family that without them she would be virtually devoid of value.

To construct Delilah as a character who actually thinks in such a way signifies the embedded politicization of blackness and the blatant propaganda that went into such screen representations. Considering Delilah's complicity, Peola's resistance is certainly more understandable. If to be black means dependence rather than independence, then we can understand why Peola is so intolerant of her own blackness.

Later in the film, Peola's development from childhood to adulthood becomes synonymous with Miss Bea and Delilah's success as entrepreneurs. Miss Bea has become so successful that she stages an elegant party at her opulent residence. The party is like a ball, featuring a live band and an expanded staff; the formally attired guests wear expensive jewelry to signify wealth. Even though it is Miss Bea and Delilah's success being celebrated, Delilah and the now adult Peola cannot attend; instead, they are confined to the downstairs. Peola makes disparaging remarks regarding the band, while Delilah notes that they sure do play good for white boys. Peola quips that they ought to since they get paid substantially, then she retreats to their quarters, expressing her frustration with having to live "beneath the veil" while the whites seemingly enjoy themselves upstairs. Conceding to her mother that her frustration stems from her desire for whiteness, Peola declares, "I want to be white like I look."

Such intolerance expressed by Peola can be read as an indication of Delilah's intolerance, too. Here Delilah is confined to the downstairs and unwelcome at the party. Although Delilah should rightfully have been treated as a partner in the success and its celebration, Miss Bea has let Delilah and Peola know that they are not welcome at the party. While Delilah is not considered "good enough" to be included in the party, she is invited to discuss the evening with Miss Bea after the party. And after the party there is Delilah, listening to Miss Bea and rubbing Miss Bea's tired feet.

In order to understand Delilah's complicity and Peola's inability to be contained, the two could be viewed as one character conflated from a divided self—a self (Peola) and an Other (Delilah), with the self reflecting the conscious while the Other reflects the unconscious. Seen in this way, the more Delilah seeks her liberation, the more aberrant Peola becomes. For example, when Peola (a young adult) agrees to comply with Delilah's proposition to attend a black school in the South—one that Delilah hopes will allow her to come to terms with her blackness and where she can escape the dilemma of having to confront whiteness—Peola attends the school for a while and then makes a conscious decision to pass as white. Unable to adjust to a black environment, Peola leaves the school and takes a job in a white restaurant where she masquerades as white.

Delilah receives a letter telling her that Peola is no longer enrolled in school. Then, with the assistance of Miss Bea, Delilah locates Peola, intending to bring her home. Peola now does the most hurtful thing she can do: she denies her own mother, telling Delilah that she is not her mother. Miss Bea interrupts and attempts to shame Peola for disowning her own mother.

It is of note that in nearly every instance where Peola resists, Miss Bea is present. This lends credence to the notion that if Delilah's resistance is displaced on to Peola, then Delilah is indirectly confronting her white employer. Peola's outburst becomes symbolic of Delilah's final public outcry against her exploitation, because it is at this point that Delilah's health begins to decline, a decline that parallels her path to liberation.

Once she is back at home, Peola declares that she intends to pass as white and seeks the approval and assistance of her mother and Miss Bea, even if they are unwilling. Delilah pleads with Peola that "you can't ask me to unborn my own child," but she reluctantly concedes—a concession that signals the beginning of Delilah's declining state of health and that leads to her ultimate death. At this point, Peola has definitively decided to live independently of both Miss Bea and Delilah and to pass as white. Peola's departure signifies the departure that Delilah makes from her white employer on her way to achieving her liberation. As soon as Peola departs, Delilah's health sharply declines, and from this point on she is rarely seen in the capacity of subservient.

Confined to her deathbed, she is no longer exploited for her labor. Now it is the whites who are positioned almost as subservient, waiting on Delilah. Miss Bea and Jessie rush to her bedside to accommodate Delilah as they realize their existence is intricately interwoven with Delilah's, emotionally if not physically. When Delilah makes demands of Miss Bea to provide an opulent funeral and to take care of Peola, she promises to comply.

Delilah's death is a symbol of her liberation (though ephemeral), and by extension, it might be thought of as a foretelling of all blacks' liberation. During the funeral scene, blacks fill the screen for the first time and spectators are provided with a glimpse of artificially constructed black life. However, this particular black liberation has been achieved through a death, which is a dangerous position in and of itself. And even in death, black liberation is still ultimately claimed by whites. This position is perhaps best articulated in a *Philadelphia Tribune* review of *Imitation of Life* that notes, "In death [blacks] have an opportunity to approach equality and they take it. But even in death the grim spectre [of] prejudice rears its head. Cold dead bodies must have separate resting places—one for white and another for colored. And in Philadelphia, a colored body may not be cremated—the ashes of colored bodies might get mixed with some white ones."[54] Though Delilah's body is subjected to segregated practices, she has nevertheless achieved her personal goal of liberation. Her labor is no longer exploited, and since Peola is now liberated (if only temporarily) from her blackness, Delilah is similarly liberated from whiteness. And though Delilah's conscious self dies, her unconscious continues to live in the aftermath of her death, which is evident when Peola returns to Delilah's funeral. It is at this point that Peola acknowledges the pain she has inflicted on her mother—a suggestion that she is coming to terms with her blackness. But while Delilah is liberated, Peola remains forever enslaved. Sandy Flitterman-Lewis argues that Peola's insistent denial of her blackness is an expression of both "the racial self-hatred of the mulatto and the sexual self-hatred of the female in patriarchal culture."[55] Peola's denial may instead represent Delilah's hatred of what she signifies as the producer of labor and her hatred of the status assigned to black women in the sociopolitical culture of 1930s America. Finally, as

Hortense Spillers characterized the mulatto as a neither/nor proposition, the black maid is similarly a neither/nor subservient.[56]

IN REVIEW: THE PRESS IN BLACK AND WHITE

Following the release of *Imitation of Life*, one reviewer noted that Beavers was omitted from the advertising material despite her unparalleled performance: "The star is hidden by the producers while the white players are given the 'write ups.' But the truth comes out when the play is seen."[57] The truth, as *Crisis* magazine and several other publications (black and white) saw it, was that "Miss Beavers 'steals' the picture. . . . That such a triumph should come to Miss Beavers demonstrates that a level head, a firm belief in one's own possibilities, and a willingness to accept small, inconsequential parts and enact them well are necessary to climb from the level of mediocrity to a place of more than ephemeral distinction in motion pictures."[58] Echoing what *Crisis* said, the *Motion Picture Herald* added that Delilah's story, as Beavers performed it, "is the more poignant of the picture's dual theme."[59] *Variety* asserted that Beavers's performance "is one of the most unprecedented personal triumphs for an obscure performer in the annals of a crazy business."[60] *Time* magazine conceded that "the real heroine of *Imitation of Life* is not Bea Pullman but Aunt Delilah."[61] The *Negro Liberator* proclaimed that for best performance, "The honors belong to Louise Beavers and Fredi Washington."[62]

Apparently, the African American press had hoped that their public lobbying on Beavers's behalf would cause the Motion Picture Academy to recognize the merit of their reviews and award Beavers an Oscar for her outstanding performance. The Academy did not, however, honor Beavers with an Oscar, a slight that the black press in particular noted with more than dismay. The *Pittsburgh Courier* claimed that "the honorable judges [for the Academy] just couldn't take it—and didn't,"[63] the *Baltimore Afro-American* added that for the Academy to do so would burnish the image of white Hollywood,[64] and the *California Graphic Magazine* reiterated the obvious: "the Academy could not recognize Miss Beavers. She is black!"[65]

Fourteen years after *Imitation of Life* was released, when the film *Good Sam* (1948) was advertised in the *Chicago Defender*, the report read, "Academy Award Winner Louise Beavers [appears] with Gary Cooper

and Ann Sheridan in Leo McCarey's *Good Sam*."[66] Beavers's picture and
the Academy Award were featured in the advertisement; the paper was
apparently taking it upon itself to bestow the award symbolically upon
Beavers, perhaps to repay her for the Academy's oversight.

With one hand the black press acclaimed Beavers for her performance
as Delilah, but with the other hand it vilified her for the role(s) she played.
Anna Everett contends that the black press took "pride in divulging Beavers's pro-studio outspokenness, her failure to be accessible to her black
audience, and her role in detracting from the community's goal of racial
uplift."[67] Everett continues that

> Ultimately, the attitude here is one of compromise. Beavers and other ac-
> tors of stock black stereotypes are deemed entitled to earn a livelihood
> in Hollywood so long as they manifest their racial pride and solidarity
> off-screen when called on to do so. According to this logic, Beavers had
> failed miserably to separate the requirements of her public persona as film
> star from her private responsibility as member of an oppressed minor-
> ity community. Adding further to Beavers's temporary ostracism in the
> black press was her dismissive attitude toward her black constituency,
> as reflected in the numerous unflattering quotes attributed to her that
> launched a good many black press missives against her.[68]

It is true that Beavers was at times alienated and ostracized by the black
press, as were other artists who provided offensive representations. Yet
some of her alienation can be attributed to misrepresentations that occurred in the black press.

For example, when *Imitation of Life* was screened for newspaper reporters, Beavers lobbied for members of the African American press to
attend.[69] Unfortunately, there was a misunderstanding, and the *Baltimore
Afro-American* falsely reported that she had expressed a lack of interest
in allowing them to attend and had even "snubbed" black reporters.[70]
In response to her alleged actions, the paper began to attack what they
deemed to be her callous attitude:

> There is something pitiful and futile, something despicable and ignoble,
> something suicidal, certainly something that strikes awfully at the very
> base of the colored man's economic status and racial self-respect when
> our own people forget their identity and perpetuate the policies that
> make them the butt of ridicule and enslavement by other races of the
> world.[71]

Beavers had in fact attempted to embrace the black press and to articulate a plea to prevent African Americans from being further marginalized on screen. Defending her, the *Chicago Defender* corrected the erroneous report and cautioned members of the African American press against circulating "malicious statements."[72] Newspaper critic Harry Levette insisted that

> For not only is she in private life just like the kindly self-sacrificing race-loving "Delilah" of the screen but neither she, Universal Studio nor Pantages showed the least disinterest for the Negro press. Mrs. C. [Charlotta] A. Bass publisher of the *California Eagle* was sent passes from the theatre; the *Defender* representative was sent sufficient [passes] for his party by Mr. Teddy McDonald, Universal's publicity ace[;] and other local newspaper folk received recognition.[73]

Such erroneous statements could damage the careers of black actors and might "endanger the future of the Race artists [who are] just now beginning to receive recognition as emotional actors."[74]

In many ways, the black community and the black press were in concert regarding their assessment of Beavers's performance as Delilah and her public and private selves. As did the black press, the black community considered the denial of the Oscar to Beavers as a slight against all African Americans whose talent had gone unrecognized and whose labor had been exploited. Although the African American community embraced Beavers, at the same time it acknowledged how she and other black actors were doubly coded, being forced to provide demeaning representations of the African American for the screen. Both the black press and the black community were critical of actors and actresses who played roles that demeaned blacks.

Discussing how she negotiated these representations, Beavers stated, "While I might interpret the roles of ignorant people at times, I have heard it said that it takes intelligence to do such a part."[75] But African American spectators were not fully convinced. In Memphis in the late 1930s, Beavers's scheduled appearances were greeted by small crowds. The press reported that "Many Beale Streeters voiced their disapproval of the various roles played by Miss Beavers. Some said her portrayals belittle the Race."[76] Even lesser-known entertainers in cinema circles garnered larger crowds than she did—perhaps because some in the African American community were offended by her continual "mammy" roles.[77] Beavers was evidently disappointed and disturbed by her poor reception in Memphis. When she toured Dallas, she expressed great appreciation of her reception there: "I have been more cordially received in Dallas than any other city in which I have made a personal appearance."[78]

This generally ambivalent reception among African American audiences was echoed in the black press. On the one hand, the press viewed Beavers as a signifier of black advancement in the cinema world, despite the marginalized roles she assumed. On the other hand, they castigated her for these roles and seldom embraced her as a leader in the movement to improve the black screen image. Seeking to improve their own plight and that of their constituency, members of the African American press were divided. Some saw their mission as hampered by conspiring with the racialized inscriptions of these representations; others felt it necessary to compromise the black screen image in order to achieve some level of progress. Their ambivalence can perhaps be seen in a 1942 press photo of Beavers wearing a handkerchief on her head, with an apron around her waist, but positioned next to a white woman similarly dressed as a maid. The caption reads, "What's Wrong with This Portrayal?"[79] In a further example, the *Baltimore Afro-American* decried Beavers's absence from the list of nominees for board members of the Screen Actors Guild in the late 1940s but referred to her as the "Buxom elfin-face Louise Beavers," thus sexualizing and marginalizing her.[80] Everett concurs that

> the press successfully navigated the choppy economic waters between agitating for black performers' rights to work in Hollywood and critical appraisals of films casting black actors in stereotypical roles. The papers were cognizant of the risks associated with alienating Hollywood, especially where the matter often pivoted on calls for access to studio publicity departments or strident insistence on black performers' employment opportunities. The press understood as well the unlikelihood of meaningful change without the demand for it.[81]

DELILAH STRIKES BACK

The character Delilah is the quintessential subservient. Although Beavers played roles before and after *Imitation of Life* of which the African American press and the African American community were highly critical,

Beavers's on-screen lives were diametrically opposed to her off-screen life. As an agent of political activism, she publicly articulated a defense of the roles she played. In response to the criticism of her willingness to assume subservient roles and her objectification as a matriarchal figure, Beavers transformed her roles into such unparalleled performances that she subverted the gaze of spectators and may have minimized some of this criticism. She was said to have deflected the gaze or "look" back onto the spectator and the stars with whom she was paired, all of whom were in awe of her talent.

One example of Beavers's public resistance to the subservience she endured on screen occurred during the filming of a scene in *Imitation of Life*, which was edited from the final version of the film. This scene focuses on Peola, who while on a train traveling South, is approached by a black male. The man is then accused of accosting a "white" woman. When it is revealed that Peola is not white, the planned lynching is halted. Peola "rushes into the center of the mob and shouts: 'Stop! Stop! I'm a N[igger] too.'"[82] The word "nigger" was to be used in the film, but Beavers met with the scenarist and asked for it to be removed because she found it offensive.[83] Her protests became public knowledge and elicited a response from the NAACP, which sent a letter to the studio expressing the organization's objection and stressing its support for Beavers. Because this had become a political issue beyond the industry, studio officials proceeded to punish Beavers, whom they considered a troublemaker: "The next day the studio sent for her and had her repeatedly pronounce the word 'Negro' and tested out its sound."[84] Such punishments were intended to deter other African American artists in the industry from asserting themselves in the future.

Beavers's acceptance of subservient roles caused her further difficulties within the African American community, but she continued to defend her choice of roles. She declared:

> As for the characters, I think that somewhere one might find a person like Delilah, a person who would not be affected by any amount of money which might come to her. A person who would be content to go along her way as long as she was assured of a place to sleep, enough to eat and a big funeral at the end. But there was more to Delilah than that. There was the trait of faithfulness, devotion, her love for her white friend and her child.[85]

Beavers understood that multiply positioned characters such as Delilah became signifiers of a variety of racial codes, which actors and actresses could manipulate and alter for their own purposes. As for the scene in *Imitation of Life* when Delilah refuses an opportunity to become a partner in the business she helped create, Beavers exclaimed, "Let somebody walk up to me now and ask me if I wanted $20,000—I'd take it and ask what for."[86] She then added, "I am only playing the parts. I don't live them."[87] In *Rainbow on the River* (1936), she was forced to say "Negroes were happier in slavery"; Beavers declared, "I have no objection to playing the so-called 'Aunt Jemima' roles, because they are period plays. I am an actress and interpret [the] characters as they are written."[88] In *Mr. Blandings Builds His Dream House* (1948), she was again positioned as a subservient, but this time her words and actions were central to the plot. In this film, it is the idea of the black maidservant Gussie (Beavers) that allows the white male advertising executive to excel in his profession: She exclaims, "Not ham! Wham! If you ain't eating wham, you ain't eating ham,"[89] and this becomes the slogan needed to revive his languishing career. This hints at the dependence of the white protagonist on the intelligence of his racial Other, in much the same way as in *Imitation of Life*.

To deny the subservience implied in her screen roles, Beavers often affirmed her blackness and applauded whites who were supportive of African Americans. Writing about Beavers, Lula Jones Garrett noted that "She likes Mae West, with whom she has played in *She Done Him Wrong* because Miss West . . . never does anybody wrong, and especially does right by always having some colored actors in her pictures. She likes Universal for the same reason, . . . because colored actresses and actors get much consideration."[90] She also appeared in all-black-cast films, such as *Dark Manhattan* (1937), produced by the Million Dollar Production Company.[91] During the Second World War, Beavers, like many black entertainers (e.g., Rex Ingram, Ben Carter, and Nina Mae McKinney), attended a rally to boost the morale of soldiers preparing for the war.[92] Undeniably, she used her position—albeit a position that was questionable to many in the community—to support causes that were instrumental to advancing African Americans.

Despite the public image that she developed as a result of her screen career, Beavers was not a "natural" for subservient roles. She had come from Cincinnati and then migrated to California, and was far removed from the southern types she often portrayed on screen. In fact, because she had never lived in the South, "she had to learn the Negro dialect just as one learns a foreign language. 'I couldn't even understand the language ... but I kept studying, reading books, and poems and finally mastered the dialect sufficiently to use [it] in screen roles.'"[93] She also had limited experience as a servant. She suggested in a 1935 interview that the only domestic work she had ever performed off screen was while employed as a maid to white actress Leatrice Joy in the early 1920s and that she did not possess the cooking skills customarily associated with maid's roles.[94] She confided that "it took her five days to learn to flip pancakes, during which time she became so tired of batter and griddles and turner that she swore she would never touch another pancake as long as she lived."[95]

Beavers's resistance to her screen representations and her dissociation from them was apparent when she was forced to appear in court for a lawsuit regarding an automobile accident. Because Beavers was working on a film, she appeared in court in a maid's uniform, but as the press reported, "the famous actress was accompanied by her personal maid."[96] Flaunting the fact that in real life she was not a maid, but instead employed one, Beavers created her own image, that of a woman of means. She was also a firm follower of the Christian Science philosophy, a religious belief and practice diametrically opposite to the religious fervor she displayed in the role of Delilah.[97] Unlike most of her on-screen characterizations, where she was denied a male companion, off screen she was married twice.

Beavers's public support of black institutions that operated in the public interests of blacks attempting to achieve equality and democracy was apparent when she endorsed Robert S. Abbott, editor of the *Chicago Defender,* and his newspaper. According to the *Defender,* "To [Beavers] the work of Editor Robert S. Abbott in building the *Chicago Defender* into an institution is the greatest single accomplishment the country can boast. 'I've loved that man for years though I had never seen him.'"[98] That she publicly supported and endorsed one of the most vigilant organs designed to achieve equality for African Americans during a period when many were denied a voice speaks to her allegiance to causes and institutions that African Americans embraced.

Beavers's political views, however, provoked considerable debate, particularly later in her career. Richard Nixon's "first campaign for public office was launched in Louise's Los Angeles home ... with Irene Dunne as co-sponsor."[99] Beavers, defending her support of Nixon, once said, "I'm not really partisan in my politics, but I'm for Dick Nixon all the way."[100] Her endorsement of a political figure who would become anathema within the African American community is certainly conceivable since most African Americans supported Republican candidates up until the 1960s.[101] Her support for Nixon could also speak to Nixon's skill at exploiting Beavers to try to gain additional African American support, or it could reveal her political naivete in her failure to foresee his future political exploits and disservice to the black community. Perhaps she genuinely supported him early in his political career, believing that he demonstrated some sympathy for African Americans. If Nixon viewed Beavers as being no different from the subservient roles she played, then he would have assumed that she was the "pleasant, likeable Negro [maid]—plump and happy and quick to laugh."[102] Beavers's frequent appropriation of this image on screen allowed her to make the transition to television when she replaced Hattie McDaniel in the *Beulah* television series in the 1950s, following McDaniel's declining health.

HOLLYWOOD'S COUNTERPUNCH

Though at times the black press and the black community treated her harshly, Beavers faced more threatening tactics from the industry itself, and she came dangerously close to having her career obliterated. In large part, her increasing alienation from the mainstream film industry was a consequence of her outspoken resistance to how the industry (and white society in general) treated and portrayed blacks and, ironically, of her stellar performance in *Imitation of Life*. As had happened to other African American actors, her parts began to be edited out of final film versions more and more frequently, thanks to "certain busy body censors."[103] She also found it difficult to acquire roles commensurate with her talent. According to the *Baltimore Afro-American*, "after *Imitation of Life* she automatically was elevated into the featured player class, [but] casting directors stopped employing her, since that meant paying her considerably more money. In other words, she promoted herself out of the maid roles which she did so effectively and frequently."[104] African American actresses found themselves in a double bind: they were vilified if they succeeded and vilified if they failed. Beavers received less money for her roles, such as the one in *No Time for Comedy* (1940, alternately titled *Guy with a Grin*) where she was cast as Clementine—the black maid to Linda Esterbrook (Rosalind Russell). In this film, Linda is the leading lady in Gaylord Esterbrook's (James Stewart) first Broadway play for which he receives critical acclaim. Taking on Linda as his wife and in view of the success he has achieved, Gaylord is then encouraged to abandon comedy and produce a tragedy, an act that nearly results in the destruction of his marriage as well as his professional career. As for Beavers's role, reports note that her hands had been contracted for several weeks at a large salary, but the studios, after utilizing a close-up of her hands, substituted a male extra, Benny Washington, for the additional scenes. The fact that Beavers's hands were used rather than Beavers herself was insulting, but even more insulting was when she was replaced by a male figure in this small scene. This was a cost-cutting measure for the studios, no doubt, but an insult to Beavers.[105]

Denigrated on screen, Beavers also was denigrated off screen. For example, the *Baltimore Afro American* reported:

> One day she . . . parked her automobile near the studio and when she re-
> turned, it had been stolen. In great haste, she went into the lunchroom,
> seized the telephone and directed her mother, in an excited manner,
> to find the license number and call the police. While she was talking, a
> young Southern white woman, waiting for the phone, drawled impatiently
> to the effect that it was a shame that any woman who wasn't white should
> be hogging the phone and what would happen to her if she were down
> South. Miss Beavers overheard her. . . . she approached the white woman,
> some words were passed, and in the twinkling of an eye, Miss Beavers
> had reached out and slapped the white woman. Astonished and pained,
> the Southern girl looked around among the other white diners and asked:
> "Are you going to let her do that to a white woman?" Nobody in the cafe
> stirred.[106]

To be sure, Beavers's characterizations in her film roles call for examination because of her contributions to cinema and her strident resistance to the caricatures inscribed in these roles. In the final analysis, it can be argued that, off screen, Louise Beavers attempted to deny and defy the subservience she was hired to portray on screen. Moreover, she used her acting talent to lessen the marginalization that came with her screen roles, and by doing so she negotiated new screen representations for subsequent actors and actresses.

FOUR

Fredi Washington

THE MASQUERADES AND THE MASKS

Louise Beavers and Fredi Washington are best remembered for their roles in *Imitation of Life* (1934), a film that spawned both actresses' film careers. While Beavers capitalized on the notoriety that her role provided by popularizing such roles in other films, Washington was much more resistant to such one-dimensional roles. According to Anna Everett, Washington was "the cinema's first reluctant black anti-hero. Her private yearning was the public demand for an acknowledgment of black humanity."[1] Although their screen careers basically paralleled each other, Washington's portrayals were diametrically opposed to those of Beavers.

As they did for Louise Beavers, many audiences and film critics praised Fredi Washington for her performance in *Imitation of Life*. Both Beavers and Washington insisted that they were unlike the characters they played in this film. While there is evidence to support Beavers's claim, there is evidence that Washington and her screen persona, Peola, were on some levels imitations of each other. Indeed, the participation of black actresses in the creation of racialized and sexualized constructions on screen is especially interesting in Washington's case. Despite her public denial that her on-screen roles, particularly her role in *Imitation of Life*, were connected to her off-screen life, there are several parallels between her private life and the role she assumed in this film. Donald Bogle affirms that Washington's "public persona and private life looked at one point as if they'd merge[d]."[2] While steadfastly denying that she sought whiteness, Washington was vilified for her screen role in *Imitation of Life* and forced to assume a defensive posture to extricate herself from the mulatto role.

Despite this controversy and some noteworthy commonalities between actress and character, the prevailing evidence is that the similarity between Washington and Peola was only skin deep and that Fredi Washington was quite unlike Peola. Though Washington and Peola were born with the mask of whiteness (they were white mulattoes), Washington's performance as Peola was merely and only a masquerade.

Fredi Washington was born Fredericka Carolyn Washington on December 23, 1903, in Savannah, Georgia, to Robert T. Washington (who died in 1965) and Harriet Walker Ward Washington (who died in 1915).[3] She was the oldest of nine siblings.[4] Following her mother's early death at the age of thirty,[5] when Fredi was only eleven years old, and following her father's remarriage, she and her sister Isabel were sent to the Saint Elizabeth's Convent in Cornwell Heights, Pennsylvania, which was operated by Reverend Mother Katherine Biddle. While Fredi was attending the convent, her stepmother died, and her father subsequently remarried again, this time to Gertrude Washington (who died in 1963).[6] After Fredi and Isabel left the convent, Fredi headed to New York to live with her grandmother and aunt.

At the age of sixteen, Fredi's schooling was briefly interrupted due to the family's strained finances, and she was forced to withdraw and seek work.[7] But she eventually managed to return to school and graduated from the Julia Richmond High School. Following her graduation, she enrolled in two professional schools, Egri School of Dramatic Writing and the Christophe School of Languages.[8]

Seeking employment after graduation, Washington worked as a stockroom clerk with a dress company for $17 a week and later worked as a bookkeeper with the W. C. Handy Black Swan Record Company. It was here that she learned of an audition for the stage show *Shuffle Along*, produced and directed by notables such as Eubie Blake, Noble Sissle, Flournoy E. Miller, and Aubrey Lyles. With the assistance of choreographer Elida Webb, Washington landed a spot with the show and went on to earn $35 a week despite having no professional training as a dancer.[9]

Washington performed with *Shuffle Along* from 1922 to 1924.[10] After appearing as a dancer and in other performances, in 1926 she managed to secure an acting role in the theatrical production *Black Boy*, which featured Paul Robeson as a prizefighter. *The Chicago Defender* noted: "When Paul Robeson appears in *Black Boy* early in September his cast will include a young girl who flourished last season in the Club Alabam and is apparently not at all depressed by being known as Freddie Washington [her name is spelled differently depending on the source]."[11] Although she gained experience as an actress, Washington discovered that acting roles were limited for black actresses, so she left the United States and headed for Europe to pursue her dancing career with Al Moore, with whom she formed a ballroom dance team billed as Moiret and Fredi.[12] The dancing team toured a number of cities in France, including Paris, Monte Carlo, Nice, Toulouse, and Dieppe. They performed in London as well as in Ostend, Belgium, and attracted audiences throughout Germany with performances in Berlin, Hamburg, and Dresden.[13]

In the late 1920s, Washington returned to the United States and appeared in a few films, including *Black and Tan Fantasy* (1929), in which she performed on screen with the jazz legend Duke Ellington.[14] She returned to the stage in productions such as *Hot Chocolates* (1929), *Great Day* (1929), *Sweet Chariot* (1930), and *Singin' the Blues* (1931). In 1932, she performed on a southern dance tour with Eubie Blake and Noble Sissle's orchestra and appeared with Duke Ellington's orchestra in several cities, including Chicago. The following year she was cast opposite Paul Robeson in the film version of *Emperor Jones* (1933, directed by Dudley Murphy, who had previously directed her in *Black and Tan Fantasy*) and in *Drums in the Jungle*. Her screen performances were often supplemented by stage shows, such as when she acted in *Run, Little Chillun* (1933).[15] It was also in 1933 that she married Lawrence Brown, a trombonist with Ellington's band; in the late 1940s she filed for divorce, citing his marital infidelity as the principal reason.

In 1934, Washington was cast in one of the most important roles of her career, Peola in *Imitation of Life*. Three years later, she returned to the screen opposite Bill Robinson in *One Mile from Heaven* (1937), which was described as "the first American[-]made picture with a mixed cast, in which there is not only no objectionable dialogue from the viewpoint of the colored moviegoer but the characters are decent, upstanding people."[16]

In the late 1930s, Washington became one of the founders of the Negro Actors Guild, serving as its first executive secretary from 1937 to 1938. The following year she landed a supporting role in the stage production of *Mamba's Daughters*, which featured Ethel Waters.[17]

During the 1940s, Washington served as theater editor and columnist for the *People's Voice*, a black newspaper edited by Adam Clayton Powell Jr., who was married to Washington's sister Isabel.[18] She also served as administrative secretary for a Joint Committee of Actors Equity and Theatre League on hotel accommodations for black performers throughout the country and was a registrar for Howard Da Silva's School of Acting in New York.[19] Meanwhile, she continued to perform on stage (*Lysistrata*) and on screen (*How Long Till Summer*), and she even appeared as a guest on the television show *The Goldbergs*. She also reportedly worked as a casting consultant for the 1943 stage productions of *Carmen Jones* and *Porgy and Bess* and the 1952 production of *Cry the Beloved Country*.[20]

Following her divorce from Lawrence Brown in 1951, Washington married Dr. Hugh Anthony Bell (a dentist who died in 1970) and moved to Stamford, Connecticut. In 1975, she was inducted into the Black Filmmaker's Hall of Fame and became a recipient of the CIRCA award for lifetime achievement in the performing arts.[21] Fredi Washington died on June 28, 1994, at the age of ninety, after being hospitalized at the St. Joseph's Medical Center in Stamford. She was survived by her sister Isabel.

MASQUERADES OF WHITENESS

To examine Washington's role as Peola in *Imitation of Life*, this study proposes that as an actress and as a person, Washington's masquerade (the character she played) and mask (the person she was) of whiteness were not the same—that her social body was not a reflection of her social being. Physiologically, Washington was what is often called a white mulatto in that she was indistinguishable from (could "pass" as) a white woman. (Within the category of mulatto, a bright mulatto was a person with distinct Eurocentric features but one whose skin tone could not pass for white.) Even before *Imitation of Life*, Washington's physical appearance had always been a point of contention in her private life, if not for herself then for those who subscribed to America's prevailing racial hierarchies. Masquerading as white, or "passing," is embedded with its own set of dynamics, raising questions of whether one is psychologically transformed in the process. Although Washington was never psychologically transformed (she never intellectually extricated herself from blackness), her physiology allowed her to be rendered as white, and it is this complexity to which she constantly responded and that can be traced to the early stages of her acting career.

In the 1926 stage production of *Black Boy,* Washington was cast in the role of Irene, the mistress of the title character (Paul Robeson). The play, written by Jim Tully and Frank Dazey and modeled on the life of prizefighter Jack Johnson, focuses on a prizefighter who is deceived and betrayed by his seemingly white mistress, Irene.[22] Under Irene's influence, Black Boy compromises a fight by becoming inebriated. At first he feels compelled to retaliate against Irene for her role in facilitating his decline—even threatening to murder her—but he changes his mind when he learns that she is actually black.[23] When Irene, "his little white missy," deserts him, he realizes "that his whole world was an elaborate illusion."[24] Irene's masquerade may be read in two ways. First, by pretending to be white and attracting the attentions of Black Boy, she is clearly establishing an interracial relationship, a provocative notion in and of itself for the time period. Second, when she reveals herself to be black, she is regarded as deceptive because she has succeeded in deluding Black Boy (as well as the audience).

The duplicity of Irene's masquerade in *Black Boy* exemplifies how the mulatto character was problematized on the American stage, a duplicity that permeated the sociopolitical climate in which Washington lived. It was a world of absolutes with respect to black and white, a world where there was no middle ground. The producers not only incorporated this duplicity into the play but they also imposed it on Washington by inducing a masquerade in her personal life. Yet Washington constantly contested the racial ascriptions imposed on her because of her physical appearance. Washington's name "was changed to Edith Warren in the playbills just in time for the performance."[25] Was this transformation necessitated by the producers' desire to conceal—that is, to mask—her true racial identity? Did the name Edith Warren sound less black than Fredi Washington? Perhaps the producers wanted to feminize her since the name Fredi could be regarded as masculine. The African American press took issue with the masculinization of her name, because her real name, Fredericka or Fredricka, evolved into Freddye, Freddie, or Fredi, suggesting another masquerade.[26] Names do have power, and language can be used to both liberate and enslave. But in these transformations, Washington was denied the power to control her identity, raising questions about the ability of all African American women to control their own image.

Her producers appear to have engineered Washington's name change to confuse theater patrons so that her white masquerade would be rendered more believable. If audiences knew that a black actress was playing the part of a white, they would be less likely to identify with her character, but if they assumed that they were watching a white actress masquerading as black, then the interracial relationship she developed would appear less threatening. Lola Young writes that "in the Hollywood 'passing' films of the 1940s and 1950s the tragic 'mixed race' protagonists were played by actors 'known' to be white. At the core of such casting was the belief that white audiences would not be able to identify with black actors in these leading roles and that the 'tragedy' of 'passing' was that basically good, honest people had their lives blighted by the [tainting] of 'negro blood.'"[27] James Snead adds that "the roles of mulatto black women passing for white are actually played by white actresses, to make sure that a visual ambiguity does not compound an already difficult conceptual leap."[28] Casting a black actress in this interracial role then distanced white audiences from identification with the character only to the extent that they knew she was indeed black. Pearl Bowser and Louise Spence further suggest that "racial mixing threatens definitions of race, challenging the idea that racial identity might be 'knowable.' By blurring the dichotomy on which whiteness depends, miscegenation throws into disarray the basis of white supremacy."[29] In this case, however, the play's producers imposed a masquerade of whiteness on Washington: "it was the producers' idea to change her name, for reasons she [Washington] never understood."[30]

It was not Washington but others who precipitated and perpetuated her duplicitous masquerade as white, who merged her stage persona and private persona. When *Black Boy* opened in Wilmington, Delaware, she was offered the same hotel accommodations at the Hotel DuPont as were the white performers, while other African American cast members were denied such access. Washington was privileged because of her white appearance, and her racial identity remained unknown to the proprietors. According to the *Baltimore Afro-American*, "the supposition was [made] that Fredi was really white, passing for a colored girl who was passing for white."[31] Explaining why she took advantage of the privileges and opportunities presented to her because of her physical appearance, she publicly stated, "I only ask my money's worth and when they know you are colored they rob you of that even break."[32] Lola Young explains that "since the success of the 'mixed race' woman who passes is based on her expectation of reaping the benefits which accrue to white women,"[33] then it is understandable why Washington availed herself of opportunities given to her on the basis of her appearance, why at times she acquiesced without internalizing the masquerade. Defending her actions on a practical level, she nonetheless continued to oppose masquerading as white on principle.

Interestingly, while Washington's mask of whiteness privileged her in private life, it also complicated her public persona. Reporting on *Black Boy,* the African American press nearly dismissed Washington because they assumed she was white, and their focus was to reveal the exploits of black entertainers. The *Pittsburgh Courier* reported:

> The Metropolitan critics have taken her quite seriously and have spoken highly of her efforts. Freddie even fooled ye scribe last week. When preparing our copy for the press her picture came along. Being lined up with Lottie Howell of "Deep River," who is really "ofay" [white], and having changed her name, we were not thinking and dubbed both "white" and passed on. It was not until the paper was off the press that we realized we had either paid a compliment or cast a reflection—we are not fully decided as yet just which.[34]

If the African American press was deceived by Washington's photo and name change, the question arises whether or not her identity was deliberately altered to deceive some members of the African American community who might have attended *Black Boy*—a play that featured some of the best black talent in the history of American theater. The ambivalent profile Washington had assumed on stage now invaded her off-stage life.

To be sure, in the entertainment industry before the 1950s, bright and white female mulattoes were privileged over African American women with darker complexions. After making a name for herself in theatrical circles, Washington was then recruited to appear in a musical short with Duke Ellington entitled *Black and Tan Fantasy* (1929). While Thomas Cripps notes that Washington's light skin is irrelevant with respect to this

short film's plot,[35] the fact that she is mulatto and thereby becomes a signifier of beauty cannot be dismissed. Moreover, that she dies even though
she is not positioned as a tragic figure certainly makes some comment
about her plight. But the point is that in this musical film, Washington
as the protagonist, while not being overtly reduced to her color, cannot
escape the association linked to the mulatto because of her color. Thus,
Washington the actress and Washington the character are forever intertwined even in this early period of her screen career.

Such screen roles allowed Washington to appear in stage productions such as *Singin' the Blues* and *Run, Little Chillun'*—for these productions, according to the African American press, she was "the best bet for
any play which requires a lovely, light-skinned girl for the lead. Producers know this well."[36] Their columns referred to her as "light-skinned,"
"green-eyed," and "straight-haired."[37]

In large part, it certainly was her physical appearance that got her
the role of the romantic interest for Brutus Jones (Paul Robeson) in *The
Emperor Jones* (1933). Although she does not masquerade as white in this
film, she is cast as the light-skinned mistress to Jones, a Pullman porter
who flees the rural South in search of opportunity; venturing north, he is
seduced by the vices of inner-city life. When Jones becomes involved in a
gambling scheme gone bad while playing craps, he accidentally murders
his friend and is sent to jail. Following Jones's escape from jail, he lands
a job on a steamship but is compelled to flee this life in search of a more
rewarding lifestyle offered by a small island. Once he reaches the island,
he establishes ties with a white trader, Mr. Smithers (Dudley Digges), and
through their machinations they manage to disrupt the island's leadership, allowing Jones to become emperor. Unfortunately, as the newly appointed emperor, Jones's corruption ultimately leads to his demise, and
his own self-destructiveness consumes him.

As Jones's mistress, Undine (Washington) signifies beauty because
of her whiteness, yet because of her blackness she is rendered violent
and uncontrollable—reflecting the dual position of the mulatto character. Her role is disturbing mostly for her hypersexualization and because
she is rendered as so impulsive that she physically assaults another black
woman who competes for Jones's attention. Denouncing Washington's
role in the film, Charles Petioni submitted a letter to the *New York Amsterdam News* and asserted, "To paint the . . . Negro woman as dissolute and

immoral and the island Negroes as superstitious savages may be pleasant for the whites, but intolerable for self-respecting persons."[38] Washington herself was conflicted about the role she played in this film, but it was a role that launched her career as a screen actress. It also solidified the negativity of her mulatto screen image—a screen image she would continue to popularize the following year in *Imitation of Life*.

THE MASQUERADES AND MASKS OF BLACKNESS AND WHITENESS

In mainstream cinema during the first half of the twentieth century, it was not unusual for studios to choose whites to play African American characters—from whites who donned blackface in the silent films to those who played white mulattoes in the talkies.[39] In fact, many films through the 1950s cast white actors in black roles (e.g., *Lost Boundaries* [1949], *Pinky* [1949], *Showboat* [1951], *Band of Angels* [1957], *Kings Go Forth* [1958], *Raintree County* [1959], *Imitation of Life* [1959]). According to Lola Young, casting whites in these roles provides "the ocular proof and visual knowledge" needed to affirm their racial origin.[40] Similarly commenting on this phenomenon, Snead notes that the use of whites in mulatto roles primarily was to prevent white audiences from confusing the social body (white mulattoes) with the social being (white people).[41] But this cross-racial casting did not always achieve its principal purpose. Susan Courtney suggests that when white actresses assumed black roles they further complicated "spectatorial belief" because the film(s) "direct[s] us when to see the white actress who plays . . . as white, when to see her as pretending to be white, and when to forget she is white at all and see her as 'really' black."[42]

It was unusual, therefore, for Washington (or any other mulatto) to be chosen to play the part of Peola (a white mulatto) in *Imitation of Life*. The usual principle and practice of cross-racial casting did not apply to the casting of this film. In the film's subplot, Peola is a very light-complexioned African American who constantly struggles with her blackness. According to Donald Bogle, director John Stahl, in recruiting actors for the role, asserted that "This girl is the daughter of a colored mammy and this point obviously makes it impossible to use an established screen player or, in fact, any girl of Caucasian birth. Such a thing, so to speak, would simply not 'go down' with theater audiences."[43] Stahl reportedly added, "I will be glad to interview at the studio any white Negro girl who fills these specifications."[44]

Although Washington's physiology ("white Negro") and acting talent seemingly made her well-suited for the role of Peola, it was almost not awarded to her. While Washington was being considered for the part, reports circulated in the African American press that she had accused studio executives of being partial when it came to the selection of "pretty Race girls"[45] endowed with talent. Apparently Washington felt it necessary to castigate studio officials; she was beginning to realize that her career would be short-lived in the cinema industry if she were only considered for mulatto roles, which were few. After she publicly aired her views, the studios were reluctant to cast her in the film, sensing that she was perhaps too outspoken, radical, or adversarial.[46] Anna Everett writes that "Even before the film's release, Washington's own outspokenness against Jim Crow practices in Hollywood made headlines in the black press to rival any of her fictional [characters']."[47] The *Chicago Defender* confirmed that Washington was almost denied the part, noting that "for a while it appeared that she was just being 'considered' for weeks passed and no word of the part reached her from the studios following the first notification. Fredi was in California . . . when called to Universal studios and told to start on the script."[48]

Directed by John Stahl, *Imitation of Life* has been heralded as a feminist film because of its progressive theme of a widowed white woman who succeeds in becoming an entrepreneur in the white-male-dominated America of the 1930s. The film is based on Fannie Hurst's novel of the same title. Hurst at one time employed black writer Zora Neale Hurston as her secretary, and it was Hurston who has been credited with providing Hurst her view of black life, with which she had been unfamiliar.[49] Affirming Hurston's contributions to her work, Hurst acknowledged that she had indeed provided valuable insights. Hurston's "mind ran ahead of my thoughts and she would interject with an impatient suggestion or clarification of what I wanted to say."[50] The symbiotic relationship between them was replicated in the novel and on screen in the characters of Miss Bea (played by white actress Claudette Colbert) and her black maid, Delilah (Louise Beavers). More central to the story, however, is the relationship that developed between their daughters: Bea's daughter,

Jessie (Rochelle Hudson) and Delilah's daughter, Peola (Washington) as the white mulatto. The film explores mother-daughter relationships and the struggles of single mothers attempting to become self-sufficient in a male-dominated culture. While numerous essays have explored the film's political and feminist dynamics, I focus here primarily on Peola as a character and on Washington as an actress.

A film that constructs a character who masquerades as white implies that whiteness is desirable and powerful, and the African American who portrays such a character attributes, if unwittingly, inferior qualities to blackness. Yet Peola does not seek whiteness for the power and privilege inscribed in it, but rather for the sake of whiteness itself—invoking the question of whether that automatically implies the negation of blackness. This is evident in that Peola chooses to work in a restaurant where she masquerades as white, even though she does not need to work because she is privileged by her mother's financial status. Peola's actions, therefore, question whether there can be an acceptance of both blackness and whiteness, or if there must be a desire for one only, with an implied denial of the other.

Largely reflecting salient issues of race during the period in which the film is set and produced, *Imitation of Life* encodes the negativity of blackness through its construction of Delilah and the other characters' response to her, particularly Peola's response to her mother. In rejecting her mother, Peola rejects the negativity encoded in blackness and consequently embraces the positivity encoded in whiteness. Delilah's dark skin is the principal signifier through which the film constructs blackness as negative. According to Sarah Madsen Hardy and Kelly Thomas, "While Peola's skin is very fair, her desire to be white is forever denied by the fact of her mother's dark complexion, which marks Peola as black. When associated with Delilah, Peola must submit to the binary racial discourse that defines her as black."[51] That Delilah's blackness becomes a codifier of Peola's blackness is similarly supported by Susan Courtney, who declares that "Whereas the 'very very light' black father is never seen, it is the black mother's visible blackness that repeatedly enforces Peola's 'true' racial identity."[52]

The film begins with Delilah arriving at Bea's residence in response to an advertisement for a maid, the first association of blackness with subservience. Delilah's speech is in dialect, a linguistic detail that also establishes difference. She is prohibited from traveling by streetcar. The white child, Jessie, refers to Delilah as a "horsey," implying that blackness is associated with animalism, and Delilah castigates herself for her large size. Yet Courtney suggests that "While this declaration partially admits that the baby does not yet understand racial difference, it insists that that difference, however inaccurately named, is self-evident even to the untrained eye. This is, presumably, why the women laugh at the baby's outrageous mistake and why Bea does not correct her."[53] Regardless as to how this inscription is interpreted, this example, among others, demonstrates some of the ways Delilah encodes blackness.

Richard Dyer posits that blackness is given meaning and importance only to the extent that it enhances whiteness—but at the same time, whiteness attests to its dependence upon blackness for its own existence.[54] The fact that Delilah is so concerned with the fate of her white mistress that she neglects her own plight as a single mother further serves to construct this purview on blackness in the film. Denial is also evident in Delilah's action of rubbing her tired mistress's feet while disregarding her own tired feet.

Blackness in the film is constructed as possessing strong religious views tainted with superstitious beliefs, as when Delilah flaunts her rabbit's foot. Blackness is also associated with ignorance and a lack of business acumen, as when Delilah fails to capitalize on the opportunity to own part of the business she helped create by sharing her pancake recipe with Bea. Blackness is further constructed to signify an acceptance of racially segregated practices and a predisposition to deprecate other blacks, as when Delilah refers to blacks with insulting and derogatory terms such as "pappy" and "mammy." Moreover, blackness is constructed to imply an absence of feelings or emotions; in those instances in the film when the black characters experience pain or suffering, they are accorded the least amount of compassion—as when Bea refers to Delilah, even as she is facing death, as a "big mountain." It is Valerie Smith's contention that the "tensions surrounding motherhood, class mobility, and abandonment [experienced by white women] are displaced onto the black plot, which performs the emotional labor in the film much as Delilah in Bea's household performs the visible domestic labor."[55]

Within the film, it is obvious, then, why Peola would be in denial of her blackness and why she might aspire to whiteness. Even when Delilah introduces Peola to Bea and praises her, Peola is embarrassed by her mother's dialect, which is devalued and coded as offensive. Racial differences are being used here to make whiteness appear more privileged, more empowered, and more desirable.

Peola's relationship with her dark mother becomes even more strained when she accuses Delilah of being responsible for her blackness, conveying to spectators that blackness is undesirable. At school, Peola seeks to deny that Delilah is her mother and refuses to obey her request to remove her rain-soaked clothes; she is disrespectful and tells Delilah to "leave me alone." Attempting to control her mother, Peola insists that Bea not be informed of her attempt to masquerade as white and of her desire for whiteness, reaffirming how white and whiteness are valued, while black and blackness are devalued. Confined to the servants' living quarters during Bea's party, Peola spurns her mother's offer to dance with her,[56] insisting that she prefers to read and revealing that she is becoming more disillusioned with her racial construction—as a black who looks white.

Even while acceding to her mother's wishes that she attend an all-black school, Peola denounces Delilah's dialect, insisting on using the term "mother," not "mammy." As her mother becomes a more potent signifier of blackness, Peola's covert resistance becomes overt and she leaves school. When Delilah finally locates her, Peola claims she has never seen Delilah before, insisting to onlookers, "Do I look like her daughter? Do I look like I could be her daughter?" Peola plays upon her appearance to reject her own dark mother. Although she is later reprimanded by Bea, her surrogate white mother, she separates herself from Delilah forever when she claims she will no longer live as black but will instead masquerade as white. Even at Delilah's funeral, while she acknowledges Delilah as her mother, in the same breath she equates her with a slave in her assertion that she "killed" her own mother as her mother "slaved" for her. The implication is that blackness is akin to slave status and that Peola still has not resolved her internal conflict with blackness.

Delilah reveals that she has previously been denied employment because of her daughter's whiteness. Thus, the whiteness theme introduced early in the film forewarns that Peola will be rejected and problematized. Delilah attempts to explain Peola's light color, revealing that her daughter inherited her looks from her father, who was equally conflicted about his appearance. Lola Young contends that the "difficult situation brought about by 'mixed' relations is the predicament of someone who 'passes' for white—that is, a person with black antecedents who lives as a 'white' person."[57] Yet it is Delilah's remarks that posit language as a powerful device for developing Peola's white masquerade both in terms of what she says and how she says it: Delilah speaks in dialect, while Peola speaks in standard English. Another device used to denote Peola's blackness is the contrasting of Peola with her white foil, Jessie, a signifier of whiteness. Jessie is referred to as an angel, while Peola, who only approximates whiteness but actually represents blackness, is portrayed as a person with negative qualities who rejects her own mother.

Peola's white masquerade allows her to penetrate racial boundaries. She demonstrates a keen interest in learning and exhibits a level of intelligence beyond that of Jessie. As the two prepare for school by quizzing each other on world capitals, Peola's masquerade begins to unravel. When Miss Bea expresses admiration for Peola's brilliance, Delilah concedes disparagingly: "We all start out that way—we don't get dumb until later." The assumption, of course, is "we" are actually unintelligent, since inscribed in blackness is the perception that blacks lack mental aptitude. When Jessie refers to Peola as black, Peola flees from her school and returns home distraught. In denial about her blackness, she resists such labeling, proclaiming, "I'm not black . . . I won't be black." It is only when Peola is reprimanded by Miss Bea, rather than by her mother, that her anger subsides, subtly suggesting that she is more responsive to a white woman than to Delilah, her black mother.

Metaphorically establishing Peola's racial origin through the lineage of her white surrogate mother is plausible, but the reality is that her racial origin is established by her black mother—from the racially dominant perspective, a signifier of Otherness. And although Lacan proclaims that the self desires to become the Other, Peola (in denial about her blackness and through the lens of the racially dominant) is very resistant to being transformed into an Other.[58] The dilemma of race is automatically problematized in that we witness a black character desirous of whiteness and in denial of her blackness. But the film minimizes the dilemma, attributing to Delilah the conjecture that it's no one's fault and that no one is to blame. This is an attempt to assuage white fears and guilt. The film avoids the real issue; it constructs race artificially and implies that virtually no one has any control over the dilemma of race. It thereby condones whites' absolving themselves of responsibility, while simultaneously ascribing power to whiteness.

Peola's masquerade as white is established early in the film. When seated in a classroom of white children, she peers above a book, trying to disguise her identity. In the words of Fanon, in this scene Peola "was going to try, in her own body and in her own mind, to bleach it."[59] Yet it is her black mother, Delilah, who arrives at school during a rainstorm to provide her with rain gear. When Delilah discovers Peola positioned in this all-white environment, it seems that Peola projects a white gaze—a gaze that resists and denies her blackness, a gaze constructed to avert her mother's black gaze. Delilah projects a black gaze, as if to construct Peola's identity for her since she is unwilling to construct an identity for herself. Spectators in turn project an "oppositional gaze" (a term introduced by bell hooks)[60] in defiance of a child who rejects her mother because she is black. Peola then becomes the object of her classmates' gaze as they objectify her after she is unveiled as black. When Delilah asks the teacher whether her daughter has been "passing" (a play on words), the teacher responds affirmatively, acknowledging both constructions of the word: Peola has been masquerading as white and achieving academically. In effect, she has merged (at least temporarily) her social body with what she desires as her social being.

Peola's white masquerade is again exposed during a party Bea gives to celebrate her recent business success. The scene exemplifies how physical space is embedded with racial codes: Peola and Delilah are confined to their quarters below Miss Bea's posh living quarters. Also in this scene, Peola's psychic tensions between her social body and her social being explode. Furious at this spatial and racial alienation, and resisting her mother, who appears to be content with such accommodations, Peola vents her frustration that she cannot enjoy the celebration because she is black. Staring into the mirror, she proclaims her whiteness: "I want to be white, like I look . . . Look at me . . . Am I not white? . . . Isn't it a white girl?" It is Homi K. Bhabha who associates "'visibility' . . . [with] the exercise of power; [visibility] gives force to the argument that skin, as a signifier of discrimination, must be produced or processed as visible."[61] Peola's light skin as reflected in the mirror then affirms and reifies her whiteness. Thus Peola's introspection reminds us of Lacan's mirror-image stage, in which the self merges with the image reflected in the mirror. Peola becomes the mirror image of herself, and since the image is white, she is transformed into the image that is reflected and desired.

Washington gave a convincing performance as Peola. The *Literary Digest* applauded her performance, commenting that "in the small role of the negro daughter, the part which should have dominated the picture, Fredi Washington is vital, straightforward, and splendidly in earnest."[62] *Variety* similarly observed that "Fredi Washington as the white-skinned offspring was excellent in the funeral scene when overcome by remorse."[63]

The black press spoke in concert with the mainstream press in applauding Washington's performance. Anna Everett observes:

> Black audiences responded so favorably to the fair-skinned Washington because the actress' own racial identity imbued the character with an authenticating aura unavailable to a Caucasian actress attempting to pass for a black attempting to pass for white. It was precisely Washington's degree zero of representational whiteness that made Peola's cry . . . so forceful and shrill.[64]

In particular, the *New York Amsterdam News* reassured its readers that "actress though she be, Fredi Washington expresses the desire for freedom and equal justice in this picture that is more convincing than any mere performer could have voiced. True to her own life, the injustices of color and race prejudices have retarded and prohibited a fuller life and freedom of expression."[65]

Despite such accolades for her following the film's release, because of its popularity and the racial issues evoked, Washington began to feel the repercussions of the role. Some reviewers and spectators asserted that Washington played the role of Peola so well because she was both physiologically and psychologically like Peola.[66] Washington's adamant response to such assertions was that though she and Peola wore the same physiological mask, psychologically she was not like Peola, that as an actress she was engaged merely and only in an on-screen masquerade. She further charged that the character of Peola, who desires whiteness and masquerades as white, is a character "created by white people and it is their conception, not mine, of the problems that our girls face when they are light enough to 'pass.'"[67] This was a position she shared with Sterling Brown, at the time a professor at Howard University, who publicly challenged Fannie Hurst for her representations in a series of editorials submitted to *Opportunity* magazine. Responding to Hurst's critique of the film, Brown asserted:

> This picture breaks no new ground. The beloved mammy is a long familiar darling in the American consciousness; vaudeville headliners, song-pluggers, after-dinner speakers (especially Southern), moving pictures, and novels have placed her there. The tragic mulatto, who adds to the cross borne by the long suffering saintly mammy, is likewise a fixture. She is so woe-begone that she is a walking argument against miscegenation; her struggling differentiates her unpleasantly from the self-abnegation of the mammy; her cheap yearning to be white is a contemptible surrender of integrity. Like her mammy, she contributes to Anglo-Saxon self-esteem. It is not easy to see any "social value" in perpetuating these stock characters.[68]

Washington vehemently resisted masquerading as white in her off-screen life. Attempting to distance herself from a role that was increasingly becoming associated with her off-screen identity, she complained that because of her white appearance, "managers, producers, and film executives have tried to get me to 'pass for white' in order to get the break they claim I deserve."[69] Refusing to agree to "pass," she began to publicly express her views against masquerading as white:

> Why should I have to pass for anything but an artist? When I act, I live the role I am assigned to do. If that part calls for me to be a West Indian half caste, a Spanish or Creole maiden, a French woman, a lady of great social distinction or a prostitute—how can I, or anyone, essay such roles with the bugbear of national heritage constantly dangled before my eyes?
>
> I don't want to "pass," because I can't stand insecurities and shame. I am just as much "colored" as any of the others identified with the race.[70]

Though she wore a mask of whiteness in her private life in that she was a white mulatto, she refused to masquerade as white off screen. In her words, "I have never tried to pass for white and never had any desire to do so."[71]

ACTRESS AND ACTIVIST

On the level of mask, there are many similarities between Washington and Peola. Washington was frequently mistaken for white, as was Peola. Whites reacted to Washington as white until her black identity was revealed, much as they had responded to Peola. Washington found her physical appearance both liberating and enslaving, as did Peola. Like Peola, Washington strongly resented racial proscriptions that invaded her life. But unlike Peola, Washington did not aspire to whiteness. In fact, the differences between the actress and the character were vast.

Nevertheless, Washington's performance as Peola was so superb that some opined that she and Peola were reflexive, and not just in their physical features. The *Chicago Defender* reported such opinions: "So realistic [is] her performance that many theatergoers have wondered if her screen role does not actually express her own attitude toward life."[72] When she was acclaimed in the African American press for her role, statements disassociating her from the character of Peola and reconfirming her blackness always prefaced these reports. For example, the *Baltimore Afro-American* introduced its interview with her by noting, "Off-stage, she is just the opposite [of] the screen role which made her famous. You remember her best as Peola. . . . But she isn't a Peola at all."[73] Yet while the newspaper seemingly attempted to extricate Washington from her Peola portrayal, it also subtly reinforced the association, titling the article "Peola Off-Stage."[74] Earl Conrad stated an opinion that persisted even a decade after *Imitation of Life:* "Fredi's portrayal of Peola was so convincing . . . many said Fredi must be like that in real life or she could not portray the part so realistically."[75]

Immediately following *Imitation of Life,* Washington was resistant to this association, a resistance that continued into later years. The *Chicago Defender* reported in 1935 that Washington "constantly [rages] against the fate which has made her near white even though she is of Negro blood."[76] Indeed, she became trapped by the film's inscription and thereafter was always in contestation with the screen image she created of the white mulatto, Peola.

Washington launched a massive campaign to refute rumors that she and Peola were psychologically the same. Either the press was not fully convinced of Washington's position or they wanted to capitalize on her screen character to attract readers. Reassuring the public of her disassociation from the character of Peola, she declared that she might have effectively conveyed "how a girl might feel under the circumstances, but I am not showing how I feel myself."[77] She added, "I am proud of my race."[78] Compelled to respond to the continuing accusations, she used the press to articulate her views. The *Chicago Defender* warned that Washington "wants the news [to be] broadcast that she does in no way wish to deny her race. The little star feels that the part she played in pictures may influence patrons to dislike her whenever she appears in legitimate houses."[79] Additional reports reiterated that "she is not such a person as was Peola."[80] So while Peola was preoccupied with whiteness on screen, off screen Washington was preoccupied with blackness and felt compelled to assert her racial identity.

Attempting to distance herself both from this film character and from whiteness, Washington became more politically active. From early in her career she had been intolerant of the discriminatory practices and oppression that prevailed in American society, and her public and political denouncements of the marginalization of African Americans now increased. In 1938, she wore a black armband in support of the NAACP, which was staging an antilynching campaign and demonstration in New York.[81] Affirming Washington's activism, the *New York Herald Tribune* described her as "a frail, defenseless ingénue, by night—a forthright, uncompromising crusader by day."[82] Washington's activism should not be viewed in a vacuum; her brother-in-law, Adam Clayton Powell Jr., was an activist and one of the most powerful black congressmen to represent the state of New York.[83] Powell's constant lobbying to improve the plight of African Americans in a racially divided America may have inspired and expanded Washington's political views.

In 1940, Washington encouraged actors to halt a boycott in protest of the segregated practices of the National Theater in Washington, D.C. She opposed the boycott, explaining to her fellow actors, "Though we are justifiably indignant, you must realize that we are bound by contractual commitments."[84] In no way did she intend this as a denunciation of the cause; indeed, she supported the protesters' plank. Her action was more a testament to her political power, influence, and activism than a reflection of her willingness to compromise her beliefs. She served as secretary of the Negro Actors Guild and became a deputy to the Actors Equity Association.[85]

By the early 1940s, Washington had become a columnist for Powell's political organ, the *People's Voice*, in which she articulated some of her harshest criticism of an entertainment industry that placated preexisting racial attitudes. She challenged black stage performers to censor their acts, charging that many comedians were perpetuating disturbing representations of African Americans, representations she viewed as a disservice to her race.[86] Washington characterized these performers as "no reading, dumb arguing, razor wielding, name calling, liquor drinking, [sexist in that they were] debasing [women], vulgar, [and] stupid."[87] Her public plea, however, inflamed African American comedian Tim Moore, who was particularly disturbed by her characterization of his and other such entertainers' humor. In defense, Moore launched a personal attack against Washington's own stage productions, which he targeted as not devoid of similar ills.[88] He pointed to her role in *Imitation of Life* as being particularly painful since the character was ashamed of her dark mother. In her reply to Moore, Washington attempted to rise above the personal affront. She defended both her actions and her position by charging that

> The fact is that ten years ago, we were a slumbering people standing still with no particular knowledge of the plight of our unfortunate brothers in far off lands or at home for that matter. There was a depression going on and each individual was interested solely in buttering his own bread.
>
> It is hardly necessary to try to point out the terrific world-wide changes which have taken place since that time. Unprecedented attention has been given the Negro since the war began because of the fact that we are theoretically free but actually part slave under a vicious system—a system which allows representatives of our government to stand on the floor of Congress and orate about our lack of responsibility, culture, education, etc., in order to keep us from the polls in the South, to segregate our men and women in the armed forces, to perpetuate the damnable jim-crow laws of the South and which are now invading the North, to keep us in ignorance of the rich history of American Negroes, etc.[89]

During World War II, Washington came to see African Americans' struggle to achieve equality as inseparable from America's effort to propagate democracy throughout the world. She argued that entertainers shared in the responsibility of elevating the black image and assisting in this collective effort to achieve democracy and equality: "Today we are shedding red blood for democracy which we do not have but for which we are waging a fight on the home front, and culture and education through the medium of every stage, screen and radio is of utmost importance. It is the responsibility of every Negro in the field of amusement to see with clarity his or her relation to this fight."[90]

Washington's strong public denouncements extended to the theater and cinema as well. In 1944 she castigated MGM studio officials for considering yet another revival of *Uncle Tom's Cabin* (1903, 1914, 1927), which she viewed as a damaging and distasteful story with no redeeming value. According to Washington, the story portrays Uncle Tom as "a selfish, back-bending, 'white-folks loving' yard man."[91] She saw no useful purpose in the dramatization for African Americans attempting to elevate themselves in 1940s America. Qualifying her position, she conceded that "while the book is informative and positive propaganda against the vicious practice of slavery which is still a blot on our country, I most definitely am against any picturization of it by MGM or any other studio."[92] She justified her position by recounting the atrocities that had been inflicted on African Americans and suggested that reviving such films added to the painful insults and injuries that they endured:

> When you realize that the country is still full of potential slave holders (could you think of Congressman Rankin from Mississippi as anything else?) you can understand why it would be suicide to show Negroes at this time on the screen under the bondage of slavery, illiterate, childlike and docile. Conditions for the Negro in the South and in many spots in the North are not too far removed from conditions which existed under actual slavery. Does not the South still keep the Negro from voting; from getting an equal education; refuse war contracts because whites refuse to train or work with Negroes; make the Negro soldier ride in the back of their conveyances if at all?[93]

Washington called for militancy to reverse the enslavement process. In doing so, she established (perhaps deliberately) a contrast with the views of her on-screen character Peola. While Peola sought invisibility so she could enjoy the privileges embodied in whiteness, Washington sought visibility as an African American. She eventually garnered enough public support for her campaign to halt the production of *Uncle Tom's Cabin*. Newspaper columnist Leon Hardwick reported that he had contacted the film's producer and informed him that African Americans, labor unions, and white liberals would stage protests upon the film's release.[94] The film never materialized, which was a tribute to Washington's political savvy and effectiveness. In this case, her campaign targeted a specific film, but its real aim was to combat a society that was both unequal and unfair to African Americans.

To increase the effectiveness of her resistance, Washington solicited support from those whose ideological views were consistent with her own. One white soldier who agreed with her views submitted a review of *The Negro Soldier* (1944) in which he denounced the film as one that supposedly commemorated the contributions of African Americans in World War II, but which according to Thomas Cripps actually promoted a racially segregated military force.[95] The white soldier asserted:

> *The Negro Soldier* in this war, is such an insidious propaganda job, I feel that you should know some of the facts. *The Negro Soldier* is a lie from beginning to end.... No movie, no story, no conversation about Negroes in the U.S. Army can even resemble the truth if it ignores, or glosses over, the fundamental problem of segregation. This, above all, is at the bottom of every act involving colored and white troops. For Negroes, segregation does not mean equal treatment with whites. It means inferior treatment.[96]

The soldier continued by describing the segregated conditions that existed in the military for black and white soldiers.[97]

Unrelenting in her attack on institutions that marginalized African Americans, Washington turned to African Americans on stage and screen. She expressed her concerns that negative representations could easily be taken out of context, and she made every effort to clarify how blacks really desired to be represented in the theater, rather than being stereotyped and transformed into mythologies:

> Many producers, directors and actors have got the idea that we object to seeing ourselves cast as maids, butlers, etc. Nothing could be farther from the truth. What we do object to is the stereotype servant with his bowed head, ridiculous dialect and idiotic, brainless stupidity. No one is or should be naïve enough to think that we object to maid or butler roles when they are a part of normal integral situations and are convincing characters.[98]

She also objected to the continual proliferation of such one-dimensional types at the expense of more redeeming representations. Her disillusionment with the industry was affirmed by Cripps, who reported, "Fredi Washington ... resented the casual racism of the crews [working in Hollywood]."[99] Washington was equally offended when white filmmakers selected white actors for black roles instead of selecting African American actors. For these reasons, Washington again launched a public attack, this time specifically targeting Alfred Werker, director of *Lost Boundaries* (1949):

> I am appalled and not a little fighting mad to think that a so-called intel-
> ligent adult could be so viciously ignorant as to give as his reason for not
> casting Negroes in [*Lost Boundaries*] that "the majority of Negro actors
> are of the Uncle Tom, Minstrel show, shuffling dancer type of performer."
> . . . In the first place, neither Alfred Werker nor Louis de Rochemont from
> the beginning of production plans ever considered using Negro actors to
> portray the roles of the Johnston family. Therefore, Negroes having the
> physical appearance and ability needed for these roles were never inter-
> viewed. . . . He [the director] simply was not interested in learning what
> he evidently did not know; that there are many legitimate Negro actors
> and actresses who are far more intelligent than Werker proves himself to
> be. . . . I would say that Alfred Werker has carved a unique niche for him-
> self in the world of picture-making. He now can take the Oscar for being
> Hollywood's number one anti-Negro bigot.[100]

Washington's political activism gained momentum with the passage of time. As she denounced the marginalization of African Americans in the cinema in 1947, she also articulated a need for them to improve their status and condition by exercising their right to vote:

> When you realize how long it took the movie industry to make up its mind
> to handle the question of anti-Semitism, it gives us an idea of how long we
> will have to wait for some protest from the screen on Negrophobia in this
> country. What we get instead is a re-release of the anti-Negro relic, *Birth
> of a Nation.* The Dixie Distributing Co., located in Atlanta, has plastered
> the South with this disgrace to a nation. . . . This is southern anti-Negro
> propaganda for 1947. Whip up hate against the Negroes and it becomes
> easier to keep them from exercising their right to vote. It makes it easier to
> get away with lynching a Negro. Again I ask the question, who said art is
> not in politics? It is, indeed, and it is here to stay.[101]

Washington's activism did not succeed in entirely disassociating her from her role as Peola, especially in later years. When she returned to the stage in the late 1940s, the African American press continued to exploit her social body. When the *Foxes of Harrow* (1947) was adapted to the screen, it was rumored that while she was being considered for an uncertain role, "she would be suited for playing a mulatto role in the film."[102] Even more disturbing was the report that when she played "the part of a

maid who had more intelligence than other members of the household" on *The Goldbergs* television show, one viewer was so impressed with her performance that she offered Washington a job—as her own personal maid.[103] This callous disregard for Washington's true talent and stature reflected the common white preoccupation with race.

The ghost of Peola haunted Washington throughout her life. Washington's black masquerade allowed her to challenge the whiteness that she visibly embodied. She was a black mind trapped in a white body. If it is conceivable that both Peola and Washington transcended their racial difference, then race is no longer an issue of difference but perhaps becomes an issue of sameness. Neither Hollywood nor the sociopolitical discourse from which *Imitation of Life* evolved was willing to explore the ramifications of this paradox.

FIVE

Hattie McDaniel

CENTERING THE MARGIN

Many people, but especially African Americans, agreed with Fredi Washington that *Uncle Tom's Cabin* (novel, 1852; film, 1927) was an extremely vicious attack on African American personhood, much like the film *The Birth of a Nation* (1915) and the novel-adapted-to-film *Gone with the Wind* (novel, 1936; film, 1939), a bestselling novel in the mid-1930s and a blockbuster film in the late 1930s. The black press and the black community reacted to *Gone with the Wind* and its black supporting actresses much as they had to *Imitation of Life* (1934) and its black supporting actresses—praising them for the performances and castigating them for the images their characters projected. For *Gone with the Wind* Hattie McDaniel, cast in the role of Mammy, and Butterfly McQueen, cast in the role of Prissy, were the principal recipients of this vacillating praise and condemnation, but especially McDaniel.

Hattie McDaniel empowered herself in *Gone with the Wind* (hereafter *GWTW*) through her transformation of the subservient (subordinate, dehumanized, and devalued) into the dominant (defiant and directing). She managed this through her commanding presence, strong posture, exertion of power, and fearlessness in the role of Mammy, and in doing so McDaniel redefined and reconstructed public images of African American womanhood. The point is debatable, but through her performance McDaniel did move this character (and character type) out of the margin into the film's center. Through her performance as Mammy, she also centered herself in the press's scrutiny of her professional and personal lives. Despite her heroism on screen, McDaniel was still positioned as the quintessential subordinate or subservient, a status that was reified by her gender and race and one that allowed her on-screen roles to be inextricably linked with persecution, victimization, marginalization, and exploitation, a characterization that permeated her off-screen life. And because of such characterizations, off-screen she fell victim to a patriarchal society that sought to contain her and render her powerless because of her race and sexuality, marking her as a tragic figure. In fact, she victimized herself through the image that was constructed for her on screen, even as she was victimized by others off screen. I do not suggest that one form of victimization takes precedence over the other, but simply that both occurred simultaneously and reinforced one another. McDaniel began to see herself in the image of the victim that was constructed for her by others, and in doing so she rendered herself a tragic figure off screen despite her tremendous—albeit marginalized—success in the cinema world. McDaniel's vulnerability and tragic circumstances are most apparent in her reported bouts with depression, suicide attempts, and troubled multiple marriages, as well as the alienation that she endured in both the African American press and mainstream press.

Hattie McDaniel, Henry and Susan McDaniel's youngest child, was born on June 10, 1895. According to biographer Carlton Jackson, Henry had been a slave and field hand on a Virginia plantation prior to joining the Union army. After the Civil War, Henry carved out a meager existence in the Virginia and North Carolina regions for ten years before moving to Nashville, Tennessee, where he worked part time as a Baptist minister. Joining a variety of gospel singing groups, he met Susan Holbert, who soon became his wife. During the Reconstruction period, Henry and Susan moved westward, where more lucrative opportunities prevailed for migrant blacks, and they settled in Wichita, Kansas. The McDaniels had thirteen children, some of whom died at birth or shortly after birth; the surviving children were Otis, James, Samuel, Ruby, Adele, Orlena, Etta, and the youngest, Hattie.[1]

In 1901, the McDaniel family, described as talented musicians and entertainers, again moved—this time to Denver, Colorado, where Hattie attended Denver's Twenty-Fourth Street Elementary School. Hattie excelled at singing, dancing, and theatrics, and by the age of thirteen she was performing with a minstrel show, J. M. Johnson's Mighty Modern Minstrels. By 1910, Henry had organized his own minstrel show—using the whole family except Hattie, who was prohibited from joining them because of her young age. Hattie quit school after her sophomore year of high school and began performing when she could secure jobs at local theaters—but sometimes she worked as a cook, clerk, or even washerwoman.[2] In 1920, Professor George Morrison gave McDaniel an opportunity to sing with the Morrison Orchestra. Billed as the "female Bert Williams" (one of the highest paid black vaudeville entertainers of the time), McDaniel soon met with tragedy—her father's death on December 5, 1922, and her first husband George Langford's death from a gunshot wound. In late December of 1924 or early January of 1925, McDaniel, performing with the Morrison Orchestra, was heard on the Denver radio station KOA, allegedly becoming the first black person to sing on that station. McDaniel began to cultivate her songwriting talent, producing songs such as "Quittin' My Man Today," "Brown Skin Baby Doll," "I Wish I Had Somebody," "Boo Hoo Blues," "Wonderful Dream," "Lonely Heart," "Sam Henry Blues," "Poor Wandering Boy Blues," and "Poor Boy Blues."[3]

McDaniel broadened her entertainment venues, performing with the Elks and the Shriners and even for TOBA (Theatrical Owners Booking Association, a chain of black-owned theaters scattered throughout the United States). Unfortunately, the pay was frequently not sustaining, and she was sometimes reduced to menial jobs to supplement her income. Still, while working as a maid for the Club Madrid in Milwaukee, she managed to convince the club proprietor that she had singing and acting talent, and he elevated her from maid to entertainer. And when her siblings, sister Etta and brother Sam, who worked as extras in the Hollywood cinema industry as well as on radio, lured her to California, McDaniel's career became more centrally focused on screen acting. But sometimes she still had to resort to working as a subservient when acting opportunities were few and far between.[4]

In 1932, McDaniel landed her first screen role, non-credited, as a servant in *The Golden West,* and acquired three additional ones that year—in *The Blonde Venus, Hypnotized,* and *Washington Masquerade* (also known as *Mad Masquerade*).[5] The next year she was hired for roles in *The Story of Temple Drake* and *I'm No Angel.*[6] During the decade of the 1930s, McDaniel secured an extensive number of screen roles in films such as *Judge Priest* (1934), *Operator 13* (1934), *Merry Wives of Reno* (1934), *Another Face*

(1935), *The Little Colonel* (1935), *Alice Adams* (1935), *China Seas* (1935), *Hearts Divided* (1936), *Libeled Lady* (1936), *Star for a Night* (1936), *Show Boat* (1936), *The Singing Kid* (1936), *Racing Lady* (1936), *Forty-Five Fathers* (1937), *Nothing Sacred* (1937), *Saratoga* (1937), *The Mad Miss Manton* (1938), *Battle of Broadway* (1938), and *Zenobia* (1939).[7] The decade culminated in her most famous role in *GWTW*—a film that allowed her to become the first black actress to win an Academy Award. Carlton Jackson reports, "In the thirties she played noticeable roles in forty different movies, averaging one movie a month in 1936 alone."[8] At the end of the decade, Hattie again married, this time to Howard Hickman; the marriage was short-lived.[9]

In the 1940s, even though Hattie had won an Academy Award, she was continually cast as a servant—for example, she appeared in the following films: *Maryland* (1940), *The Great Lie* (1941), *They Died with Their Boots On* (1941), *Affectionately Yours* (1941), *The Male Animal* (1942), *In This Our Life* (1942), *George Washington Slept Here* (1942), *Thank Your Lucky Stars* (1943), *Since You Went Away* (1944), *Janie* (1944), *Hi Beautiful* (1944), *Song of the South* (1946), *The Flame* (1947), and *Mickey* (1948).[10] Accepting such roles resulted in public criticism of her by the NAACP, an organization that targeted black actors who accepted subservient screen roles. The NAACP's labeling was particularly harsh during World War II, when the organization was lobbying to achieve equal rights for people of color in America.[11]

The decade was especially active for her personal and professional lives. McDaniel again married—James Lloyd Crawford in 1941 and Larry C. Williams in 1949.[12] Both marriages deteriorated, and by the late 1940s, McDaniel returned to radio to perform on *The Beulah Show*. She negotiated her own contract, increasing her initial salary of $1,000 per week to a salary of $2,000 per week, for some seven years. When the show was converted to television, Ethel Waters assumed the primary role for a while, but McDaniel was cast in the role until her health declined after she was diagnosed with breast cancer, which resulted in her death on October 26, 1952, in San Fernando Valley, California. Hattie McDaniel requested that she be buried in an all-white cemetery, Rosedale, and despite some objections because of her race, she became the first black to be buried in this cemetery.[13] During her career, Hattie McDaniel appeared in more than three hundred films.

MCDANIEL'S SCREEN ROLES BEFORE
GWTW: THE SHADOW REFLECTS

Before her Academy Award–winning performance in *GWTW,* McDaniel appeared in several films. In most of these, her roles were typical for black actresses in minor parts during the period between the world wars—as a shadow who reflects the positivity of the leading white female character. In a few of her films, her roles were different enough to be worthy of note. In *Alice Adams* (1935), a film that centers on the class politics that infiltrated middle America in the 1930s, McDaniel appeared as Malena Burns, a house servant to the Adams family rather than a personal maid to the white female protagonist. The father in the Adams family, Virgil Adams (Fred Stone), is temporarily bedridden and cannot work. His wife (Ann Shoemaker) constantly harasses him to do better financially so that their daughter, Alice (Katherine Hepburn), will remain competitive with the socialite daughters of the affluent families with whom the Adamses interact. The mother pressures the father to establish his own factory to make glue—a product that he helped to design with his current boss—in an effort to make enough money to sustain Alice's future among the socialites to whom she is being compared. Although Alice is affected by the lack of material accoutrements, she is more concerned with the harmony, health, and stability of her family than with the class dynamics she faces. Alice's situation becomes more complicated when she manages to attract the attentions of her wealthy friend's fiancé, Arthur Russell (Fred MacMurray). Infatuated with the young wealthy businessman, Alice is intent on camouflaging her class origin. When she brings him home, she rarely invites him inside the house and is frequently apologetic for the small and less ostentatious home in which she resides.

The pivotal moment in the film is when her love interest is invited to a family dinner to meet her parents. It is here that McDaniel, as Malena, is introduced for the first time—the film is more than half over before she appears. In her effort to prepare for the family gathering and give the illusion of wealth, Alice's mother hires Malena to serve the dinner. It is of note that Malena has only a few lines in the film, delivered while she is preparing and serving the meal. She enters in a dark uniform, and the white dollet on her head continually falls off while she is serving the family dinner. Her walk is rather slow and wobbly, and she chews gum while serving food. These and other behaviors make it clear that Malena is not professional and is therefore a representative extension of (rather than a contrast to) the family, who because of their class status are Othered.

As a black, Malena's role as an extension or a reflection of the family's class status becomes more evident as the family masquerade begins to unravel. Alice's brother, Walter Adams (Frank Albertson), plays craps in the closet at a black tie affair and fraternizes with a black bandleader. Even Alice comments that her brother is so ingratiated with blacks that he might be predisposed to write "darky" stories some day. In this instance, Malena's inclusion in the film is to signify the oddity associated with this family, who are different primarily because of their class position, and her blackness reifies the lower-class position the family occupies. Of course, at the film's end, the father reunites with his boss to establish the glue factory and Alice receives the object of her desire, despite her class position.

China Seas (1935) is a love story designed to showcase the talent of Clark Gable and Jean Harlow. The film features McDaniel in a small role as Isabel McCarthy, the maidservant to Dolly (Harlow), also referred to as China Doll. Dolly is on a quest to attract the attentions of the ship's captain, Alan Gaskell (Gable). Although romantically linked, Captain Gaskell and Dolly are torn apart on board a ship sailing the Chinese seas when a young English widow, Sybil Barclay (Rosalind Russell) arrives to renew her former love interest in Gaskell. Dolly is distraught that Sybil challenges her genuine affections for the ship's captain, and Jamesy MacArdle (Wallace Beery) takes advantage of Dolly's weakness for the captain by coaxing her into a conspiracy to obtain the gold the ship is transporting.

After a mutiny erupts on the ship with the assistance of Asian pirates, Dolly admits that she participated in the mutiny only to the extent that when the captain refused to hear her revelation about the mutiny, she sought allegiance with Jamesy by acquiring the key to the arsenal on his behalf. At the film's end, while admitting her involvement in the mutinous plot, she expresses her genuine affection for the captain and he expresses his affection for her, as well as his admiration for the bravery she exhibited by attempting to halt the mutiny. It is at this point that the captain dissolves his relationship with Sybil and unites with the nobler of the two women, Dolly.

In this film, McDaniel's character, like her character's role in *Alice Adams,* is more an extension of the white female character with whom she is paired than a contrasting figure to aggrandize the white female character's whiteness. (In *China Seas* it is the Asians, not Isabel, who function as the whites' Other.) Even though McDaniel appears at only three points in the film, she is incredibly convincing in her role as Isabel.

Her first appearance in the film is when Dolly, threatened by the presence and refined manners of Sybil, questions her own beauty by glaring into a mirror. Isabel, dressed more like a star than a maid, wears a robe lined with ostrich feathers and reclines in a chair with her feet elevated on a stool while reading a magazine. Her hair is noticeably straightened. Yet, to affirm her caricature as a subservient, her eyes bulge with excitement as she reads a magazine. Isabel is frank and honest in her reply to Dolly's question regarding what Sybil possesses that she does not. First, Isabel becomes comic relief for the film since Dolly is such a whimsical character with her platinum blonde hair. Dolly poses, "Would you say that I look like a woman?" In reply, Isabel states, "No suh Miss Dolly—I been with you too long to insult you that way." Then Isabel remarks that Sybil is more refined in comparison to Dolly and declares that she would never wear that dress with all those shiny beads. Of course, this is an attempt to acquire the dress for herself, and Dolly understands Isabel's implication and hands the dress over. Isabel then commends Dolly and remarks, "You sho have the right instincts no matter what they says." Her interest now aroused, Dolly forces Isabel to explain just what is being said about her on the ship, and Isabel remarks, "They say you got yourself [so] hooked on that Captain Gaskell—that he shaking himself like a wet hound dog and can't get you loose no how." In this instance, Isabel, while serving as the comic relief, also serves as the informant regarding Dolly's image among others. At the same time, she even hints at Dolly's weaknesses, yet reassures her that the captain finds her attractive. The fact that Isabel is elegantly dressed nearly displaces the maidservant position she occupies, as her attire becomes an extension of the attire Dolly wears. It is only in later brief scenes that we see Isabel appear in maid's attire.

One scene occurs when the ship is enduring a storm and passengers are instructed to put on life jackets. Isabel walks in, dressed in her maid uniform, and wearing a life jacket while looking for Dolly, signaling that she might be lost at sea. In this instance, the maid is used to warn audiences of a climactic moment in the film. The crew members and the captain then launch a search for Dolly, who is in a cabin drinking, betting, and fraternizing with Jamesy until she realizes his plan to attack the ship.

The final scene in which Isabel appears is toward the end of the film when the ship reaches Singapore and Dolly has to face authorities for her involvement in the mutiny. Dolly reaffirms her affection for the captain and begins to rid herself of her possessions, in particular her clothes, which Isabel is eager to receive. Isabel, in her maid uniform, receives the clothes and remarks, "Lordy, Lordy I got enough clothes to last me a million years." The film subtly hints at Isabel's desire to be as glamorous as Dolly even though we know they are not the same size. So although Isabel is a maid, it is certainly not her desire in life to remain one, which is evident by her constant preoccupation with the beauty signified by the white Dolly—who is made to resemble a China doll.

Nothing Sacred (1937) features McDaniel (as Mrs. Walker) in a role in which she, again, is more an extension of the positive white characters than a contrast to them. In fact, Mrs. Walker's positivity contrasts sharply with the negativity of the film's leading white female character. Mrs. Walker appears only in the film's opening scene, and her character establishes the film's moral tone and implications. In this opening scene, she is a mother who exposes her spouse, posing as a sultan at a banquet for newspaper journalists celebrating the proposed *Morning Star Temple Newspaper.* She disrupts the banquet with her four children and a police escort to reveal that her spouse, Ernest Walker (Troy Brown), is an imposter.

The film centers on the deception created by a white female protagonist from Vermont, Hazel Flagg (Carole Lombard), who is allegedly suffering from radium poisoning. A New York newspaper journalist, Wally Cook (Frederic March), becomes interested in her story and brings her to New York to expose her illness as well as garner sympathy for this dying woman. Of course, Hazel Flagg is an imposter; she takes advantage of the many opportunities presented to her in New York and capitalizes on the sympathy of those concerned with her plight. However, by the film's end, she falls in love with Wally, who has accompanied her to the city. Wally and his editor recognize that they have been deceived, and in their attempt to salvage their reputation as credible journalists, they construct a fake disappearance of Flagg.

The film opens with a warning that New York is a city of skyscrapers, "Where the slickers and know-it-alls peddle gold bricks to each other and where Truth, crushed to earth rises again more phony than a glass eye." Thus, the film is about deception, and McDaniel, who appears only in the opening scene, uncovers the deception her spouse perpetrates. Dressed in a blue dress, hat, and sweater, she seemingly represents the moral fiber lacking in this sea of immorality and deception in which her husband takes part. In this instance, blackness could signify both the morality that most of the white characters lack and the immorality embodied by her husband and the other characters in the film. Ernest is revealed to be an imposter who is a bootblack and later becomes the janitor for the *Morning Star* newspaper. That he is marked as an imposter represents the deception that occurs throughout the rest of the film.

MCDANIEL IN *GWTW:* THE PRESS SPEAKS OUT

GWTW was, by most accounts, a commercial and artistic success, and as such it has often been the focus of numerous articles in the print media. This includes the black press, since the film included a black actress in a supporting role and focused on a topic germane to the black community's interests and concerns. Notable about this coverage in the print media is the black press's and the mainstream press's ambivalent treatment of McDaniel and, at times, the mainstream press's erasure of her in its coverage of the film.

The roles McDaniel popularized as the black subservient on screen (before and after her award-winning performance) were marked by ambivalence. Film scholar Michele Wallace speaks to the ambiguity that McDaniel's on-screen image invokes. This image, Wallace argues, helped blacks make strides in the movie industry but at the same time perpetuated representations that they sought to escape. According to Wallace,

> Given the narrow restrictions on the roles that Black actresses could play in the thirties and forties (either maids or entertainers), McDaniel excelled at her craft. She was so perversely commanding in the "Mammy" role that Jamaica Kincaid was moved to write in *The Village Voice* in 1977 that she had always wanted a Mammy.

> As an adult, as a woman, as a Black woman and feminist, I strongly identify with both the restrictions McDaniel and [Butterfly] McQueen faced, and their efforts to surmount them.[14]

Wallace's critique points to the dilemma that McDaniel faced as a talented black actress working in an industry that offered her limited roles, and to the harsh treatment she endured from a press that was ambivalent regarding how blacks should reconcile this dilemma.

This ambivalence became the center of the African American press's reporting on McDaniel. In fact, while the black press mentioned McDaniel for her minor roles in films prior to her appearance in *GWTW*, it was actually following her role in this film that the black press began to cover her extensively. Thus, this extended coverage serves as the starting point of this examination of her contentious relationship with the black press.

The African American press took particular delight in flaunting her success, although their commentary was often tempered with criticism. For example, when McDaniel was being considered for an Academy Award, the *Baltimore Afro-American* proclaimed, "She's on the Ballot,"[15] but prefaced its report by featuring a photo of McDaniel from *GWTW* in which her expression was one of suspicion—a photo that personified her as the quintessential subservient and one in which the look of inquisition, often directed toward Scarlett in an attempt to second-guess her motives, now was directed at the Academy. Never before had the committee bestowed the award upon an African American, so even though she and the African American community knew it was well-deserved, McDaniel's nomination was indeed a surprise. While the *Baltimore Afro-American* headline was optimistic, this optimism was tempered by the implications of the photo selected to accompany the story.

McDaniel's Oscar nomination was already beginning to be politicized, as the African American community used it to express its anger at the Motion Picture Academy for its prior snub of other black actresses. In acknowledging Hollywood for its recognition of McDaniel, the African American press also voiced its strong displeasure with the Academy regarding its snub of Louise Beavers for her performance in *Imitation of Life*. When it was officially announced that McDaniel had indeed won the Academy Award for Best Supporting Actress, the *New York Amsterdam News* took the opportunity to remind its readers of the pain that had followed when "Louise Beavers, who stole the show in *Imitation of Life* . . . received only an 'Honorable Mention' from the Academy."[16] The African American press used McDaniel's award as a weapon to battle the industry over recognition of blacks that was long overdue. Why had not many other talented African American actors and actresses received awards? Although these reports were not targeted at McDaniel, she was at the center of the debate, and such reporting eventually began to have the effect of victimizing McDaniel.

The *Baltimore Afro-American* was particularly preoccupied with the way McDaniel's win was perceived in the African American community. Among blacks, the award seemed to represent all African Americans of stature in public settings, even though, according to Donald Bogle, Mc-Daniel and her escort were seated at the awards ceremony at a "special table for two at the rear of the room."[17] The *Baltimore Afro-American* made a point of reconstructing the emotions of the awards night and noted that "Tears were in the eyes of Fay Bainter, actress, winner of last year's identical prize, as she presented the prize to McDaniel, and tears were in both Miss McDaniel's eyes [and Bainter's eyes] . . . as she graciously thanked the group for the honor bestowed upon her."[18] By emphasizing the emotional climate at the ceremony, the paper was introducing a deeper question: Did this emotionalism signify a new era of liberalism? If whites could so publicly and openly display seemingly sincere warmth, affection, and respect for an African American actress, could this attitude transform the racial boundaries that divided the nation? The press also seemed intent on portraying McDaniel's emotionalism as a response to the marginalization and exploitation she had endured as an African American actress, and even as an attempt to question the racial politics of Hollywood.

Nevertheless, the African American press's ambivalence in its response to McDaniel's success could not have escaped McDaniel's notice. On the one hand, the press eagerly acknowledged her talent, but on the other hand, it was disturbed that she was reduced to no more than a mere subservient. Members of the black press wanted the actress to receive the applause that she deserved for her talent, but they also wanted her to be cast in roles that were more representative of the wide range of black life, rather than roles that reduced blacks to caricatures. McDaniel's success made her both a heroine and a victim, in that while she was perceived as making strides in a white-dominated industry, at the same time she was seen as doing a disservice to black advancement by perpetuating racial stereotypes. Thus the press used McDaniel's successes and failings to articulate its own views regarding racial advancement in American culture.

In covering McDaniel's acceptance of the Academy Award, the *Baltimore Afro-American* characterized her evening attire as "dull,"[19] which was one of many uncomplimentary comments (deliberate or innocent) in the press's coverage of her. This stance toward her is evident in the *Philadelphia Tribune*'s coverage, which noted, "Metropolitan paper reviewers who covered the [award ceremony] say that her entrance was the big moment of the evening."[20] The choice of the words "big moment" would have no significance but for McDaniel's size and the press's preoccupation with her physical appearance. Even if this pun was unintentional, it could have been an awkward Freudian slip that devalued McDaniel's talent and reduced her to her body. The *Philadelphia Tribune* reviewer continued in this same vein: "As the lights dimmed and the crowd danced to the music of Guy Lombardo, the manager of the Ambassador asked Miss McDaniel to come with him on the mezzanine floor, where hundreds of private guests of the hotel stood to catch a glimpse of the smiling Negro actress."[21] This time McDaniel is rendered as a spectacle, as something to be looked at. She is not objectified because of her stardom but because of her Otherness. This description of her as "the smiling Negro" played upon the stereotype of the "happy darky," who smiles incessantly to placate whites.

In some instances, mainstream publications were ambivalent in their coverage of McDaniel. The *Chicago Tribune* applauded her accomplishments, but in the same breath denigrated both McDaniel and McQueen. The news columnist wrote, "Laurels to big, colored Hattie McDaniels [*sic*] as Mammy, and to little, black Butterfly McQueen for a dandy 'bit' work as Prissy."[22] The *Chicago Tribune* was both racializing the two women and reducing them to their bodies. Even some of her African American peers in the industry echoed the press's unflattering (ambivalent, at best) remarks. African American actor and columnist Clarence Muse observed that "Hattie McDaniels [*sic*] stood in silence and accepted the token, which says to the world that as a supporting artist she is Hollywood's best."[23] Muse's use of the term "token" reflected on Hollywood's years of neglect in acknowledging African American talent and it implied that McDaniel belittled herself by accepting the award at all. Refusing the award, though, would have been a questionable act for McDaniel. Receiving the award may have seemed not just a personal tribute but also an accomplishment for all African Americans. She may have felt an obligation to receive the award gracefully.

Muse's ambivalence, whether intentional or not, is evident in his description of McDaniel's path as an actress: "An astute showman, she quickly changed her approach to the cinema art, which has a great love for typing people, and became what they wanted, 'the mammy.'"[24] The implication, of course, is that McDaniel consciously compromised her principles to elevate her career as an actress. Muse, attempting to qualify his position, later added: "'That the old South is beautiful. That days of slavery and the happy slaves singing in the windows at night were lovely' is indeed not the creation of Hattie McDaniels [sic]. She is only the servant to the play."[25] Muse held McDaniel responsible for compromising her principles, yet pardoned her for popularizing such caricatures.

Crisis magazine, the official publication of the NAACP, took a more even-handed position toward McDaniel and the other blacks in the film. Rather than targeting the actors for their compromising roles, the magazine directed its criticism at white Hollywood. Following McDaniel's acceptance of the Academy Award, *Crisis* featured her on its April 1940 cover. The combination of the cover photo, a caption lauding McDaniel, and a later critique denouncing Hollywood gave McDaniel increased visibility and more objective treatment. Attacking the racial climate that prevailed in the cinema industry, Dalton Trumbo, writing for the *Crisis*, leveled the following charges:

> In Hollywood the most gigantic milestones of our appeal to public patronage have been the anti-Negro pictures, *The Birth of a Nation,* and *Gone with the Wind.* And between the two, from 1915 to 1940, we have produced turgid floods of sickening and libelous treacle. . . . But if we shy from Negro themes, we also shy from Negro writers. A shocking and, to us, most pertinent example of the race myth in operation may be found in Hollywood's failure to tap the great reservoir of creative Negro talent.[26]

In its coverage of McDaniel's Academy Award, the mainstream press differed little from the African American press. *Daily Variety* found it necessary to report that "Not only was she the first of her race to receive an Award, but she was also the first Negro ever to sit at an academy banquet."[27] This "achievement"—becoming the first African American to attend an Academy Awards banquet—would not have been defamatory had it not been seen as newsworthy by the mainstream press. It was ignored entirely by the African American press, but the mainstream press wanted to call attention to what it viewed as "privileging" African Americans. This same publication, affirming McDaniel's resemblance to and effectiveness at reconstructing the matriarchal figure, surmised that, "In addition to her ability as an actress, Hattie McDaniel could pose as an ad for Aunt Jemima."[28] Variety was not alone in the mainstream press in deliberately devaluing, maligning, and commodifying (with stories that sold publications) McDaniel and promoting her as a model subservient. The mainstream press appeared unwilling to relinquish the negative image that they had constructed for McDaniel—an image that would have greater meaning after GWTW.

Some mainstream publications were more cognizant of McDaniel's talent and less harsh about her as a person. The New Yorker asserted that "The Mammy of Hattie McDaniel is truly distinguished."[29] In the same vein, the New York Times reported that "Best of all [performances], perhaps, next to Miss Leigh, is Hattie McDaniel's Mammy, who must be personally absolved of responsibility for that most 'unfittin' scene in which she scolds Scarlett from an upstairs window. She played even that one right, however wrong it was."[30] Newsweek observed, "As the bossy Negro Mammy, Hattie McDaniels [sic] turns in a first-rate job that frequently amounts to scene stealing."[31]

Some of the other mainstream publications displayed a less enlightened racial consciousness. Theatre Arts failed to even mention McDaniel in its review of the film. This neglect is particularly striking when we note that this publication made a point of comparing GWTW to The Birth of a Nation, a film enshrined in cinema history for both its cinematic achievements and its racially inflammatory themes, with the latter picture provoking riots in major cities following its release.[32] The reference to The Birth of a Nation in Theatre Arts may have been a subtle attempt to re-invoke the racist white supremacist views the film articulated. It may have been a riposte to those mainstream press publications that praised McDaniel.

The *Nation* also marginalized McDaniel, and although mentioning her name, the paper's reviewer made no additional reference to her role. Reducing McDaniel's performance to one sentence and barely even mentioning Butterfly McQueen reads as an overt attempt to slight both actresses. Apologetic for his oversight, the *Nation's* reviewer claimed, "I have only space to mention Hattie McDaniel as Mammy and Butterfly McQueen as Prissy."[33] Both the slight and the apology illustrate not only how McDaniel was marginalized in much of the mainstream press, but also how this exclusion could be read as one way of deliberately minimizing her contribution to the film.

POINTS AND COUNTERPOINTS: "AND ALL THE MEN AND WOMEN MERELY PLAYERS"

Two familiar lines from Shakespeare's *As You Like It* read thus: "All the world's a stage, / And all the men and women merely players." These lines apply to the debates in the black press about the roles Hattie McDaniel (who is centered in the debates) and other black actresses and actors played in *GWTW*. On the one hand, some members of the black press argued that despite the negativity of the role she played, McDaniel was merely a player, and an excellent one. This was the stance, in part, that Al Monroe took when proclaiming McDaniel's undisputed talent and characterizing her performance as a "show stopper."[34] Monroe both praises and condemns the black actors who appear in the film. In this instance, Monroe implied that the talent of African Americans prevented the film from being a failure. Citing McDaniel's performance in particular, Dan Burley of the *New York Amsterdam News* also noted the centrality of her brilliant and convincing performance in a film that he considered basically flawed.[35] Writing in the *Philadelphia Tribune,* the syndicated columnist Jimmie Fidler concurred that McDaniel's performance "steals that picture," and added that she rendered "one of the greatest dramatic performances of all time."[36] The *Washington Afro-American* asserted that "Hattie McDaniel does as much for her race with her portrayal as Mammy as anyone in history."[37]

While reviewers and commentators in the African American press often cited particular scenes in which McDaniel's acting talent was especially brilliant, Harry Webber of the *Baltimore Afro-American* thought her acting was equally excellent in every scene in which she appeared, "From the moment she comes on in the upstairs window scene ... until her last poignant appearance."[38] These stellar evaluations of McDaniel as an actress in this role are representative of the black press's positive assessment of her award-winning performance, an assessment echoed by those in the black community (and the white community) who viewed her performance in a positive light. For example, one moviegoer's letter to the *Baltimore Afro-American* stated, "I felt proud when the acting of Hattie McDaniel, in the role of Mammy, brought hearty laughs or heartfelt tears to the eyes of many in the audience. No colored player provoked unnecessary criticism, scorn, or hatred from those whom I sat near. I heard as many favorable comments for the colored actors as for the white actors. Truly, I felt proud."[39]

Though positive evaluations of McDaniel and other black actresses and actors in the film were effusive, negative attitudes expressed in the black press and from the black community were often caustic. In the black press, the naysayers often included praise and condemnation in the same article. Some members of the black press argued that McDaniel and other black actors and actresses in the film (and similar films that depicted black characters) were not merely players but representatives of their race and that their performances reflected negatively on the race. Al Monroe, writing in the *Chicago Defender,* held African American actors who appeared in *GWTW* responsible for their offensive representations. He declared, "Thus when we saw Miss McDaniels [*sic*], Miss Butterfly [McQueen] and also Oscar Polk cast to portray, for cash, a role that some slaves enacted in order to lessen their burdens at the whipping block, we weren't surprised, however disturbed we may have been."[40] Although he had earlier praised McDaniel, he later denounced these actors, McDaniel in particular, for compromising their supposed principles in order to display their talents and advance their positions in the film industry. So, too, did a reviewer in the *New York Amsterdam News,* who quipped, "If, in the case of Hollywood and *Gone with the Wind,* Negroes are wanted for parts that do their race or cause no good, there's a flock of them lined up at the employment window."[41]

In a letter to the *New York Amsterdam News,* Ross Hawkins castigated the paper, the film, and McDaniel: "Neither your endorsement, nor the award of an 'Oscar' to one of the players, will erase that foul odor arising from *Gone with the Wind*."[42] Some of the most venomous condemnation of the film and the black performers came from William Patterson of the *Chicago Defender*, who charged the film with staging character assassinations against African American women. In his view, the film "'morally justifies' the slave breeding pen and the degradation of Negro womanhood and manhood" and "made of Negro womanhood a wanton wench ready to accept the advances of any man."[43] An editorial in the *Chicago Defender* alleges that in the film "The Negro woman becomes by inference the free prey of any sex-crazed beast. The ravishing of any and every black woman is justified."[44] Though the sexual exploitation and abuse of black women is implied through the recreation of the slave experience, there are only a few instances in which the African American woman is sexualized, as when Rhett Butler (Clark Gable) approaches Mammy and requests that she unveil her red petticoat. From the purview of sexual exploitation, therefore, Patterson and the *Chicago Defender* overstate their case.

As the warring factions of praise and condemnation continued their dispute in the black press and the black community, African American actors who were caught in the debate surrounding the film began to emerge from the shadows and publicly defend their involvement in the film. Oscar Polk was among the first to defend his role. He publicly declared that, as a southerner, he felt that many of the characters were consistent with southern tradition. He argued that "As a race, we should be proud that we have risen so far above the status of our enslaved ancestors, and be glad to portray ourselves as we once were, because in no other way can we so strikingly demonstrate how far we have come in so few years."[45] Polk's defense gave other actors the courage to break the code of silence that had enveloped the film. More began to step forward. One month later, in May of 1939, Hattie McDaniel, the performer whom the naysayers targeted most frequently, defended her participation in the film. As a counterpoint to negative criticism of her, McDaniel revealed in the *New York Amsterdam News* that she was attracted to the Mammy role because "I naturally felt I could create in it something distinctive and unique."[46] She countered critics such as William Patterson of the *Chicago Defender*, who saw the film as a vicious assault on black womanhood, and milder critical opinions that the film caricatured black womanhood. Notwithstanding the costume of Mammy and what it connoted, McDaniel said she saw and accepted "an opportunity to glorify Negro womanhood. Not the modern, streamlined type of Negro woman, who attends teas and concerts in furs and silks, but the type of Negro of the period that gave us Harriet Tubman, Sojourner Truth, and Charity Still. The brave, efficient type of womanhood which, in building a race, mothered Booker T. Washington, George [Washington] Carver, Robert Moton, and Mary McLeod Bethune."[47] She confessed, "I knew that Mammy in the Civil War picture would have to wear a handkerchief on her head, to depict her people in slavery, but this would only serve to emphasize the improved status of our race today."[48] She concluded her public declaration by stating, "I saw in the Mammy of the O'Hara household the type of womanhood which has built our race, paid for our elaborate houses of worship, and sustained our business, charitable, and improvement organizations."[49] That McDaniel drew upon the strong will demonstrated by black leadership supports the assertion that she transformed the black stereotype into a strong characterization and attempted to defuse the subordination implicit in the Mammy role. McDaniel's defense of her role received some consideration from the public. Although most were disturbed by her role, McDaniel's allegiance to the African American community led some African Americans to accept her explanation that she took the role to elevate the African American community. This did not make the Mammy figure more acceptable, but it allowed the public to empathize with her decision.

McDaniel claimed that her portrayal of Mammy was an attempt to reconstruct and glorify black womanhood. Her position was that being a servant in itself was not offensive; rather, it was the cultural connotations and the assumption that blacks could not attain positions beyond this capacity that were disturbing. McDaniel referred to her subservient status as Mammy as a reminder that "members of that class have given so much. Bending their backs over washtubs, they have smiled encouragement to daughters who wanted an artistic career. Hobbling about kitchens, they have inspired their children to become doctors of philosophy and law."[50] She contended that she used the role as a means to an end, making her decision more understandable and acceptable to the public and perhaps to herself as well.

THE AFRICAN AMERICAN PRESS
DENOUNCES THE FILM

While ambivalent about the black actresses and actors who worked in the film, overall the black press and the black community (sometimes with support from whites) were uniform in their denunciation of the film. Objections to the film began even while it was still in production. Earl Morris, for example, objected to the film's intent to use derogatory terms such as "nigger," and he criticized those African American actors who during auditions for parts were forced to forget "all about self respect, pride, and duty to their race" by reading a script that demeaned them and others of their race.[51] After the film's release, protests against it became more active, more organized, and more widespread. Several people called for a boycott of the film. *GWTW* thus became a political weapon with which African American activists could assert their positions and lobby for their causes.

Benjamin Davis publicly denounced *GWTW* and expressed his dissatisfaction with its African American representations. In his view, "The faithful slave servants of the heroine's family are supposed to be symbolic of all the Negroes and their love for the 'benevolent' slave masters. . . . According to this picture, slavery was a blessing to these Negroes who appreciated it."[52] Davis viewed *GWTW* as a political weapon strategically designed as propaganda to create a wedge between blacks and whites of the labor and progressive movements for "Negro rights." Like several other publications, the *Chicago Defender* framed the racial and sexual aspects of the film as a political struggle whereby whites attempted to exert control over blacks through their historical preoccupation with the black body. William Patterson considered the film a direct attack on the constitutional rights of African Americans and asserted that "Black America has won its right to sit at the table of democracy and to enjoy every bounty heaped upon that board."[53] An editorial in the *Chicago Defender* affirmed, "This is the essence of *Gone with the Wind*. It makes [a] mockery of civil liberties."[54] Citing what he considered the film's weaknesses, Dan Burley of the *New York Amsterdam News* characterized *Gone with the Wind* as "the pus oozing from beneath the scab of a badly healed wound and aggravated by the subtlety of its presentation by the master directors and technicians of Hollywood."[55]

In Philadelphia, the president of the National Baptist Convention publicly fanned the growing criticism of the film, resulting in an effort to halt any screening of the film in that city.[56] The resistance spread to New York, where the Harlem–Washington Heights Council of the Workers Alliance submitted a letter to MGM informing the studio of the alliance's intent to protest the film.[57] The *New York Amsterdam News* reported that "Seventeen Union locals on behalf of their thousands of white and Negro members . . . urge[d] the American Federation of Labor and the Congress of Industrial Organization to go on record against the film *Gone with the Wind,* and we call upon these great labor organizations to declare a national boycott of the picture throughout the country."[58] These organized protests were later translated into public action as protesters gathered support for their position and staged boycotts of local theaters.

When the film opened in Chicago at the Woods and Oriental Theaters, it was met by a hundred protesters affiliated with the International Labor Defense, the National Negro Congress, the Workers Alliance, and the American Student Union. William Patterson, one of the film's harshest newspaper critics, was among the protesters.[59] The film met similar resistance at the Lincoln Theater in Washington, D.C., where a picket line was formed by Howard University law students.[60]

MAMMY LOCATES A SPACE FOR HERSELF IN *GWTW*

Many if not most African American actresses who had significant (though minor) roles in films through the 1940s functioned as a shadow for the leading white female star's character (and sometimes for the star herself). This is true for Hattie McDaniel, whose character Mammy in some ways was a shadow for Vivien Leigh's character, Scarlett O'Hara. Some no doubt would argue that it was McDaniel's projection of the quintessence of the Mammy stereotype, with all its dimensions of negativity, that earned her an Oscar. For this outstanding performance, some in the black press and black community praised her while others condemned her. I argue that it was her exceptional talent in subverting the Mammy stereotype that should account for the Oscar-level accolades for her performance.

Viewer expectations and filmic devices (costume, makeup, script, language, setting, characterization, etc.) situate Mammy in a defined space. Hattie McDaniel as Mammy defies this fixed space. I concur with

Maria St. John, who concludes insightfully that "Ultimately, though, Mammy is Scarlett's insides, and her comment, 'It ain't fittin', it just ain't fittin',' echoed throughout the film, betrays the fact that the projections with which Scarlett wants Mammy to be coincident will always fit her ill. 'It,' the projected image, doesn't fit because 'it,' the mammy stereotype, embodies the contradictions 'it,' the dominant cultural imaginary, disavows through secretly nursing the fantasy [of the black stereotype]."[61] Indeed, though the film positions her in the role of the stereotypical Mammy, the shadow, McDaniel steps out of this space, reconfigures the role, and locates a different space for herself within the film. She defines this reconfigured space through her acting talent—the gaze, the inflectional language, the (re)interpretation of the script, the symbolic actions, and other acting techniques that she brings to the role. In doing so, not only does she "steal the show," as some of her contemporary critics maintained, but she in effect controls it by elevating her supporting role to a leading performance. Her performance overrides costume, scripted language, makeup, and other filmic devices associated with the stereotypical Mammy. McDaniel becomes Mammy, but not in the negative way her detractors claimed. Rather, she becomes Mammy in the same way that any first-rate actress becomes on screen the character she portrays. Perhaps cast as a stereotypical Mammy, through her acting expertise McDaniel redefines this one-dimensional role and produces a complex character.

Though Mammy's identity is intricately interwoven with that of Scarlett and other white characters in the film, in configuring her own space in the film she establishes an identity distinct from the one assigned through her connection to her white mistress. Mammy seeks to define herself rather than simply allowing others to define her, and in so doing she successfully challenges the limitations of Otherness that her role implies.

Mammy's reconfiguring of her own space can be observed in virtually every scene in which she appears. It is most apparent when she assumes multiple voices, speaking for and to Scarlett, and speaking for herself to other characters in the film. Mammy's voice articulates a wide range of functions. At times, her voice functions much like the chorus in a classical Greek play, which comments on the action and provides a perspective on the play's moral implications. Indeed, at times her voice is the voice of reason and moral and ethical persuasion, not only for Scarlett but also for other characters and groups of characters (such as Confederate and Union soldiers). Additionally, when she speaks to Union soldiers, black slaves, and even Rhett Butler, it is through a different (her own) voice—a voice that ranges from being commanding to being sympathetic, and a voice noteworthy not only for what she says but, more important, how she says it. She refuses to remain silent, and when she speaks it is with conviction and authority, particularly when she assumes the role of Scarlett's conscience. I use the term ventriloquism to refer to Mammy's voice as the voice of Scarlett's conscience. As a speech act, Mammy often articulates words and thoughts and perspectives that should be and can be attributed to Scarlett (whether they are a part of Scarlett's conscious, unconscious, or subconscious). As I use the term ventriloquism in this discussion, it is a dramatic situation in which both women usually are on screen and the thoughts that emanate from one (Scarlett) are actually spoken by the other (Mammy). In this film, ventriloquism reinscribes the conventional function of the black woman as the white woman's shadow.

One of Mammy's functions in the film is indeed as a shadow for Scarlett, much in the manner that the black shadow-self functions in other films of the period to aggrandize the positivity associated with the leading character's whiteness. (One indication of this is Mammy's statement that she has applied buttermilk to Scarlett all winter, certainly a cosmetic procedure designed to maintain or even increase Scarlett's whiteness.) The two women are shown to be direct opposites, with Scarlett as the self and Mammy as the Other. From this purview, Mammy is desexualized and portrayed as unattractive due to her size and weight, in a culture where such characteristics are all-important. In addition, Mammy is masculinized by her deep voice, a deliberate contrast with Scarlett's feminized, high-pitched voice. Mammy also signifies blackness as she is dark in complexion, in stark contrast to Scarlett's whiteness. When Scarlett is informed that Ashley, the object of her desire, intends to marry another woman, she is anguished and disillusioned. She starts to leave the plantation, but Mammy opens a window and yells at her, shouting a variety of commands. In this scene, Mammy's round, dark face contrasts sharply with Scarlett's thin white face. Mammy, boisterous and demanding, uses her deep (masculinized) voice to assert her power, as she exclaims: "Miz Scarlett, where you going without your shawl an' night air fixin' to set in. And how come you didn't ask the gentlemen to stay for supper. You ain't got no more manners than a field hand. Come on in the house befo' you catch yo' death of dampness. Come on in y'ere."

From this scene and in subsequent ones, it becomes apparent that Mammy is more than a mere shadow used to aggrandize Scarlett's supposed assets and that McDaniel's interpretation of the role elevates Mammy out of the one-dimensional category to which such character types typically were assigned. Despite their physical differences, it is the two women's sameness that is intriguing. In the context of time and place, both of these antebellum women are relegated to the category of Other. Linda Williams astutely observes that the "affinity between nineteenth-century white women and their slaves [is witnessed in the fact that] as disenfranchised persons with no rights, white women and black slaves were liminal beings who derived whatever power they had from the moral virtue of their very powerlessness."[62]

Williams suggests that the moral fortitude exhibited by black slaves, and in some instances by white women, was derived from the disenfranchised position they assumed in the antebellum community. The similarity between Scarlett and Mammy (shadowed selves) is evident not only in the alienation they endured from the white plantation patriarchy but also in the fact that the two are assertive, strong-willed, and defiant characters. They both resist containment—Mammy resists the subordination inscribed in her characterization and Scarlett resists the moral codes imposed on white Southern womanhood. They are defined by and identified through each other; their identities are inextricably interwoven.

In examining the mammy figure, it is necessary to observe the strategic positioning of the character in relation to her white screen foil, for Mammy's construction in *GWTW* is, on one level, inextricably bound to Scarlett. Grace Elizabeth Hale observes that "the figure of the mammy, then, both eased and marked the contradiction at the heart of that new home-based white womanhood, its dependence on a gendered influence and yet possession of a racial authority, its masking of the new with a conscious celebration of the old."[63] She continues, "The mammy figure revealed, perhaps more than any other construction of the culture of segregation, a desperate symbolic as well as physical dependence on the very people whose full humanity white southerners denied and the centrality of blackness to the making of whiteness."[64] As a maid to the O'Hara family, Mammy is physically inseparable from Scarlett. In fact, one rarely appears in the film without the other. On another level, that of the performative, McDaniel separates Mammy from Scarlett as she creates her own filmic space.

The interdependence established between the white mistress and her black maid drew them together in close proximity both spatially and psychologically. This proximity helps explain how the two characters shared their thinking, with one (Mammy) articulating the views of the other (Scarlett). Through this association, Mammy becomes Scarlett's ventriloquized voice and echoes her internal sentiments. For example, when Scarlett proceeds to leave the plantation without her shawl, Mammy reminds her that she should not subject herself to the night air without adequate protection. Scarlett is aware of the consequences but seems to be in defiance of Mammy (the voice of maternalism and authority), who represents her internal thoughts and in some ways her inner self. Scarlett resists these internal views and instead voices whatever she is intent upon conveying, regardless of her internal inclinations. In support of this position, Herman Vera and Andrew Gordon note that Mammy "enters the film scolding Scarlett and continually upbraids her for her lapses in etiquette and morality, even if Scarlett usually ignores or rebels against her advice."[65] In this instance, it seems that Mammy, as Scarlett's servant and protector, is articulating a maternal voice as demonstrated in her desire to protect her white mistress. But while some scholars interpret Scarlett's relationship to Mammy as simulating that of a child who is resistant to a mother figure, I argue that Mammy much more closely represents Scarlett's conscience. This contradictory position that Mammy assumes as both servant and voice of authority reflects the multiple positions she occupies as well as the power she signifies and manages to wield over characters in the film.

That Mammy assumes multiple positions in *GWTW* and articulates multiple voices is particularly evident when Mammy assists Scarlett with her corset. Scarlett holds the bedpost while Mammy roughly tightens the straps and commands Scarlett to "Just hold on and suck in." These remarks, accompanied by a commanding gesture, suggest that an element of suspense and intrigue is about to be introduced. Mammy's voice is used at this juncture to alert spectators to an alteration in the film's emotional intensity. At the same time, her remarks remind the viewer of the two characters' strong personalities and interconnected identities. While Mammy assumes the commanding position of securing her white mistress, Scarlett does not resist being confined by the corset, eagerly awaiting the forthcoming adventure to which Mammy symbolically alludes. Mammy's position behind Scarlett as Scarlett holds onto the bedpost simulates the control one might exert over a thoroughbred and links Mammy to animalism because of her blackness. However, the tightening of the corset can be understood to represent Scarlett's need (and subconscious desire) to be contained or controlled in spite of her expressed desires to the contrary.

In creating her own film space, Mammy, to some extent, parallels the function (though not the form) of the mulatto as a character type who, according to Hortense Spillers, is neither black nor white.[66] Mammy is neither a field hand nor mistress of the house, but at times she becomes the voice for both. For example, early in the film Mammy tells Scarlett that she doesn't have any more manners than a field hand. This remark is as much intended to berate the field hands and set Mammy apart from this "lowly" group of slaves as it is designed to chastise Scarlett.

Frantz Fanon, exploring the psychology of mulattoes, argues that they seek to establish a unique space for themselves. Fanon states that mulattoes profess their difference by making assertions such as "I am not a Negro, and in order to prove it to you, I . . . am going to show the genuine Negroes the differences that separate me from them."[67] The mulatto attempts to both deny and acknowledge her or his white patriarchy and "black blood." Mammy assumes a social space similar to the mulatto in that she denies and acknowledges her likeness to and difference from both field hands and whites, particularly those whites whom she views as powerless. She comments that "Miss Ella [Scarlett's mother] has no business acting like a wet nurse" to those Mammy characterizes as "low down po' white trash." Helen Taylor claims that "Far more than Ellen O'Hara herself, Mammy voices the conservative views and values of her mistress, usually in order to scold or express shock at Scarlett."[68] Mammy knows herself to be different from all whites, both the aristocracy and the lower class. Having become the ventriloquized voice of Scarlett, she still recognizes that she is not Scarlett. But although she is black, Mammy will not allow herself to be associated with the field hands; as a house servant, she knows she is different from them. Therefore, she struggles to locate her own space—a space different from both her white mistress and the black field hands. Thus Mammy positions herself duplicitously in that she both resists the inscription of Otherness imposed by white southern codes and accedes to this inscription.

In resisting the inscription, and in her attempt to reposition herself and locate a space for herself in the film, Mammy to some extent escapes the inscription and liberates herself from the identities that have been constructed for and imposed on her. In her quest to establish a space for herself, Mammy is constantly contesting and challenging her role in the film. For example, while most of the characters have themselves gone with the wind by the film's end, Mammy remains intact, both literally and figuratively, due in part to her inner strength and continued endurance.

To contest her role and create a space for herself in the film, Mammy employs a range of devices. In virtually every scene in which she appears, she attempts to make her mark and establish her own identity. For example, in the film's introduction when she yells at Scarlett from the upstairs window of the plantation house, Mammy's round face is a circle extending through a square window—a juxtaposition that conveys how she attempts to challenge and defy the space that has been created for her. Mammy even appears to be too large for the window's opening, implying that she has exceeded the confines that have been designed for her. Mary Anne Doane suggests that feminism can be equated with windows:

> Within the "woman's films" as a whole, images of women looking through windows or waiting at windows abound. The window has special import in terms of the social and symbolic positioning of the woman—the window is the interface between inside and outside, the feminine space of the family and reproduction and the masculine space of production. It facilitates a communication by means of the look between the two sexually differentiated spaces.[69]

The space that Mammy occupies in the window suggests her unique subject position and may very well be equated with femininity, as Doane contends. From this study's purview, however, Mammy utilizes this space to emphasize her unique subject positioning as the ventriloquized voice of Scarlett.

Mammy's transgressions of assigned place and space are revealed in other scenes. She is often shown either ascending or descending the massive stairwells that adorn the plantation house. Although this symbolic action does not necessarily make her distinct from Scarlett, it does convey her distinction from many of the other characters denied such mobility. This unique foregrounding is a testament to her power and privilege; she is rarely seen in the kitchen, despite her repeated association with food and the connotations typically associated with her stereotypical role. Moreover, her association with stairwells distinguishes her from Scarlett, from other whites, and from the other subservients. Such positioning reflects on Mammy's mobility. She is the one character who has access to all the worlds the film envelopes: the world of white males, Confederate soldiers, white aristocrats, slaves, carpetbaggers, free blacks, and even Union soldiers. No other character, not even those with the greatest power and prestige, has as much mobility as Mammy. Because she is aware of her difference from other subservients and has liberal access to spaces denied to other characters (blacks and whites), she claims a privileged space in the film. For example, in Atlanta at the end of the war, she and Scarlett walk through the ravaged streets and pass a group of black soldiers. Mammy, asserting her power and authority, walks between rather than around the soldiers, suggesting through this symbolic action that she does not intend to be contained by anyone—whites, blacks, even black Union soldiers.

Mammy continually defies the formal and informal codes that conjoin race and space, place and space, codes that dictate what spaces a black (or any subservient) is allowed to occupy. Mammy's claim to her space is particularly apparent in the scene in which she assists Scarlett and ties her corset. The corset strings are reminiscent of the reins used to guide and direct thoroughbreds, as previously noted, implying the power associated with being allowed to guide and direct. While Mammy, because of her blackness, would normally be associated with bestiality (an association between beasts of burden and slaves), she to some extent subverts this racial inscription and instead controls Scarlett, who becomes linked with animalism because of her behavior. Mammy's control over Scarlett is both figurative and literal. As she tightens the corset, she advises Scarlett on what is morally appropriate and thereby articulates Scarlett's conscience.

Seen from the interpretive perspective of Mammy creating her own filmic space, this same scene reveals the multiple positions and articulates the multiple voices that Mammy assumes in *GWTW*. Among other things, the full scene reveals the protective, maternal, ethical, and moral positions Mammy assumes, as well as the voice of Scarlett's conscience. Included among these multiple positions is that of a surrogate male figure for Scarlett. Rhett Butler hints at the sexuality socially imposed on black maids when he requests that Mammy reveal her red petticoat. Linking Butler to black sexuality invites reference to Joel Williamson's view that Margaret Mitchell, the author of the novel upon which the film was based, constructed Butler as a black character.[70] And if it is tenable that Butler is constructed as a black character in both the novel and the film, then what is Scarlett's racial identity? Linda Williams hints at Scarlett's subtextual ethnicity when she observes that "this selfish, unreflective heroine earns respect either by taking over the natural, close-to-the-earth, biological functions of slaves or by connecting with earth, dirt, and blackness. In this way, the Depression-era Irish heroine, no less than the Jazz Age Jewish hero, becomes a representative American through yet another form of posing as black."[71] The joke between Butler and Mammy could also play upon the fact that while Mammy reins in her prey (as in exerting control over Scarlett), Butler intends to rein in Scarlett. And if Mammy represents the surrogate male denied to Scarlett, when Butler enters the picture as the personification of (black) maleness, he intends to replace the surrogate male (Mammy). But Mammy is in control, and her assertive posture underscores the fact that she recognizes this threat and does not intend to be displaced, as is evident in her initial virulent dislike for Butler.

Mammy's dislike for Butler becomes obvious to him, and he questions Mammy, a subtle way of also discovering the reasons for Scarlett's avoidance and distaste for him. Mammy informs Scarlett, "I told him you was prostrate with grief," further reflecting her association with the body. Moreover, Mammy articulates the desire of Scarlett, who wants to deflect Butler's advances but at the same time is fascinated by him. That Scarlett is now attracted to a more assertive male (Rhett Butler) rather than a more passive male (Ashley Wilkes) is a sign of her maturing sexuality, since Butler is portrayed as the embodiment of the overtly sexualized male, evident through his sexual advances to Scarlett (as well as his command to Mammy to show him her red petticoat, a not-so-subtle hint at the sexualization rather than desexualization of the black maid) and his sexual exploitation of her (a scene that is implied rather than explicitly shown).

However, this is not to imply that one's maturing sexuality automatically becomes associated with sexual exploitation.

Butler's presence in Scarlett's life now affects Mammy's unique subject position and in some instances diminishes Mammy's multiple roles. This position is affirmed by Helen Taylor, who argues that Mammy is denied a voice because she is absent from "the final act of the film [which] has the effect of silencing and marginalising her even more thoroughly than before."[72] I agree that Mammy is silenced in the final act of the film, but I maintain that through her multiple voices she is anything but silenced up to this point, and that McDaniel's interpretive performance rescripts this character and moves Mammy out of the margins into the filmic center, where she remains until the film's final scene. This absence at the film's end, then, could be viewed as a silencing not only of Mammy, but also of Scarlett, as she is silenced in order to empower the leading male character, Butler, and to give him voice. Thus, the usurping voice of the male protagonist is given control of the film at its conclusion. (Some critics contend that the film was specifically designed to showcase Clark Gable's talent.)[73] Mammy's absence from the film's conclusion also follows logically from the fact that the black maid often served as a surrogate male for her white mistress when the male figure was absent. Therefore, once Butler assumes a more dominant role in the film, Mammy is no longer needed as Scarlett's superego—her confidante, protector, and advisor.

Mammy's unique subject position is also evident through her gaze, a symbolic action (in a variety of forms and meanings) that McDaniel executed with exceptional expertise. Mammy's gaze is a surrogate for the gaze of cinematic spectators, who become increasingly aware of Scarlett's machinations. It is through Mammy's gaze that Scarlett's immorality is made ever more transparent to viewers. While according to bell hooks, blacks (slave or free) were denied the right to look,[74] Mammy, despite her role as the black racial Other, is self-empowered to look. She is privileged with this gaze, even though her gaze is theoretically controlled by whites. At times, her gaze becomes Scarlett's gaze, establishing an introspection that reveals Scarlett's inner thoughts.

Mammy's gaze also represents the gaze of spectators as it directs our attention to important points in the film. She forces us to see through Scarlett's deceptions. In her feminist critique of cinema, Laura Mulvey argues that "The man controls the film phantasy and also emerges as the representative of power in a further sense: as the bearer of the look of the spectator, transferring it behind the screen to neutralize the extra-diegetic tendencies represented by woman as spectacle."[75] If Mammy assumes the position of surrogate male in the absence of a male figure for Scarlett even though she similarly serves as a subservient and represents a maternal figure, it is conceivable that Mammy then becomes the bearer of the look. According to Mulvey, spectators identify with the symbolic male character; in this instance, that is Mammy. When the audience identifies with Mammy, she becomes an agent of the look both for Scarlett and spectators and thereby locates a space for herself in the film that allows her to defy the inscription imposed on her as a subservient.

Even while Mammy controls the look, she is also engaged in deflecting the look back onto her audience. While she represents the subordinate Mammy figure for those spectators who view her as such, Mammy thwarts their looks, redirecting the look back to spectators through her (McDaniel's) outstanding performance. By the end of the film, spectators become aware that she is much more than the servant she portrays. Through her performance McDaniel redefines and reconstructs black womanhood, in the words of Hazel Carby;[76] and in McDaniel's own words, as a counter to her critics who asserted that her performance degraded "Negro womanhood,"[77] she (McDaniel as Mammy) brought "something distinctive and unique"[78] to the stock character and thus glorified black womanhood through her performance. As bell hooks argues, it is at these margins—as a black subordinate exploited because of her race and sexuality—that Mammy reconstructs and reshapes her marginalization as a site of resistance when she returns the look that has been projected onto her and reflects it back to the spectator.[79] It is at this juncture—the juncture when McDaniel/Mammy looks back at her audience through her outstanding performance—that she overcomes the marginalization normally imposed on the Mammy figure because of race, gender, and historical origin and claims the film as her own.

The adages that actions speak louder than words and that a picture is worth a thousand words are applicable to McDaniel's Oscar-winning performance as Mammy. Through her talent, McDaniel obviously embellishes the screenplay with gazes, gestures, speech inflections, symbolic actions, and other techniques that reinterpret the script, exhibit her exceptional acting talent, and reform the stereotypical role of the mammy, moving the character out of the shadow(s) and into the spotlight in a manner that an actress with less talent could not and would not do.

FROM THE PROFESSIONAL TO THE PERSONAL

As the first African American Academy Award winner, McDaniel could not combat the relentless and ubiquitous criticism she received in the press. McDaniel defended herself on professional grounds. Perhaps in part as a counterpoint to her defensive posture (and certainly in part because of her national visibility), the African American press turned to a closer scrutiny of her personal life. Some of the coverage was benign and some was pernicious, but all of it was intrusive. For example, when Mc-Daniel appeared in Washington, D.C., for an engagement, the very first question posed to her by a reporter (presumably black since the report appeared in the black press) was whether or not marriage was imminent. The article was headlined "'No Romance For Me' Says Miss McDaniel."[80] The effect was to diminish McDaniel's professional accomplishments by focusing on her private life, an approach not very different from those of most tabloid and gossip publications then and now. The article also reduced her to her body when it referred to her as "the stoutish and talented star."[81] The Academy Award reporting typically referred to her large size and dark complexion, but in the counterpoint to her defensive posture, these physical attributes became more decidedly negative in the press.

Continuing to foreground the negative regarding her personal life, one report revealed that prior to her role in *GWTW*, she had actually worked as a maid for seven dollars per day, implying that she was a "natural" for such roles on the screen. Before her role in *GWTW*, she had in fact worked as a maid in order to continue her career as an actress, a dilemma that confronted many African American actresses.[82] White actresses also were sometimes employed in menial capacities, but at least they had the luxury of having access to a wider range of employment opportunities.

Several press reports focused negatively on her marital life. One ended with the following comment: "Married twice, she describes herself as 'Widow by Death and Left.'"[83] Another noted that she had eloped for her third trip to the altar[84] when she married James Lloyd Crawford, a Detroit realtor. The newspapers were basically unsympathetic to her when her third marriage dissolved. McDaniel's "failure" to maintain a long-lasting marriage and her divorce from Lloyd Crawford became well publicized.[85] A reporter referred to her as the "lone colored actress,"[86] implying either that McDaniel experienced increasing loneliness because of the failures in her private life, or that she was bound to experience a degree of loneliness as one of the few African American actresses working in predominantly white Hollywood.

The gist of this negative reporting about her personal life was that she was a failure as a wife and a mother; after three marriages, she remained childless, a fact that the press in general noted with more than a negative tinge. The *Chicago Defender* announced that "Hattie McDaniel . . . pleasantly surprised both the ofay [white] and sepia movie colony with the announcement of expectancy of the stork's arrival next fall."[87] A later report alleged that McDaniel's "first-born died at birth" or that physicians had erred in diagnosing her pregnancy.[88] McDaniel's disappointment was further news. Reports were published that she had made elaborate plans for the birth of her young one by creating a nursery and had received gifts from well-known colleagues such as Clark Gable, Vivien Leigh, and Claudette Colbert. These stories were woven among gossip about marital troubles.[89] Public exposure exacerbated the personal disappointment that she experienced and inflicted additional injury. The press, meanwhile, assured its readers that McDaniel would not remain childless and declared she would seek adoption.[90] Dovetailing with this were reports that she intended to adopt a child.[91]

Negative reporting about McDaniel's personal life extended beyond the intimate. Along with other successful African American actresses, such as Louise Beavers and Ethel Waters, McDaniel soon found herself fighting to retain her property and having to go to court to oppose a city plan to build a freeway through her affluent Los Angeles community.[92] Her problem in this regard also became negative grist for the press's mill. Because of her stardom, McDaniel found herself continually at the center of news reports, and her personal difficulties were often magnified for public scrutiny.

Another event that exacerbated her frustrations and personal difficulties was when the NAACP met with studio executives in 1943 to improve the screen image of African Americans. McDaniel was excluded from the meetings, while less prominent actors were invited to attend. McDaniel, responding to the exclusion, publicly asserted:

> I have no quarrel with the NAACP or colored fans who object to the roles some of us play but I naturally resent being completely ignored at the convention after I have struggled for eleven years to open up opportunities for our group in the industry and have tried to reflect credit upon my race, in exemplary conduct both on and off the screen. You can imagine my chagrin when the only person called to the platform was a young woman from New York who had just arrived in Hollywood and had not yet made her first picture. This put not only myself, but other established artists in an embarrassing light with our studios.[93]

Shortly thereafter, McDaniel was featured at a program sponsored by the Committee for Unity in Motion Pictures where "she referred to Miss Lena Horne as 'a representative of the new type of n---- womanhood.' Caught by immediate surprise exhibited by the silence of more than 3,000 colored and whites who attended the gathering, Miss McDaniel corrected herself in this wise: 'I said Negro womanhood.'"[94] This Freudian slip evokes the question of whether McDaniel genuinely made a mistake or if it was a personal attack against her competitor, Lena Horne. Whatever the case, the black press eagerly reported on McDaniel's "slip of the tongue."

McDaniel appeared in several films during the decade that followed *GWTW*. Most of her roles in the 1940s typified the subservient, a casting decision over which she had little control. Occasionally, the black press lauded her talent, but generally it subjected her to increasing criticism for playing these roles. Her performances in *They Died with Their Boots On* (1941), *George Washington Slept Here* (1942), and *Since You Went Away* (1944) typify the films and the roles she played during the 1940s.

They Died with Their Boots On is a dramatic reconstruction of George Armstrong Custer's contribution to the Civil War effort along with his involvement in the annihilation of Native Americans during the westward expansion. In the film's foreground is a love story involving Custer (Errol Flynn) and Elizabeth (Olivia de Havilland), the daughter of the distinguished Samuel Bacon (Gene Lockhart). The film explores Custer's notorious exploits as a soldier, but he is so committed, unwavering, and courageous that he is hardly believable. To buffer this portrait and to humanize this nearly inhuman character, the film develops his pursuit and brief courtship of Elizabeth, and their later marriage. It is in conjunction with Elizabeth's storyline that Hattie McDaniel (as Callie, Elizabeth's personal maid) first appears in the film. The film uses Callie as a vehicle to embellish the characterization of the white mistress with whom she is paired.

Callie's first appearance is when Elizabeth solicits her supernatural help in getting Custer, the object of Elizabeth's romantic desire, to return to her. Elizabeth and Callie sit in the kitchen and Callie performs her "magic" with the use of a teacup. Elizabeth asks Callie, "Do I have to drink the tea every time?" And Callie responds that "If you want the fortune to come true. . . . That's the fourth time I done read the tea leaves for you Miss Libby. . . . If you keep drinking tea like that, you will turn as yellow as a canary. . . . You gonna get that wish wore out before it can come true." Callie then spins the teacup around and it sits upside down in the saucer. To carry out the spell, she lifts the teacup above her head and then lowers it, an indication that she has finally received a message. Callie looks into the teacup and states, "What's this I see . . . appears like a bird with his wings spreading out; he's flying this way." Elizabeth, excited that Callie has received a message, hurries to have her interpret it, and Callie warns her, "Don't touch it Miss Libby . . . you will spoil the spell." Callie continues that it's a message being directed at Elizabeth: "It's straight and tall, walking beside the bird—a man; he's pulling something—taint a horse; taint a sword, . . . it's a bell . . . I'se got it, it's a door bell." As soon as Callie indicates that it is a doorbell, the bell at the house actually rings, and both are startled that this superstitious ritual really works.

Afraid to answer the door, Callie picks up a frying pan and heads for the door, with Elizabeth close behind. Callie asks for her rabbit's foot and states, "Oh feet keep me from slipping down. Oh rabbit work your charm and keep this child away from harm . . . Ain't got time to kneel and pray. Don't let me down today." When they reach the door and it opens, it is none other than Custer; Elizabeth's wish has been granted. Callie remarks, "Here he is Miss Libby. Here he is . . . You done got your wish." Elizabeth, surprised by Callie's power as well as by the results of the spell, stands in shock and amazement. Callie then urges her to extend an invitation to him and remarks, "You standing there like your feet glued to molasses. . . . Don't get uppity Miss Libby . . . the tea leaves never forgives and never forgets."

This full scene reveals that the black maid's principal functions are as servant, as the executor of supernatural beliefs, as a reflection of her white mistress's hidden emotions, and as a facilitator of her romantic desires for Custer. For example, when Callie serves the tea to the two of them, Elizabeth makes an unusual request for green onions. Callie remarks, "Onions! . . . I know what you love and it ain't onions." Later in this scene, when Elizabeth's father returns and recognizes Custer as the soldier who previously disrespected him at a local tavern, he orders Custer out of the house. Callie escorts him to the door and reflects Elizabeth's emotions by chanting: "Brother Rabbit work your charm and keep this big boy out of harm" and "Out . . . you is going but not for good . . . you is coming back." Then she also facilitates Elizabeth's desire by arranging for Custer to meet Elizabeth at nine o'clock that evening. At nine, Callie meets Custer at the gate and says that unless he is color blind, he knows it is she, not Elizabeth, and that she will escort him to Elizabeth. She says that she will hoot like an owl when it is time for him to leave or when Elizabeth's father, who opposes his presence, nears. Callie sits on the porch while Custer climbs the balcony to meet Elizabeth. Callie hoots when the father, suspecting that Custer might return, enters the porch and inquires about Custer's return. Callie vows that she has not seen anything. Shortly thereafter, an owl seated in a tree begins to hoot and Custer rushes to make his escape by jumping from the balcony to a tree. Callie chastises the owl and remarks, "What you have to wake up for . . . you devil. . . . Don't wink at me." Callie, as the black maid, therefore, also serves as comic relief. Indeed, she has multiple functions, even though she is allowed only brief appearances in the film.

The only other time Callie appears in *They Died with Their Boots On* is when Custer and Elizabeth are married and one of the servants asks, "Where did Miss Libby get such a fine gentleman?" Callie responds with pride, "While child, I found him in a teacup." At this point, Callie virtually disappears from the film but solidifies her position as being responsible for Elizabeth's fate and happiness.

In *George Washington Slept Here*, McDaniel assumes the role of maid to a white family that is relinquishing city living for a more rural lifestyle and is moving from an apartment into an old home where the former president, George Washington, is believed to have resided. McDaniel, interestingly, is more prominently featured in this film than in some of her other screen roles, even though she is relegated to the role of a maid. McDaniel, as Hester, enters in the film's first scene, in which Connie Fuller (Ann Sheridan), wife to Bill Fuller (Jack Benny), stands with Hester observing an antique music box. Hester remarks, while viewing the mechanics of the box, "Look at them birds gone to town." Connie tells her that the box once belonged to Ben Franklin and that it is now an antique. Hester replies, "It's old too, ain't it." And Connie notes that this is what antique means. In this and the following scene, Hester's dialogue as the black Other is designed to display her lack of intelligence (such as her ignorance of the word "antique") and to make her the conveyer of humor, the object of derision, and the brunt of jokes. She misspeaks and often speaks out of turn, she is uninformed about things Connie and Bill consider general knowledge, and Bill mocks her by repeating her comments in her tone and accent.

But she is not exclusively a character for comic relief. In reference to the music the box is playing, Hester says, "That one wouldn't start no jam session in Harlem." Clearly she is knowledgeable about what characterizes black music and her blackness affirms her knowledge of or association to Harlem. Repeatedly reminding Connie and Bill that she must leave because it is her night off, she adds, "If I miss my first day at class, it's all your fault." That Hester aspires to be educated certainly seems to suggest that the black maid is given a wider range of attributes in comparison to a maid in earlier years. Yet she still cannot escape derision, because Bill comments that he would not be surprised if she turned out to be a foreign agent. Bill adds that all Hester does is rearrange the dust, suggesting that being a maid (and not a good one) is the measure of her value and worth.

When the Fullers move from their inner-city apartment to their dilapidated home outside the city, Hester moves with them and endures as much agony as they do in their new house. The house is without plumbing, the roof leaks, and the floor is unstable, among several other problems. According to Hester, "George Washington should have chopped this house down instead of the cherry tree." Several incidents (a horse walks into the house; people fall through the floor; and the table floats away during a rain storm, among others) reveal the house's dilapidated condition and lack of basic housekeeping utensils and provide humor in the storyline. Hester becomes frustrated with the living conditions and threatens to quit.

Hester's frustrations and tribulations are compounded when Bill's mischievous nephew (whom Hester calls a "bad boy") comes to visit and when a neighbor forecloses on the house because he claims it is on his property. The Fullers develop a scheme to retain the property despite all of the endless repairs and problems. Their rich Uncle Stanley (Charles Coburn), who is visiting, and whom they counted on to give them money to save the house, reveals that he is broke. Yet he concocts a scheme by fooling the neighbor into believing that he is still rich and that his lawyers are likely to become involved. Stanley's scheme unravels when Hester arrives and reveals that she attempted to pawn his personal effects and accumulated $150, which is only a small portion of the money needed to save the home. The family, however, is rescued when a document signed by George Washington is discovered and its value is enough to allow them to pay off their debt and retain the house.

What is noticeable about McDaniel's role in this film is that her character is intricately woven into the film's plot even though she is a maid. Nevertheless, Hester serves primarily as a tool for comic relief and to accentuate the humor of the film's other characters. Unlike Hester, the white characters are afforded the luxury of not being read only on the basis of their humor.

Since You Went Away, a World War II propaganda film, focuses on the Hilton family, who are forced to readjust their lives when the father, Timothy, goes off to war. The father never physically appears in the film, but a photo of him is displayed throughout the film. In his absence, his wife Anne (Claudette Colbert) and their two daughters, Jane (Jennifer Jones) and Bridget (Shirley Temple), attempt to carry on a normal life with the assistance of their black maid, Fidelia (Hattie McDaniel). Because the family is struggling financially, Fidelia is forced to assume employment elsewhere and the family decides to take on roomers to generate additional income. The children, distraught over the loss of their father, are now equally distraught over the loss of Fidelia. Fidelia consoles Bridget with the comment that "The Lord himself will have to take care of some of the calamities."

Fidelia clearly is marked as the housekeeper who struggles to maintain some semblance of normalcy in the family in view of the absent father, yet at the same time she serves as the comic relief through the use of comical quips. Her deliberate misuse of the language signifies how she is constructed as the black Other. At the same time, Fidelia represents normalcy in a world of confusion.

While Fidelia displays undying devotion to the Hilton family and affirms how important it is for them to remain intact, it is her own absence of family that provides the contradictory position she assumes when juxtaposed to the Hiltons. When Fidelia returns to the family and tells them that her own employment efforts are not materializing as she had hoped and that she would like to rent a room from the Hiltons, the interdependency between whites and the racial Other is established. Fidelia even offers to work for the family on her days off from her other job, but she insists that "I want my solitude and my privatization." She seems so beholden to the Hilton family that what once appeared to be interdependency now seems to be a relationship in which Fidelia's existence is totally defined by the white family.

When Fidelia is reunited with the family, others also arrive: an elderly roomer named Colonel William Smollett (Monty Woolley); Smollett's grandson, William "Bill" Smollett II (Robert Walker), who is stationed nearby and who returns to greet his grandfather while becoming friends with Jane; and Tony Willett (Joseph Cotten), best man to Tim and Anne at their wedding. In fact, when Tony arrives and Fidelia greets him, Tony teases her and remarks, "If it isn't my old girlfriend Fidelia." Tony brings with him a poster that was to be used as an advertisement for the navy; the poster depicts Anne lifting her skirt and a caption that reads, "Come on in! Join the Waves!" Fidelia, embarrassed by Anne's display of sexuality in the poster, tells Tony to cover up the poster. In this instance, Fidelia serves as the moral conscience that should be exhibited to this overt display and exploitation of white female sexuality.

After Anne and Tony are reacquainted and as Jane exhibits her adolescent desire for Tony, he too is called off to war. At his departure, Fidelia packs his luggage as though she begrudges his presence. Yet when he presents an illustrated drawing of Fidelia elegantly dressed and pleasingly posed, Fidelia develops a renewed affection for Tony. When she sees the drawing, she comments, "It is just the way I always wanted to look. . . . I must have been blind not to see what a nice gentleman you are." The drawing is in stark contrast to the way Fidelia appears in her robe and pajamas with her hair pulled back, and it is in direct contrast to her earlier appearance when she wore a brimmed hat and trench coat. While

Fidelia admires the portrait (as if by looking at the picture she stands to become the image pictured), we as spectators are puzzled by the question of why Fidelia's attractiveness in the picture could not be duplicated on screen. The film subtly suggests that if the picture is a mirror image of how Fidelia desires to be seen, then for Fidelia, this is an image that only can be achieved in a dream. Therefore, the screen as a mirror image of the black maid depicts Fidelia as she is and not as she desires to be, which is as an attractive, desirable, and sophisticated woman. The screen seemingly deludes us as spectators by recognizing what Fidelia desires, yet at the same time indicating that this desire is unattainable for Fidelia or for spectators who want to see her as the woman in the drawing. When Tony departs, Fidelia informs him that the taxi has arrived, and she vows to leave the room before she starts to cry. However, the subtle reference to Fidelia's expressed sorrow could be targeted to her own sorrow over the fact that she cannot be depicted in the way she desires, as reflected in the drawing.

Fidelia has several functions in the film. She enters the film at pivotal moments to motivate or to comment on the action, as in the case of Tony's departure and Jane's graduation ceremonies. Later in the film, she delivers Anne a letter indicating that her husband, Tim, is missing in action, to which Anne responds by fainting. Fidelia celebrates the colonel's birthday by presenting him with a cake—a celebration that comes on the heels of the death of his grandson, who has died in the war. At the celebration, the doorbell rings and none other than Tony returns to the Hilton household. When the Hiltons celebrate Christmas, Fidelia opens the door to Christmas carolers, and when they engage in a game of charades, with each participant acting out a word or phrase, only Fidelia is able to guess the colonel's phrase "Bottom's-Up" as he attempts to recreate his antics on the floor. In the final scene of the film, Fidelia places gifts under the Christmas tree—gifts she claims were sent by Mr. Hilton, who even provided a gift for her. Fidelia gets emotional about his absence as well as his kindness and says that he never forgot me "even when fighting them devils." She recognizes that although he is missing in action, she must maintain her faith and be a true believer. Then Anne opens her gift from Tim and gets emotional and teary-eyed when the phone rings and she receives a message that Tim is scheduled to come home. Fidelia's emotionalism is reflected by Anne's emotional display, but, more important, Fidelia's presence signals Tim's return to the family. Thus Fidelia's role is characteristic of the black maid who serves as the bearer of news, who is the signifier of emotionalism, and who signals pivotal points in the film.

To be sure, in the decade following *GWTW*, African American press coverage of McDaniel's personal and professional lives (often a reflection of the black community's views) was decidedly more negative than positive and her screen roles were increasingly more scrutinized. Soldiers dissatisfied with her screen portrayals protested her film *Three Is a Family* (1944), a film in which she was characterized as "exceedingly obnoxious."[95] Another McDaniel film, *Hi Beautiful* (1944), also was harshly criticized by soldiers, who "contended that pictures of that type are 'poisoning Pacific Islanders toward colored Americans by playing Uncle Tom roles.'"[96] The timing of her success may have contributed to her difficulties. African American soldiers in World War II experienced a new sense of liberty and wanted to improve their status, so they responded to media images they found defamatory. Unable to disempower predominantly white Hollywood, they castigated African American actresses such as McDaniel, whom they viewed as unwilling to relinquish roles and profit to uphold personal and racial principles.

The African American press viewed the behavior of these African American soldiers as unsettling. But they too continued to take issue with McDaniel's screen roles. For example, when she was cast in *George Washington Slept Here* (1942), the *Chicago Defender* asserted, "Period pictures seem to be the proper diet for Miss McDaniel."[97] The implication of this remark was that McDaniel would always be associated with films that reconstructed the mythical representation of Mammy even though in this film, McDaniel is the black maid to a family located in the North yet forever dependent on its black maternal figure.

However, following McDaniel's performance in *Since You Went Away* (1944), the African American press came to her defense once more. According to the press, the white film director, John Cromwell, taunted McDaniel as a scene stealer, commenting, "'You must be planning to carry off another Academy Award this year' . . . and then broke into a big laugh."[98] The African American press viewed such insults to McDaniel as attacks hurled at the entire African American community. The press interpreted the director's behavior as indicating either that he knew that because of her race she would not win another award, or that he was so intimidated by her talent that if she did win an award, her winning would be an insult to the white actors in the picture. McDaniel appears to have been subjected to a backlash, if not from the Hollywood community as a whole, then certainly from at least some in the industry because of her success in *GWTW*.

McDaniel's scene stealing was often heralded by the African American press. Referring to her performance in *The Great Lie* (1941), the *Chicago Defender* wrote, "They are predicting that several scenes showing Miss McDaniels [*sic*] will be cut to save the face of the billed star, Bette Davis.... Certainly, it would be pridal suicide for Hattie McDaniels [*sic*] to win the Academy Award in successive years and while playing minor parts in a picture that carries a billed star like Bette Davis."[99]

By the late 1940s McDaniel married a fourth time, attempting to salvage her private life from the struggles that plagued her professional life. But the marriage to interior decorator Leroy Williams was dissolved within five months—a marriage that may have ended because she was the victim of cruelty[100]—and McDaniel's personal trials were again made public.[101] Suffering from bouts of depression, McDaniel attempted suicide, according to Carlton Jackson.[102]

THE CLOSING OF A CAREER AND A LIFE

Second only to her role as Mammy in *GWTW*, Hattie McDaniel is probably best remembered for a radio and television show that carried her character's name in its title, *The Beulah Show*. She began playing the character Beulah on the radio version of the show in 1947, replacing white males who played the part, and continued in the part when the show moved to television. *Time* magazine's coverage of McDaniel's entry into radio for this program focused on McDaniel's racial construction. According to *Time*, "Since her [Beulah, the character's] introduction to Fibber McGee's cluttered household in 1944—fat, jolly, colored Beulah [the housemaid]—had been impersonated by two thin, tense, white men. Now, at long last, the new Beulah show had a Beulah that was really fat, jolly and colored: Cinemactress Hattie McDaniel. Everyone agreed that she made an ideal Beulah."[103] Like other radio shows of the period, *The Beulah Show* had garnered an audience in radio that was later transferred to television. Radio performers are of course invisible to listeners and can engage their audiences' imaginations primarily through voice, but on television the African American servant Beulah needed to provide "visible evidence" of the black subservient. It was necessary to satisfy the visual/racial expectations of the audience by presenting an actress who epitomized this mammy figure. The *Time* article implied that on television it would be necessary to present a Beulah whose physical construction was the important feature. When the show transitioned to television in 1950, Ethel Waters assumed the role of Beulah, but because of her demanding stage engagements, McDaniel was later cast in the television version, and she worked in both radio and television productions of this dramatization.

In a more positive tone, the *Baltimore Afro-American* applauded her landing a job on television in *The Beulah Show* and praised her achievements in general, particularly the power she had garnered as an actress:

> She has used this power in helping many young aspirants who have tried to break through many closed doors in Hollywood. With money, earned in menial roles, Hattie has put that money to best advantage, owning property and aiding those less fortunate, all of which have made her a credit to her people. . . . She's created for herself, through hard work and persistence, a name among the fabulous, and in her own right.[104]

For McDaniel, the year 1950 began with an upbeat (the *Baltimore Afro-American* article in January), but the decade of the 1950s proved even more problematic for McDaniel than had previous decades. Her financial resources declined further, and she was forced to sell her house.[105] Shortly after she began working on *The Beulah Show,* she was diagnosed with breast cancer, an illness that ultimately resulted in her death on October 26, 1952.[106] After McDaniel's death, the African American press paid tribute to its black star by publishing lengthy articles on her screen career.[107] The mainstream press often merely mentioned McDaniel's death without referring to her extensive career in the cinema industry. For example, *Time* magazine provided only one sentence on McDaniel's death, noting that she appeared in *The Beulah Show* and *GWTW*.[108] *Newsweek* similarly provided only one sentence, mentioning that she had received an Academy Award but failing to even name the film.[109]

McDaniel's marginalization continued even after she died. In contemporary writing, for example, references to her sexuality take precedence over references to her talent. In 1991, *Vanguard* reported that "despite her fame, as a black, a woman, and a lesbian, she never knew life free from discrimination."[110] While this may not be a deliberate attempt to marginalize McDaniel, it places her sexuality (which according to her biographer has never been confirmed as heterosexual, homosexual, or bisexual) as central to her identity. One factor that might have contributed to the ambiguity surrounding her sexual orientation is that some in the gay rights movement have sought support from public figures, and the private lives of some actors and actresses such as McDaniel have been unearthed for political purposes.[111]

The tragic circumstances that McDaniel endured in life surrounded her death as well. Whites opposed her burial in a segregated cemetery in Los Angeles. Her estate's value had declined from $200,000 to $10,000 by the time of her death, and her talent had been reduced to one sentence in the mainstream press.[112] McDaniel, who on screen subverted her Otherness through her strong-willed performance as the quintessential Mammy, off screen internalized the Otherness that had been projected onto her by a press that became more intolerant of her stereotypical roles, by an industry that failed to capitalize on her talents, and by a sociopolitical culture that marginalized her on the basis of her race and gender.

FIGURE 2. Nina Mae McKinney, center; William Fountaine, right of center, in *Hallelujah!* (King Vidor, 1929). MGM/Photofest.

FIGURE 1. Louise Beavers and Mary Pickford in *Coquette* (Sam Taylor, 1929). United Artists/Photofest.

FIGURE 3. Madame Sul-Te-Wan and Dorothy Burgess in *Black Moon* (Roy William Neill, 1934). Twentieth Century-Fox Film Corporation/Photofest.

FIGURE 4. Paul Robeson and Fredi Washington in *The Emperor Jones* (Dudley Murphy, 1933). United Artists/Photofest.

FIGURE 5. Louise Beavers, Claudette Colbert, Curry Lee, Hazel Washington, and Madame Sul-Te-Wan in *Imitation of Life* (John M. Stahl, 1934). Universal Pictures/Photofest.

FIGURE 6. Beulah Bondi and Madame Sul-Te-Wan in *Maid of Salem* (Frank Lloyd, 1937). Paramount Pictures/Photofest.

FIGURE 7. Vivien Leigh, center left, Hattie McDaniel, center right, in *Gone with the Wind* (Victor Fleming, 1939). MGM/Photofest.

FIGURE 8. Eddie "Rochester" Anderson, Ethel Waters, and Paul Robeson in *Tales of Manhattan* (Julien Duvivier, 1942). Twentieth Century-Fox Film Corporation/Photofest.

FIGURE 9. Ethel Waters, Eddie "Rochester" Anderson, John W. Sublett
(a.k.a. John Bubbles), and Lena Horne in *Cabin in the Sky* (Vincente Minnelli,
1943). MGM/Photofest.

FIGURE 10. Hazel Scott shown at piano in *I Dood It*
(Vincente Minnelli, 1943). MGM/Photofest.

FIGURE 12. Ethel Waters, Julie Harris, and Brandon de Wilde in *The Member of the Wedding* (Fred Zinnemann, 1952). Columbia Pictures/Photofest.

FIGURE 11. Lena Horne, right, in *Broadway Rhythm* (Roy Del Ruth, 1944). MGM/Photofest.

FIGURE 13. Dorothy Dandridge and Harry Belafonte in *Carmen Jones* (Otto Preminger, 1954). Twentieth Century-Fox Film Corporation/Photofest.

FIGURE 14. Dorothy Dandridge and Stuart Whitman in *The Decks Ran Red* (Andrew L. Stone, 1958). MGM/Photofest.

SIX

Lena Horne

ACTRESS AND ACTIVIST

When at a gathering of blacks and whites in 1944 Hattie McDaniel used the "N-word" to refer to Lena Horne as "a representative of the new type of [African American] womanhood" in Hollywood, she shocked the audience, but she made a valid point.[1] This new representative type of black actress was "new" primarily in the sense that she (a certain physiological type, a mulatto) was being privileged over the physiological type to which McDaniel belonged. As white Hollywood transformed an endless variety of representations that often reflected America's social and political ideals, it also reconstructed its racial Other, and Lena Horne was indeed a representative of this reconstructed Other.

Jacques Lacan argues that one's sense of self is often mediated through the construction of its Other.[2] African American screen actresses could not escape the inscriptions that emanated from a sociopolitical context that marginalized, devalued, sexualized, and often erased them. In this regard, this new type was not so new, either in form or in function. Indeed, representatives of this "new type" had preceded Horne—Sul-Te-Wan, Nina Mae McKinney, and Fredi Washington among them. Many were aware of being exploited, and Lena Horne was among those who contested and challenged the inscriptions. Rather than internalizing these representations, at one point in her career she responded to her marginalization by publicly denouncing the sociopolitical discourse that sought to contain its racial Other.

This chapter discusses the way Horne launched a campaign to defy Hollywood, viewing it as enslaving and marginalizing, a denial of voice, and a disenfranchisement. Horne found herself preoccupied and even obsessed with aggressively challenging the hegemony in both the reel and the real.

When Horne was recruited by the cinema industry, she, like Hazel Scott, was already an established entertainer. Unlike most white actresses, most African American women did not have the luxury of pursuing a career in acting unless they could sing or dance or both; many were established nightclub entertainers before being recruited, and the pre-existing myth was that African Americans were automatically quintessential entertainers. According to Peter Stanfield, since "the connotations of racial and gender transgression must be carried by sound,"[3] then the black jazz artist occupies a unique position or assumes a significant space. Thus many well-known black women entertainers were attractive to the cinema industry, which hired them with blatant disregard for their dramatic talent (or lack thereof). In this respect, Horne also was representative of this "new" type.

Lena Calhoun Horne was born June 30, 1917, in Brooklyn, New York, to Edwin F. Horne and Edna Scottron Horne, who divorced three years later. Prior to her parents' divorce, Lena resided with her parents and her paternal grandparents, one of whom was Cora Calhoun Horne—an avowed suffragist and defender of black rights who was affiliated with the Urban League, the NAACP (National Association for the Advancement of Colored People), and the Ethical Culture Society. At the age of seven, Lena joined her mother, who traveled constantly as a struggling actress. Being reunited with her mother forced Lena to live a transient life, yet she eventually spent several years in Brooklyn, where she attended public school and a girl's high school. When she was fourteen, her mother married Miguel Rodriguez, whom she had met on a tour in Cuba, and the family relocated from Brooklyn to the Bronx.[4]

Two years later, when her mother became ill, Lena was forced to quit school and landed a job at the Cotton Club, thanks to the assistance of Elida Webb, the club's choreographer. During this period, Horne enrolled in music classes to perfect her singing talent while performing as a chorus line dancer at the club for prominent entertainers such as Count Basie, Cab Calloway, Billie Holiday, and Ethel Waters. In 1934, Horne appeared on Broadway in *Dance with Your Gods,* and the following year she abandoned the Cotton Club and appeared on stage with Noble Sissle's Society

Orchestra in Philadelphia. While performing in Pittsburgh, Horne met Louis J. Jones, a printer, and in 1937 the two married. Horne bore two children—a daughter, Gail, who was born in December 1938, and a son, Edwin (Teddy), who was born in February 1940. In 1938, Horne appeared in her first film, *The Duke Is Tops*. The following year, she left Noble Sissle's Orchestra and landed a prominent role in Lew Leslie's *Blackbirds,* but the stage production was short-lived and Horne was forced to return to domestic life.

In 1940, Horne returned to the stage as a singer with Charlie Barnet's band and supplemented her stage career by working in radio and recording music. When Barnet's band toured the South, Horne was prohibited from performing with the group because of racial intolerance; though she continued to be paid, monetary compensation could never offset the pain of segregation. In the early 1940s, Horne's marriage began to dissolve, and she returned to Pittsburgh to retrieve her children. Her daughter came with her, while her son remained with Jones. It was not until 1944 that their divorce became final. While performing with Barnet's band, she had the opportunity to appear at the Café Society in New York City, and it was here that she met both Paul Robeson and Walter White of the NAACP—black political figures who would greatly influence her views.[5] "As 'a solid classy night club entertainer,' with radio assignments behind her and a voice permanently recorded in two RCA-Victor record albums, Miss Horne next received an invitation to open in Hollywood's Little Troc cabaret in February 1942 and at the Mocambo in July."[6]

Based on this success, Horne was recruited by Metro-Goldwyn-Mayer and received a small role in the picture *Panama Hattie* (1942). When MGM signed her, she became the first black actress to land a seven-year contract with a major motion picture studio. In 1942, Horne left the West Coast and returned to New York to appear at the Capitol Theatre and the Savoy-Plaza Hotel, but she returned to Hollywood the following year and appeared in numerous films, including *Cabin in the Sky* (1943), *Stormy Weather* (1943), *I Dood It* (1943), *Thousands Cheer* (1943), *Swing Fever* (1944), *Broadway Rhythm* (1944), and *Two Girls and a Sailor* (1944). Despite her successful screen career, she continued to make nightclub appearances. During World War II, Horne frequently performed for U.S. soldiers and was declared the favorite pinup girl of black soldiers. At the end of 1944, Horne was one of fifteen women nomi-

nated by the National Council of Negro Women as among the most outstanding of the year.[7]

In December 1947, Horne married Lennie Hayton, a white musical
director with MGM, but she kept the marriage secret from the public
until 1950. By 1948, Horne was earning a substantial sum of money for
her performances at the Copacabana in New York. Although she had
severed her ties with MGM, she was cast in the MGM production *Duchess of Idaho* (1950). It was also during the 1950s that Horne became more
politically involved as a member of the Hollywood Independent Citizens'
Committee of the Arts, Sciences, and Professions, among other organizations. During the McCarthy era, Horne appeared in the *Red Channels* and *Counterattack,* and she, like many performers, was regarded as
a communist sympathizer. Horne returned to the screen in 1956 in *Meet
Me in Las Vegas* and the following year in *The Heart of Show Business.* In
1957 she also performed on Broadway in *Jamaica,* a production that ran
through 1958. After that, Horne appeared in *Nine O' Clock Revue* until it
closed in 1961.[8]

In the 1960s, Horne became actively involved in the civil rights movement. "She was one of the most visible black celebrities involved with the
civil-rights movement, traveling [to the] South to sing and speak at rallies;
taking part in a 1963 meeting between black leaders and Attorney General
Robert F. Kennedy; and adding songs with civil-rights messages to her
repertoire."[9] In 1965, Horne's autobiography, *Lena* (which she wrote with
Richard Schickel), was published by Doubleday. Four years later, Horne
appeared in *Death of a Gunfighter* (1969) and performed in her own concert on national television.[10]

In the 1970s, Horne was faced with the death of her father, her son,
and her second husband, Lennie Hayton. Despite these hardships, she
returned to public life in 1974, appearing on Broadway with Tony Bennett
in a show titled *Tony and Lena.* She also performed in clubs and toured
the United States with Bennett, Alan King, and Count Basie. She was
also cast in the screen production of *The Wiz* (1978), playing the part of
Glinda, the Good Witch. At the end of the decade, in 1979, Horne received
an honorary L.H.D. degree from Howard University.[11]

At the age of sixty-four, she opened on Broadway in *Lena Horne:
The Lady and Her Music,* a show that became the longest-running one-
woman show on Broadway. It also earned her the New York City Handel

Medallion, the Drama Desk Award, a Drama Critics' Circle citation, two Grammys for the original cast album, and the Emergence Award from the Dance Theatre of Harlem. Following the close of her show, Horne toured London in the summer of 1984. Her achievements resulted in her receiving the Governor's Arts Award from New York State Governor Mario Cuomo, the Paul Robeson Award from Actors' Equity, an Image Award, and the Spingarn Medal from the NAACP, among other accolades.[12]

In later years, Horne has appeared in several screen productions designed to document the black cinema experience or to showcase her own singing talent. These include *Small Steps, Big Strides* (1997), *That's Entertainment! III* (1994), and *Lena Horne—An Evening with Lena Horne* (1994).[13] These screen appearances coincided with a revival of her recording career.

A NEUTRALIZED RACIAL IDENTITY

Lena Horne's commodification as a mulatto entertainer can be traced directly to her early years (the mid-1930s), when she debuted as a stage performer with Noble Sissle's band. She had been billed as Leana Horne and promoted by the African American press as a "beautiful, glamorous, glorious" performer who moved with "grace and rhythm."[14] Film historian Donald Bogle contends that Horne's hybridization and appropriation as neither black nor white was evident even during this period in her career.[15] She was deliberately promoted as a Latin star in an the attempt to "neutralize" her blackness so that she would seem more acceptable to white audiences.

This neutralization of Horne did not necessarily offend African Americans in her audience, many of whom, themselves in denial about their blackness and internalizing the negative connotations of blackness, similarly sought to distance themselves from this negative construct. She even allowed her lightness to be used for commercial gain, advertising skin lighteners to transform one's skin into alluringly lovely skin, "whiter, brighter,"[16] a feat that could be achieved only through the use of Dr. Fred Palmer's skin ointment. Implicit in these advertisements was the assumption that whiteness was synonymous with beauty. In Horne's first screen performance in the all-black-cast film *The Duke Is Tops* (1938), produced by the Million Dollar Productions Company, she was promoted as a "glamorous [and] romantic star."[17] She was being commodified not only racially but also sexually, and she was thus rendered an object of the male gaze.

In his review of *The Duke Is Tops,* Arthur Knight contends that the film foregrounds the black male protagonist, Ralph Cooper, more than his female lead, Horne. Knight reveals that the film "depicts an all-Black world, but here its implications—in keeping with the musical genre—are more clearly utopian. In *The Duke Is Tops,* individual but lawful initiative of Black individuals in concert with Black audiences makes Black stars, but only when the individuals have a group with and against which to perform and from which other stars may emerge."[18]

Horne's objectification occurred again when she became one of the few black female performers to accompany a white band—Charlie Barnet's band—and was touted as having "unusual beauty."[19] The implication, of course, was that as an African American entertainer, her unusual beauty allowed her to be exoticized, thus titillating white male fantasies. The black actress/white band combination invites a discussion of Freud's "dark continent" trope, with blackness becoming linked to female sexuality.[20]

Actually, Horne's association with Barnet's band was short-lived. According to the African American press, she endured much the same treatment as had other black singers such as Billie Holiday and June Richmond. Whites, although fascinated by African American singers, were nonetheless disturbed by any privileges that were accorded them. As previously mentioned, Horne was prohibited from performing when the band toured the South because white audiences objected to the association; for their northern tour, she rejoined the band.[21] Again, there was an attempt to neutralize her: reviewers described her as "olive-complexioned," suggesting she might be Italian, Spanish, Portuguese, Argentinean, Chilean, Jewish—anything but black.[22] In erasing Horne's blackness, whites may have been dealing with fears about themselves, finding support for their "superiority" by appropriating blackness as something to be devalued, rejected, and dismissed.

Arthur Knight observes that "Remaining a singer, a principally live, nonnarrative, nonnarrativized performer, allowed Horne to maintain continuity with other Black stars—athletes, musicians, dancers, and theater performers—that *The Crisis* favored for its covers."[23] Returning to the stage, Horne performed at the Café Society of New York, where she was billed as "Helena Horne," and she became well-known in other circles as "La Horne,"[24] again being promoted as a performer of Latin or French descent. Rendered a cultural hybrid, she found herself gaining in popularity. At Carnegie Hall, her performance solidified her reputation as a sex symbol and elicited the following commentary: "Lena, who is so breathtakingly beautiful that nobody usually stops to consider whether she [also] can sing, provided a real surprise chanting some blues."[25] Horne, a symbol of beauty to the African American press—"charming," "copper-colored," "sepia toast of Broadway's nite life," and "darling"—was destined to be sexualized and transformed on the screen.[26] If she elicited the male gaze on the stage, then she would certainly do so in cinema.

HORNE'S MGM MOTION PICTURE CONTRACT AND ITS AFTERMATH

In 1941, Horne found herself on the West Coast negotiating a major motion picture contract with MGM; the contract was not without its own set of polemics. According to Gail Lumet Buckley (her daughter), Louis B. Mayer of MGM consulted both Horne's father, Teddy Horne, and Walter White of the NAACP regarding the terms of her contract.[27] White, representing the interests of the African American community, was concerned with the defamatory representations that had proliferated in Hollywood. White warned against casting Horne in subservient roles and called for her to have the latitude to "establish a new kind of image for black women."[28] As Horne later wrote:

> Walter's concern and mine too, was that . . . they would force me to play roles as a maid or maybe even as some jungle type. Now these were the roles . . . that most Negroes were forced to play in the movies at that time. . . . But Walter felt, and I agreed with him, that since I had no history in the movies and therefore had not been typecast as anything so far, it would be essential for me to try to establish a different kind of image for Negro women.[29]

Horne's father was determined that his daughter was not to be subjugated, compromised, or exploited for the sake of landing a motion picture contract. At his meeting with Hollywood studio officials, he insisted that Lena not be cast in maids' roles.[30] Studio executives acceded to these demands and reached an agreement stipulating that "part of any contract Lena Horne signs from now on will be a clause [indicating] that she be given only romantic leads."[31] Arthur Knight, Michele Wallace, and others affirm that Horne never played a subservient or a comic character, but that she also never landed a dramatic or nonmusical role either.[32]

Yet this was a landmark contract. Its signing was regarded as a major achievement for Horne, but also for all African Americans. It established MGM as the vanguard of democracy in Hollywood, while studios such as Republic and Paramount held on to their "openly racist" views.[33] According to Buckley, the negotiation of this contract became a bargaining tool by which other African Americans could lobby for improved screen roles.[34] As news of the contract spread, the African American press eagerly embraced this perceived liberal gesture by Hollywood as an opportunity to invade a terrain that had previously been restricted to whites: the ability to acquire redeeming roles. The *Chicago Defender* asserted,

> [MGM] studio early this week did what many studios wanted but hesitated doing when it hired beauteous Lena Horne to a long term contract.... It only remained for a time when some produce[rs] would find the right vehicle to further exploit this rare combination of beauty and acting ability. ... Miss Horn[e] is the type of actress that can be put into many variable roles and still be "in cast."[35]

The *Chicago Defender* saw MGM's gesture as a progressive development toward improving race relations in the cinema industry. The *New York Amsterdam News* credited the actress with creating an opportunity to elevate the entire African American community. Horne herself assured readers, "I hope to really accomplish something of which my entire race will be proud."[36] Vowing to use this opportunity to improve conditions for the masses of African Americans, she pointed to the contract as not only a career move but, more important, a political move.

Horne, already sexualized and racialized, now placed herself in the position of being politicized. To the African American press, she signified the struggles of all blacks to elevate their status in a sociopolitical discourse from which they had been alienated and disenfranchised. Reports swirled in the press: a new black star had obtained a contract that excluded maids' roles! If Horne was not regarded as a bona fide star in the African American community prior to this incident, she certainly was elevated to star status at that point. She became doubly determined in the African American press as both a star and a political leader. The *Pittsburgh Courier* complimented her for her effectiveness in merging these two profiles successfully: "She has recently signed a contract with Metro-Goldwyn-Mayer. She is as beautiful in her ways and manners as she is physically and everybody who meets her 'raves' about her. But she remains unaffected and charming."[37] The *Chicago Defender* suggested that "her quietness, lack of conceit, willingness to listen and reticence for ballyhoo, an unknown quantity among performers on the way up, were assets that made her the toast of all."[38]

Now came the first test and Horne admitted that her Hollywood debut was immediately problematic. When she and Eddie "Rochester" Anderson came together in romantic roles, according to Horne,

> They wanted me to match Rochester's color so they kept smearing dark makeup on me. And then they had a problem in lighting and photograph-ing me because, they said, my features were too small. . . . In the end, the test was a disaster. I looked as if I were some white person trying to do a part in blackface. I did not do the picture; Ethel Waters got the part.[39]

Reacting in a different way to Horne's release from the role, however, the African American press responded, "A recent role originally planned for Lena was given to another actress because the tests showed Miss Horne as definite competition to the famed actress in the starring role—and that would never do! Besides Lena wasn't crazy about the type of role anyway."[40] Meanwhile, so that her unique color would not continue to be a dilemma, studio officials had the cosmetic "Light Egyptian" assigned to her, a cosmetic that had been used for white actresses taking black roles.[41]

Having overcome the "color" issue, Horne was transformed as an African American screen goddess in the films *Cabin in the Sky* (1943) and *Stormy Weather* (1943). These all-black-cast musicals, while allowing her to assume romantic leads, were enveloped in controversy. The tension that erupted between Horne and Ethel Waters during the production of *Cabin in the Sky* has become legendary, and in *Stormy Weather* Horne was cast opposite Bill "Bojangles" Robinson, a much older male steeped in criticism in the African American press. In fact, in these films most of the black characters simply conformed to white Hollywood's racial precon-ceptions. The fact that Horne was being racialized in these all-black-cast films is perhaps less important than it would have been in films of racially mixed casts. Therefore, while racializing is endemic in the black star/ white Hollywood environment, this discussion will concentrate instead on the way Horne was hypersexualized.

In *Cabin in the Sky*, Horne (as Georgia Brown) is rendered a mulatto whose black blood makes her a pawn for Lucifer, an agent of the devil. Lucifer struggles with God for the soul of Little Joe (Eddie "Rochester" Anderson). Flaunting her high heels, short skirts, and low-cut blouse, Brown attempts to lure Little Joe away from his wife Petunia (Ethel Waters), who becomes an instrument of God (the General), fighting to save her husband from a life of sin and evil. The much younger and more sexually alluring Horne is a direct contrast to the matriarch Petunia. (Although Waters evokes memories of the "mammy" figure, in one scene in the film she looks more like an entertainer and less like a matronly figure, and she provides competition for Horne as a screen seductress.) Regarding Horne's role in the film, Richard Dyer observes that "as a very light-skinned black woman, she was unplaceable except as the ultimate temptress in an all-black musical, *Cabin in the Sky*, where the guarantee of her beauty resides in the very fact of being so light. Otherwise she could not really be given a role in a film featuring whites, because her very lightness might make her an object of desire, thus confusing the racial hierarchy of desirability."[42]

With this film, Horne established herself as a black sex symbol and was promoted by the African American press as one of the first black sex symbols since Nina Mae McKinney of *Hallelujah* (1929)—nearly twenty years earlier.[43] That Horne was hypersexualized or overdetermined with sexuality in this role is confirmed by reports that the Will Hays office ordered her characterization to be "toned down."[44] Her hypersexualization also earned press criticism. One *Chicago Defender* reviewer declared, "I am sure critics and patrons alike must have resented Lena's sitting on a piano lifting her skirt to prove that the clothing beneath her dress was highly colored, silk and of the finest. That simply does not rate in our book of fancies, for leading players; anymore than does the continual display of teeth as in *Cabin in the Sky*."[45]

The filming itself was a stormy process. Tensions reached an all-time high when Ethel Waters and Horne engaged in a verbal dispute. Horne, recalling their unpleasant encounter, wrote:

> The atmosphere was very tense and it exploded when a prop man brought
> a pillow for me to put under my sore ankle. Miss Waters started to blow
> like a hurricane. It was an all-encompassing outburst, touching everyone
> and everything that got in its way. Though I (or my ankle) may have been
> the immediate cause of it, it was actually directed at everything that had
> made her life miserable, the whole system that had held her back and ex-
> ploited her.[46]

Many of the actors received injuries. Horne's ankle fracture halted production, while John Bubbles damaged his spine and Eddie "Rochester"
Anderson hurt his knee.[47] But a greater tragedy than these accidents was
the image Hollywood provided, assigning talented African Americans to
highly objectionable screen roles that characterized them as "downright
criminal."[48] Even the mainstream press took note of this; one reviewer
observed that "the Negroes are apparently regarded less as artists (despite
their very high potential of artistry) than as picturesque, Sambo-style
entertainers."[49] The *New Republic* demonstrated unusual insight, observing that the "film is no less Jim Crow than a bus where whites sit in front
and Negroes in back, because the film is owned, operated and directed by
whites, even to the song writers."[50] Most disturbed were members of the
African American press, such as E. B. Rea of the *Baltimore Afro-American,*
who attacked the *New York Times*'s Bosley Crowther for observing that
the film treated blacks with "affectionate respect."[51]

Equally controversial was the all-black-cast production of *Stormy
Weather* (1943). Thomas Cripps notes that

> *Stormy Weather*... was a more prickly subject. Culturally black in its
> roots, wearing its black patriotism on its sleeve, larded with cross-over
> black performers, it surely promised to be an ornament of conscience-
> liberalism. It had begun as a Hollywood rarity, an original story, a pet of
> Hy Kraft, an old lefty who had been tossing it over transoms for months.
> Yet whatever coherence it might have derived from its leftist sources
> would seem compromised by the same all-black quality that made black
> liberals wince.[52]

Horne, the romantic lead, costarred with Bill "Bojangles" Robinson. In
this film a romance between the two entertainers is undermined by their
vast age differences: Robinson was in his mid-sixties, and Horne in her
mid-twenties. The lack of attraction between them was apparent on the
screen. The African American press claimed that Hollywood had made a

mistake casting these two actors in a romantic comedy, and that some of the scenes had had to be reshot to make the couple appear more romantically involved.[53] Although Hollywood evidently meant to showcase Robinson, Horne was characterized as "the romantic lure all by herself."[54]

Horne's dislike of Robinson is confirmed in her biography: "Lena loathed Bill Robinson and nearly everything connected with *Stormy Weather*. . . . Robinson was a male Ethel Waters, and the biggest Uncle Tom in show biz. He carried a revolver, was poisonous to other blacks, and truly believed in the wit and wisdom of little Shirley Temple."[55] Perhaps Horne's view of Robinson's politics, rather than his talent, was what caused her disenchantment. But she overcame her feelings and (as with *Cabin in the Sky*) again became an object of the male gaze: "Lena Horne, star of the picture, isn't star anymore—she's barbecue."[56] Her sexualization was rendered not only through her singing style and body movements, but also through her costumes. Her roles spanned the gamut from an elegantly dressed goddess to an exoticized "native" dancing to jungle rhythms with an exposed midriff and swinging a grass skirt that exposed her legs and midriff. One critic observed that because of her costuming, "audiences will divide on whether she is truly elegant or merely too refined."[57]

Stormy Weather's title aptly describes the production. Robinson was accused of imitating an Uncle Tom, a label that riled his friends.[58] Some of the players refused to do additional stunts unless their pay was increased; they were replaced by Robinson's understudy (Milton Shockely), who stepped in to perform the scenes. William Grant Still, the music supervisor, was dismissed because he refused to sexualize and racialize the music to conform to Hollywood standards. To add to the ongoing saga, three African American actresses were accused of defaming the African American community when the black press exposed them for "engaging in too bold interracial affairs with male stage employees."[59] Controversy also erupted when it was reported that MGM had "loaned" Horne to Twentieth Century Fox for some $7,000, yet Horne's contract remained at only $450 per week and she did not benefit from the pay difference.[60] Disenchanted with white Hollywood, the African American press made this exploitation known in the African American community to demonstrate how its black stars were being marginalized. Many other stars of the period encountered similar problems with management, but virtually all had endured them in silence. Now at least the inequities were being reported.

Stormy Weather received mixed press reviews. While *Variety* commended its "cream-of-the-crop" cast,[61] the *New York Times* referred to it as more of a "super-vaudeville bill than motion picture."[62] One member of the African American press declared that Horne, "because of her talent, beauty, and recent publicity campaign is the flicker's star," but another reviewer cautioned that "the picture . . . has something, but it likewise lacks something."[63] The harshest criticism came from a reviewer who targeted the hegemony of Hollywood: "The Uncle Tom attitude still reigns supreme in Hollywood. . . . It is a revolting hotch-potch of comico-pathetic 'nigger characterisation.' . . . The . . . long romance [between] Bill Robinson and Lena Horne . . . becomes sickening, it's so doggy! Big black faithful spaniel snuffling in the tracks of dainty yellow bitch."[64] If there had been any doubt about how the African American screen image had been compromised with this film, this reviewer made it quite clear, even attacking Horne's undeniable mulatto figure association. The African American screen image, as well as Horne herself, had been damaged by the production. Compounding these difficulties, Cripps reports that "*Cabin in the Sky* and *Stormy Weather* went into release during three nasty race riots that simultaneously drew attention to the persistence of racism and seemed to point to movies and other pressures for enhanced black status as causes of riots."[65]

HORNE'S MIXED-CAST FILMS

My purpose here is to explore how Horne was constructed in films made primarily for white spectators. Despite her starring roles in the all-black-cast productions, it became increasingly clear that she would be only an addendum to the roles of the leading white stars with whom she was paired; functioning in this shadow position, she became the representative of Hollywood's new racial Other. As Horne herself acknowledged, "They didn't make me into a maid . . . but they didn't make me into anything else either. I became a butterfly pinned to a column singing away in Movieland."[66] Arthur Knight suggests that "the isolated quality of most of Horne's film appearances, the very quality that forced her departure(s) from Hollywood, also supported her as a Black star."[67] He continues that

"Horne's isolated numbers also allowed an oddly, complexly pleasurable sign of, response to, and prompt to resistance of racism."[68] While Knight contends that this isolation could have been read as a form of resistance, this is less believable when we consider that as Hollywood was attempting to incorporate blackness into the white landscape, it was actually positing blackness as an additive.

This was particularly apparent when Horne and the Berry Brothers were added to the cast of *Panama Hattie* (1942), which had not included any African Americans when it was a Broadway musical. The press noted that the talent of African Americans was very much needed, particularly "after a sneak pre-view of the film revealed that a great deal was lacking."[69] Hollywood studio executives knew that a film lacking in narrative development or excitement could be easily improved with the addition of talented African Americans. According to Horne's biography, in *Panama Hattie* she was promoted as a "Latin singer" and then accused of trying to "pass." However, she still remained unnamed and unmentioned in the screen credits.[70] Because filmmakers pandered to white audiences' fears regarding blackness and negotiated Horne's racial construction, she was rendered as an Other but not a black Other, which might offend audiences and result in decreased proceeds at the box office.

Although Horne's racial construction was subverted, she became a success. *Collier's* magazine asserted that while her success was "the most spectacular occurrence known in Hollywood since Rudolph Valentino's funeral . . . such adulation could lead only to lucrative servitude in one of the cinema's concentration camps."[71] This reviewer commented, "They rewarded her rather evilly for such surrender of her poverty by casting her in *Panama Hattie,* which will run well up in competition with any collection of the screen's worst bores."[72] Adding Horne to the cast had not been enough to salvage the film. According to the same reviewer, the musical interludes allowed audiences to "crawl out from under the seats 'without danger of asphyxiation.'"[73] Hollywood executives provided Horne with a fifty-piece orchestra, which so intimidated her that she requested that some sixteen band members be removed.[74] Studio officials apparently were aware that the film was failing long before they recruited her, and they were either eager to provide her with assistance or they were trying to turn a marginal production into a successful production. But whatever the motive, the result was failure. Horne sang "It Was Just One of Those

Things" and "The Spring," neither of which left a lasting impression on the spectator.[75] As for Horne herself, even if she had been able to provide a stunning and memorable performance, she still was there as a singer, not as the actress she desired to be.

Off the screen, she was marginalized by the studios. According to the African American press, during the production of this film Horne and several "sepia players" were refused admission by a doorman at the MGM commissary. During that era of segregation, it was unusual for African Americans to be employed in any capacity other than as menials, and thus they were halted by the studio's security. To compensate for this humiliation, Horne and others were invited to a private luncheon at the commissary—an act designed to placate them, which merely caused Horne to grow increasingly disillusioned.[76]

Following this incident and responding to her unsettling treatment, Horne began to display her interest in the political scene. Her on-screen exploitation became symbolic of the ongoing African American actors' struggle to achieve equity within the motion picture studios. At the same time the *Chicago Defender* was advertising Horne's role in *Panama Hattie*, Walter White (the black executive secretary of the NAACP) and Wendell Willkie (a white Republican presidential candidate and NAACP member) were attending a luncheon at the Twentieth Century Fox Studios hosted by Walter Wanger and Darryl Zanuck. Their mission was to discuss the plight of black actors in the cinema industry. It was the opinion of the African American leadership that cinema was an "important medium for molding public sentiment."[77] Horne, recently appointed by the NAACP as Hollywood's representative black screen actress, allowed herself to become politicized, both for her own self-interest and for the African American community.[78] Knight reveals that "Unlike the Black Hollywood players who so frustrated the NAACP, Black critics, and increasing numbers of ordinary Black viewers around 1940, these Black stars remained collaboratively connected with their audience(s)."[79] Having achieved stardom, she began using her fame and position to publicly articulate her political views.

Ironically, white Hollywood provided Horne with a superb public forum. Both her films and nightclub performances were being reviewed in the mainstream press. As her public image continued to be racialized and sexualized, she became increasingly resistant to her subjugation.

Horne was forced to return to the nightclub circuit between screen performances, despite her lucrative contract with MGM.

Reports circulated that she had been exploited at the Savoy-Plaza and had been underpaid for her services, and two Savoy-Plaza employees who had booked her performance at this previously all-white establishment were forced to resign. The Savoy managers, however, acted quickly to keep the controversy from becoming public; they wanted to maintain a pristine image untainted by racial politics and social codes.[80] *Newsweek* magazine reviewed Horne's Savoy-Plaza Café Lounge performance, pointing out that this was the first time an African American was allowed to perform at this establishment. "Visually there is Miss Horne herself, who has not been called the Negro Hedy Lamarr for nothing. Her dusky glamour and sex appeal are an addition to any song."[81] As usual, *Newsweek* racialized and sexualized Horne, adding the insult of referring to her as a black version of Hedy Lamarr, using the white star as the standard. Then *Newsweek* opined that while Horne's singing ability did not equal that of other black singers, "she knows well how to sell a song."[82] The African American press applauded Horne's performance at the Savoy-Plaza, but it was still concerned with the marginalization she had experienced, which it saw as related to all African Americans operating within the racially segregated America of the 1940s. Each public performance provided an entrée into white America; the treatment she experienced in transgressing the racial divide reflected on the community as a whole.

While it is true that Hollywood had marginalized and sexualized Horne, the African American press participated also, referring to her as "Miss Sex in Sepia" and "the pulchritudinous" Horne.[83] Her private life (for example, her divorce from Louis Jones) was no longer private. She was receiving some 1,500 to 2,000 letters a month from fans, and press copy made a point of providing extensive coverage of her screen roles and her activities, such as "Lena Horne Packing Bags to Trip East" and "Lena Horne Still Idol."[84] Her sexual appeal was transferred to her screen persona and was exploited also by the African American press.

In 1943, the African American press was reporting, "Metro has turned out several noteworthy colored sequences in grade A white musicals."[85] It was assumed that Horne would be given the usual sequences, yet she should have been able to have an entire film woven around her character, as a "real Hollywood star" would have. Even though she was becoming ever more marketable for the studios, her roles were generally still disconnected from the plot. The black Other was thus both present in and absent from white life: present in that she was part of the landscape, but absent in that she was considered irrelevant, insignificant, and meaningless with respect to white life.

Films that reflect how Horne was disassociated from "white life" include *I Dood It* (1943), a film in which she was cast with Hazel Scott, Butterfly McQueen, Ford Lee Washington, and John William Sublett of Buck and Bubbles; *Broadway Rhythm* (1944), again with Scott and Eddie "Rochester" Anderson; *Thousands Cheer* (1943); *Swing Fever* (1943); *Two Girls and a Sailor* (1944); *Ziegfeld Follies* (1946); *Till the Clouds Roll By* (1946); and *Words and Music* (1948). Despite her dissociation, she provided a different brand of black and female sexuality. According to Richard Dyer:

> Her whole act in these films—and often it is no more than a turn inserted into the narrative flow of the film—promotes the idea of natural, vital sexuality, with her flashing eyes, sinuous arm movements and suggestive vocal delivery. That people saw this as the ultimate in unfettered feminine libido is widely attested, yet as an act it has an extraordinary quality, a kind of metallic sheen and intricate precision that suggests the opposite of animal vitality.[86]

I Dood It focuses on an actress, Constance "Connie" Shaw (Eleanor Powell), who becomes the fiancé of a man, Joseph "Joe" Rivington Renolds (Red Skelton), posing as the owner of a gold mine. Horne's role in the film is that of an entertainer who, according to *Time* magazine, "proficiently marshals Count Basie's band and numerous choristers through a particularly unpleasant stretch of suboperatic Africorn about the walls of Jericho."[87] Highlighting Horne's contributions to the film, Philip Hartung of *The Commonweal* wrote, "The musical part of this film wakes up in a big way when a group of Negro entertainers come to the theater to try out for a show. . . . After [Horne's] first-rate number ['Jericho'], the film relaxes again to its humdrum course."[88] The *New York Amsterdam News* reported that director Vincente Minnelli was "highly pleased with the Negro actors."[89]

In the opening scene of *I Dood It*, a stage show (backgrounded by Jimmy Dorsey's band) features a rodeo with a cowboy demonstrating his skills by roping in a cowgirl, as well as a woman selling kisses to a long line of men to generate proceeds for the promoter's show. African American women, doubly determined because of their race and sexuality, had to endure being both sexualized and racialized in this film, for it is heavily inscribed with racial codes. For example, even before Horne is introduced, a Civil War drama is re-enacted, featuring black cotton pickers and a handkerchief-head matriarchal figure. Perhaps the matriarchal figure's insertion is designed to alert spectators to Horne's direct opposition to the "mammy figure." Unfortunately, whether it is intentional or not, such a disturbing representation of African Americans juxtaposed with a desirable representation of them negates whatever positive impact the desirable representation might have had on public opinion.

The white character actress in *I Dood It* is accompanied on the set by her real-life maid, none other than Annette (Butterfly McQueen). The intensity of the white actress, who in a fit of anger breaks a mirror, is displaced onto her anxious black maidservant, who becomes the vehicle for her emotions. This black subservient figure is a reminder of the status that African Americans typically occupied and diminished the sophistication and independence of Horne and Scott, who also appear on screen. Because of these directly opposed representations, African American spectators are forced to identify with both a desirable and an undesirable image of themselves. This complexity associated with the black spectator is supported by Manthia Diawara's critique of black spectatorship and his assertion that "the Black spectator is placed in an impossible position"[90] of both being drawn to the representation and at the same time resisting the representation. Wanting to identify with the Horne/Scott representation, African American spectators feel they are being forced to reject the McQueen representation, but since she is also an African American woman, they are thus rejecting themselves. It is conceivable that this was a subtle device used by the hegemonic discourse of white Hollywood to remind blacks of their subordinate status while at the same time tantalizing them with fantasies of what they might become, knowing that only a few would be able to achieve such status.

When Horne and Scott appear on screen as jazz singers, African American spectators are temporarily transcended into a world of black splendor and glamour. For one brief moment they can forget the race's diminished status. Appearing ahead of Horne, Scott wears a black sequined t-strapped gown, a jeweled bracelet, and white mink. Escorted by an entourage of black men dressed in overcoats, suits, and top hats, she strides in with confidence and self-assurance. Her jazz piano demonstrates a rare command of the instrument as she hits every single note with conviction and voraciously traverses up and down the keyboard. The scene nearly erases the film itself. Scott's act is followed by Horne's entrance. She is attired in a white satin off-the-shoulder gown split nearly to the waist; beneath the split she flaunts a contrasting satin. Horne's mink is dark. Surrounded by a bevy of elegantly dressed background singers and jazz band members, she sings "Jericho." Her sophisticated style is conservatively voluptuous; her slow-moving song, although a jazz rendition, alludes to biblical characters.

Horne was not willing to acknowledge the fact that regardless of their talent and their desirability, both she and Scott would remain distanced from the plot—in this film and in future films. It is important to remember that in the years before desegregation, black artists were deliberately cast in this mode so that when a film toured the South they could easily be edited from the film without disrupting its plot. Southern spectators objected to African Americans appearing on the screen as anything but servants. According to Arthur Knight, "Her structurally isolated numbers signaled Hollywood's racism, and, as a consequence, served as prompts to Black solidarity, expressed via the Black press, which never missed an opportunity to report the excision of Horne's numbers by Southern censors."[91]

Returning to the screen in *Swing Fever* (1943), Horne joined big Hollywood names such as the orchestra leader Kay Kyser and leading white actress Marilyn Maxwell.[92] At this point, Horne still believed that if she continued to receive exposure and association with white Hollywood talent, she was certain to advance her screen career. She hoped that such association eventually would translate into screen roles that showcased her dramatic abilities. And, indeed, in this film not only was Horne's singing talent the main point of appeal, but her positioning next to white screen stars reflected the beginning of an experiment in insinuating the black star into the social milieu of the white life portrayed on screen. Unfortunately, she would find herself rendered as a foil, a shadow for the white actress, and a mere embellishment.

The director of *Swing Fever* (Tim Whelan) cast Horne as herself, an entertainer, while he cast Kay Kyser as Lowell Blackford, a mild-mannered musician who ventures to New York to publish a symphony he has written. He also has the power to hypnotize people, and he is embraced by a group of prizefight promoters until they learn that he is more astute than they originally believed and has the power to dismantle his victims.[93] Ginger Gray (Marilyn Maxwell), who is engaged to boxing promoter "Waltzy" Malone (William Gargan), tricks Blackford into using his skills on a boxer, "Killer" Kennedy (Nat Pendleton), to fix the outcome of a fight. The boxer is revealed to be Ginger's brother, and to keep him from being hurt in the fight they capitalize on Blackford's hypnotic ability. The extent to which Horne is racialized and sexualized in *Swing Fever* is unknown.

Horne next appeared in *Thousands Cheer* (1943). Playing the part of herself in a role not unlike her off-screen life, she is cast as a seductive African American entertainer designed to elicit the male gaze; she performs a "patriotic" vaudeville show to entertain soldiers prior to their departure overseas. In this World War II propaganda film, the entertainers include (in addition to Horne) Kathryn Grayson, Mary Astor, Judy Garland, Mickey Rooney, Red Skelton, Eleanor Powell, Ann Sothern, Virginia O'Brien, June Allyson, Marsha Hunt, Kay Kyser, Marilyn Maxwell, Donna Reed, Gene Kelly, and Lucille Ball, among others. Film critic Dan Abramson observed that "no racial trouble of any sort is evident on screen in *Thousands Cheer*. . . . Horne's sultry rendition of 'Honeysuckle Rose' was sandwiched in between a Gene Kelly dance number, a Lucille Ball comedy sketch and Judy Garland singing 'The Joint is Really Jumpin'.' Mickey Rooney appeared as the emcee."[94]

After Judy Garland and Lena Horne played together in *Thousands Cheer,* Vincente Minnelli (who was Judy Garland's husband at the time and was affiliated with MGM) directed many of Horne's screen roles.[95] Her first appearance in the film is prefaced by the introduction of the black musician, Bennie Carter, and the formally attired horn section of his band—they perform while positioned in a circle with their horns elevated. The scene is dark, and the faces of the band members are barely discernible. Horne enters in a floor-length white gown with one shoulder exposed. She performs alone onstage, but mirrored walls give the illusion that a bevy of similarly dressed Horne look-alikes surround her. Thus although Horne is a solo artist, the cinematic illusion provides additional stage performers without having to employ African American dancers.

Judy Garland, less elegantly dressed than Horne, wears a blouse, vest, and skirt. As she sings, accompanied by a pianist, she directs her attention to the piano player and later seats herself on the piano, elevating her skirt (undoubtedly to elicit the male gaze). Garland is sexualized much as Horne is, and she also sings a "boogie-woogie" tune, traditionally more closely associated with African American entertainers. This raises the question: Were filmmakers attempting to infuse Garland with blackness, while infusing Horne with whiteness? Were they attempting to reverse the codes normally inscribed in blackness and whiteness? And by disrupting such codes, were they attempting to erase differences that might exist on the basis of race and therefore make both women acceptable to both black and white spectators? As with her other films, Horne's scenes in *Thousands Cheer* were edited out by the Memphis "one man" censor board.[96] No matter how liberalized Hollywood might be and how talented a musician Horne was, she could not escape being defaced because of her race.

In 1944, Horne appeared on screen with Hazel Scott and Eddie "Rochester" Anderson in the musical *Broadway Rhythm*. The film was compared to *Cabin in the Sky*,[97] and in the black press the black actors were billed as stars alongside their white counterparts, who included George Murphy (cast as Johnny Demming), Ginny Simms (cast as Helen Hoyt), Charles Winninger (cast as Sam Demming), and Tommy Dorsey along with his orchestra.[98] The black community appreciated the talent of these black entertainers who were elevated to star status, but, unfortunately, in this film the black roles again were disconnected from the plot, allowing the Memphis Board of Censors to delete Horne's scenes from *Broadway Rhythm* because it believed she was too prominently displayed.[99]

Horne appears on screen as Fernway de la Fer in a nightclub scene, when a stage producer attends the nightclub, referred to as the Jungle Club, to recruit big-name talent for his musical show. While Felix (Ben Blue) and his budding actress are seated in the nightclub, the stage show opens with a black character wearing a hat and vest in striped pants playing the bongo drums backgrounded by a grass wall. The camera then cuts from the bongo player to a dancer's feet and then pans upward to Lena Horne, dressed in a low-cut halter top with flowers in her hair, a midriff top, and a skirt. She sings a "Brazilian Boogie Woogie." In this instance she dances with one of the black male dancers as she wiggles to the beat of the music. Her skirt has high slits so that when she moves on stage her thighs are visible. She is surrounded by several black dancers who are part of the dance routine and who present a flurry of gloved hands that enter the screen's frame with Horne positioned in the middle. As Horne dances and sings to this Brazilian boogie-woogie, the song's lyrics state, "Down in Brazil, they do a dance that's gonna give you a thrill. It's just a half-breed cause its Mammy was a Samba and its Pappy was swing. They got together [and] made a new kind of swing." The song undoubtedly reflects on the hybridity of Horne's own racial construction as a mulatto as well as the marginalized status of African Americans apparent in the continued use of the stereotypical assertions. The dance continues when Horne is then backgrounded on stage by barefoot black female dancers similarly dressed in midriff tops and short skirts. These dancers are replaced by another group of women who wear headscarves and short skirts as they accentuate Horne's dance across the stage. A black man then joins her in the dance wearing gloves, hat, midriff top, and striped pants as though he is a hybrid of the Sambo stereotype and a Brazilian dancer. This is one of the few instances where Horne is allowed to appear on stage with other dancers and is accompanied by a male dancer. Interestingly, she is promoted in the film as a Latin entertainer, a position inscribed with its own racial and political codes. That her racial construction was subverted suggests that her blackness was being neutralized so she would be seen as less threatening.

Later in *Broadway Rhythm,* Horne appears on screen for a second time, this time auditioning to be a singer. She appears on stage, more elegantly dressed, with a piano player and her manager, played by Eddie "Rochester" Anderson. Horne's hair, more conservatively coiffed, is now pulled back in an upward hairstyle, and she sings a seductive love ballad with lyrics that state, "Somebody loves me, I wonder who." During her performance she dances around the stage and around Rochester, who is seated on stage with her. At the end of her performance, the audience claps and Rochester lobbies to have Horne accepted as part of their show.

Despite Horne's success in this film and the relative success the film had, not all of Horne's appearances were in Hollywood hits. In 1944, she appeared in *Two Girls and a Sailor,* a failure described as "disappointing to both white and colored fans; one song 'Paper Doll' not justifiable for

[Horne's] great talent and wonderful personality."[100] Not only were the spectators annoyed with the song, but so was Horne; she complained that "it's a boy's song."[101] Horne's being forced to sing a song with masculine themes suggests that her sexuality was deliberately distorted in this film, permissible perhaps because white Hollywood already had rendered her a racial Other. Film roles for African Americans often entailed a marginalization that resulted in the subversion of their racial and sexual identities. When members of the African American press reported on this film, it may have been no accident that they referred to the film as *Two Sisters and a Sailor*.[102]

On the screen with white stars such as Harry James, Xavier Cugat, June Allyson, Van Johnson, Gloria DeHaven, and Jimmy Durante, Horne sang the song "Trembling Leaf." Her performance was backgrounded by a bevy of black talent provided by Olivette Miller, daughter of Flournoy Miller; Phil Moore, pianist and one-time singing coach for Horne and Dorothy Dandridge; and Aaron (T-Bone) Walker.[103]

In film after film, promoting Horne as an entertainer seemed to be the Hollywood technique for negotiating the competing views of spectators. For some white spectators, appropriating Horne served to appease their objections to African Americans' talents being showcased; and to accommodate this group's pre-existing notions of the black Other, Hollywood too often made it possible to completely edit out these scenes. Quintessential entertainer or not, the black Other thus remained distanced from the films' plots, which was particularly important for the distribution of films in the South. On the other hand, because Horne approximated whiteness and her physical appearance was therefore deemed less threatening to some whites, she eased white fears about blackness. Although rarely cast in leading roles, at least she was not a subservient figure. In fact, despite the polemics, an African American's appearance on screen with leading white stars in major motion picture productions was viewed as progressive.

Horne's status received a mixed reception in the African American community, who wanted the industry to provide her with more meaningful roles. In 1944, the Committee for Unity in Motion Pictures chose Horne as the most outstanding black actress of the year, through "whose dignity and personal charm a new light has been cast on the American Negro race."[104] Shortly thereafter, the African American press hinted at the troubles Horne faced while working in Hollywood. Her interview with David Hanna, associated with a mainstream publication, was reprinted in the *Baltimore Afro-American:*

> To be a symbol to one's race and at the same time remain a realist is an uneasy position to maintain—one requiring more than the usual appurtenances of character and a patience that often can become oppressive.
>
> Yet with a dignity, intelligence, a way of parrying words and a beauty that is dazzling, Lena Horne has managed to accomplish both in the troubled waters of the motion picture industry.[105]

Hanna appeared to be hinting at Horne's troubled relationship with the motion picture studio. She began to publicly articulate her frustration at being cast primarily as an entertainer, with cameo appearances that disconnected her from the plots and that denied her any dramatic depth. Expressing her desire to be known as a "straight actress," Horne stated, "I'm very gratified that people accept my singing but that's frustration too. I really wanted to be an actress. It's easier for a colored person to be a singer than an actress."[106] The *Chicago Defender* restated her position: "Lena Horne's ambition now centers around two projects. One is to quit singing and be an actress, and the other is to 'fight' for an honest portrayal of Negro life by the film industry."[107] Horne was not alone in her disenchantment with Hollywood; the African American press also was complaining about Hollywood's unwillingness to honor its black star's dramatic talent.

By 1946, Horne was still being popularized in musicals such as *Ziegfeld Follies* (1946), *Till the Clouds Roll By* (1946), and *Words and Music* (1948). In *Ziegfeld Follies,* she was again cast opposite some of the leading white talent of the period—Judy Garland, Fred Astaire, Lucille Ball, Fanny Brice, Lucille Bremer, Kathryn Grayson, Gene Kelly, Red Skelton, and Esther Williams. According to Horne's biography, the film was an "all-star extravaganza in which every MGM player except Lassie [the dog] had a part."[108] The film basically reconstructs the similarly titled stage show produced by Ziegfeld as he reminisces about his contributions to the theatrical world. Lucille Ball is glamorous and elegantly dressed, Esther Williams performs her water ballet, and Fred Astaire provides sweeping dances on a moving floor. In contrast, when Horne appears on screen, she sings in a dark and dilapidated nightclub, surrounded by impoverished-looking black patrons. Recognizing the contrived contrast as an insult, the African American press castigated white Hollywood.

But by concentrating on the nightclub as a "cheap water-front night [spot]," the press almost seemed to overlook the minimizing of the film's African American star that was also occurring.[109] The nightclub appears to be situated in the West Indies. Women wear turbans and parade in wraparound skirts, while one woman balances a parrot on her shoulder. Horne, reflecting the West Indies atmosphere, adorns her hair with tropical flowers, wears an off-the-shoulder blouse, and flaunts a tightly fitting draped skirt with a belt encircling her hips—sexualizing and constructing her to elicit the male gaze. The film, unable to escape the racial and sexual codes associated with blackness, suggests she is an islander. Horne's coding is mirrored by both the setting and her sexualized body movements. Undoubtedly, she represents an exotic black beauty; the problem is that blackness itself is rendered as a negative construct, automatically denoting impoverishment and squalor. The two black women in the film, seated at a bar and competing for the attention of a male figure, later engage in physical assault, a scene that illustrates vividly how black women were hypersexualized, rendered aggressive, and portrayed stereotypically as being unable to control their emotions.

More important, a reading of this scene of *Ziegfeld Follies* suggests an intent to contrast Garland, signifying the white, with Horne, signifying the black Other. When Garland enters, she is elegantly dressed in a long gown and is surrounded by a bevy of men attired in formal wear, who accentuate her star status. As she bellows her songs, the men kneel around her, responding to her voice, and she walks between them, demonstrating confidence and dominance—a song stylist who captivates audiences. Garland, like Horne, is hypersexualized; as part of her stage performance, she poses seductively for male photographers, men who affirm her star status and alluring beauty. But unlike Horne, she is respected by the men who surround her, and she epitomizes whiteness through the grandeur, the well-lit stage, and the affluence (expensive furnishings, sparkling jewels) of this scene. Thus, the film creates a dichotomy between white star and black star.

Richard Dyer has written (referring to still another film) that Garland developed a gay following. According to Dyer, she was embraced by gay males because "her image spoke to different elements within male gay subcultures."[110] He contends that her "relationship to the male dancers is ambivalent. . . . She is centered by them and this, plus her stockinged legs, insists on her femininity, but they do not surround and present her as other male choruses do in musical numbers centered on a female star. They are choreographed in a balanced (but not uniform) style around her, and her dancing picks up on the movements of different men at different times."[111] Given the period and in a culture in which gays were branded as immoral, the implied diminishment in their morality may then have been transferred to Horne, her co-actress, who was already racialized and sexualized.

Dyer further contends that Garland "and other musicians have already been described as jazz musicians, thus linking them to a music tradition that is assumed to be based on unpremeditated musical expressivity (it is assumed that improvisation in jazz just happens, immediate and spontaneous, unrehearsed); and behind that, there is the link with black culture, which has always functioned as a marker of authenticity and naturalness in white discourses."[112] This raises the question of whether Horne's presence as the black Other was essential for developing Garland's image as a songstress (even though Garland earned such a reputation in her own right). Had Horne's presence elevated the quality and style of Garland? Was Horne's pairing with white entertainers vital to their status, allowing them, by association, to be rendered as authentic entertainers, assuming that authenticity was synonymous with blackness?

Despite such rendering, Horne was "well pleased with her special sequence"[113] in *Ziegfeld Follies*. Equally pleased with her performance was the African American press: "With plenty of everything—smoldering voice—figure divine—and combustible charm, Miss Horne makes 'Love' a sultry song sensation in one of the biggest production numbers in the colorful entertainment spectacle."[114] These pleasing moments often turned to despair, as when Lloyd Binford, chairman of the Memphis Censor Board, edited out her sequences when the film was shown in Memphis.[115] To Horne's dismay, a scene featuring her with African American dancer Avon Long was edited from the final film version because it was "overcrowded." Too much black talent would have taken attention away from the white stars. Black stars were never allowed to outperform white stars—whiteness must suggest superiority, while blackness must be identified with inferiority. According to a review in the African American press, "The 'Liza' number was brilliantly costumed with Lena in an old fashioned gown being wooed by Avon. It was her eighth role, yet it was the first time Lena had danced on the screen in 1900 attire."[116] It is of note that during the production of this film, Horne became acquainted with the film's white musical director, Lennie Hayton, who would later become her second husband.

Horne appeared as a nightclub singer in most of her screen roles, but in the production of *Till the Clouds Roll By* (1946), she was cast in a showboat sequence. While she avoided appearing as a field hand, she was still thrust into a southern milieu in which a host of black actors assisted in reconstructing the slave South in front of a riverboat decorated with bales of cotton. Thomas Cripps reveals that Horne "as Julie the mulatto in *Show Boat* performed as a play-within-a-play in the Jerome Kern biopic *Till the Clouds Roll By*."[117] A deep baritone singer (Caleb Peterson, an African American) provided a rendition of "Old Man River" in Paul Robeson style. It is noteworthy that white performer Frank Sinatra sang "Old Man River" at the film's end. The rendition seemed ill-placed and ill-suited to Sinatra's sophisticated style, particularly when he attempted to sing in dialect. According to Gail Buckley, "MGM was roundly derided for *Clouds*, especially the 'all-white' finale in which Lena leaned against a pillar in a white Grecian gown to sing 'Why Was I Born?' and Frank Sinatra, in snow-white tails, sang 'Ol' Man River.'"[118] Again, Horne appeared with an impressive cast of white stars, including Van Johnson, Dinah Shore, Judy Garland, June Allyson, Kathryn Grayson, and Lucille Bremer. Horne's second spouse, Lennie Hayton, served as the film's musical director.

Till the Clouds Roll By is a tribute to the musical composer Jerome Kern, chronicling his life and tracing the origins of his songs. The film opens with the showboat sequence in which Horne appears. This is an early entrance for Horne compared to her previous films. The innovation may have been strategically designed to appease the growing criticism of her continued marginalization by the motion picture studios. Horne, dressed as a southern belle, sings a solo, "Can't Help Loving that Man of Mine," but there seems to be a mismatch: she is dressed as a southern belle yet sings in a sophisticated urban nightclub style. But she provided a convincing performance. According to the *Chicago Defender*, "In the great *Show Boat* sequence in the technicolossal show, Miss Horne does the greatest singing of her brilliant career."[119] The African American press seemed relieved that in this film "her wardrobe omits red-heeled shoes, slit skirts and peekaboo blouses which Hollywood has virtually made her trademark."[120]

Garland first appears alone as an overworked dishwasher who dreams of overcoming her impoverishment. This may have been a Hollywood attempt to equate the white actress with the black actress—isolated, alienated, and ostracized. But then, true to form, when Garland returns to the screen, she floats down a stairwell in a long gown-cum-scarf, surrounded by the predictable group of men dressed in tuxedos, tails, and top hats. She dances with them, radiating her star status. Yet for Horne, as might have been expected, there is no similar transformation. The title of her last song in the film, "Why Was I Born?" seems to play on how the mulatto is problematized, being of mixed ancestry—neither black nor white and therefore rejected by both worlds.

In an effort to appease Horne, Hollywood now offered "her [the] best marquee billing to date in the picture."[121] Such billing was considered significant, but it was not sufficient compensation for her continued marginalization. The African American press noted that with this film, as with others, Horne's racial construction was subverted; she was lightened, because offstage she was definitely "darker" and more "freckled."[122] And the Memphis Censor Board still censored *Till the Clouds Roll By,* leaving Horne's scenes on the editing room floor.[123]

The African American press lamented that "people can't understand why they haven't given Lena Horne a decent role in such a long time—The talk along Hollywood and Vine is that some of the other top companies are bidding for the beautiful star's service. That MGM lion isn't roaring, it's crying!"[124] However effective Horne may have been in her roles, they were much the same from film to film, whether or not other studios were vying for her talent. The African American press began to worry that she might be fading as a box-office attraction: "Photogenic Lena Horne has come closer to the distinction than any other performer, but she has missed the mark by so great a margin, it is possible that she will soon fade unless she gets a break of some consequence almost immediately."[125] Disturbed at Hollywood's exclusionary practices, the same reviewer stated that some claimed that Horne lacked acting talent, "and they could be right, but the truth is, she has never had a chance."[126] It was his opinion that "for all the vaunted liberalism of Hollywood studio personalities, there isn't the slightest hope that a colored actor of the highest ability will get a chance to rise to stardom."[127] In an effort to determine who was ultimately responsible for such maligning, the reviewer charged that far too often script writers who are blamed contend that it's the film's producers, and the producers claim that it's the whims and tastes of the southern market; yet, he continued, "Actually, the situation derives from an unwritten agreement by all concerned to carry out the pattern of lily-whitism, while proclaiming a desire to act without stand."[128]

Both Horne and the African American press were annoyed with MGM, and one report asserted that she was "quarreling with the Metro-Goldwyn-Mayer Studio."[129] By 1947, she decided to distance herself from her difficulties with Hollywood; rumors circulated that she was leaving MGM.[130] According to Arthur Knight, "This type-casting frustrated some Black critics, and it certainly frustrated—enraged, even—Horne."[131] In Europe, she performed for both Parisian and British audiences. In Paris, the mainstream press referred to her as the "cafe au lait beauty." Parisian audiences "shouted, cheered, and—a rare event even in France—whistled."[132] In London, the African American press observed, "In the eyes of the English people, colored women appear to be a kind of psychological enigma because among them, you can get from black to blonde with varying types of features."[133] Commenting on her performance, the same writer conceded that while "Horne is not a singer in the accepted sense of the word . . . she can give romantic gloss to a song. . . . Her subtly gliding serpentine phrases fascinated her London audiences just like the piping of an Indian snake charmer to a cobra."[134]

Time magazine frequently compared Horne to Josephine Baker, but unlike Baker, Horne returned to the United States despite her treatment there and America's racial polemics.[135] MGM continued to meet the terms of their contract, but once again they offered her another musical, *Words and Music* (1948). This film, a biographical tribute to the genius of lyricist Lorenz (Larry) Hart and composer Richard Rodgers, focuses on the struggles of Hart (Mickey Rooney) to promote his work in a competitive industry. While he eventually succeeds, he fails at romance and meets an untimely death. Again, Horne was cast with leading white talent, including Gene Kelly, June Allyson, Ann Sothern, Perry Como, and Judy Garland.

Words and Music includes a black character, Larry's maid, Mary (Marietta Canty). This maid figure seems a strategically devised reinforcement of the subservient status assumed by African Americans; black subservients were a part of America's social landscape in the 1930s and 1940s. Horne's portrayal in her dignified role, which was diametrically opposed, did not lessen African Americans' pain. Hollywood was elevating them on the one hand, yet denigrating them on the other, accommodating the racial politics that prevailed in American society. Excusing black subservience by pointing out that some whites also were cast as servants did not make it less offensive. For African Americans, such portrayals were uniquely problematic because of their history of slavery, and because even freedom from slavery had not opened the way for alternative roles or positions. Moreover, the African American was cast in a subservient role in a special way, as in this film: when a black maid greets a guest (a white male) at the door, he responds to her affably by using her shoulder as a hat rack; that is, she is an object. In another scene, her white employer is shown reading to her, implying that she is illiterate—another disturbing and insulting way of characterizing the black maid. Horne, although allowed to appear more star-like, was still constrained to conform to the prevailing racial codes. It is unlikely she could have become anything other than an entertainer.

In *Words and Music,* Horne is introduced as a performer at a nightclub frequented by Larry's associates. She appears on screen as herself, in a lavender mid-length dress and a matching bow in her hair, and sings "Where or When?" in her usual sultry style, appearing almost doll-like. Sexualized, she also has an aura of sophistication. Then, singing "That's Why the Lady Is a Tramp," she accentuates the song's seductive lyrics with body movements, at times swishing her gown around her calves and elevating her skirt, playing upon the sexual theme embedded in the song's text. One African American reviewer claimed that "Lena was the only one in skirts who didn't show above the ankles, besides the . . . wife of the famous composer."[136] Despite such defensive denials, however, Horne's role was not only that of an entertainer, but of an entertainer who was hypersexualized and associated with the immoral or illicit. Reviewers evidently found this quite acceptable, but they did have one complaint: "It was with regret that we watched Lena Horne at Radio City Music Hall in her latest film, *Words and Music,* in technicolor. The girl has everything—

charm, glamour—such natural good looks. And even a voice. But Lena can't dance."[137]

In *Words and Music*, Horne is again juxtaposed with white actress/entertainer Judy Garland, who plays herself. Garland signifies whiteness while Horne signifies blackness. When Larry achieves success as a lyricist and moves into a Hollywood mansion, he celebrates by throwing a lavish party attended by Hollywood's Who's Who. Garland performs at his party and the two sing together. When Horne performs on screen in white Hollywood pictures, she is rarely allowed to perform opposite a male in close intimate contact and is seldom allowed to dance with a white male. Garland, on the other hand, both sings and dances with males (that is, white males). With reference to this unique subject positioning in white Hollywood, Horne once wrote:

> Even though I was a star now, I was still a Negro. I am eternally grateful to M-G-M for all they have made possible for me—I have sung in musical films, I have played in dramatic pictures, my contract permits me to appear annually on the stage at big presentation houses and to make night-club engagements as well—but when I sing in a picture I sing alone or with other Negroes. In dramas, I act only with other Negroes; indeed, I have never spoken a word before the cameras except to a Negro.[138]

Horne attributed Hollywood's containment of its black Other to the social codes that prevailed in American society and to the legal codes imposed by the Motion Picture Producers and Distributors of America:

> For the studios seemed to interpret this section of the Code [referring to interracial relations] to mean that Negroes and whites could not be shown together in any manner which suggests equality. Any normal relationship between a Negro and a white person—two friends standing together in conversation or seated at the same table or attending the same school or working side by side, would inevitably lead to "sex relationship"—and this was strictly forbidden![139]

And if the Motion Picture Producers and Distributors did not regulate the industry with respect to racial codes, then the film censor boards would step in, as was the case when the Memphis Censor Board edited Horne's scenes. The *Pittsburgh Courier*, expressing its frustration with censors' decisions, asserted that "Memphis' one-man censor board, from which there is no recourse once a decision is made, is the most flagrant offender in cutting scenes of Negroes from films, especially if the Negro performers are shown on an equal basis with white stars."[140] For what it was worth, this writer was accusing the censor board of vilifying African American screen stars. Exclusionary practices also typified award committees. It became known that Horne's film was not listed among the 1948 Oscar nominations and that she was excluded from a list of some thirty-one "sepia actors" deemed eligible to receive an Oscar for best supporting roles.[141]

As Horne's pessimism grew, her increasing resentment toward Hollywood was revealed: "Asked if she saw any hope for MGM to change and give Negroes more of a break in story purchasing and casting, she replied frankly, 'Not so far.'"[142] She made her denunciation of MGM public and finally dissolved her contract even though it had not been scheduled to end until 1951.

HORNE'S DEPARTURE FROM HOLLYWOOD AND GROWING POLITICAL ACTIVISM

Horne probably could have renegotiated her contract with MGM instead of dissolving it because, according to *Negro Digest,* in 1947 she was reissued a contract that "requires only ten weeks of her time each year for one Metro picture and five more for an appearance in one theatre designated by the film company—the other 37 weeks she's free to do café jobs, records, other theatres, even an outside picture in which her pulchritude can be used for more than mere decoration to add to the scope of Negro artists, perhaps."[143] Later reports confirmed the details of the contract dispute and noted that she had attempted to dissolve her seven-year contract with MGM because she actually worked only about ten weeks but was contracted for fifty-two weeks per year, thus making it impossible for her to capitalize on other offers.[144] Horne's biography notes that she bought her own contract and renegotiated an agreement that was less confining and more liberating, so that she could earn a living on stage during the long lapses between screen roles. The *Chicago Defender* claimed it would actually have been cheaper for MGM to hire Horne on a per-picture basis since they rarely used her for pictures and were therefore eager to renegotiate.[145] Increasingly, Horne became aware that white spectators were not yet ready to accept African Americans in leading roles in Hollywood films. She wrote, "The American movie public would rather see films acted by white people rather than the Negro cast film . . . but the American people are still very young."[146] Richard Dyer notes that

> It is rare for performers to understand and state so clearly both how they worked and the effect of it, but this catches exactly Horne's image in the forties and fifties, its peerless surface, its presentation of itself *as* surface, its refusal to corroborate, by any hint of the person giving her self, the image of black sexuality that was being wished on her. This could not, did not stop audiences reading her as transparently authentic sexuality; but it was some sort of strategy of survival that could also be seen for what it was, a denaturalising of the ideas of black sexuality.[147]

The transporting to the warehouse of a mannequin the studios used for customizing Horne's costumes was both the symbolic and actual ending of her contract.[148] Horne apparently renegotiated her contract in late 1947 or early 1948 but by 1950, following her role in *Duchess of Idaho*, she finally dissolved her contract with the studio.

When Horne appeared in the MGM production *Duchess of Idaho* (1950),[149] her relationship with MGM remained strained, a tension aggravated by the fact that when Horne was greeted by members of the African American press in Washington, an MGM representative dismissed them. Horne, embarrassed by this event, was apologetic. She was well aware that to alienate members of the African American community was to condemn herself, since she had become a revered extension of that community.[150]

Horne's disillusionment with both Hollywood and MGM increased when she was denied the mulatto role in a revival of *Show Boat* (1951). She felt that the role "might have been written especially for her."[151] According to her own account:

> I asked to play it. But I was having a difficult time at the studio at the moment. They didn't like it because I had refused to do a Broadway show they wanted to do . . . and I think to finish the punishment they were giving me they refused.[152]

The loss of the role reverberated throughout the African American community. As one letter writer to *Ebony* magazine charged, "Having seen all of Lena Horne's pictures, some of them twice, I think she could do more with the role of Julie than any other actress in Hollywood. . . . I think Lena has gotten a rotten deal from the very start."[153] What caused special pain to all African Americans was that the part was awarded to Ava Gardner, one of Horne's closest associates in white Hollywood, which made the rejection slightly more acceptable—but this was an added jab since Horne then couldn't complain without losing a friend. As Horne asserted, "[Ava] was a nice Southern White girl. We liked each other because we both respected each other. Besides, we both knew that we were being screwed out there by M-G-M—I for racial reasons, she for being liberated long before it became acceptable. She was a unique person in that she felt that she had as much right to be human as a man had."[154]

Horne's daughter Gail, commenting on her mother's Hollywood career and the racial politics that prevailed, reflected, "My mother and I . . . entered the great 'white' world, where we lived not as white people, but like white people."[155] This implies that because of blackness she was denied "white" opportunity and access; but because of lightness, she became an "acceptable African American" to both whites and blacks. According to this source:

> Lena was the first black Hollywood star—a title of great symbolic value, though she actually did very little in movies. But as long as she existed as a symbol of black aspiration and American brotherhood, Hollywood was not racist. . . . As Hollywood's first black glamour symbol, [she] was practically a "token" of a token. Lena paid the dues for all the black stars who came after her, but she never felt free to enjoy herself as a performer, or to step out of her symbolic persona.[156]

In later years, Horne made public her real feelings about white Hollywood, stating, "I really hated Hollywood and I was very lonely. The black stars felt uncomfortable out there."[157] Despite their exploitation, Arthur Knight contends that the relationship between the industry and its black stars was reciprocal in that black stars were at least being allowed to construct their stardom.[158]

Horne internalized her experience in Hollywood, translating it into political activism; throughout her career she publicly challenged discriminatory practices. She, like Hazel Scott, parallels the resistant spectator identified by Manthia Diawara in that they actively engaged in refutation and resisted the offensiveness inscribed in the black screen image. Yet her activism was never so blatant as when she defied white Hollywood "standards" by taking a white spouse, one of their own, MGM musical director Lennie Hayton. Their marriage in Paris in December 1947 was kept secret for some two years. In a culture where the pervasive racial politics took a dim view of interracial marriage, Horne and Hayton could both expect their careers to be affected, since they were both under contract with MGM. They also could expect public censure and even private disapproval from family members. Hayton's family was more accepting of their marriage than was Horne's family.[159]

The marriage was well-publicized in the African American press, which sought to protect its black star but at the same time held her accountable for her behavior. One report asserted:

> The public has been good to glamorous movie and disk star Lena Horne. It went along with her when she left her husband and kids to make a stab at personal fame. It stuck by her when she could neither sing nor act. It did all of this because she was a pretty girl who always behaved in a ladylike manner. Lena is now on the top, but—according to many quarters—she is forgetting the public which still idolizes her as "the cream of Negro womanhood." This is not good, especially so since it is creating nasty rumors about her which may wreck her future.... Rumors are flying and confirmed stories are published saying that she is married to a white man. Nothing is wrong with marrying a white man.... The question is this—Is she married?[160]

The marriage sparked articles on mixed marriages. The *Baltimore Afro-American* titled an article about Horne "Who Worries About Race When Dan Cupid Strikes?"[161] Years later, she revealed that she had married Hayton primarily because he was white and because of what whiteness signified in the America of the 1940s: "It was cold-blooded and deliberate. I married him because he could get me into places a black man couldn't. But I really learned to love him."[162] Despite the way Horne rationalized her marriage to Hayton, the marriage was politically empowering for African Americans. It was an act that "turned the tables": a white was having his whiteness exploited by an African American.

Horne never permitted her marriage to minimize, dilute, or interfere with her political activism. Symbolically, the marriage could be read as an act of political defiance. Her public display of her interracial marriage—to an MGM employee, no less—subverted MGM's refusal to confer on her the access and privilege enjoyed by white actresses. Increasingly, her political activism caused her to become estranged from the cinema industry and more closely associated with the political world, an apparent response to the marginalization she endured both on and off the screen. While some actresses internalized their exploitation, Horne elicited what bell hooks terms an "oppositional gaze,"[163] becoming more intolerant of the discriminatory practices that she and all African Americans endured and resisting the inscriptions that whiteness connoted power, access, and privilege, while blackness connoted their deprivation. Her activism was threefold. First, she refused to conform to the social and legal codes designed to promote segregation both in the theater world and in her public life. Second, she aligned herself with a variety of organizations whose purpose was to eradicate racial decisions implied by the legal and social codes of pre-integration America. Third, she defended her political views and position publicly, laying herself open to charges that she was a communist sympathizer.

The unwillingness of Horne to conform to racist legal and social codes came to the fore on numerous occasions. For example, in a performance sponsored by the Hollywood Victory Committee and the USO for military troops stationed at Camp Robinson in Little Rock, Arkansas, Horne was asked first to perform for white soldiers and then to perform for Nazi war prisoners. Discovering that African American soldiers also were stationed at the camp, she asked permission to perform for them as well, but she was informed that the African American soldiers were not allowed in the post theaters, so she would have to perform for them in the dining hall. When she arrived at the dining hall, she discovered that the Nazi prisoners also were in attendance and she refused to perform.[164] Segregating African American soldiers and lowering them to the same status as Nazi prisoners was a double insult to Horne and to all African Americans. Horne also charged that the Camp Robinson commander had been unusually "rude and definitely unfriendly."[165]

On this same trip to volunteer her services for a patriotic cause, Horne was confined to a Jim Crow car on a train traveling from Jackson, Mississippi, to Little Rock, Arkansas. Her tour was headlined by the African American press as "Snubbed and Jim Crowed from Mississippi to Little Rock, Arkansas" and "War Dept. Awaits Probe of Camp JC Against Lena Horne."[166] Horne's refusal to perform signified a challenge to the establishment. It was her way of telling America it would not be a postwar world power until it stopped denying African Americans their rights and freedoms and upheld the principles of democracy it claimed to espouse.

In a more personal matter, "Lena Horne cancelled her trip from Chicago to New York in order to rush home and thwart attempts by ofay [white] neighbors to toss her out of that exclusive Hollywood home the star owns."[167] She had acquired a home in Hollywood's Nichols Canyon, and the disturbed white residents tried to impose restrictive covenants to prevent her from occupying it.[168] The Valley Homeowners Association was forced to abandon its effort, however, after it was reminded by a local newspaper editor that similar cases involving June Richmond and Benny Carter had been resolved in court and that the covenant would not stand if challenged in court.[169]

Horne often had to contend with racial bias in accommodations. For example, in 1949 she sued Caruso's restaurant in Chicago for refusing her service.[170] Having to file charges against a restaurant did not deter Horne; she was willing to fight for the access and privileges to which she felt entitled. Adamant about resisting discriminatory practices, she also publicly protested a Chicago nightclub's "anti-Negro" policy. When management urged her "to be meek like the Jews," Horne retorted, "No, what we should learn from the Jews is this, mister; when you find a place lousy and crawling with prejudice like this one—buy the joint."[171] Her fight for access to public accommodations extended to hotels as well. She succeeded in gaining admittance to the Chase Hotel in New York, which had previously excluded boxer Joe Louis and baseball's Jackie Robinson.[172] Disillusioned with the racial dynamics of America in the 1940s and 1950s, Horne publicly denounced the social and legal codes imposed by Jim Crow that were not only humiliating but also inconvenient: "We hate driving across town to eat when there's a restaurant right around the corner. We hate having to live in a restricted neighborhood that's miles from our work."[173]

In the entertainment world, Horne expanded her political activism. For example, she revealed that when she insisted on referring to a white male actor by his first name on radio, as other white actors were doing, editors removed her remark from the script. She declared:

> Almost every day, I hear someone on the radio hailing America as the home of democracy. Yet almost every network is guilty of discrimination against the Negro performer. There are a few isolated cases of Negroes

in broadcasting, but the lily-white policy is seldom violated. When I was on the Ed (Archie) Gardner show, the script had to be revised so that I wouldn't address the star as "Archie." They wanted me to call him "Mr. Gardner." It wasn't considered proper for a Negro girl to speak a white man's first name.[174]

She also refused to accept certain roles she considered degrading. Horne declined a role in the stage production of *St. Louis Woman*, according to the *New York Amsterdam News*, because, she argued, it "sets the Negro back 100 years, is full of gamblers, no goods . . . I'd never play a part like that!"[175] According to Cripps, "African Americans needed only a major movie against which to stake out an ideological position with greater clarity than they had brought to *St. Louis Woman*."[176] Horne might have been influenced to decline the role, because the Inter-racial Film and Radio Guild castigated the play for its continual defaming representations of African Americans.[177] The guild found it "vicious in its stereotyping of colored, makes exorbitant use of dialect of the worst kind and that it insults colored womanhood by having the leading character cast as a loose woman."[178]

Horne's opposition to such marginalization can be observed in the political organizations she joined, most of which lobbied for the eradication of discriminatory practices that disenfranchised African Americans. As early as 1943, she joined the NAACP; her membership was widely publicized in the African American press, perhaps to urge other black artists to follow suit.[179] *Crisis* magazine, an organ of the NAACP, frequently noted her contributions.[180] She also extended her support to the National Non-Partisan League for the Re-election of President Franklin D. Roosevelt, who seemed concerned with minority issues. While hedging his support for Roosevelt, Walter White asserted that "the Democratic minority plank resembles more a splinter than a plank. Yet we at least know what Roosevelt has done for the Negro in the past. And I'd rather take a small piece of cake now than wait for the big one that might never turn up."[181]

Horne used her access to the public platform as an entertainer to lobby for political leaders and causes she thought would advance African American status. For example, joining with African American veterans who sought recognition for their contributions to the military and improvement of their work status, she endorsed the campaign for "Operational Terminal Leave Pay," sponsored by the United Negro and Allied Veterans of America.[182] As a member of the executive board of the Screen Actors Guild, she used her influence to try to provide visibility to African American entertainers whose contract agreements prohibited them from earning additional money when their studio "loaned" them out.[183] To resist the decentering that African Americans endured in the industry, she associated herself with the International Film and Radio Guild (IFRG), an organization that promoted racial harmony and included such Hollywood personalities as Bette Davis and Orson Welles.[184] The IFRG was "designed to protect the interests of minorities in the fight against racial stereotyping in the entertainment world."[185]

Horne also supported rallies and demonstrations. In 1947, she attended a deportation rally at the Manhattan Center in New York sponsored by the Committee for the Protection of the Foreign Born. For Horne, the rights of foreigners were inseparable from the rights of African Americans.[186] Her most radical and politically charged act was her address to some twenty-five thousand at the Progressive Counter-Attack Citizens of America. Publicly castigating the historic separation of accommodations for African Americans in the nation's capital, she reflected:

> That was Washington then. That is Washington today. It hasn't changed. Colored Americans still have to buck through traffic, rain or shine, and wait outside for colored cabs. The restaurants—many of them in Government buildings—amusement parks, theatres . . . and the like are no more friendly.
>
> Nor are the hotels any more hospitable, the all-white hospitals more merciful, the department stores or fine women's shops any more inviting, or the housing any less restricted. . . .
>
> This is the Washington I know. This is how the men we trust to pass price control, housing legislation . . . health, education, housing, old-age farming and all other forms of legislation to safeguard the welfare of the people of an entire nation—this is how they govern a single city.[187]

By the late 1940s Horne was even more politically active and increasingly intolerant of discriminatory practices. In 1947, she publicly remarked that she was influenced by Paul Robeson's ideological views: "The first half of my life I hated my own people because I saw them getting pushed around and taking it. And I hated whites for doing the pushing. But one night Paul Robeson came into Café Society where I was singing and that night changed my whole life."[188] Horne's affection for Robeson also rose from a family tie: her grandmother Cora had assisted him in attending college. This connection, in addition to her affinity for his ideology, caused her to embrace Robeson in spite of growing criticism against him from both white Americans and the African American community.[189]

In 1949, during a period characterized as the "Red Scare," Senator William Tenney included Horne among the entertainers whom he believed to be un-American, which automatically rendered her a political threat.[190] According to Horne's biography, she was never actually declared a communist and never had to publicly testify to defend herself, but because she supported a variety of organizations associated with communists, she suffered from the label of "un-American." It was asserted that "Lena knew perfectly well that communists were active in many of the causes she supported."[191] Some newspaper columnists, such as Jack O'Brien of the Hearst papers, were unrelenting in their attempts to expose Horne's political leanings as a communist.[192] For financial reasons and to salvage her career, she was forced to defend herself against charges by *Counterattack,* a publication that accused many Americans of communist leanings. Horne's manager, Ralph Harris, declared, "To clear up once and for all the propaganda emanating from *Counterattack* charging her with having been associated with 'subversive causes' and implying that she was unfit to entertain Americans. . . . She's been given a clean bill of health. But she'll try to avoid groups which are called subversive."[193]

The African American press rumored that Horne's communist associations were responsible for her departure from MGM, alleging: "She is so accused because of appearances on same programs as Caleb Peterson, John Howard Lawson, Rex Ingram, and others accused by the House Un-American Activities Committee."[194] They came to her defense after *Life* magazine's editor Jimmy Tarantino accused Horne and white actress Rita Hayworth of preferring communism over democracy and charged that Horne had been blindly led into supporting such organizations and causes. "Lena Horne's name would not have been connected in any way with front organizations had she not been so easy to approach and had not leftists here who needed 'names' ill-advised her."[195]

Film critic Dan Abramson, responding to *Red Channels* (an organ directed against suspected communist entertainers), claimed, "What *Red*

Channels did not mention was the publicly known fact that Horne was married to a white man named Lennie Hayton. During the early- to mid-1950s, this was not the stuff of which good public relations were made as far as [Senator] McCarthy was concerned."[196] The African American press questioned: "Have so-called communist charges killed her in pictures? ... The movie colony is wondering whether Lena will become a parallel to Paul Robeson, now the forgotten man of Hollywood. ... Will Lena be replaced by Dorothy Dandridge?"[197] Despite the efforts of the African American press to revive Horne's career and protect their black star, she never escaped the label placed on her because of her political activism. Harassed but unyielding, she again found herself politically active in the civil rights movement.

Horne's political activism is symbolic of how African American women in general, and actresses in particular, resisted the inscription imposed on them because of their race and sexuality both on and off the screen. Marginalized, Othered, and decentered, Horne employed a variety of strategies to resist being contained by a hegemony that sought to restrain all African Americans. Using her public platform to argue against such practices, she supported rallies and demonstrations, joined organizations whose goals and objectives were consistent with her own political beliefs, and refused acting roles she viewed as denigrating to the African American image. Unlike many other African Americans who were consumed by decentering and who internalized their victimization, Horne transformed herself from actress to political leader.

SEVEN

Hazel Scott

RESISTANCE TO OTHERING

There are those who would object to the term "actress" being applied to Hazel Scott. Though she appeared in several films, she usually played herself, an entertainer and exceptionally accomplished pianist who had few speaking lines in the films in which she appeared. Even in *Rhapsody in Blue* (1945) she appeared as herself, though she had a larger speaking role in this film than in her others. Like many African American entertainers and actresses of the pre-1960 period, Scott was dismayed by the stereotypical roles available to black actresses, yearned for the opportunity to do dramatic roles, and abhorred the screen images of blacks the Hollywood studios perpetrated. Unlike most of the actresses, however, Scott launched a public campaign against what she and others considered Hollywood's demeaning of blacks in general and the (sexual and other) exploitation of black female actresses in particular. Lena Horne left the Hollywood industry in protest of such treatment; Hazel Scott in effect was ejected from Hollywood because of her protests against such treatment.

To resist the commodification of Otherness so deeply inscribed in the black screen image, some black actresses forged their own unique forms of resistance. Manthia Diawara, among others, has alluded to how black (and sometimes white) spectators resisted identification with the "persuasive elements of Hollywood narrative and spectacle."[1] As a black actress, Hazel Scott embodied the on-screen equivalent of the "resisting spectator" by similarly refusing to be constructed as a spectacle. Of course Scott had only limited control over how she was depicted on screen; the industry still strove to present her as the quintessential entertainer. But off screen, she constantly sought to reconstruct herself and establish her own space, alerting the public to the motion picture studios' attempt to exploit her. She refused to accept certain roles and refused to be used in a manner inconsistent with her ideological beliefs. Her claim was that "black women were too often cast as whores and maids."[2] By publicly articulating her political views, the resistance Scott engaged in off-screen was entirely different from her on-screen representations.

Hazel Dorothy Scott was born on June 11, 1920, in Port of Spain, Trinidad, to Alma Long Worrell Scott and R. Thomas Scott. Hazel's mother was a musician and played the saxophone with her own group, the Alma Long Scott All-Woman Orchestra, with whom Hazel also went on to play. Her mother was a concert pianist in Trinidad, and it was she who provided Scott with her early introduction to music. By the age of three, Scott was playing the piano publicly. When the family moved to the United States in 1924, Scott's father was hired as a professor at Fisk University[3] and Scott received more formal training. She made her U.S. debut at New York's Town Hall. Shortly thereafter, at the age of eight, Scott received a scholarship to the Juilliard School of Music. By the age of twelve she was performing as a soloist at Carnegie Hall, playing a Tchaikovsky piano concerto. Scott attended a Harlem girls' high school, but her school attendance was often interrupted by musical performances.[4]

As a teenager she pretended to be four years older than she was so that she could join the musicians union. By the age of fifteen, she was playing with her mother's all-female band in a Brooklyn nightclub. Around this same time, Scott's father died. In an attempt to earn money and provide for her family, she turned from classical music to swing music, which was more marketable. At sixteen, Scott became a radio star on the Mutual Broadcasting System while she played at the Roseland Dance Hall with Count Basie's band.[5] Scott even referred to herself as a "child prodigy" but professed, "There were times when I thought that I just couldn't go on. At one stage, for example, I was going to high school, studying at Juilliard, and playing in a swing orchestra at night."[6]

In New York, Scott managed to perform on Broadway, where she garnered the attention of critics. By 1939, Scott made her first record with the Rhythm Club of London sextet.[7] She then worked for six months directing a male band.[8] *Ebony* reported that "she gave a sultry rendition of *Franklin D. Roosevelt Jones* in the musical *Sing out the News*."[9] She later performed with the stage production of *Priorities of 1942*.[10]

Scott gained a national reputation when she opened at the Café Society in New York, where she earned $65 a week, a salary that would quickly increase to $4,000 a week because of her growing popularity.[11] This popularity also gave her the opportunity to appear on screen in several films, such as *Something to Shout About* (1943), *I Dood It* (1943), *The Heat's On* (1943), *Broadway Rhythm* (1944), and *Rhapsody in Blue* (1945).

At the peak of her screen career in 1945, Scott married Adam Clayton Powell Jr. Powell had been a minister at the Abyssinian Baptist Church in New York, where he preached black nationalism and passive resistance in the 1930s. He was the first African American appointed to the New York City Council in 1941 and was elected to Congress in 1945, where he went on to become chairman of the House Education and Labor Committee in the early 1960s.[12] Scott's marriage to Powell was greeted by large crowds. The Powells had one son, Adam Clayton Powell III, whom Hazel affectionately referred to as Skipper.

During the 1950s, Scott appeared in her own television show, but it was short-lived.[13] It was during this period that Scott was called to testify before the House Un-American Activities Committee, as were many entertainers during this era who were characterized as communist sympathizers.

Following her divorce from Powell in 1961, Scott moved to Europe, and while residing in Paris she married Enzio Bedin, a marriage that was short-lived and ended in divorce. She continued to perform, and she received accolades from critics for her performances in Paris.[14] At the same time, Scott managed to return to the cinema, appearing in the French film *Confessions at Night* (1958)[15] and in a second unnamed film.[16] She appeared in her last film, *Night Affair*, in 1961.[17] In the 1960s she suffered from mononucleosis and other health problems. Scott later said that some of her memories of Paris were painful because of the deaths of her friends and fellow musicians Lester Young and Billie Holiday.[18]

After disappearing from the public eye for much of the 1970s, she made a brief return to public life and performed in some New York clubs. In 1978 she was inducted into the Black Filmmakers Hall of Fame. Prior to her death in the fall of 1981, Scott battled alcoholism.[19]

SCOTT'S SCREEN CAREER

Scott first made her mark in the entertainment world as a pianist by perfecting two styles of music—classical music and jazz music—to create a hybrid sound that garnered her attention and popularity in music circles. As a result, Scott was recruited to personify the entertainer on screen, and her undeniable musical talent won her the attentions of studio executives. Off screen, however, she could not escape the inscription associated with the black jazz artist. Peter Stanfield observes that black jazz artists as actresses were commodified on screen because of their race and gender, resulting in what Stanfield calls "theft of the body."[20] He goes on to say that "the captured sexualities provide a physical and biological expression of 'otherness,' which then translates into the potential for pornotroping and embodies sheer physical powerlessness that slides into a more general 'powerlessness.'"[21] Stanfield adds, "This project of 'othering' is continued in Hollywood's more general representation of blackness and in the 'darkening' of white women through their proximity to, or use of, recordings" so aptly perfected by the black jazz artist.[22] The black actress is not only exploited for her talent, race, and gender but is now exploited for what she can provide the white actress.

In addition to this exploitation, the black jazz artist on screen could not escape the multiple complex meanings ascribed to her image as an entertainer. Stuart Hall asserts that the "clown" or "entertainer" "captures the 'innate' humor, as well as the physical grace of the licensed entertainer—putting on a show for The Others. It is never quite clear whether we are laughing with or at this figure: admiring the physical and rhythmic grace, the open expressivity and emotionality of the 'entertainer,' or put off by the clown's stupidity."[23] Hall further states, "One noticeable fact about [this image] is [the] deep ambivalence—the double vision of the white eye through which [this image is] seen."[24]

In view of the double determinacy inscribed in the black screen image as entertainer, Scott's resistance was often complicated by her desire to respond to the ambivalence complicating this image. Certainly she desired to be acknowledged for her talent, but to be seen exclusively because of her talent as an entertainer was bound to invite disdain. Such one-dimensional positioning narrowed her range as an actress and helps to explain her resistance.

Scott was often referred to as Lena Horne's rival, but she more closely resembled Horne's mirror image. Paralleling Scott as the performer on screen, Horne similarly assumed Scott's defensive posture off screen. Michele Wallace notes, "Like Scott clinging to her piano, Lena Horne clung to her roles as a chanteuse in 'a long line of movies where she was pasted to a pillar.'"[25] Although relegated to one-dimensional roles on screen, Horne attempted to reposition herself, and though she was silenced, as a "black cultural producer" (to capitalize on the words of Jacqueline Bobo) she began to re-center herself with "a vengeance"—an approach not so different from the one Scott employed.[26]

According to Jacqueline Bobo, black women's resistance is reduced to a struggle over power. Bobo writes that:

> Black women are rendered as objects and useful commodities in a very serious power struggle. By centering these images of black women in public perceptions the women seem powerless, lacking the initiative to change their social conditions. No recognition is given that black women are and have been powerful agents conscious of their historical circumstances and deliberately working toward bettering their lives.
>
> Within the last several decades [and perhaps even earlier] black women have effectively written themselves back into history; they have retrieved their collective past for sustenance and encouragement for present-day protest movements.[27]

Scott and Horne often were grouped together, not only because of their political activism but because their paths as entertainers frequently crossed. The African American press noted of Scott that "Out of the West Indies, through the Bronx and Harlem to Café Society downtown and uptown, then to Hollywood . . . [Scott, like Horne] too, passed through the Café Societies, played leading clubs on the coast and landed a lucrative movie contract."[28] But the similarities really ended when the two women began their Hollywood careers. Was the African American press deliberately counterposing the two actresses to construct a rivalry between them? According to Bogle, Scott's transition from the stage to the screen was negotiated by Café Society's Barney Josephson, who stipulated that she would not be presented in a "derogatory manner."[29]

Scott's introduction to the cinema industry occurred in *Something to Shout About* (1943)—playing the part of herself, a role that she replicated in most of her screen appearances. When Scott auditioned for *Something to Shout About,* she was so impressive that the film's director had a special part written for her.[30] According to Thomas Cripps, Scott, "a bundle of intellect, brass, and musicology, was spotted at Café Society by Gregory Ratoff, who made a spot for her [in the film]."[31] This may have been a Hollywood first for an African American actor. According to *Negro Digest,* "Columbia officials saw the sequences, quickly revamped the film, wrote a fat part for her, [and] brought her out to Hollywood."[32] She negotiated a contract that paid her some $4,000 a week and that stipulated that she "[wouldn't] wear a handkerchief or dirty clothes in a film."[33] Donald Bogle adds that her contract indicated, "No bandana on her head. . . . No apron upon her waist. And they took her. They wanted her that much."[34] These were similar to the demands Horne had negotiated earlier when she had contracted with the motion picture studios. With respect to her on-screen representation, however, Scott still exercised little control. When she appeared with the Teddy Wilson band in *Something to Shout About,* the African American press was disappointed that the film's black actors had "nothing more than 'flash' roles."[35] She did assert herself when she refused Cole Porter's request to introduce "You'd Be So Nice to Come Home To," declaring that "she had no feeling for the lyrics."[36]

Reporting on *Something to Shout About,* one newspaper columnist, Frederick Othman (Hollywood writer) titled his review "Why Dusky Hazel Scott Sings in the Movies."[37] Reporters sometimes used their critiques to articulate their own views. That Scott was characterized as "dusky" demonstrates how black actresses were maligned and thus fell victim to the same kind of politics that many ethnic stars endured. In her assessment of ethnic female stars, Diane Negra claims that "One of the ways in which [the] . . . modern girl was neutralized was through a discourse of masculine production. . . . [The actress] was represented as having been filtered through a layer of male sponsorship."[38] Though black actresses were denied their own voices, the black press could articulate their voices at least within a restricted realm, even though these actresses could not count on support from the mainstream press. Attacks on black artists, black newspaper critics said, wouldn't happen if "colored readers of white newspapers show enough resentment by not reading papers that direct their reflective whims against them."[39] Castigating both black leadership and white newspaper columnists, the African American press further declared that "the capricious fancy of the white press, tainted an otherwise banner story on Miss Scott by attaching a reflective heading," which the black press labeled "stinky."[40] Scott then came to her own defense. Since she now wielded power in the capacity of the film's screenplay supervisor, she was able to edit "all the dialogue spoken by colored players in the film—to make sure that no phrases offensive to her race will be injected into the script by overzealous writers."[41] Scott's determination to control how she was commodified on the screen forced her to assume a defensive posture, a prelude to her later politicization.

Scott's increased visibility on screen soon translated into increased visibility off screen. Racial slurs or assaults were ever-present, albeit sometimes humorous. While she was performing at the El Morocco nightclub, a white southerner approached the club's owner and inquired, "'Do you allow the n----ers in here?' 'Why yes,' replied Perona, 'come right in!'"[42] Scott refused to allow such assaults to interfere with her career.

She returned to the screen in *The Heat's On* (a 1943 film adaptation of the Broadway stage show *Tropicana*), with Mae West.[43] West's liberal sexuality, which disturbed the Production Code censors, was complemented and offset by Scott's innate dignity. Somehow the pairing of the African American woman and the white sex symbol created a fusion of race and sexuality that made their appearance together acceptable. The white female's devaluation here becomes synonymous with black devaluation. At the film's end, one is left wondering: While Mae West (because of her hypersexualization) is supposed to embody the "heat," perhaps it is really Scott who generated the genuine "heat."

Transforming her style of music on screen in *The Heat's On* made this Scott's most controversial film. She was once again commodified, appearing on screen seated at a piano and flaunting a strapless evening gown.[44] But the sexualization was not the pivotal point for Scott. The film erupted into controversy when she held up Columbia's production for three days because she refused to be marginalized racially. According to *Negro Digest,* Scott, dressed as a WAC officer, appeared in a scene with eight African American actresses attired in aprons. "The producer wanted the girls to wear soiled aprons 'to make them look lived in.' Miss Scott refused to participate until clean aprons were secured."[45] Because she refused to be compromised, "Harry Cohn [Columbia studio executive] vowed to end her Hollywood career, and [he] did."[46] Her screen career was indeed short-lived; following her appearance in this picture, she landed only a few other screen roles.

The Heat's On centers on the stage career of actress Fay Lawrence (Mae West), who is ambivalent about participating in the revival of the stage show *Tropicana*. As the producers prepare for the show, Hazel Scott, appearing as herself, auditions and performs for the production. Seated at the piano, she engages in her boogie-woogie style of music, complemented by her singing. Her long, low-cut, black gown with polka-dot sleeves emphasizes the jazz rhythms of her music while her facial expressions accentuate the musical tunes. Her strong persona is evident in her posture; she radiates confidence, presence, and style. The film is nearly half over before she is introduced, but unlike some of her other cameo roles, in this film she is allowed to appear on screen more than once. In her subsequent appearance, she is positioned between two pianos and plays both simultaneously! Her long, low-cut, white gown accented by white sleeves with black circles is designed to offset the black-and-white piano keys that appear to dance beneath her fingers. At the end of her performance she bows to the audience, with composure.

In her final appearance in *The Heat's On*, Scott is set in a symbolic representation of African American life, complete with dilapidated structures, but she uses her music to transform this misery into merriment. The scene itself suggests that blackness is somehow coded ambiguously, since it is symbolic of both despair and happiness. Because black soldiers parade on the screen, *The Heat's On* could be regarded as a war propaganda film. Even Scott deviates from her usual style of dress, wearing an army uniform and cap, playing her boogie-woogie to entertain marching soldiers, and saluting them while singing. This role may have been consistent with her own ideological views. Showcasing African American soldiers may have alerted audiences to the important contributions these soldiers made to winning World War II. It also may have been a subtle attempt to support the integration of African American soldiers into the military.

Scott usually played herself in her movie appearances, an entertainer seated at the piano. Unlike Horne, she did not perform on stage alone. The piano allowed her to appear less isolated, and because of its large size and its color, it can be seen as symbolic of an all-powerful black presence.[47]

Scott's next film was *I Dood It* (1943), which boasted such talented white stars as Red Skelton and Eleanor Powell. Cripps revealed that Vincente Minnelli, the director of several MGM productions, "remembered *I Dood It* [as] 'a comic potboiler' salvaged from 'footage and sets' of a stalled project into which they tossed Hazel Scott and Butterfly McQueen."[48] The alleged rivalry between Scott and Horne first surfaced during the production of *I Dood It*. Horne's biography states that she arrived at the studios in "California style, in pigtails, slacks, and loafers. Hazel, fresh from New York, was dripping silver fox. The next day Lena wore her Irene canteen suit, and Hazel appeared in slacks."[49] Walter Winchell gossiped that the two entertainers engaged in a hair-pulling match at the Café Society; both women denied the story, which seems unlikely in view of their sophistication.[50]

I Dood It was believed to be an improvement in the way African Americans were represented on screen.[51] Although they were still rendered as entertainers, Horne and Scott appeared "in evening dress," in "one of the classiest scenes in the picture."[52] Other African Americans who appeared in the film included Ruby Dandridge (mother of Dorothy Dandridge) and Joel Fluellen.[53] Their elegant dresses supposedly provided a more redeeming representation of African Americans on screen. The African American press felt that at least to some extent they were being compensated for the exploitation they had endured. But it could be argued that the film industry was in need of the talents of Horne and Scott, since the song "Jericho" suffered from unimaginative musical direction.[54]

Because *I Dood It* was another film whose comic plot was loosely woven around a variety of stage skits to justify featuring a variety of stage talent on screen, entertainers such as Scott and Horne could be inserted into the film and yet easily excised from the plot. Scott arrives on screen at the stage entrance in a glittering, black, full-length gown covered by a white mink and accompanied by an entourage of black men dressed in overcoats and top hats. It is clear that she is a star, and a star to be reckoned with. Walking with a confident stride and rapid pace, as though this show is merely one stop among many, she and her following are approached by the doorman and asked to identify themselves. She states emphatically, "I'm Hazel Scott," and of course immediately gains entrance to the stage—suggesting that her name itself has prestige within entertainment circles. As the African American band members assemble on stage, Skelton, an anomaly, follows. While Skelton connotes social difference, the band members are racially different, sharing in their Otherness.

Scott is foregrounded on the stage as she plays the piano with assurance, hitting the keys emphatically, while band members complement her playing with rhythmic jazz. The music is upbeat and reaches a crescendo, but then slows in pace. Smiling and utilizing her body to accentuate the rhythms, Scott rocks her head back and forth to the music, exhibiting pride in her ability, delight in her musical talent, and a passion for her work. Photographed primarily in waist shots to emphasize the sexuality of her bosom, she ends her performance by bowing to her audience as the film segues to Lena Horne.

Covered extensively by the African American press because of her contributions to *I Dood It,* Scott was heralded by the *Chicago Defender* as the "race's number one pianist today," while the *New York Amsterdam News* laid claim to its artist by announcing "New York's Piano Darling Goes Hollywood."[55] But although the black press applauded Scott's success, they were disturbed by reports that she was attempting to distance herself from the African American actors working in Hollywood. Perhaps her on-screen confidence was viewed by audiences as a sign of arrogance, which they assumed transferred into her off-screen posture. Expressing its anxieties, the *Chicago Defender* informed readers that "Writer Fears Hazel Scott Has Become Hollywood."[56] These fears apparently stemmed from Scott's public snub of Bill Robinson, one of the biggest African American stars working in Hollywood, at a popular Hollywood establishment. Scott also ignored African American newspaper columnists Lawrence LaMar and Herman Hill, who were visiting the Vitagraph Studio for a Columbia production, while Mae West acknowledged them. That certainly did not help her case.

It was rumored that she had remained aloof from the black actors working on *The Heat's On* during production, which further problematized her in the African American press. Assuring his readers that some of these reports were well-founded, Lawrence LaMar proclaimed that "Hollywood writers have noticed this as have several blonde and brunette women and have wondered what it's all about."[57] However, since LaMar was the very writer who complained of being alienated by Scott and since no additional reports to substantiate the complaint have been located, it is possible that this development represented a personal conflict between Scott and LaMar.

Despite these reports, Scott's public appeal did not decline either in the African American press or in white Hollywood; she was embraced by both. Her next appearance was with Horne in *Broadway Rhythm* (1944). The film had "created 'Brazilian Boogie Woogie' especially for Lena," and Scott's boogie-woogie style as a pianist lent itself perfectly to the film; Scott's role revolved around the filming of a "Jungle Night Club" sequence.[58] This film, of course, exploited the racial codes that equated the jungle with blackness. Stuart Hall observes that

> "natives" always move as an anonymous collective mass—in tribes or hordes. And against them is always counterposed the isolated white figure, alone "out there," confronting his Destiny or shouldering his Burden in the "heart of darkness," displaying coolness under fire and an unshakeable authority—exerting mastery over the rebellious natives or quelling the threatened uprising with a single glance of his steel-blue eyes.... No Royal Tour is complete without its troupe of swaying bodies, or its mounted tribesmen, paying homage. Blacks are such "good movers," so rhythmic, so natural.[59]

Therefore, if the jungle becomes linked to the native, then it is glaringly apparent that the black jazz artist is associated with the natural and becomes transfigured in this reproduction of naturalism. Because of Scott's performance in this film, the African American press touted her as the "pianist who has reached fame by playing the classics in boogie woogie time, in her interpretation of Chopin's 'Minute Waltz' [in *Broadway Rhythm*]. [Scott] not only ... [plays] the piano in her inimitable fashion, but she 'complicates' the love life of Lena and Eddie 'Rochester' Anderson."[60] Scott does not appear in the jungle nightclub scene as does Horne. However, Scott does appear in a scene immediately subsequent to Horne's scene, and because of its proximity to Horne's scene, she automatically becomes connected to blackness.

Scott's scene opens when Anderson, dressed in a top hat and tails, enters a stage door and passes a billboard displaying several pictures of Scott, the pianist. The camera then cuts from the billboard to Scott, who is seated at the piano in a white gown with a neckline trimmed in ostrich feathers. She starts playing a conventional style of music in the beginning but suddenly converts to a jazz style accentuated by a two-piece band, which becomes illuminated in the background when Scott converts to the jazz style. As the music proceeds, the horn section of the band is revealed, and they play in unison to the music created by Scott on piano. Scott's face is reflected by the piano's surface as she smiles endlessly and shakes her head back and forth to the rhythm of the music. At the finale of her performance, she stands and bows to the audience. Her scene, like Horne's, was disconnected from the film's plot and could easily be edited so as not to offend audiences who objected to seeing blacks prominently displayed on screen.

After an interim stint on the stage, Scott returned to Hollywood to appear in *Rhapsody in Blue*.[61] Bogle suggests, though, that "Hazel Scott—high-minded and haughty—clashed with Columbia Pictures mogul Harry Cohn over stereotypes in a film on which she worked. . . . She had already signed to do *Rhapsody in Blue* at Warners."[62] Bogle claims that Scott declared "I never made another Hollywood film."[63]

Rhapsody in Blue chronicles composer George Gershwin's life, show-casing his musical talent and his compositions as they transformed 1940s American music. The film, adapted from one of Gershwin's classic com-positions, presents a series of stage shows and performances interspersed with his failed romances and his compulsion to succeed as an artist. It presents genius as inseparable from insanity, portraying Gershwin work-ing at a nonstop, health-endangering pace. Cripps characterized *Rhapsody in Blue* as

> one of a cycle of show-business biopics into which it should have been likely to work black acts. This George Gershwin life provided a neat open-ing for Hazel Scott, an actual friend of the subject, and Warner Bros. indeed engaged her for a sequence in which she appears in his *Porgy and Bess*. But as production dragged on and the "nut" rose, the bosses went for only the safest of material, thereby shelving its urbanity, its director Reuben Mamoulian (who had done the first *Porgy* on Broadway), its leftist writer Clifford Odets, and gradually all of its black parts.[64]

The *Baltimore Afro-American* ascertained that Scott was hired to "recreate the character of a colored pianist who inspired [Gershwin] one afternoon while strolling [through] the streets of Paris. He listened, hur-ried to his study and wrote the incident into music. So Miss Scott will be both seen and heard when the great feature is finished and released."[65] Her assignment to both act and sing on screen, as well as to serve as a prime device to advance the film's narrative, was regarded as a significant achievement by African Americans. The *Chicago Defender* referred to her expanded role as a milestone, noting that she was not only a pianist and singer, but also demonstrated fluency in French: "It is doubtful that anyone who has followed films over the years can remember when a Negro artist was permitted to display her cultural abilities as does the glamorous Hazel in *Rhapsody in Blue*."[66] Although pleased, Scott did not see this role improvement as being inseparable from the typecasting and marginalization that African Americans commonly endured. As she put it, "There's one thing about being typed as myself. When people ask me what my favorite role is, I can answer with all modesty—Hazel Scott."[67]

In *Rhapsody in Blue*, Gershwin leaves America. In Paris, he attends a nightclub performance featuring Hazel Scott. When Scott is introduced, the camera pans to a gate leading to the club's entrance, perhaps to suggest that Gershwin is exploring uncharted territory. The gate becomes a metaphor for the boundary he attempts to transcend, a boundary that connotes difference not only in his music but also in race—the introduction of Scott implies that he is beginning to experiment with Otherness. Scott, dressed in a white t-strapped gown that reveals her bare shoulders and wearing a floral ornament in her hair, stands and sings for the formally dressed, all-white audience. She delivers her tunes in French with a perfection, fluency, and level of familiarity with the language that most whites did not associate with African Americans.

While applauding Scott's appearance in the film, reviewer David Platt was condemnatory of film censors. Platt revealed that "This scene in which Miss Scott renders Gershwin's music in a Paris night club was easily the most outstanding thing in the picture. That is precisely why the scene has been heavily chopped in Memphis, Tenn. where Jim Crow rules with an iron rod. According to the trade papers, the Memphis Board of Censors ruled against the famous Negro artist because she had a featured role in the picture. To these worried gentlemen, this amounts to a threat to white domination in the South."[68]

Reviewing Scott's performance, *Ebony* magazine noted, "In *Rhapsody in Blue*, Hazel sings and plays 'My Man' in a Paris cabaret setting. She uses both English and French. The French accent may be more Hazel Scott than Parisian but it manages to get by."[69] Nonetheless, being allowed to speak in both French and English certainly added to her stature as a performer. As for the marginalization to which she was subjected, Scott, like many other black actresses, radiated such a commanding presence that she managed to deflect the gaze projected onto her.

In a more extensive critique of her performance, Donald Bogle writes that "the sequence [in which Scott appears] is not without irony. After all Scott, performing for a very hoity-toity white crowd, seems cut off from her community. There's not one black face in the room. She is indeed a black woman put on display for the perusal and pleasure of a white audience."[70] Scott, undeniably a signifier of black female sexuality, was rendered an object of the gaze to white spectators in the film. Bogle continues: "Still she's so supremely confident you know here's an above-it-all black goddess who cannot be touched."[71]

In a subsequent Paris nightclub scene, Scott is again shown elegantly dressed: her white gown with a bodice decorated with white fringe is low-cut, revealing her bosom, and her bare arms flaunt diamond bracelets. This time, however, she speaks in English. Playing her boogie-woogie music, she sings the lyrics "Clap your hands, slap your thighs." The dress, the music style, and the lyrics all combine to suggest that an African American woman is identified purely because of her body. As if that were not enough, Scott is displaced and seemingly rendered invisible as the film attempts to center Gershwin. When her face is shown on the screen, a man in the audience inquires, "Who is that?" It is assumed that he is referring to Scott, but then an off-camera voice blurts out, "George Gershwin." The camera continues to cut back and forth from Gershwin's table to Scott playing the piano, her fingers dazzlingly working the keyboard, arms gyrating to the rhythms of the music. At the end of her number, she bows to the audience but remains unnamed and unidentified. Standing and dancing, Scott delivers her next song as she flaunts an ostrich-feather fan to accentuate the lyrics. Her black body, backgrounded by white male jazz members, constructs a dichotomy between black female sexuality and white male sexuality. Her performance is even politicized, as she sings "Yankee-Doodle Blues," a song that counterposes the politically divided American North and South. Interestingly, it is being sung in a Parisian nightclub, albeit one frequented by American visitors.

According to Bogle, "Scott was about as elegant and sophisticated as they come, a blazing symbol of the contemporary black woman completely at home in the most continental of settings."[72] The African American press attributed this quality, and "her ability to get more money for working a few weeks in pictures than several topnotch Negro stars who spent the major portion of their time before the magic lenses," to her West Indian ancestry.[73] Scott was promoted in the African American press as the "best stock in trade."[74] She is not the only Black to appear in *Rhapsody in Blue:* Anne Brown also sings in a dramatization of *Porgy and Bess,* previously mentioned. Earlier in the film, when Gershwin's "Blue Monday" is performed on stage, the setting is a smoke-filled nightclub featuring dancers who appear to have been darkened. (Darkening whites for black roles, rather than employing African Americans, was a typical Hollywood tactic in the first half of the twentieth century.) At the end of this scene the camera cuts to a melancholy African American couple located off stage, with the woman shedding a tear; the assumption is that sadness or emotionalism is best conveyed by, or embodied in, the black body. As Dyer suggests, "whiteness is related to blackness, materially and emotionally dependent on it yet still holding sway over it."[75]

Although Scott returned to the screen in a few later roles—in *Confessions at Night* (1958), in another unnamed French film, and in *Night Affair* (1961)—the ending of her screen career coincided with the dissolution of her marriage to Powell. The African American press seemed less enamored with Scott than they had been in previous years. They reported, "Hazel Scott, brilliant pianist-vocalist, who gained a few pounds and sports a $300 black wig since her engagement in the French film *Confessions at Night,* starring Danielle Darrieux and Jean Gabin, left Paris for a two-months [*sic*] holiday in Cannes, on the French Riviera."[76] And when she returned to the United States and attempted to revive her career, she declared,

It's difficult for a woman alone in this industry. Everyone wants to sleep with you. If you don't, you've got problems. When you brush off the bosses and geniuses in the front office, you automatically become a lesbian. If you do go along with these idiots, you're a bum. Name it and take your choice. This is the story of my life. I have been called a lesbian since I entered this business at 15 and made it clear that I did not intend to go along with shoddy practices.

This, strange to say, is the accepted practice in show business. Some girls on the way up find it easier if they accept the attentions of certain powerful individuals. This is not always the case and I am a case in point. ... I am sick and tired of being stepped on and talked about and called names because I will not compromise.[77]

Responding to the marginalization that she endured in the cinema industry, Scott set the record straight: "I turned down four singing maid's roles in movies during the past year. Some producers want you to come on the set, dust off a piano, and then sit down and play. There are plenty of white performers who can play maid's roles and then step out into a penthouse or a classroom."[78] Some have questioned whether Scott might have been willing to compromise her position on screen if more lucrative opportunities had not presented themselves off screen. Despite this argument and regardless of Scott's response, it is clear that she remained true to her stated position while retaining her employability.

The struggle to achieve dramatic status, however, was ongoing, and even as her screen career neared an end, she, like Horne, was trying to obtain dramatic roles. Scott asserted, "I want[ed] to do some real acting. What room is there for a Negro dramatic actress? Well, a lot of room. I could play some of the Negro characters of history like Sojourner Truth, the Civil War abolitionist, or maybe I could play the part of a Negro WAC today."[79] Her marginalization in the Hollywood cinema industry is easily documented. First, Hollywood constantly depicted her as a performer, denying her any serious dramatic roles. Second, her sequences were edited out of the final versions of her films when they toured the South. Third, she was denied credit for some of her roles. Fourth, filmmakers sexualized her (as they did all women working in the industry during this period) and racialized her on screen. Rather than internalizing her frustrations, Scott, like Horne, became more politically active.

HAZEL SCOTT OBJECTIFIED IN THE AFRICAN AMERICAN PRESS, MAINSTREAM PRESS, AND ON STAGE

Diawara argues that spectatorial resistance involves refutation, reinscription (based on one's own historical accounts or beliefs), reading (meaning imposing one's own gaze), and disidentification (failing to impart identification with the representations on screen).[80] Therefore, it appears that Scott's resistance to Hollywood's commodification of her race and gender parallels practices employed by the resisting spectator. Diawara emphatically declares that "resisting spectators [transform] the problem of passive identification into active criticism."[81] Scott assumed a defensive posture by resisting such representations through her active criticism in ways that link her to the resisting spectator. And although she had little control over how she was commodified on screen, off screen she waged a vigilant battle. To reconstruct Scott's resistance to her off-screen objectification, it is necessary to unveil how she was covered primarily in the African American press and secondly in the mainstream press.

Diverting attention away from Scott's music to her physical appearance, the African American press often featured photos of her wearing low-cut or strapless gowns that exposed her bustline. In these photos, Scott, thrusting her bosom forward, was seductively positioned on a piano or the arm of a couch decorated with satin pillows. Apparently she was a participant in this objectification, inviting scrutiny from both the mainstream and the black press. The *Baltimore Afro-American* recounted the observation of Earl Wilson, a columnist for the *New York Post,* who suggested that "in a strapless evening gown she makes most sweater girls look underfed."[82] Wilson's article was not only excerpted by the *Baltimore Afro-American* newspaper but was also reprinted in *Negro Digest.* He added, "Some . . . have attributed her success largely to her extreme good looks and her sensational 36-inch bust."[83] Continuing to sexualize Scott, Wilson titled his article "Keeping Abreast of Hazel."[84] That Scott's sexuality was appropriated by the press was similarly noted by Elizabeth Hawes, who stated, "Some people tell her she must always cover her arms and back because they don't like to see the muscles move when she plays. Others say, 'Oh, Hazel, you should always wear a low back and no sleeves because it is so beautiful to see your muscles when you play.'"[85] In this instance, it seems that a female reviewer was less accusatory than were male reviewers. Many actresses, reduced to the body by the entertainment industry and by the press, sexualized themselves. Sex and sexuality sold. Whether this is read as a form of self-exploitation or of business acumen, the unfortunate fact is that in the male-dominated entertainment industry, women felt themselves compelled to succumb to or comply with such exploitation—or even to self-exploit.

Wilson continued in his *New York Post* article, "Hazel Scott boasts buxom bust and deft touch on piano."[86] Constructing Scott primarily in terms of her body, he stated that when they met at a restaurant to conduct the interview, "I noticed everybody looking at Hazel as we walked across the room, and I was sort of proud, in a hammy way, to be with her, and hoped they'd notice me, too. Remembering her figure, I doubt whether they did."[87] According to this source, Wilson had even questioned Scott's dressmaker to determine whether or not her breasts were false, thus further demeaning her by suggesting that she resorted to deceptive techniques (which are much more socially acceptable in a later age of saline and silicone implants) to promote her sexuality.[88] Even more disturbing was that the African American magazine *Ebony* repeated Wilson's words in a story that was presented as a defense of Scott. The *Ebony* review then reported that Scott had vowed that "she no longer stands for publicity like *New York Post* Saloon Editor Earl Wilson's frothy piece."[89]

While it may be argued that Scott (and other actresses of that period) collaborated in the sexualization discussed here, the real issue is the extent to which the controlling forces—males solely in the position to hire and fire—resorted to sexual exploitation. Rather than condemning Scott and her "sisters" for participating in their own victimization (blaming the victims), it is more important to identify the dynamics of an industry that thrived on the sexual exploitation of women. This is not to absolve her from any blame or responsibility for participating in her own exploitation, but rather to suggest that she was encouraged and even compelled to promote herself in this manner. Jacqueline Bobo contends that "Rather than simply say a representation is negative or positive, the historical and cultural impetus that gives rise to the images needs to be analyzed along with the presentation of the ways in which black women creators politicize the images."[90] Catering to a male-dominated industry that sexualized women in a culture where sex and sexuality are marketed, Scott stood to gain attention and ultimately to increase her earning potential. Members of the mainstream press such as the *New York Post* sought to malign her, while the African American press, though not above participating in Scott's sexualization, attempted to provide wider and more thorough coverage of her stage and screen career.

Scott was further sexualized on stage—an observation that was acknowledged by her spouse, Adam Clayton Powell Jr. Reminiscing about Scott's stage performance, he revealed:

> All the lights would go out, Hazel would make her way to the piano, and then suddenly a spotlight would catch her. For a moment the audience would gasp, because it looked as if she were seated there nude—the height

of the piano, the bare-shouldered dress, nothing but the golden-brown shoulders and arms, the super-talented fingers.[91]

Transformed on the stage, Scott's appeal was her sexualized image.

Because Scott had perfected the boogie-woogie style, she, like a number of other entertainers, was accused of promoting the moral decline of a younger generation. Artur Rodzinski asserted that "'boogie-woogie,' which appeals to hep cats, is the greatest cause of delinquency among American youth today."[92] Such criticism sounds a familiar chord with respect to hip-hop music throughout the 1980s and 1990s; the warning has been repeatedly sounded that rap is leading to the moral decline of today's youth. Scott, defending her music and style as an artist, retorted that juvenile delinquency existed long before the introduction of swing music.[93]

A WEDDING TO AN ACTIVIST AND TO ACTIVISM

Scott's political activism did not occur in a vacuum. Her spouse, Adam Clayton Powell Jr., exerted considerable influence over her off-screen activities. The Scott-Powell marriage was covered extensively by the African American press, primarily because of the prestige and social standing each held within the African American community, but also because their marriage was controversial. Powell, previously married (to Fredi Washington's sister, Isabel), had difficulty obtaining a divorce. As early as 1944, the press circulated reports of Scott's relationship with Powell and their imminent marriage.[94] There was endless news reporting: an African American minister, recently elected to Congress, was seeking a contested divorce and planning to marry an entertainer, Hazel Scott— a performer whose profession and reputation might be considered diametrically opposed to the sanctity of black religion. Could the church possibly approve?[95] Fredi Washington became linked to the scandal; she was the theatrical editor of Powell's newspaper, The People's Voice, and he suspected she had interfered in his domestic affairs.[96]

Although in July 1945 the press reported that Scott had become ill and required several blood transfusions, two weeks later, on August 1, she and Powell were married.[97] Their marriage was regarded by some as a move to elevate Powell's political career, since it was believed that "if Powell's marriage to a West Indian helps in any way to mitigate the unfortunate misunderstanding between Negro Americans and West Indian Negroes, then all that has happened in Powell's domestic life in the recent period may be overshadowed by that one important fact."[98] The wedding and reception held in New York City were attended by an impressive array of politicians, including Democratic mayoral candidate William O'Dwyer, congressmen Samuel Dickstein and Emanuel Celler, borough president James J. Lyons, and postmaster Albert Goldman.[99] According to *Ebony* magazine, the wedding reception at the Café Society turned into "a political demonstration" for Powell.[100] "Some 3,000 well-wishers, mostly excited Harlem women, turned out at Café Society. The climax of the affair came when Hazel fainted away while shaking hands with friends."[101]

The transformation from entertainer Hazel Scott to the wife of Adam Clayton Powell Jr. was reflected in Mrs. Powell's dress, which became notably more conservative. Yet her political views became less and less conservative as she increasingly denounced discriminatory practices, articulating a position similar to Powell's. He was one of the most active African American leaders in Congress, working for more legislation than any of his predecessors to improve the plight and upgrade the status of African Americans in the state of New York.[102] Characterizing Scott's political activism, one source wrote, "Scott was . . . equally spirited offstage, a factor of her personality that was seldom appreciated."[103]

While obviously complementing her husband's activities, Scott's political activism was not new. It seems to have accelerated with the rise of her career. Even in the early 1940s when she performed in nightclubs such as Loew's State, she had publicly denounced white comedians who made racial jokes. During such performances, the African American press also responded to racializing. According to the *New York Amsterdam News*, Lou Holtz, an emcee at Loew's State on the same program with Scott, received a telegram from the African American press protesting his disparaging remarks. The telegram read:

> Possibly you are unaware that your Negro dialect and use of "darky" are in bad taste and an insult to Hazel Scott and all Negroes. Like "kike" it is a term used to belittle a minority group. The present international situation behooves both your race and ours to make every effort at mutual understanding and respect.[104]

Although Scott admitted that she had been offstage when the remarks were made and therefore had not heard them, she informed the newspaper that Holtz had agreed to eliminate the offensive material from his routine. The implication was that had she been fully aware, she herself would have taken action immediately. That she publicly responded to the press's concerns demonstrated her lack of tolerance for racial defamation.

In similar public gestures, Scott contributed her talent in support of World War II, performing for a British Aid project and participating in a war bond rally. This thrust her into the same league with many white Hollywood entertainers, including Edward G. Robinson, Cecil B. DeMille, Bing Crosby, Dinah Shore, Betty Hutton, George Burns, Gracie Allen, Kathryn Grayson, and Rudy Vallee.[105] Attesting to Scott's support of political causes, Sherrie Tucker noted, "Another favored pinup of black GIs was jazz pianist Hazel Scott, also a champion of desegregation and public antiracist protests (and one of the few black artists of the era to integrate the jazz and classical genres without being accused of 'inauthenticity' by the white critics)."[106] Now married to Powell, she was bound to become even more politically involved and even more politically covered by the press. One report stated, "[Scott] has been active in progressive circles in New York and during the last election went out to soapbox for President Roosevelt."[107]

In 1945, Scott challenged the Daughters of the American Revolution (DAR). She had been invited to perform at Constitution Hall, but was then uninvited because a DAR ruling prohibited African Americans from performing in their auditorium. Taking this as a personal insult to his wife as well as a racial insult, Congressman Powell used his political savvy to respond to the DAR: he approached President Harry S. Truman. A precedent had already been established by Eleanor Roosevelt, who cancelled her DAR membership in 1939 after the organization denied the world-renowned concert artist Marian Anderson, an African American, access to Constitution Hall.[108] Truman responded to Powell's complaint and to the publicity surrounding the case by denouncing the DAR, but he stated that "he could not interfere in the 'management policy of a private enterprise such as the one in question.'"[109] Although Truman publicly suggested that his wife might refuse to attend the tea sponsored by the organization, Mrs. Truman did no such thing; she had accepted her invitation prior to the eruption of the controversy. Powell made it known that although he agreed with the spirit of Truman's response, he desired action. He therefore suggested an oft-used political tool, the Internal Revenue Service (IRS). The DAR enjoyed tax-exempt status and Powell posed the question: "Can we as a nation exempt from taxation the property of people who claim to be charitable, religious, and philanthropic and they use that property against the best interest of the people?"[110] He vowed to propose legislation to end the DAR's tax-exempt status. Shortly thereafter, the DAR's board met and decided to rescind their rule prohibiting African American entertainers from performing at Constitution Hall.

Despite the interestingly timed new ruling, however, the DAR's actions provoked a rash of criticism throughout the African American community. Mary McLeod Bethune, president of the National Council of Negro Women, charged: "The Japanese and Axis propaganda addressed to the smaller nations tried to discredit the United States on the grounds that its democracy was not sincere. The DAR by its official action now picks up where the Japanese and the Axis left off."[111] The African American press, infuriated by the DAR's actions, continued their unfavorable coverage. They reminded readers that the DAR had similarly denied Paul Robeson access to Constitution Hall in the previous decade and had "closed their doors to one of the descendants of Crispus Attucks, the first colored American to shed blood and die in the Boston massacre ... for the freedom of America."[112] They then proclaimed that Hazel Scott was "a true daughter of the Revolution."[113] She had challenged the DAR, forcing a national debate that ended in their abandoning racial bans on performances at a public building. Such a victory for herself and, more important, for her people and for her country reflects upon Scott's capacity and her will to translate her star power into political activism.

Scott's intolerance for discriminatory practices was again made public by the press when she accepted an invitation to appear before the "lily-white" National Press Club. Members of the African American press in the Capital Press Club charged that they had been refused admission, and Scott now found her scheduled appearance before the club problematic. The press wrote, "If this is the extent of democracy being practiced by the National Press Club, then we would find some difficulty in reconciling Miss Scott's appearance at the dinner with the dramatic protestation for justice often voiced by her husband, Congressman Adam Clayton Powell, Jr."[114] Scott, concerned with the way her invitation might be perceived in the African American community, declined to attend.

She attributed her decision to two precedents: "'One, the fact that the National Press Club excluded Negro journalists, even though they are members of the American Newspaper Guild whose membership consists of both white and Negro correspondents.' ... Two, 'as you know, Negro journalists have been excluded from the press galleries of the House and the Senate.'"[115]

By the mid-1940s, the African American press began to cover Scott's campaign against race discrimination more than they covered her performances. As December 1945 approached, she announced that "she would tour the country fighting 'DAR-ism' much the same as Frank Sinatra is combating racial prejudice."[116] Sinatra's defense of black entertainers subjected to segregation was well-known, particularly his defense of Sammy Davis Jr., with whom he performed extensively. Scott became affiliated with the People's Council, an organization Powell had founded to lobby against racist practices. Scott contended, "I am ready to fight now, not for myself alone, but for all [members of] my race. Since V-J Day, three Negroes have been lynched in this democracy."[117] Her anger was further fueled by conditions that she was experiencing herself while touring: in St. Louis, she was denied hotel accommodations, and in Booneville, Missouri, she was refused service at a bus terminal restaurant.[118] Scott's tour was characterized as a "tolerance tour," and it exposed the segregated practices she endured.[119]

By 1946, Scott was being heralded in the African American press as "an eloquent and effective fighter against discrimination and intolerance."[120] Refusing to compromise her convictions, in 1947 Scott refused to perform for a mixed-race audience of some seven thousand at the University of Texas at Austin after noticing that African Americans were restricted to segregated seating. She had already been refused housing accommodations in Austin prior to her scheduled performance. After consulting with Powell and before publicizing her decision, she made it known that she would not perform, declaring, "I am proud of the fact that I am the first colored artist to refuse to play to segregated audiences. I started this, four years ago."[121] Scott's contract stipulated that she would not perform for segregated audiences, and *Negro Digest* affirmed: "She has never played a Jim Crow theater and her contract contains a clause prohibiting the segregation of colored people."[122] Aware that her actions had political implications, Scott wrote, "At this time when our President has been elected on the issue of civil rights and also when my husband is sponsoring all the civil rights legislation in the House of Representatives, I can do no less than refuse to be a silent partner of Jim Crowism."[123] Unfortunately, several months later, in a case of two steps forward one step back, Marian Anderson did perform at the University of Texas and was complicit in Austin's Jim Crow practices. Anderson, who had been supported by the press in the DAR issue, might have anticipated the bitter criticism she received from the African American press. The *Chicago Defender* charged, "Miss Anderson is endorsing all the Jim Crow and prejudice they have fought against so long. . . ."[124] By utilizing these sagas of popular African American entertainers, the black press strove to promote new racial policies that they viewed as germane to the nation.

Scott was barred from restaurant service in Pasco, Washington, when she arrived for a concert in 1949. When she complained of this racial affront to police, they endorsed the restaurant's policy. Infuriated by such blatant disregard for her civil liberties, Scott reported the incident to the press.[125] She later filed a $50,000 lawsuit against the restaurant for damages. As the case unfolded, it was noted that when she reported the violation of her rights to the police, they ordered her to leave their office, and arriving at her hotel after a considerable delay, she reportedly had not eaten for twenty-seven hours.[126] She received only $250 in damages, an insult but a victory in principle.[127] Scott's tour was a relatively profitable one, earning her approximately $120,000 for seventy-five concerts, but she nonetheless had to endure the same discriminatory practices faced by other African Americans of the period.[128]

In January 1949, Scott and Powell received considerable coverage in the African American press for their positive contributions to the social and political struggles of the times. They were featured in an *Ebony* magazine article with a family photo on the front cover. The article is best described as a sentimental essay that focused on their attraction to each other, their success in their professions—the merging of entertainment with politics—and their marital pleasures and woes.[129] It received a variety of responses from the African American community, with one letter to the editor that declared, "I for one am nauseated from looking at and hearing about Hazel and Adam. It was a great shock to me to learn that Congressman Powell would permit publication of any such article over his name. It seems in very poor taste. It also seems in bad taste for the Powell[s] to continue to parade their wealth so brazenly. I wonder if many people are interested in that or in their intimate private lives."[130]

The *Ebony* article included Powell's characterization of Scott, whom he described as a political activist:

> very militant in terms of her peculiar position as a Negro Artist and in rela-
> tion to the struggle of her people for equality everywhere. She accepts no
> Jim Crow bookings nor will she play in a town where [desegregated] hotel
> facilities are unobtainable. Her contract with Columbia Concerts contains
> a very significant clause which says that if hotel accommodations for her-
> self and party cannot be arranged without strings the engagement is off.[131]

Despite or because of her militancy, Scott was continually marginalized as an entertainer. In May 1949, the *Pittsburgh Courier* announced that she had again been barred from performing at Constitution Hall by the DAR, but I have not found any corroborating reports to substantiate this accusation.[132]

One of the most turbulent events in Scott's career occurred in 1950, when she encountered segregated practices at the University of North Carolina at Chapel Hill and refused to perform. She was scheduled to perform on March 22 and 23 at Memorial Hall, the campus's main concert hall.[133] She apparently arrived late due to inclement weather. Her flight was redirected to Richmond, Virginia, and she had to travel to Raleigh by train and from there to Chapel Hill by car. Upon her arrival, she did perform, but she altered her originally planned program.[134] On the second night, Scott refused to perform when she discovered that African Americans were confined to one section of the balcony. She later agreed to perform only before a student audience; others who had previously purchased tickets were issued a refund.[135] The university stated that it had been unaware of Scott's policy of refusing to perform in segregated facilities; this policy had been inserted in her contract in the years 1945 through 1947, but had been removed because its very inclusion was considered offensive.[136] Reviewing her Chapel Hill performance, one critic observed, "Hazel Scott, a graduate of the Never-Let-Your-Right-Hand-Know-What-Your-Left-Is-Doing school of piano playing, gave her third concert last night in Memorial Hall in less than two years, and it was the usual howling success."[137]

One white ticket holder, John Poindexter Jr., submitted a letter to the editor of the UNC's student newspaper, the *Daily Tarheel*, expressing his

disturbance at the auditorium's having acceded to the "situation" that
Scott had caused:

> the balcony was reserved for Negroes and tickets were sold to them long
> before eight o'clock, while Carolina students shivered in line, awaiting
> seats they had already paid for and were even then unsure of obtaining.
>
> Frankly, the situation "reeked" to high heaven and I, for one, suggest
> that the practice be discontinued immediately. I am a native of this state
> and I did not enter this tax supported institution to have tolerance shoved
> down my throat or to have the services that I have paid for denied me in
> preference to some rank outsider. . . . Is it not indeed possible that a minor-
> ity might persecute a majority on occasion?[138]

It is of note that in a later period, Scott referred to the clause in her
contract. She affirmed that "I come from a very proud people and from the
very beginning my contracts had a clause stating I would not perform for
segregated audiences. It cost me quite a few contracts. It all seems funny
now . . . and that's one of the reasons I stayed in Europe. All of a sudden
these Johnny-come-lately-instant-Africans started asking me where I
stood in The Fight. I needed a vacation from them too."[139]

SCOTT'S POLITICAL VIEWS IMPACT HER CAREER

Scott's popularity began to decline as she became more politically active.
Reports surfaced that although she had signed for a twenty-six-week television show sponsored by a facial tissue manufacturer, the show was canceled.[140] Donald Bogle wrote, "Despite good ratings her television show
was not renewed."[141] Scott's political positions rendered her threatening to
the entertainment world, particularly after she was listed in Red Channels,
a publication designed to identify entertainers suspected of communist
leanings. In the late 1940s, Scott, Paul Robeson, Langston Hughes, and
others were declared communist sympathizers and were "accused of pro-
tecting Communists who run afoul of the law by the House Un-American
Activities Committee."[142] Specific charges against Scott, according to Red
Channels, were that she was affiliated with a large number of subversive
organizations, including the National Citizens Political Action Committee, the Citizens' Non-Partisan Committee to Elect Benjamin J. Davis
Jr., the Progressive Citizens of America—the Citizens Committee of the
Upper West Side, the Musicians Congress Committee, the American

Committee for Protection of Foreign Born, the American Peace Mobilization, the Artists' Front to Win the War, the Joint Anti-Fascist Refugee Committee, and the Civil Rights Congress.[143] She was forced to defend herself against such charges and restore her good name for the public. Investigated by the House Un-American Activities Committee, she testified on her own behalf before the Committee on September 22, 1950. According to the *Baltimore Afro-American*, "Miss Scott desired to appear before the committee because her name was included in *Red Channels*."[144]

In defending herself, Scott stood by her convictions, much as she had done throughout her life. Among her remarks, she vowed that she would not be deterred by attempts to defame her character, proclaiming, "We should not be written off by the vicious slanders of little and petty men. We are one of your most effective and irreplaceable instruments in the grim struggle ahead. We will be much more useful to America if we do not enter this battle covered with the mud of slander and the filth of scandal."[145] Attempting to refute claims that she was a communist sympathizer, she declared:

> *Red Channels* mentions my name as "reported" connected with nine organizations it considers subversive. One of these listings was for an appearance, by direction of my employer, which was perfectly proper at the time. Another was ostensibly a series of benefits for orphaned children. As soon as I found out otherwise, I discontinued my activity. Still another involved use of my name [three] years after I played a benefit for a group which thereafter merged with one that developed a bad name. A fourth advertised that I was guest of honor at a dinner I never went to or even heard of.[146]

As for her "association with communism," Scott emphatically denounced communism, but asserted:

> While I am unalterably opposed to communism and all other forms of totalitarianism, I am also wholeheartedly for the alleviation of poverty and oppression at home and abroad....
>
> Furthermore, I will maintain my fight for the application of our liberties to all, regardless of color and creed. Those of the far left and far right have no place in this fight. The latter have no respect for liberty; nor do the former, although they mouth the slogans. But the fact that Communists pretend to stand for the causes for which I stand will not make me abandon the battle.... But I refuse to surrender the burning issue of our day to the enemies of democracy.[147]

Despite the efforts of her accusers to marginalize Scott because of her race, sexuality, and political orientation, she, like Horne, remained politically active. One source affirmed that "troubles began for her [Scott] when it became obvious that this black woman believed she had all the rights and privileges of a white male."[148] Scott endured tax troubles with the Internal Revenue Service in 1954 when it was reported that she failed to pay some $10,844—an amount due on her income taxes that she should have paid.[149] Added to her woes, following the dissolution of her marriage to Powell in the 1950s, she moved to Paris, where she continued her political activism:

> In fact, a march on the American embassy in France (to coincide with the 1963 March on Washington) was organized from her Paris bedroom. She was laid up with a broken hand when writer James Baldwin, actor Bill Marshall, and photographer Richard Avedon came to talk to her about some sort of sympathy demonstration, Hazel enlisted actor Anthony Quinn in the project and later she marched with her arm in a sling.[150]

During the more turbulent decade of the 1960s, Scott declared that her activism was evident in that she was among the first to wear her hair in a natural style. Added to this, she wanted to respond to those critics who accused an older generation of being less politically active. Scott stated,

> I have a deep and abiding resentment for the so-called "new Negro," because I think he has been a little late in arriving, Number one.... Number two: I'd like to know where were they—and they're going to say they weren't born, but their parents were here—25 years ago when I put myself out of work, when I was called, among some of the kinder things, a black Joan of Arc, a Communist and radical, a professional black lady and an apologist for my race. I was told that I waved my color like a banner. I am not about to sit still, now, and let anybody tell me that nothing was done until these "new Negroes" started letting their hair grow long. I didn't wear my hair in its natural state, that is to say combed high ... and with various costumes, because I was angry about being black. I did it because I thought it was beautiful, and I still do. But if somebody is going around wearing a large scowl to go with the hairdo as a badge proclaiming, "I have this hair and I am better than you," then they are quite wrong. There are a great many Negroes who will never be able to have what is known as a "natural" because their hair is just not nappy enough. Let's not go in the other direction and become reverse snobs.[151]

Scott further revealed that following her return to the United States after living in Paris, the government wanted her to testify against her husband, who was being prosecuted for tax evasion. She stated, "When I returned to America last March, when it was thought that perhaps the government had brought me back as a prosecution witness in the Powell tax case, the enemy loved me. When it became clear that I had timed my arrival to coincide exactly with the trial of my son's father, and that I refused to be used by anyone, the picture slowly began to change. Doors that stood ajar slowly closed."[152]

Although commodified throughout her professional life as the quintessential entertainer, Scott always fought against the marginalization she endured. She also fought for causes that extended beyond her own career. Becoming politically active and increasing her political involvement despite the danger to her person and her career, she served as a beacon of determined resistance to racialization, sexualization, and social oppression in all its manifestations. Her political activities may have led to her tragic demise; life for this singular African American performer, actress, and woman of conviction and courage ended in alcoholism and obscurity. Yet throughout her life, "the most notable element was . . . what could have been."[153]

Scott's response to her commodification is perhaps best understood by returning to Diawara's assessment that if the "dominant reading [of the story] compels the Black spectator to identify with the racist inscription of the Black character—and the resistance, on the part of Afro-American spectators, to this version of US history [in reference to *Birth of a Nation*], on account of its Manichean dualism," then the black spectator is dually positioned.[154] Thrust into the positions of both the spectacle and the spectator, Scott was positioned ambivalently and at times responded ambivalently, unable to consistently resist the inscription implied by her role as an entertainer.

Scott remained uncompromising in her principles and committed to her political views. She epitomizes the black actress who resisted her on- and off-screen objectification despite the marginalization she endured. Even toward the end of her career, she was still holding dear to her beliefs and principles.

EIGHT

Ethel Waters

PERSONIFICATION OF OTHERNESS

Lena Horne recounts an incident that happened during the filming of *Cabin in the Sky* when Ethel Waters blew "like a hurricane," lashing out at Horne and at "the whole system that had held her back and exploited her." It seems true that Horne was "the immediate cause" of Waters's outburst, for what Horne represented certainly could have been at the heart of Waters's frustration and anger.[1] Horne represented what Hattie McDaniel, naming Horne specifically, had referred to as the "new Negro womanhood" (the sultry, mulatto sex symbol) that Hollywood was privileging over another group of African American actresses to which McDaniel and Waters belonged, the mammy-maid group of darker-complexioned black actresses who were not necessarily sex symbols. To be sure, two of Waters's outstanding dramatic screen performances placed her in this second group: Berenice (*The Member of the Wedding*, 1952) and Dilsey (*The Sound and the Fury*, 1959). But Hollywood exploited both of these groups of black actresses—though perhaps for different purposes—and these two groups were not the only groups subjected to exploitation in the Hollywood film industry.

As the African American actress became a signifier of racial and sexual codes that allowed Hollywood to explore its repressed fears and desires, the African American woman became central to what was problematic about Hollywood. This is particularly evident in films regarded as feminist films or women's pictures, in which the African American actress, as racial Other, is rendered vital to the development of narratives that foreground white women. Though the African American woman remains curiously visible in these narratives, she still is a form of the shadow. It is as though white female liberation was thought to be unachievable without the presence of a racial Other.

While this inextricable link between the black female and the white female is evident in other films (e.g., *Imitation of Life*, 1934), it is especially marked in *The Member of the Wedding*. Featuring African American actress Ethel Waters and white actress Julie Harris, the film explores the bond that develops between these two women and, at the same time, reconstructs Waters's biography. *The Member of the Wedding* best illustrates how the cinema industry used Waters as a black actress and provides one of the best representations of Waters's rare dramatic screen performances (with the possible exception of *Pinky*, 1949). Although Waters did appear in other films, it is her appearance in this film that best captures what she contributed to the cinema industry and that resonates most closely with her own personal life experiences.

Ethel Waters, born October 31, 1896, in Chester, Pennsylvania, was the daughter of Louisa Tar Anderson and John Wesley Waters, a white pianist who died when Ethel was three years old. Some reports allege that Louise became pregnant with Ethel after being raped by John Waters when she was only twelve years old. In her early years, Ethel was reared by her maternal grandmother, Sally Anderson, in Chester and in nearby Philadelphia, in abject poverty. As a youngster, Ethel frequently ran errands for people affiliated with the sex industry in order to earn money for herself. At the age of thirteen, she married Merritt "Buddy" Purnsley, a marriage that lasted two years. Shortly afterwards, Waters was forced to work as a chambermaid and laundress in a Philadelphia hotel. On the advice of two young men, she was encouraged to sing on stage, where her performance was observed by Arthur Braxton and Clarence Nugent, vaudeville agents who then recruited her to appear in a two-week performance at the Lincoln Theatre in Baltimore. It was here that she received permission from W. C. Handy and his music publishers to perform his song "St. Louis Blues," becoming the first woman on stage to present an American jazz classic.[2]

These early ventures launched Waters's career as a nightclub singer, allowing her to tour the United States, where she was often billed as the "Sweet Mama Stringbean." In 1921, she made her first recording with the Cardinal Company and popularized the songs "New York Glide" and

"At the New Jump Steady Ball." These recordings spawned a series of hit records over the next two decades, including "Dinah," "Stormy Weather," and "Am I Blue?" Later, working with the Black Swan recording company, she became the first prominent black recording artist who was not classified primarily as a blues singer. Returning to the nightclub scene, Waters frequently performed with entertainers such as Fletcher Henderson and established herself as a successful musical entertainer even though she could not read music. In 1925, she served as a substitute singer for Florence Mills at the Harlem Plantation Club. Despite such lucrative invitations, she declined an opportunity to travel to Paris because of her reluctance to perform for white audiences. Two years later, however, Waters had her first Broadway appearance on stage in *Africana,* giving her a level of exposure that resulted in Earl Dancer serving as her manager.

Waters first made the transition from stage to screen in 1929 when she appeared in *On with the Show.*[3] The 1930s was a decade marked by numerous performances both on stage and screen, as well as marriages. Temporarily interrupting her career, Waters married for a second time, this time to Clyde Edward "Eddie" Matthews. After that marriage dissolved, she married a third time, to Eddie Mallory. These marriages occurred as she advanced her stage and screen careers. For example, she performed on stage in Lew Leslie's *Blackbirds* and Sam Harris's *Rhapsody in Black.* In 1933, she was cast in the stage musical *As Thousands Cheer,* along with Clifton Webb and Marilyn Miller, while also appearing on screen in *Rufus Jones for President.* The next year she appeared in the films *Bubbling Over* and *Gift of the Gab,* and in 1935 she costarred with Beatrice Lillie in the play *At Home Abroad.* These stage and screen performances drew the attention of DuBose and Dorothy Heyward, who recruited her to appear in *Porgy.* She then expressed interest in performing in the stage production of *Mamba's Daughters*—a production that garnered her a first-rate dramatic role.[4]

During the 1940s, Waters starred on Broadway in *Cabin in the Sky* and later reprised her starring role when the play was adapted for the screen. Prior to her role in the film version of *Cabin in the Sky* (1943), Waters landed two additional screen roles in *Tales of Manhattan* (1942), where she was cast opposite Paul Robeson, and *Cairo* (1942), in which she was cast as a maid. Waters was able to combine her increased stature as an actress as well as a singer in the film *Stage Door Canteen* (1943), which fea-

tured her in a singing role. During the spring of 1945 Waters starred in the
stage revue *Blue Holiday,* and by the year's end she sang at the New York
Embassy Club. After assuming a number of small engagements between
1946 and 1948, Waters returned to the screen in *Pinky* (1949), playing the
grandmother of a black woman who passes as white. For this performance
she received an Academy Award nomination and was recognized for her
acting talent by the Negro Actors Guild.[5]

By the 1950s, Waters returned to Broadway to appear in *The Member
of the Wedding*—a stage production that would later be made into a film.
In both the play and the film, she was cast in a primary role as the surrogate mother figure to a white adolescent, played by Julie Harris. This role
garnered Waters her second Academy Award nomination.

Waters worked in radio and also appeared on television in *The Beulah Show,* but she left the show within a year. In 1951, Waters published
her autobiography, *His Eye Is on the Sparrow* (written in collaboration
with Charles Samuels), a book that became the Book of the Month Club
selection for March of 1951. Waters also frequently returned to the stage,
appearing in her one-woman show titled *An Evening with Ethel Waters.*
By the late 1950s, despite having made at least a million dollars as a performer, Waters became frustrated with her entertainment career, and as
her health began to decline she renewed her commitment to her religious
faith and joined evangelist Billy Graham's crusade at Madison Square
Garden in New York City. When the crusade ended, Waters returned to
Los Angeles. There her health continued to decline as she suffered from
heart disease, diabetes, hypertension, and sight problems. Yet despite her
ill health, in 1958 she appeared in the religious-themed film *The Heart Is
a Rebel,* and the following year she appeared in *The Sound and the Fury,*
where she was cast with Yul Brynner and Joanne Woodward.[6]

In the 1960s, Waters continued to appear in her one-woman show
and also performed in a stage revival of *The Member of the Wedding* in
Pasadena, La Jolla, and Santa Barbara. She remained with this revival
well into the 1970s, when it toured Chicago. During this period she continued to perform with Billy Graham's crusades and to give concerts at
churches and religious conventions. In 1971, Waters was invited to sing
at a Sunday worship service at the White House, and a year later she
returned as a guest at the wedding of Richard Nixon's daughter Tricia.
In 1972, Waters published her second autobiography, *To Me It's Won-*

derful, and was honored by Billy Graham at a testimonial ceremony in California. On September 1, 1977, Waters died at the home of Juliann and Paul DeKorte of Chatsworth, California, after suffering from a bout with cancer.[7]

REFLECTIONS OF THE SELF:
WATERS AND BERENICE

Waters's performance in the screen version of *The Member of the Wedding* reflects how she personified Otherness. No matter how powerful a performer she was, she could not escape being cast as either a subservient or a matriarchal figure. Despite such typecasting, however, Waters's role is this film is significant because of the parallels between this role and her off-screen life: Waters's matriarchal stature, her adolescent marriage, her multiple marriages, her identity as a singer, and her strong religious faith. While the parallels might have been unintentional, Waters's "interpretation" of the character certainly brings such parallels to the fore. Undeniably, the Waters/Berenice parallel became a box-office boon for Hollywood. By linking the real-life Waters with the character Berenice, filmmakers could generate appeal for the film and capitalize on the popularity Waters had previously enjoyed as an entertainer.

While she eventually transformed the character of Berenice in such a way that it mirrored her own life, initially Waters declined the role, adamantly declaring, "No, I won't do it. Berenice Sadie Brown, the cook you want me to play, is a bitter woman. She's a chain smoker, drinks heavily, and has lost her faith in God. I won't deny there are characters like her in real life. I've met such women. But Berenice is sordid and ugly and she's not for me to play. I wouldn't work well in that channel."[8] Berenice, as the filmmakers originally conceived her, was a mask Waters would not parade. But she was an actress and therefore could have been expected to take on whatever role she was asked to portray, to wear whatever mask she was assigned. It was not until she was allowed to adapt this character to her own style that she accepted the role: Waters met with Carson McCullers, the author of the novel from which the film was adapted, and was given permission to "interpret the role in her own way."[9] She wrote, "Free to give my own interpretation, the character of Berenice satisfied me. She had been buffeted plenty, but now she was not without humor, and she had retained her faith in God. Besides this, she was moved and guided always by the memory of her one great love."[10] Taking such a stand took great courage on Waters's part; she personified the liberated female in real life, in control of her professional career.

Based on McCullers's novel of the same title, *The Member of the Wedding* was first adapted to the stage and later modified for the screen. The film focuses on the internal conflict of Frankie Addams, a young white adolescent (Julie Harris), as she makes the transition from adolescence to adulthood. Frankie's conflict is brought to the foreground when her brother Jarvis Addams (Arthur Franz), a soldier and a signifier of white maleness, marries Janice (Nancy Gates), a signifier of white femininity, beauty, and desirability, qualities that Frankie believes she herself sorely lacks. Suffering from feelings of alienation and ostracism that emanate from a variety of sources, Frankie wants to become a member of the wedding, which for her would mean a transformation from the "Me" to the "We." For Frankie, the wedding is symbolic not only of marital bliss, but of her passage into adulthood. Family life has largely escaped her following her mother's untimely death, and happiness has eluded her during these formative years. The wedding is also symbolic of a utopian existence that she feels she has been denied. Frankie is also conflicted about her sexual identity, which the film handles clearly but not blatantly (as might have been the case had the film been produced decades later). Berenice's (Ethel Waters) facilitation of Frankie's transition into adulthood includes Frankie coming to terms with her sexual identity.

Struggling with the pain of being raised by her father after her mother's death, Frankie turns to the African American domestic Berenice, who becomes a sort of surrogate mother. It is Berenice who provides advice, guidance, and assurance to Frankie. She becomes the sounding board by which Frankie can express her inner conflicts and introspection as she comes to terms with herself. The inextricable emotional connection between Berenice and Frankie allows Waters to infuse the character of Berenice with a performative intensity derived from Waters's own life experiences. It is this emotional and performative intensity, rather than a list of specific incidents in Waters's personal life (though there are several), that forms the basic parallel between Waters and Berenice, and it is Bernice's interaction with Frankie that brings these parallels—and Berenice's character—to the film's dramatic foreground.

Berenice is vital to the existence and self-discovery of the young white female, and therefore she is central to this feminist film's narrative. She is centered in Frankie's conflict as she serves both to unveil the conflict and to respond to Frankie's dilemma. A film that might have been claimed by a white woman now revolves around a black woman; it ends when the white woman achieves her liberation and the black woman claims the film as her own. Linda Williams observes that "With a black servant in the home, white women could both remain ladies and at the same time more fully exercise the privileges and authority granted by white skin."[11] While Williams affirms the relationship that existed between the black servant and her white mistress as reconstructed in *The Member of the Wedding,* the empowerment associated with the white mistress is now displaced onto her black servant.

By the time the film went into production in the early 1950s, it was not necessary to use excessive makeup and costuming to make Waters look the part of Bernice as a matriarch and surrogate mother figure. Waters was past fifty years in age, heavy-set, and resembled in other ways the type of character the filmmakers envisioned for Berenice. Because Berenice is a matriarchal figure, the attributes customarily associated with the matriarch (such as wisdom, insight, strength, and power) are also inscribed onto her. She is, therefore, a dominant figure both physically and intellectually.

In many films of the pre-1960 period, the physicality of the black actress as shadow was used as a contrast to enhance the whiteness (sexuality and beauty) of the leading white actress. Lola Young argues that "Standardized notions of beauty are one reason why black women's appearances in mainstream cinema have been so limited. Images of white European women as the standard of beauty are pervasive: those images are the polar opposite of and yet dependent on images of black women's femininity and sexuality."[12] It is of note that Berenice's body is contrasted to that of her white costar, who is thin, small-framed, and small-bosomed. Yet this constructive contrast is not to aggrandize the whiteness of Frankie (who lacks, at least in her mind, beauty and sexual appeal); it is a construction designed to emphasize that Frankie is undeveloped physically, socially, psychologically, and sexually.

Berenice embodies both the mother figure denied to Frankie and the sexuality for which Frankie searches. Ironically (when compared to films of the period), Berenice becomes a signifier of sexuality as rendered in the body. She is stout, large in stature, and full-breasted; she wears the feminine trappings of hat, high-heeled shoes, purse, and so on. Although sexualized and feminized, Berenice is not constructed as sexually alluring; her appeal is implied through her reference to multiple marriages. There is also a hint that T. T. Williams (Harry Bolden) finds Berenice attractive. Williams is a character who represents black maleness and becomes a subordinate who is rendered non-threatening in Berenice's presence. His weakness functions to enhance her strength.

Waters ostensibly draws upon her own maternal instincts, emotions, experiences, and role as a "surrogate" mother herself to shape the character (of Berenice) as a surrogate mother for Frankie. Waters experienced a fulfilling maternal relationship with her godchild, Algretta Holmes, whom she adopted when the child was only eighteen months old.[13] Waters once observed, "You are a person of greatest importance when you are a mother of a family. Just do your job right and your kids will love you. And for that love of theirs there is no satisfying substitute."[14] Waters never had children of her own, and perhaps her failed relationships with men demonstrated a quest for love and affection that seemingly escaped her. Thus her multiple marriages, her maternalistic pursuits, and her close relationships that ultimately ended were infused into her interpretation of Berenice.

Waters's real-life failed relationship with Archie Savage reflected not only her maternalism but also her vulnerability when it involved males. According to Glenda Gill, "The Mallory affair [Waters's third marriage] was in trouble, and Waters took [Archie] Savage as her protégé, or so she said."[15] Zora Neale Hurston asserted that Savage was more than Waters's protégé or secretary:

> She is in love with Archie Savage, who is a talented dancer, and formerly of the [Katherine] Dunham group. They met during the rehearsals for *Cabin in the Sky* and the affair is on! It looks as if they will make a wed, because they are eternally together.[16]

While Waters may have been romantically attracted to Savage, "this was the beginning of her undoing."[17] Perhaps instead of or in addition to a romantic relationship, Waters certainly had a maternal relationship as a surrogate mother to Savage. She allowed Savage to live in her home during her absence. Upon returning from a stage engagement, she discovered that he had stolen some $10,150 in cash and $35,000 worth of her jewels. Disappointed and angered, she took legal action.[18] Savage confessed to the theft, but Waters agreed to his proposition: he would return her possessions contingent upon receiving the deed to her home and ownership of her automobile. The African American press reported that "Miss Waters had earlier startled investigators for the State's attorney's office when she broke into sobs and cried 'God will take care of everything' in refusing to sign a complaint against her ex-secretary [an appointment that Savage later denied] whom she had accused of purloining the valuables from her Blueberry Hills mansion."[19] Ultimately, Savage was required to serve jail time, but some of the facts and certainly the emotions of this relationship bear a striking resemblance to Berenice's and Honey's (James Edwards) relationship in *The Member of the Wedding*.

When Frankie is announcing her plan to leave town after her brother's wedding so that she can be a "We" (desirable) rather than a "Me" (undesirable), she is interrupted by the arrival of Berenice's relative, the jazz trumpeter Honey Camden Brown and his associate, T. T. Williams. Frankie transgresses her racial difference, telling Honey Brown that she is very impressed with his music. He becomes the quintessential black male through his predilection for jazz and perceived violent nature. It is of note that as the surrogate mother to Frankie, Berenice has her racial identity affirmed through the other black characters in the film. That the black males she refers to or encounters are dead, equated with violence, or reduced to subordinate status illustrates how blackness is rendered a negative construct and reifies the blackness embodied by Berenice.[20]

Prior to John Henry's (Frankie's six-year-old cousin's) death, Frankie writes her father a note and leaves home. Her departure is mirrored in Honey's hasty departure. Honey rushes to inform Berenice that he is being pursued by the police because he fled the scene of an accident involving a white man. In an effort to protect Honey, Berenice asks T. T. arrange for his clandestine departure. Distraught over her decision, she understands that this may be the last time she will see Honey. This finality is symbolic of the finality associated with Frankie's departure because it represents Frankie's transformation into an adult, and Berenice recognizes that the transition will spell the end of their relationship.

One circumstance that precipitates Frankie's departure is that she feels intensely the emotions that derive from being ostracized and alienated, largely because of her physical appearance and sexuality, which are interrelated. From Waters's own private life (particularly her failed marriages) and her public life (in particular, her Otherness based on her race, gender, age, and professional marginalization in the film industry), Waters was well-versed in the pain that emanates from ostracism and alienation (actual or perceived). It probably was this pent-up pain and frustration that caused her to verbally explode during the filming of *Cabin in the Sky*.[21]

Waters could and did infuse the character Berenice with these residual emotions. Likewise, Berenice, who also has firsthand knowledge of the experiences that produce these emotions, empathizes with Frankie and, doing what a surrogate mother does, helps her surrogate child cope with the pain of feeling alienated and isolated.

Indeed, Waters's firsthand experiences with ostracism and alienation particularly because of her race are too numerous to recount here. Certainly Waters was subjected to the same kinds of racial discrimination and racist treatment that other actresses and entertainers of the period suffered. A few racist incidents are exemplary of several that compounded the burden for her. Reports circulated in the black press that racial ostracism was evident when southern audiences objected to Waters's radio performance. According to the *Chicago Defender,* "One of the most vicious forms of race prejudice is attributed to the rumored withdrawal of Ethel Waters, singing comedian, from the radio. Southern listeners-in are said to have complained of the star of *As Thousands Cheer* in their letters to the sponsors, [one of] which is the American Oil Company. . . . Miss Waters may [have been] forced to withdraw in favor of some inferior artist."[22]

On Broadway, Waters was maligned in a controversy in which she was charged with contributing to the failing mental health of the white dancer Eleanor Powell.[23] Apparently, because Waters was competition and Powell did not take well to her competitors, particularly those who were marginalized because of their race, Waters was deemed as threatening to Powell's self-concept. Some speculated that this might have exacerbated Powell's mental decline. The African American press contended that blaming Waters was simply a technique to defame and damage the reputation of a black star, because Broadway "does not want women of color [acquiring] top honors on the main stem."[24]

Disturbed that black patrons were charged higher admission prices than whites to attend her Kansas City performance, Waters became even more disillusioned with the racial politics that prevailed in segregated America.[25] Like Hazel Scott, Waters was also barred from performing at Constitution Hall by the Daughters of the American Revolution (DAR).[26] When she was injured in an automobile accident while touring the South, she was ignored by white passers-by. After she was finally taken to a hospital for treatment, the physician scolded Waters: "You needn't holler, gal. This is what all you niggers should get when you wreck white people's cars."[27]

Her response to the discrimination was unfailingly compassionate:

> We are close to this earth and to God. Shut up in ghettos, sneered at, beaten, enslaved, we always have answered our oppressors with brave singing, dancing, and laughing. Our greatest eloquence, the pitch of the joy and sorrow in our unbreakable hearts, comes when we lift up our faces and talk to God, person to person. Ours is the truest dignity of man, the dignity of the undefeated.
>
> I write all of this to explain why I am not bitter and angry at white people. I say in all sincerity that I am sorry for them. What could be more pitiful than to live in such nightmarish terror of another race that you have to lynch them, push them off sidewalks, and never be able to relax your venomous hatred for one moment? As I see it, it is these people, the Ku-Kluxers, the White Supremacists, and the other fire-spitting neurotics who are in deep trouble.[28]

Of African Americans who engage in self-hatred, Waters observed:

> Dicty's and the others among my own people who despise Negroes who are poor and ignorant and condemned to live like animals arouse my fury as no white people ever can. We Negroes have lived through so much together—centuries of slavery, terror, segregation, and unending concentrated abuse—that I'll never understand how some of us who have one way or another been able to lift ourselves a little above the mass of colored people can be so insanely brutal as to try to knock the hell out of our own blood brothers and sisters.[29]

Though she did not allow this array of disturbing experiences to interfere with her career, she probably was not as emotionally resilient as she suggests. Nevertheless, she infuses this emotional resilience into the character of Berenice and uses it to guide her surrogate child, Frankie, into adulthood.

Summarizing Waters's career, Glenda Gill avers that "However 'mean' Waters was, her childhood, her treatment on the T.O.B.A. [Theater Owners Booking Association], her Mammy roles, her segregated world, her bout with the IRS, and her men gave her reason to be. Beautiful and fiery in her youth, vivacious in her middle age, poignant in her twilight years, Waters knew victory and defeat."[30] Her firsthand knowledge of "victory and defeat" is recognizable in what she brings to the character of Berenice. Her comments about how she saw this character were equally applicable to her own life: "She had been buffeted plenty, but . . . she had retained her faith in God."[31]

Though Waters was a victim of racism, it probably was the pain she suffered from the victories and defeats in her private life that helped her shape more fully the character of Berenice. Waters reveals in her autobiography that she was thirteen when she married Merritt "Buddy" Purnsley, a man nearly twice her age. She writes, "There was something terrible about him I disliked and feared, even though he was attractive."[32] Her claim that "it seemed to me that he wanted to marry me only because he couldn't get me any other way"[33] is strikingly similar to the tale of her screen character Berenice, a tale designed to reconstruct how a woman comes to terms with herself. The tale is designed to help Frankie come to terms with herself, and Frankie is reassured when she learns that Berenice married at thirteen, an age close to her own, and so she believes that she, too, can soon become desirable.[34]

Even when Frankie tells Berenice that Janice (her sister-in-law) regards her as beautiful, Berenice reins her in, forcing her to come to terms with herself and suggesting that such comments should not be taken out of context. Frustrated that no one takes her claims of desirability and femininity seriously, Frankie bursts into tears. Her fear is that she has not made a good impression on her future sister-in-law. It seems that Frankie is attempting to displace her frustration with her physical appearance onto Janice, who may not have recognized Frankie's beauty, value, or importance. In a fit of anger and frustration at the rejection she has endured as well as the internal conflict she experiences, Frankie throws a knife into a door. It seems that in an effort to assert her femininity, Frankie decides to excise the maleness in her body and reaches for Berenice's butcher knife. She soon succumbs to Berenice's maternal concern and releases the knife, forcefully throwing it into the back of a closed door. This is another explicit symbol: The knife is the male phallus that penetrates the door or the female, suggesting that Frankie is claiming her feminine self through the penetration of the female body by the phallus. Of course, the knife's symbolism also reflects Frankie's desire for the sex act, or the excision of the maleness that still lingers in her body.

When Frankie questions Berenice about Berenice's own experiences and marriages, she learns that Berenice was married more than once. So was Waters—three times. After Waters's multiple marriages were chronicled in her autobiography, an article appeared in *Ebony* magazine titled "The Men in My Life," which described her tumultuous marriages and reflected on her relationships with several men. Published primarily to promote her newly released autobiography, the article exposed the sensationalism of her private life.[35]

Waters characterized her third spouse, Eddie Mallory, as a fine trumpet player, but their relationship dissolved when the property holdings he encouraged her to invest in never materialized: "Whenever I mixed up romance and my bank account, I seemed to end up with no dough and even less romance."[36]

Waters admitted that she was attracted to her second husband, Clyde Edward Matthews, because "he was a handsome devil, with a courtly air, a real charmer."[37] By this time Waters was a popular song stylist. She credits Matthews with inspiring her to perfect her rendition of "Stormy Weather," a song that in her words signified "my misery and confusion . . . the misunderstandings in my life that I couldn't straighten out . . . the wrongs and outrages done to me by people I had loved and trusted."[38] Her singing allowed her to come to terms with her inner turmoil, and that turmoil provided her with a depth of feeling that gave her songs their power and impact: "Only those who have been hurt deeply can understand what pain is, or humiliation. Only those who are burned know what fire is like. I sang 'Stormy Weather' from the depths of the private hell in which I was being crushed and suffocated."[39]

Summarizing her multiple marriages and endless relationships with men, she declared, "All the men in my life have been two things: an epic and an epidemic."[40] This is a trait that she may have shared with Berenice. If Waters took something valuable from her third failed marriage (to Eddie Matthews), it was a full understanding of the power of song as a cathartic. The function of "Stormy Weather" in her internal life seems to be replicated in Berenice's rendition of "His Eye Is On the Sparrow." Waters's version of "Stormy Weather" was very personal; in her words, it expressed all the "misery," "confusions," "misunderstandings," "wrongs and outrages" she had suffered, especially from the people she "loved and trusted." When Berenice sings "His Eye Is On the Sparrow," the song is a cathartic for her (and for Frankie) for those miseries, confusions, misunderstandings, wrongs, and outrages the two of them have suffered. It is an expression of Berenice's retention of her faith in God. After the film, the song became the signature song of Waters's unwavering faith in God, despite her many trials and tribulations.

As a stylist, Waters's music frequently expressed the pain and agony she endured in the discriminatory treatment she faced. In fact, she once was described as

> Tragedy and comedy all rolled into one. Long limbed, lithe, natural, with a winsomely winning smile which seems to reach right across the footlights to go deep into the hearts of those who hear her, this star typifies with the lifting of an eyelid, the sway of her body, the expression of her eyes, and the haunting melody of her husky voice that something which is typical of the entire Negro race. She appears at times to be a little bird in a gilded cage, crying for liberty; at other times she is the personification of that comedy streak in the Senegambian which peeps forth even in the face of oppression. In short, Ethel Waters is the artiste supreme....[41]

Waters's transformation into Berenice, described as "perfection itself" and "richly compassionate,"[42] is fully captured in her singing style, which she perfected off screen. Commenting on the spirit in her music, she once recalled, "There was one emotional outlet my people always had when they had the blues. That was singing. I'd listen, fascinated by the stories told in the songs. Later, when I sang those same old songs, both folk songs and popular numbers, on the stage or on the radio, they gained nationwide attention."[43] As she reinterpreted the character of Berenice from the original script, Waters drew upon her life experiences and her expertise as a song stylist to bring both humor and tragedy to the character she played. She saw Berenice as originally scripted as "a bitter woman."[44] Enduring physical and mental abuse in her marriage to Purnsley, Waters "felt defiled and besmirched.... Maybe my disillusioning experience with Buddy had made me bitter."[45] Nevertheless, she does not bring this intense bitterness from her own experience to the character she plays because as an actress (and as a person), she "wouldn't work well in that channel."[46]

BERENICE AND FRANKIE: REFLEXIVE OTHERNESS

To deconstruct the way in which filmmakers positioned Waters in *The Member of the Wedding*, I will examine both her role and that of her white costar to determine how the white female in search of femininity locates herself through the black female Other. As I see it, Frankie and Berenice are inextricably bound in this film; in several ways they are reflexive and reflections of the Other. To examine Frankie's search for femininity and adulthood through her black maidservant, we must first analyze Frankie's discontent, internal struggles, and neurotic behavior. Frankie enters the film walking alone on the narrow sidewalk of an empty street, surrounded only by hedges. Her isolation and loneliness are palpable. She walks toward the camera, giving the illusion that she is on a journey, as a voice-over narration both distances her from the world that surrounds her and foregrounds her internal conflict. The scene invites spectators to question Frankie's sexuality: she wears a short, boyish haircut, jeans, and a short-sleeved shirt. When she speaks, her feminine voice directly contrasts with her physical appearance. This juxtaposition of Frankie's feminine voice and masculine appearance plays on the internal discord she harbors—a conflict accentuated by her masculine name, Frankie. "Her lithe—almost boyish—body is often emphasized by the camera . . . [and seems] to call into question [her] sexual identity."[47] The physical codes connoting maleness and femaleness provide the drama and heighten Frankie's conflict. The film also plays with racial and ethnic codes. Frankie hangs a Mexican hat around her neck, which connotes Otherness. Conceivably, the signifier of one type of racial Otherness draws an association to another form of Otherness. Although this nexus is never developed, her association with African Americans and African American culture is developed.

Returning home, Frankie volunteers to serve mint juleps to Jarvis, Jarvis's fiancé Janice, and Frankie's father as they gather to plan the wedding. Her entrance almost appears to be an intrusion; she stands while they remain seated. In the discourse of what follows, Frankie's clumsy appearance as a gawky twelve-year-old contrasts with the pristine femininity of Janice, who is well-dressed, well-spoken, well-mannered, and neatly coifed. Janice also represents desirability because she is the bride-to-be. Frankie (played by an adult actress) appears to be much older than twelve years old; had her age not been established by the film, her signification as an adolescent would have been impossible to discern and thematically disruptive. Although Frankie expresses delight at Jarvis and Janice's marriage, her delight is undermined by her pain at not being accepted as an adult. Her conflict, established in the film's opening scene, is not fully developed until she encounters her racial Other. As she discusses the couple's wedding plans with Berenice, she expresses sadness that she is losing her brother and will become even more isolated. Lola Young contends that "white women—both middle and working class—and black people are again both implicated here as both were characterized as being dependent on others, and as being defined only through their oppositional relationship to white middle class men."[48] Frankie's dependence on Jarvis, who in her estimation becomes a signifier of her own self-worth, is made glaringly apparent. It is at this point, when she exposes her feelings to Berenice, that Frankie's internal conflict is metamorphosed—a conflict that is best understood by providing a psychoanalytic reading.

Freud contends that while girls experience penis envy, boys experience castration anxiety.[49] Frankie, who occupies a space transfixed between maleness and femaleness, seems to experience both. Lacan contends that as a woman desires the phallus, she is forced to reject some aspects of her femininity, while for men who desire the phallus, no woman is adequate.[50] It is conceivable that Frankie's internal conflict is related to desire and to a rejection of both the masculine and the feminine position.

In a similar vein, Judith Butler has challenged this distinction between masculine and feminine positions and questions whether or not they are actually distinguishable.[51] The idea that Frankie's femininity is being sacrificed for the sake of masculinity is certainly plausible in this film. Her internal struggle can be read as a conflict about her own sexuality, as the two competing forces, masculinity and femininity, engage in a struggle for dominance. When Frankie laments, "I've been just an 'I' person but I want to be a 'We' person," the dichotomy of self versus Other, of adolescence versus adulthood, and of masculinity versus femininity becomes explicit. In her effort to resolve her dilemma—to end the quest to become desirable, united, connected, or even a whole person—she declares her intent to move in with her brother and his bride; they will then become the "We of Me." The implication, of course, is that her unification with them not only qualifies them to be referred to as "We," but also gives her meaning and an identity: she refers to herself as the "Me" who is now transformed as "We." But more than that, this unification will resolve her internal conflict with respect to her sexuality as she moves between masculinity and femininity.

Frankie's sexual ambiguity is not confined to her body and is heightened when she rejects a doll she once enjoyed in childhood, symbolizing a rejection of her childhood and, to some degree, of her femininity. Her questions prompt Berenice to ask if Jarvis's marriage has caused her to be envious or jealous. Frankie's innermost complexities are exposed when she remarks that it is all so "queer"—the screenwriter's not so subtle attempt to call attention to her ambiguous sexuality. Frankie then reveals that her brother and future sister-in-law represent the ideal; she characterizes them as "the two prettiest people I ever saw." Preoccupied with beauty, she uses Jarvis and Janice as the standard by which to reject her former playmate, her six-year-old cousin John Henry (Brandon De Wilde). She proclaims that she is not interested in playing outside with the other children, whom she regards as "just a crowd of ugly silly children." Her standard of beauty reflects her unique subject position at the intersection of masculinity and femininity, adulthood and childhood, and self and Other. It also reflects the way she both accepts and rejects herself and may even reflect the difference between her and Berenice.

Because Frankie's internal conflict has been rendered as sexual, the black woman, through her sexuality, comes to Frankie's rescue. In her examination of the racial and sexual implications of photographs, Sander Gilman provides a useful analysis by linking the white employer to the black servant through their sexuality. Gilman ascertains that "the illicit nature of their sexual relationship [meaning the subjects displayed in the photo] . . . is thereby linked to the appearance of the figure of the black servant."[52] This link is particularly useful for exploring the relationship established in *The Member of the Wedding*. Examining Freud's dark continent trope, Mary Anne Doane argues that "a metonymic chain is constructed which links infantile sexuality, female sexuality, and racial Otherness."[53] Acknowledging that racial and sexual codes are inscribed onto the black female body, Gilman notes that "Freud ties the image of female sexuality to the image of the colonial black and to the perceived relationship between the female's ascribed sexuality and the Other's exoticism and pathology."[54] By this analysis, Frankie turns to her black maid Berenice to locate her own sexuality. Her voyeuristic gaze at the black female's body may resolve her own quest. This is conceivable when we consider Frantz Fanon's assertion that "When the whites feel that they have become too mechanized, they turn to the men of color . . . for a little human sustenance."[55]

In the words of Kaja Silverman, Berenice becomes "the acoustic mirror" by which Frankie looks at herself, engages in self-reflection, and examines her competing sexual identities.[56] Berenice, as a black woman, connotes sexuality, and therefore she becomes the site where Frankie can explore and challenge her own conflicted sexual construction. Gilman further notes that "the concupiscence of the black is thus associated also with the sexuality of the lesbian."[57] But it is not only her feminine sexuality that she seeks to reclaim through Berenice, it is also her intellect.

Berenice is the vehicle by which Frankie makes the journey to her own sexuality, maturity, and self. An exclusive neighborhood girls' club denies Frankie admission; here the women are feminized in dress and demeanor. Again, Frankie turns to Berenice for solace and guidance. Attributing her rejection to the fact that she has boils on her skin (from an infection), Frankie is forced to use an ointment that emits unpleasant odors, thus rendering her more undesirable, an Other. As an Other, she becomes inextricably linked to disease; this is a position affirmed by Gilman, who maintains that "the function of the sexualized female [is] as the sign of disease."[58] Berenice advises Frankie to start her own club. Frankie, who is really attempting to escape the masculinization that is written onto her female body, proposes changing her name, as though that will alter her identity. Changing her name from Frankie to Janice or even Jasmine will allow her feminine self to escape from her masculine body. She sees naming as a way to transcend sexual confusion in her attempt to claim or locate her sexuality and as a way to validate her feminine identity by linking herself to the male she has come to idolize, her brother.

Explaining why she cut her hair, Frankie tells Berenice that she wanted to minimize her height (she is 5'5" and only twelve years old) and to compensate for her awkwardness. When she realizes that instead of compensating for her height, the haircut has intensified her masculine appearance, she feels like a "freak, like the freaks exhibited at the fair."

The term "freak" is used strategically here; it plays upon her ambiguous sexuality, since gays have been demeaned through the use of the term. Berenice reassures Frankie that she is certainly not a freak, for she will "fill out" or mature in adolescence. It is Gilman who contends that "we can see the link established between the ill, the bestial, and the freak."[59] Thus, the black subservient becomes integral to the young white female's search for liberation from her maleness.

With her father's approval, Frankie purchases a dress for the wedding, but in her attempt to be especially feminine, she selects a long satin gown. When Berenice sees the gown, she exclaims that it is excessive, in much the same way that femininity has been characterized as excess.[60] Berenice remarks, "I'm not used to seeing . . . Christmas in August." Frankie, disappointed with this reaction, concedes that the dress is inappropriate. Meanwhile, as her double, John Henry mimics Frankie, entering the room dressed in an angel costume, mocking her extravagant claims of femininity. In response, she calls him two-faced and a Judas; and as she attempts to come to terms with herself, she vows that while the gown may be inappropriate, her intent to leave town (an act that will allow her to claim her femininity) is still very real.

Berenice suggests that Frankie invite a young male to the wedding as her escort—an act that will allow her to establish her femininity. Frankie then would be positioned to form her own union and become a "We," and thus desirable. Frankie resists Berenice and parades around with a bucket over her head to reflect her feeling of being an "ugly duckling." In her whiteness, she parades in the blackness of the bucket, nearly masquerading as a black Other.

While Frankie's wearing of the bucket is symbolic of her desire to transgress racial difference—to vicariously experience blackness—this desire becomes transfigured in her conversation regarding death. She wishes death upon the girls who rejected her and discusses death with Berenice. Fanon contends that blackness has become associated with death, thus it is "natural" that Frankie engage in this discussion of death with her black surrogate mother.[61] Frankie inquires about death, proclaiming that it must be terrible to die and forcing Berenice to recall the death of her spouse Lutte. Frankie even admits that she was sadder at Lutte's death than at the death of her own mother. It is Frankie's internal struggle between femininity and masculinity that precedes the death of her masculine self as she claims her feminine self. Death signifies a kind of liberation that Frankie ultimately achieves.

The discourse on death also leads Frankie and Berenice to attempt to define and identify love. Berenice tells of the shivering that overcame her and penetrated her body when she observed two boys in an alley from the corner of her eye, and she says this is synonymous with being in love. Thus, Frankie's search for love and self is achieved through Berenice's unraveling of her own life experiences. When Berenice tells Frankie that despite her attempts she could never reproduce the love she felt for Lutte, she introduces the idea that some things cannot be duplicated, and that love is one. She warns Frankie to avoid attempting to reproduce love, because it will only result in wedding after wedding in an endless, unsuccessful quest. Berenice starts to share her experiences in her second marriage but abruptly stops, claiming that she cannot reveal this to Frankie and John Henry. This makes Frankie furious because it thwarts her attempt to vicariously experience adulthood through her black surrogate mother.

John Henry again mimics Frankie, and Berenice as well, by parading in high-heeled shoes and carrying a handbag. Decorated in feminine accessories, he is hinting at Frankie's inevitable transformation into her feminine self and suggesting that as she embraces symbols of desirability she moves further into adulthood—an adulthood that in her words will allow her to become the president, a member of the United Nations, a beauty pageant contestant, or whatever she chooses. She will become known, and she will belong. Berenice, empathizing with Frankie's frustration in her struggle to achieve adulthood, cautions her that she is trying to grow up too fast. She embraces Frankie, holding her on her lap and singing "His Eye Is On the Sparrow" (the title of Waters's autobiography and a song she popularized). This is a religious song, reflecting Berenice's spiritual belief and her faith in an omnipotent being who is keeping his eye on even the tiniest sparrow—on Frankie, on John Henry, even on herself. One line of her song has meaning for both the singer and her surrogate child, who must continue her journey to achieve liberation through her quest for feminization: "I sing because I'm free."

Jarvis's wedding represents the culmination of Frankie's transformation. Frankie, elegantly dressed, attends the wedding with a male escort. Before the end of the ceremony, she picks up her suitcase and exits, intent upon leaving town with the newly married couple. Berenice sees this and tries to halt her but is unable. As the bride and groom exit the building, they discover Frankie sitting in the back of their car. Frankie's father tells her she must not interfere with the couple's plans. Trying to arouse her sympathy and induce her to leave without making a scene, Janice explains to her that because Jarvis's military leave is so short, they will have only a little time together. But Frankie still refuses to leave the car, and she is jerked out by her father and thrown to the ground.

This severe treatment is the most painful scene in the film. This physical assault on Frankie is symbolic of the castration of her masculine self, which is necessary for her feminine self to exist. Because this castration is executed by a desexed father, it may also be thought to have allowed him to reclaim the phallus he is denied. When John Henry, Frankie's alter ego, subsequently becomes fatally ill, his death symbolizes the death of her adolescence, the death of her masculinity, and the death of her internally conflicted self. It is Frankie's father who goes to John Henry's bedside, evidently having become much more emotionally liberated.

Frankie's escape from home in search of herself and her femininity brings her face to face with danger; she encounters a deserted street, a family brawl, a nightclub—all signifiers of an alien world. She is propositioned by a soldier, who attempts to rape her. She manages to escape, but the attempted rape (as associated with female victimization) alerts her to the dangers that accompany the female sexuality she has yearned for. Yet, dressed in feminine attire—a pinafore dress with a collar, and a tam—and in the company of a male admirer, Frankie returns home to discover that John Henry is dead. She accepts John Henry's death easily because he was feminized, although male, and the femininity that he represented has now been transferred to her. It is as though her liberation could not be achieved without the death of John Henry and the signifier of her internally conflicted self. Her transformation is now complete. She has achieved adulthood, femininity, and self, and thus Berenice is no longer needed.

Although Waters assumes a powerful role in the film, both for what she signified as well as for the importance of her position as the surrogate maternal figure to a white adolescent, she could not avoid the typecasting to which most black actors were subjected in this period. Nor could she escape African American newspaper critics, such as Alfred L. Levitt of the *New York Amsterdam News,* who castigated her for her role in *The*

Member of the Wedding, referring to Waters's character as "a devoted (to the white folks, of course), warm-hearted, over-amorous, spiritual, singing, childwise 'Mammy.'"[62] For Levitt, the greatest insult rendered by the film was that

> When the Ad[d]ams family moves from the house to other quarters at the end of the film, Berenice is left with little or nothing to live for. A note of sadness is sounded: not because Berenice is out of a job, but because she's lost "her white folks."
>
> It is certainly valid that any woman who has raised a child would face a permanent parting from her with sadness. But here the genuine pathos of such a situation is exploited to convey the idea that Berenice without the Ad[d]ams family is somehow cut adrift; that the life purpose of Negro women is to serve white families.[63]

I read the film's ending differently than Levitt because I read the storyline, Frankie, and especially Berenice differently than Levitt and others who see Waters as playing just another typecast mammy. Indeed, in reinterpreting the character of Berenice before she accepted the role, Waters's performance succeeded in reinterpreting significant portions of the original script. Wearing a black dress, Berenice prepares to leave the family, which is in the process of moving. She sheds tears as she and Frankie embrace for the last time. The black surrogate mother has served her purpose. Because she is the vehicle by which the white female achieves her liberation, it is Berenice who emerges as the film's star and who claims the film as her own despite the secondary role assumed in the film. In this context, Berenice epitomizes in the words of Toni Morrison, "the power of blackness . . . upon which the imagination could play; through which historical, moral, metaphysical, and social fears, problems, and dichotomies could be articulated."[64]

THE SIGNIFICANCE OF VISION IN
THE MEMBER OF THE WEDDING

The film is undeniably about looking, seeing, and visibility/invisibility—about how the gaze of characters and spectators are transmitted and controlled. For example, that Frankie is not seen by her brother, sister-in-law, or father establishes the invisibility that is the seed of her internal conflict. Moreover, if Frankie is invisible to those relatives deemed important to her, then Berenice's value to Frankie and her role in her liberation are presaged early in the film. This interpretation hangs on the belief that the blackness Berenice embodies is central to assigning meaning, awarding value, and giving visibility to Frankie as an individual and as a signifier of whiteness.

As the film foregrounds Frankie's dilemma of standing transfixed between masculinity and femininity, adolescence and adulthood, and self and Other, Frankie controls the gaze of spectators as she looks at herself. Yet Berenice becomes a mirror by which Frankie engages in her self-examination. Because Frankie attempts to control the gaze of spectators, Berenice deflects the look back onto Frankie as she observes her conflicted emotional state. At other times, it is Berenice's gaze, rather than Frankie's, that forces us as spectators to dissect Frankie's motives and to participate in her inner struggles. Frankie's voyeuristic gaze of Berenice is the means by which she achieves her liberation; Berenice's gaze allows us to explore Frankie's complexity. John Henry's gaze represents a kind of third eye that allows us to examine Berenice and Frankie from afar and to examine his role in Frankie's development.

Berenice's gaze is metaphorically rendered by the fact that she has a glass eye. At the film's beginning, she wears a patch over one eye to suggest that she has limited vision. It is significant that at the end of the film she removes the patch and displays both eyes—implying that she now is full-sighted, as her vision is concomitant with Frankie's transformation of herself or her claim to femininity. Although Berenice's sight is impaired because she has lost an eye, this does not mean she is unable to see. We are aware that Berenice, with or without an eye, embodies an authentic look—that she can see without being seen. John Henry curiously remarks that Berenice has three eyes, and he asks which one she uses for seeing. Berenice is multiply sighted: she can see Frankie, see through Frankie, see for Frankie, render Frankie visible, and understand Frankie's invisibility. Moreover, Berenice affirms her sightedness or ability to see through others when she proclaims that gray-eyed persons (i.e., whites) are jealous of her ability to see. Perhaps the ability to see is what Frankie desires when she looks toward her racial Other, since it is Berenice's insight that Frankie lacks.

Berenice equates vision with the mind and refers to the "mind's eye." It is she who suggests that the mind is a source of vision, a vehicle by which to see and interpret the world, a vision that is symbolically represented in her song "His Eye Is On the Sparrow." Therefore, the insight she possesses allows her to effectively provide spiritual guidance and direction on life's course as Frankie embarks on her journey.

At the film's end, the camera traces a tear coursing from Berenice's eye to suggest that while her vision has been restored, her pain has not lessened. Thus, while the white female's search for her liberation and conflict with herself have caused agony and pain, this agony and pain are now displaced onto the black woman, who is alone, isolated, alienated, and without purpose since Frankie has matured and disappeared from her life. As Richard Dyer has pointed out, the black characters in cinema often express the emotions reserved for the white characters.[65]

WATERS'S ADDITIONAL SCREEN ROLES

As early as 1929, Waters was recruited by film director Darryl F. Zanuck to appear in *On with the Show*. According to Bogle, "Composer Harry Akst, who was writing the score of the movie, saw Waters's performance at the Orpheum and afterward visited her backstage. He discussed the proposed film, the studio, and his music. He showed her a tune on which he was working. The song was 'Am I Blue?' Later, Akst and Waters spent time working together to get the song in shape for the studio to hear."[66] Before inserting it into the film, Waters skillfully negotiated her salary for her appearance in *On with the Show* and established a reputation in the film industry as driving a hard bargain. This was nothing new for her. When she performed on stage and her salary was abruptly cut, Waters immediately quit the show rather than work for less than she felt she rightfully deserved.[67] Bogle claims that, regarding *On with the Show*, "With only two numbers ['Am I Blue?' and 'Birmingham Bertha'[68]] to perform . . . Waters knew her performances were considered by the studio to be a specialty act, which soon became the way most studios usually handled big-name Negro performers. Rather than cast the black stars as characters integral to a film's narrative, they simply filmed their musical numbers."[69]

Although Waters's role in *On with the Show* was limited to that of an entertainer—in part because of her popularity as a singer—she did appear in musical shorts that included acting roles for her. One of these musical shorts was *Rufus Jones for President* (1933) in which she was cast with the young Sammy Davis Jr. However, when Waters accepted this screen role of a matriarchal figure who is transformed into a sexy singer, the black press denounced her acceptance and questioned her motivations for taking such a part. According to Ralph Matthews, "The scene, for instance, where you were giving away pork chops to get votes for your boy during the election may have been a little degrading and a reflection on the value of the votes of your race, but honestly, Ethel, I liked the psychology [behind] it."[70] Matthews, despite his criticism of the film's other aspects, attempted to absolve Waters and other black performers of the guilt they might feel for accepting such roles by forcing them to become conscious of the roles they select. He concluded, "I wouldn't want you looked upon with hostile eyes, as the woman, who while at the top held us up as a laughing stock and proselytized her remarkable talent by ridiculing the group to which she belonged, when she might have exalted them instead."[71] Despite such criticism, one reviewer acknowledged Waters's talent and stated, "Miss Waters not only acts well, but breaks up the show with a number of song hits that she uses on the radio."[72] An additional review revealed that

> Ethel Waters scores an undeniable hit in the movie short, *Rufus Jones for President.* Take Ethel out of the film and there is nothing left. . . . Miss Waters, as is always the case, just Miss Waters and when she sings her three numbers, there is nothing left in the film. Her "Am I Blue" is a classic, but when she lilts "Underneath the Harlem Moon," she doesn't miss a thing—especially panning the whites who are in the numbers racket along with the colored folk. Yep, the *Rufus Jones for President* film has no place except to bring the charming Ethel Waters before an already adoring public.[73]

Henry T. Sampson noted the film's strengths as well as its weaknesses and surmised that

> In *Rufus Jones for President,* brilliant performances by Ethel Waters and Sammy Davis, Jr. (his first screen appearance) are marred by scenes showing blacks, in roles as U.S. Senators, checking razors, shooting craps in the halls of Congress, and passing laws to make chicken—and watermelon—stealing legal. From a historical view, however, the films above and other black musicals made during this period are the only existing record on film of black music and dance performed by many of the best American entertainers of the era.[74]

The film opens with Ethel Waters hanging clothes on a clothesline in her front yard while standing behind a fence wearing a handkerchief on her head and apron around her waist. This image of Waters would solidify her screen image as the quintessential matriarch; she is depicted in a similar manner in her later and most important film roles—*Pinky* and *The Member of the Wedding* and maybe even *Cabin in the Sky*. While hanging clothes, Waters overhears a youngster crying after being teased or berated by nearby children, and the boy returns to her poverty-stricken home to seek refuge and comfort. She embraces the youngster, Rufus Jones (Sammy Davis Jr.), by sitting him on her lap while she sits in a rocking chair, and attempts to console him. Waters reassures Rufus that one day he is going to be a great man and predicts he will be president. She begins to sing, but what is immediately apparent is that while she speaks in dialect, she sings in "standard English"—a characteristic observed of many black actors transformed on screen. Rufus falls asleep and assumes a dream-like state where he envisions himself being elected president. While the film is designed to showcase the talent of Waters and Sammy Davis Jr. and serves as an entertainment vehicle, one cannot ignore the political implications of this parody. It plays on both black desire to assume power through the presidency as well as the superficial, trivial, and stereotypical issues likely to be invoked if blacks did assume power, such as debating the use of loaded dice, padlocking the chicken coop, and overseeing the watermelon patch.

Yet during Rufus's dream-like state, he observes a parade in which crowds are dancing, flogging the streets, and holding signs promoting Jones for president. One sign at the election site reads "Rufus Jones for President—Two Pork Chops Every Time You Vote." While voters cast their votes, some are seen eating chicken as the election results are announced (incidentally, there are no other contenders mentioned in this race) and Rufus Jones is elected president. Jones, on accepting the presidency, proceeds to the microphone and breaks into a dance. During the inauguration ceremony, Jones wears a top hat and tails, while Waters follows, elegantly dressed in a long white tight-fitting gown with a fur collar. Following the inauguration, when the all-black Senate convenes, the members are checked for razors before meeting on the Senate floor. Waters nominates herself "presidencess" and establishes a poultry commission, which is followed by the establishment of a watermelon investigator and, later, dice president. During the Senate session, Waters sings "Am I Blue?" to which the senators fall asleep; to re-invigorate them, she sings "Underneath the Harlem Moon," and they awaken and sway to the music. One lyric of the song popularized by Waters hints at smoking reefers while feeling low, which reflects Waters's risqué style as a singer and the counterposing of these lyrics to her strong religious views. As the newly elected president, Jones seems to be a lame duck figure during this session; the Senate commands him to do something. In response to the command, he again dances and is joined in the dance by others, among whom are chorus line girls and a dancing couple. As the film ends, photographers begin to photograph Jones, the president. When the camera clicks, a cloud of smoke fills the screen and Jones awakens from his dream-like state with Waters embracing him—a dream that ends when she declares "my pork chops is burning." This musical short, though infused with negative representations of blackness, certainly seems to be a precursor to music videos and attests to Waters's popularity as a singer as well as Davis's talent as a performer. The film managed to capitalize on the star status and singing talent of Waters as well as the talent of Davis, both of whom personify the entertainer.

On the heels of *Rufus Jones for President,* Waters was cast in *Bubbling Over* (1934), a film that featured Frank Wilson, Hamtree Harrington, Joe Byrd, the Southernaires, and J. Rosamond Johnson's choir. A review of this musical short revealed that "Miss Waters put over two songs in her inimitable manner, which fit right in to the story, concerning Ethel as a married woman, whose husband is a lazy gent that refuses to work. All his relatives come to visit and 'live off' them. It is packed with laughs and music."[75] This musical short led to Waters being cast in another short picture, titled *Gift of the Gab* (1934), in which she similarly assumed a prominent role. One report noted, "This musical photoplay, *Gift of the Gab,* boasts of more stars of radio, the stage, and the screen than any picture ever produced in Hollywood. It has 30 star names. It is virtually a 'play within a play,' for not only does it tell the story of Lowe's rise from an humble auctioneer in a cheap Broadway store to the position of America's foremost broadcaster and radio reporter, but it also shows several broadcasting programs."[76]

After these films in the late 1920s and mid-1930s, Waters did not return to the screen in a feature-length film until 1942, when she appeared in *Cairo*. Although cast as a maid to white actress Jeanette MacDonald, Waters sang two numbers and performed a humorous duet with the white star.[77] In this case, the African American press asserted that "the role of domestic servant in the films, once the sore spot to those seeking a more realistic portrayal of colored people on the screen, has been raised to a new standard of dignity by two of the actors."[78] Regarding Waters's appearance in *Cairo*, Cripps points out that the *Richmond News-Leader* reviewed the film and observed that "There were plenty of times when it seemed the camera hunted her out to the exclusion of the other actors."[79]

Escaping the servant typecasting, yet still cast as a black matriarch, Waters found herself in *Tales of Manhattan* (1942), a role no less redeeming than her subservient role in *Cairo*. *Tales of Manhattan* is a series of brief skits woven together by the thematic device of a tattered coat that is passed along from one person to another—a tailcoat that initially was considered bad luck but later was predicted to bring good luck to anyone who touched it. Those who receive the coat experience a combination of good luck and bad luck. For example, in one of the first segments of the film, an actor who is involved with another man's wife wears the tailcoat to visit the woman at her home following an outstanding stage performance of his. The woman's husband, aware of the actor's machinations, confronts him and shoots him. The actor stumbles as though he is seriously injured and observes the husband and wife conspiring to cover up the crime. Recognizing that his lover may not really love him as she declares, in that she is willing to conspire with her husband regarding his death, the actor then proclaims that he was actually shot with a blank and is faking his death. Yet when he leaves the home and reaches his chauffeured auto, he directs his chauffeur to take him to a hospital, when we learn that he really was shot. Thus, the tailcoat that he wears brings him good luck in that he achieves an outstanding performance on stage, nearly convinces his lover to leave her husband for him, and does not die from the gunshot wound he received. Yet, the actor/stage performer also endures the bad luck of being physically injured and losing the object of his desire.

The coat continues to symbolize the contradictory positions of good and bad as it is passed from the actor to a couple preparing to marry; then to a struggling orchestra conductor; to a man who although well-educated is living in a shelter for the needy; later to an elderly gentleman who swindles money from supporters of a health drink he has concocted;

and finally into the arms of criminals who rob a local casino and flee the country on board a plane. As these criminals stage their escape, they throw the tattered coat out of the plane and it lands on barren farm land, to be discovered by desperate black farm workers Luke (Paul Robeson), who appears in a worn hat, suspenders, and overalls, and Esther (Ethel Waters), who wears a handkerchief on her head and an apron around her waist. Luke, pointing to the coat, exclaims, "Where did that come from?" to which Esther replies, "Heaven." The black actors in this film do not appear on screen until the last five minutes of this two-hour film.

After Luke and Esther discover $43,000 hidden in the coat, Esther proclaims that it is sinful to have so much money, despite their impoverished condition. She and Luke take the tattered tailcoat to the local preacher (Eddie "Rochester" Anderson), who distributes the money to those in the community, particularly to those who have prayed. Since it is near Christmas, their dreams are answered. The gifts they ask for reflect their plight and condition: Luke desires a tractor, Esther desires a brindle cow, another desires a mahogany coffin, and another adamantly proclaims, "I got all I need." After the preacher distributes a portion of the money, the recipients decide to use the rest to develop the community. In line with this plan, Luke vows to buy land, work side by side with others, and share resources so that there will be no more rich and no more poor.

That Robeson and Waters assumed stereotypical roles in this film in view of the stature they had attained off-screen diminished their appeal among black spectators. Moreover, because of the socialist views appropriated by the film's depiction of wealth being distributed to those less wealthy, casting Robeson and Waters in the roles of poor illiterate black farmers undermined the progressiveness of the film's intent. Additionally, the film gives the impression that they cannot think seriously about their plight because their judgment has been clouded and overshadowed by their preoccupation with religion. At the film's end, they hang the tattered coat on a post to deter scarecrows from devouring the crops and sing happily while waving their hands in the air.

As Thomas Cripps views the black segment in the plot line of *Tales of Manhattan*, when the coat falls:

> into the rough hands of a village of Southern Negro farmers . . . their enclave is sketched in stylized, almost hillbilly, imagery—as though [Julien]

Duvivier had reached the limits of French capacity for comprehending Southern American racial arrangements. The dramatic conflict was symbolized by Robeson's openhanded communal vision of a black sharecropper as opposed to Eddie Anderson's raspy-comic venal preacher who has a sharp eye for the main chance.[80]

Cripps continues that "the well-meaning populism of the black sequence in *Tales of Manhattan* clashed with its residual echoes of stock Negro characters who sang either for glory or supplication."[81]

According to Waters, "When *Tales of Manhattan* was released, various Negro organizations picketed the theaters showing it. Their placards protested picturing us colored people as wretched, dirty, and poorly clad. I didn't understand that. These same organizations were forever complaining that we Negroes in America are underprivileged. So why did they object to anyone showing us that way on the screen?"[82] In defense of her role in the film, Waters claimed that one of the more sentimental parts of the film that allowed her to draw upon her strong religious beliefs was edited from the final version of the film even though executives had raved about it.[83] Waters rationalized her position by contending that because African Americans represent a wide variety of personalities and characters, this variety should be displayed on screen. But she failed to acknowledge that in the cinema, these one-dimensional representations of African Americans were the norm. In assessing the roles accorded to blacks in the industry, James Snead wrote that

Chauffeurs, domestics, porters, jazz musicians, and other blacks are marked by the black/white codings. . . . Aprons, gloves, dresses, scarves, headbands, and even white teeth and eyes are all signifiers of a certain coding of race in Hollywood films that audiences soon came to recognize. This is not to say that whites on film would not bulge out eyes, or wear servants' clothes; only that (1) blacks seemed to do it exclusively; and (2) these signifiers have a different coding when whites are associated with them.[84]

Incidentally, Robeson, though he had accepted the role, was offended by the film's depictions of African Americans and threatened to boycott the film's opening.

The following year, Waters returned to the screen in *Cabin in the Sky* (1943) in the same role she had played in the stage production. Her onstage performances had garnered considerable praise from critics, one of whom reported that "As Petunia, Little Joe's long suffering wife, she wrings your heart like the great actress she is, beguiles you with tunes in that lovely old cracked voice, sets you roaring as she resists the temptation to dance or execute a massive conga."[85] Waters was then transformed as the black matriarch and wife to Little Joe (Eddie "Rochester" Anderson) in the screen adaptation of this production, a role not so different from the one she played in *Tales of Manhattan*. Revealing her experience with the film, she asserted that

> when we made *Cabin in the Sky* there was conflict between the studio and me from the beginning. For one thing, I objected violently to the way religion was being treated in the screen play. . . . But all through that picture there was so much snarling and scrapping that I don't know how in the world *Cabin in the Sky* ever stayed up there.
>
> I won all my battles on that picture. But like many other performers, I was to discover that winning arguments in Hollywood is costly. Six years were to pass before I could get another movie job.[86]

Rethinking that statement, Waters later remarked, "At one time I suspicioned [*sic*] that the Hollywood tycoons, angered by my outbursts of temper while making *Cabin in the Sky,* were using their power to blackball me out of show business. . . . Today I blame only certain agents for my long eclipse as a public entertainer."[87] Cripps supports these views and affirms that "performers such as Ethel Waters with a reputation for being 'difficult' sometimes lost jobs and regarded with suspicion Negroes such as Bill Robinson who got along too well with whites."[88]

Cabin in the Sky featured Ethel Waters (as Petunia), Eddie "Rochester" Anderson (as Little Joe), and Lena Horne (as Georgia Brown) in a dramatization that pits a black matriarch against a sexy, sultry nightclub singer, both of whom are competing for the attentions of a black male who gambles, has difficulty maintaining employment, and is caught between God and the devil. Arthur Knight contends that "With its story of a devout woman struggling to keep her wandering man from the interrelated, sinful temptations of gambling, jazz, and brassy women, it still appeared to be—especially if distilled into its narrative outlines—a refashioning of *Hallelujah!* by the way of *The Green Pastures*."[89] And although the film has been largely characterized as a Lena Horne vehicle (see chapter 6), Waters, as Petunia, assumes such a dominant role in the film that she appears on screen as much if not more than does Horne. Added to this, she certainly sings more songs than does Horne.

First, most noticeable about Waters's role is that when the film opens, Waters appears in her front yard wearing a hat and returning a basket of clothes to her front porch. Thus her association with being a washer-woman is inescapable and is reminiscent of her earlier appearance in *Rufus Jones for President* and later appearances in *Pinky* and *The Member of the Wedding,* even though as Petunia she was cast as a sexy nightclub singer. In fact, Paula Massood notes that "the connection between Petunia and the idyllic, already apparent through her name, is emphasized by what she wears. Her simple, everyday work / house dresses are light in color and usually tight-fitting, but not in order to reveal a sexualized or sensuous body. Instead, they emphasize Petunia's large physique, which while not exactly conforming to the physical conventions of most mammies, resembles the archetype."[90] For fear that Little Joe, whom she is attempting to reform from his gambling ways, is backsliding and may be stalling as they head for the church meeting, Petunia is greeted by the minister, who senses that she might need some assistance. With his encouragement, Petunia and Little Joe head for church. During the service, Petunia, delighted that she is on the pathway to saving Little Joe's soul, joins the church congregation in singing "Little Black Sheep Come Back Home," a song specifically designed to reflect on Little Joe. However, before the service is over, Joe reunites with his former friends outside, who claim that he owes them gambling money. In order to repay the money owed, he vows to gamble one last time even though he is attempting to make a spiritual transformation.

Petunia, distraught over his departure from the church, hears a gun-shot in the background and knows that it is her beloved, Little Joe, who has been shot at John Henry's Paradise nightclub. As Little Joe lies in bed wounded, a physician and minister visit him, and Petunia prays passionately for his life. She exclaims, "Lord, please don't take Little Joe.... He ain't wicked, he's just weak. And Lord, forgive me for loving him so much." Petunia, the black matriarch, is deeply religious, and the agents of the Lord/General who are contesting with the devil/Lucifer for Little Joe's soul, hear her prayers and give Little Joe a second chance. Recognizing that Little Joe is not dead, Petunia rejoices and sings "Happiness Is a Thing Called Joe."

While Little Joe recovers, Petunia is greeted by gamblers attempting to lure him back to his old ways. She intervenes on Little Joe's behalf and, realizing that the gamblers have exploited her husband, decides to gamble with them herself. Petunia engages in a crap game with the extortionists, fully aware that they are playing with loaded dice and that this was how they got money from Little Joe. Winning their money, she then prays for forgiveness and proclaims, "Lord, please forgive me, but sometimes when you fight the devil, you have to jab him with your own pitchfork."

Following Little Joe's recovery and his vow to overcome his wicked ways, Petunia sings "Cabin in the Sky" in celebration of his transformation. When Little Joe gives gifts to Petunia on her birthday, she sings "Taking a Chance on Love." Despite Little Joe's best efforts, of course, the devil attempts to lure him away from Petunia. He wins money on a sweepstakes ticket that, incidentally, is delivered by none other than Georgia Brown (Lena Horne). Petunia, overhearing a conversation between Georgia Brown and Little Joe in which he promises to reward Georgia for delivering the ticket, banishes Little Joe from their home and forces him into the arms of Georgia Brown.

When Georgia Brown enters the film, Petunia nearly disappears. But at the film's end Petunia reappears and visits John Henry's nightclub; she is elegantly dressed and tries to make Little Joe jealous by aligning herself with Domino Johnson (John "Bubbles" Sublett), Little Joe's assailant. Massood suggests that "When Petunia enters Club Paradise in an attempt to rekindle her relationship with Little Joe, the iconography identifying good and evil, and by connection the antebellum idyll and the city, changes. Until this point, Petunia had been contained within spaces exclusively defined in familial, domestic, and idyllic terms.... When she enters the club, she is a changed woman."[91] This time she sings "Honey in the Honeycomb" and dances in the nightclub, but when Domino Johnson becomes overly aggressive, she calls for Little Joe and a fight ensues, resulting in the deaths of both Petunia and Little Joe. The two plead for Little Joe to get into heaven, and the film seems to end, but we then realize that Little Joe has merely been dreaming. When he awakens he immediately asks Petunia to destroy both the sweepstakes ticket and his dice. Waters closes the film by again singing "Taking a Chance on Love."

Even though Waters assumes a matriarchal role in the film, her talent as a singer manages to reverse or at least minimize the implication associated with this typecasting, particularly in the scene where she performs as herself, a sexy nightclub singer. In fact, Michele Wallace affirms that "In *Cabin*, Waters is clearly still a hot momma, although not as thin or as young as Lena Horne, her competition."[92] Regarding her singing, Arthur Knight suggests that the songs in the film as they connect to the film's narrative development reify the film's theme of good/bad and morality/spirituality, but do so "shiftingly rather than uniformly."[93] He contends that "*Cabin in the Sky* was not a radical break with Hollywood black-cast musical practice, so its rewards, pleasures, and resistances must be seen as heavily qualified at best. And it will not do to forget that some—perhaps many—black viewers saw no reward, pleasure, or resistance in the film at all."[94]

Waters, however, could not escape being relegated to such one-dimensional roles. Responding to those who criticized her for portraying subjugation on the screen, she insisted that she sought to elevate the African American screen image. According to the *Chicago Defender*, Waters "has an aversion to playing parts that reflect on her people. She will not under any circumstances accept maid parts in pictures.... 'I stand by my guns' she has repeatedly told reporters and casting agents."[95] Some two years later the *Chicago Defender* wrote that

> She has done little in pictures because she does not care for the typed roles offered most of the Negro players, stars and otherwise. "I'd rather stay home and look after little Ethel than accept some of the parts offered me," she told reporters recently. That is why you'll find the nation's number one artist resting in her Harlem apartment instead of beating the boards of Hollywood.[96]

Despite Waters's claims of having presented Hollywood with a standoff based on her principles, only a few years later she accepted the role of a domestic in both *Pinky* (1949) and *The Member of the Wedding*. In *Pinky*, she played Granny, the stock mammy figure—a role she landed with the assistance of Ward Bond, a close friend of director John Ford: "All I had to do to play Granny [Dicey Johnson] well was remember my own grandmother, Sally Anderson. The Granny in *Pinky* was much like her, being proud of her blood, hard-working, fierce-tempered, and devoted to her white employers."[97]

Waters, as Dicey, attempts to convince her granddaughter Pinky (Jeanne Crain), who is a nurse passing for white in the North, to return south to take care of Dicey's elderly white employer, Miss Em (Ethel Barrymore). Pinky, who has established a relationship with a white physician, Dr. Thomas Adams (William Lundigan), is reluctant to abandon the life that she has created for herself while passing as white, but she concedes to Dicey's wishes. When Pinky returns to the South, she is accosted by two white men who assume she is black and therefore an object of their desire; she is arrested when she squabbles with Jake (Frederick O'Neal) over money he extorted from her grandmother; and she is refused the ownership of property deeded to her by the elderly Miss Em and is forced to engage in a court dispute. Even as she initially provides care to Miss Em, the elderly employer chastises Pinky and makes her perform tasks outside of her nursing skills. Yet the two later develop an affection for each other and at Miss Em's death, she wills Pinky her property, which Pinky transforms into a nursing school for blacks.

Of course, the film's plot is complicated by (1) the fact that Pinky is played by a white actress, thus raising the problematic issue of what Susan Courtney referred to as representing race on screen. Pinky's racial origin is never really established in the film because her parental origin remains obscure; (2) the black female is displaced in a story designed to presage her experience; (3) Dicey extends unending commitment to Miss Em even though she serves as her washerwoman; (4) Pinky's fiancé is willing to marry her on the premise that she keep her racial identity secret;[98] and (5) Pinky comes to terms with her blackness with help not from her black grandmother but from the elderly, white Miss Em. The film illuminates these and other complexities. Regarding Pinky's racial identity, Courtney asserts that "Pinky confronts [the racial dilemma] through a complex series of inscriptions that direct us when to see the white actress who plays Pinky as white, when to see her as black pretending to be white, and when to forget she is white at all and see her as 'really' black."[99] Yet despite the film's complexities, most important for this discussion is Dicey's role in the film.

When the film opens, Pinky is walking through streets marred by the impoverishment that has ravaged the black South. She reaches her grandmother's dilapidated shack lined with white clothes hanging from the clothesline, a scene that marks Dicey's status as the black washerwoman for her wealthy white employer. Dicey fails to recognize Pinky, mistaking her for white, but then realizes that this is her granddaughter. This lack of recognition signifies both Pinky's uncertain racial identity and Pinky's uncertainty as she returns to the South. Elspeth Kyyd declares that this scene "plays on several aspects of recognition and misrecognition."[100] Yet, proudly wearing an apron draped around her waist and a handkerchief tied on her head, Dicey welcomes her granddaughter home. After their reunion, Dicey confronts Pinky about her desire to have Pinky return to and remain in the South.

Though Dicey figures prominently in Pinky's decision to return South, she appears in the film less frequently than do Pinky and Miss Em. Therefore, Dicey's relationship to Pinky and Miss Em is viewed as central to constructing her role. When Pinky rejects Dicey's proposition to take care of the ailing Miss Em, Dicey becomes frustrated with Pinky and assists her in packing her clothes. Dicey provides a moving testimonial, nearly demanding that Pinky return not only to the South but to her black self—"not because she wants Pinky to live a life of deprivation, but because she believes that Pinky can find fulfillment through 'belongingness.'"[101] Dicey, appalled that Pinky desires to pass as white while remaining in denial about her blackness and insistent that she repay Miss Em for what she has done for Dicey, commands Pinky to return to the South. It seems that in making her case, she plays on Pinky's guilt and on her own moral conviction to do what is right despite her subservient status. First, Dicey confronts Pinky, contending that when Dicey had fallen ill during Pinky's absence, Miss Em had nursed her back to health. Then, Dicey claims that Pinky's training as a nurse has resulted in an erosion of her emotions, causing her to distance herself from any affection for Miss Em. Finally, Dicey constructs Pinky as an Other by referring to her own granddaughter as "trash."[102] The use of this term demeans not only Pinky but also Dicey and it absolves whites of any responsibility for holding such views when these views are articulated by black characters. Dicey is stern in her treatment of Pinky and at the same time unrelenting in badgering Pinky to come to terms with her identity. After Pinky concedes to Dicey's wishes, Dicey becomes a background figure in a story that foregrounds Pinky and Miss Em until the film's end, when Pinky goes to court to fight for the property that she feels she rightfully deserves.

As for Dicey's relationship with Miss Em, Dicey epitomizes the quintessential subservient. "Dicey is the very embodiment of subordinance among whites. She is compromising, subservient, and placating even in the face of racial degradation. To Miss Em, however, Dicey is also religiously steadfast in her loyalty. Although Dicey reminds us of the not too distant slave past when some African Americans remained loyal to slave masters even after achieving their liberation; some characterize this behavior as a demonstration that they were morally superior to their white slave owners."[103] Indicative of Dicey's subordinance in the film is, of course, her overbearing allegiance to Miss Em and her eagerness to withhold her support of Pinky when Pinky fights to retain the property inherited from Miss Em. Dicey concedes to Pinky, "If it is something that white folks don't want you to have, you might as well forget it."

Although Waters gives a moving performance in the role of Dicey—a role that earned her an Academy Award nomination—black newspaper critics were critical of her role even as they supported her Academy Award nomination. In support of Waters one member of the African American press wrote, "This year's Academy Award program at the Pantages theatre was the greatest of all the years, but we were disappointed because Ethel Waters did not win an award for her supporting role in Pinky. . . . It was 'so near yet so far.'"[104] The mainstream press joined in criticizing her role, even as they applauded Waters's performance. Time magazine noted that "the Ethel Waters role [is] a 'symbol' of Aunt Jemimaism,"[105] while the New Republic characterized her role as exhibiting "doglike devotion."[106] Some, especially blacks, did not view comments such as these in the mainstream press as positive ones. The Chicago Defender took a slightly different view and condemned the roles of both Ethel Barrymore and Waters by stating that "the roles given them are absolutely nothing but worn out stereotypes of the domineering old mistress of the plantation and the blindly faithful servant."[107] Ebony magazine echoed the negative criticism and referred to Waters as "an out-and-out Dixie mammy."[108] Fearing public scrutiny for her role, Waters declared that one newspaper columnist "was not welcome to scribble about handkerchief head roles and misquote her."[109]

During the 1950s, Waters returned to the screen in The Member of the Wedding and appeared in two additional films, The Heart Is a Rebel (1958) and The Sound and the Fury (1959). One review of her performance in The Heart Is a Rebel observed that "Ethel Waters is quite an enjoyable presence throughout this movie, both for her heartfelt renditions of a number of gospel standards (most notably 'Sometimes I Feel Like a Motherless Child') and for her cheerful portrayal of the ideal nurse/

nanny character who watches over the sick little child."[110] *The Sound and Fury,* based on William Faulkner's novel of the same title, cast Waters in the role of Dilsey. However limited many of her screen roles were, it was because Waters commodified Otherness on the screen that she became one of the few leading African American jazz artists to have an illustrious screen career in Hollywood as a dramatic actress, receiving more prominent screen roles than did either Billie Holiday or Lena Horne. As we have seen, this commodification is exemplified by her role as Berenice in *The Member of the Wedding.*

Referring to Waters's complexity and contradictions as a prominent black person, Glenda Gill surmises that she "died a misfit who was at home with neither whites nor blacks. Ethel Waters embraced, with zeal, [Billy] Graham, but took no notice of Martin Luther King, Jr., who by 1955 was equally as popular. She was also friendly with President Richard Nixon, who invited the star to the White House to Julie Nixon Eisenhower's Rose Garden Wedding."[111] However, as a relatively successful actress, Waters's on-screen representation became inextricably linked to her off-screen reputation as a jazz artist. The industry's exploitation of her musical talent is an element she shares with other black actresses.

NINE

Dorothy Dandridge

INTERTWINING THE REEL AND THE REAL

"LIFE IS BUT A WALKING SHADOW"

Dorothy Dandridge belonged to that group of "new Negro womanhood" actresses in which Hattie McDaniel placed Lena Horne. Indeed, Dandridge and Horne shared several characteristics as aspiring actresses in Hollywood of the 1940s and early 1950s—young, sexy, beautiful, light-complexioned, nightclub singers turned actresses, exploited by the industry for their beauty and sexual appeal, and subjected to essentially the same kinds of racial discrimination in the society at large that other blacks faced. They differed, however, in that Dandridge rose to the level of leading lady in films of the 1950s in a way that eluded Horne in the 1940s. In several ways, Dandridge occupied a transitional position for African American actresses in the pre- and post-1960 periods. Her career blossomed about the same time the civil rights and women's rights movements began to move into high gear in the late 1950s and early 1960s, but it faltered before she could reap the full rewards of the changes these movements wrought in Hollywood and in the society at large.

About half a century separates the beginning of Sul-Te-Wan's movie career primarily as an actress in minor and subservient roles from the rise of Dorothy Dandridge's career as a leading African American actress in the 1950s. During the period between the two world wars, the Hollywood movie industry confined African American actresses to minor roles or, in a few exceptional instances, to major roles in which they played subservients, practically all of whom shadowed the leading white actress in the films in which they appeared. In some respects, Dandridge's life and career also invite a comparison to lines from Shakespeare's *Macbeth* (act v, scene v): "Life's but a walking shadow, a poor player / That struts and frets his hour upon the stage, / And then is heard no more." But the role of the black actress as a shadow of the white female Other in films took a significant change with Dorothy Dandridge's career: She became a shadow of herself as her on-screen identity and off-screen identity collided, merged, and became reflexive. One might say that she became "a walking shadow" of her film personae, and that after about a decade of playing a particular type of character, she died, and the memory of her as a Hollywood (dark) star almost faded from public memory.

In the period from 1950 to 1960, African American actresses who were cast in leading roles with male costars were constructed as objects of desire in much the same manner as were white actresses. The typical leading man was projected on and off screen as powerful, dominant, and privileged. The leading lady was presented to the world as a sex object, a product designed to elicit the male gaze and to be marketed to mass audiences. According to Marguerite H. Rippy, "There lies in objectification a fundamental inhumanity that derives pleasure from the flight of the object toward subjectivity (the act of pulling away from the grasp, the hand thrust toward the camera in an attempt to block the lens): there is a sadism in our desire to return the woman-as-object to her photographic frame that feminist film theory has thoroughly interrogated."[1] Therefore, it is not surprising that spectators began to identify with these mediated constructions and to desire for themselves the established standards of beauty and desirability these stars symbolized.

Although there were very few African American leading ladies in Hollywood before the 1950s, the industry created their images in basically the same manner and for the same purposes as it did those of white actresses: beautiful and sexually desirable objects of male desire. Positioned as objects of desire, both white and black actresses had their images packaged and marketed to mass audiences. However, the racial hierarchies of American society relegated African American actresses to on- and off-screen roles that exploited their race as well as their sexuality. Unlike many white actresses, they could not keep their off-screen lives separate from their on-screen constructions. White actresses had the luxury of living lives associated with the white privilege afforded them—they could live relatively normal lives and had access to opportunity generally denied to black women. Black women, in comparison, were forced to assume the subordinate status off screen to which most blacks were confined. White actresses had more opportunity to move beyond their screen roles than black actresses. Because of the social, political, and economic discursives that often defined and influenced perceptions of them, black actresses could not escape the conscriptions of race and sexuality inscribed by their screen representations, could not (as was the case with their white counterparts) escape being objectified, and could not escape much of the exploitation or victimization they endured in the cinema industry because of their race.

Among African American leading actresses in 1950s Hollywood, none is more exemplary as a mediated construct than Dorothy Dandridge, a nightclub singer and actress who ultimately evolved into a tragic figure. Dandridge provides a striking example of Hollywood's construction of the "dark star" and provides an excellent case study of the intersection of race and gender in predominantly white Hollywood.

Like many of the African American actresses before her, Dandridge's early childhood set her on an entertainment road that eventually led to Hollywood. She was born Dorothy Jean Dandrige on November 9, 1922, in Cleveland, Ohio, to Ruby Dandridge (formerly Ruby Jean Butler, born to George Butler and Nellie Simmons in Wichita, Kansas, March 1, 1899) and Cyril Dandridge (born to Henry Dandridge and Florence Locke in Cleveland, Ohio, in 1895). Dorothy was the younger of two daughters. After a divorce, Ruby Dandridge went on to pursue a theatrical career and encouraged her daughters to follow a similar path. As youngsters, Dorothy and her sister Vivian performed skits and readings at local churches. With the assistance of Geneva Williams, a former Fisk University music student who had formed ties with their mother, the two children began to receive professional performance training. When they toured a number of southern cities for the National Baptist Convention, they were billed as the "The Wonder Children." Later, when Etta Jones joined their group, the three of them became known as "The Dandridge Sisters."[2] One report noted, "The Dandridge Sisters [are a] youthful and charming trio who took the capital by storm in their first appearance at the Howard Theatre this week, after a successful run at the Cotton Club."[3]

Leaving Cleveland for the better opportunities that Los Angeles provided to entertainers, Ruby enrolled her children in school. Initially, the Dandridge sisters attended the Hooper Avenue School, later McKinley High School, and finally Jefferson High School. As Ruby struggled to carve out a living in the entertainment industry, she was instrumental in landing small film roles for her daughters through the Central Casting Bureau, headed by Charles Butler, whose job involved locating roles for black actors. Ruby's efforts paid off in 1935 when the Dandridge trio appeared in *The Big Broadcast of 1936,* when Dorothy was only a teenager. That same year, the group toured in Honolulu, and when they returned to California they were met with offers to tour Europe. Throughout the rest of the decade, Dorothy Dandridge managed to land small roles in films such as *A Day at the Races* (1937), *It Can't Last Forever* (1937), and *Going Places* (1939). During this time Dandridge also continued to tour with the trio. Following a trip to London in 1939, the Dandridge Sisters reported to the black press on the war climate that they experienced while on tour in Europe.[4] After they returned from Europe, they made appearances with Jimmie Lunceford's band, which resulted in the dissolution of the trio when Etta married Gerald Wilson, one of Lunceford's band members.[5]

In the 1940s, Dandridge's film career escalated with several screen roles. She appeared in *Irene* (1940), *Four Shall Die* (1941), *Sun Valley Serenade* (1941), *Lady from Louisiana* (1941), *Sundown* (1941), *Bahama Passage* (1941), *Drums of the Congo* (1942), *Lucky Jordan* (1942), *Hit Parade* (1943), *Since You Went Away* (1944), *Atlantic City* (1944), and *Pillow to Post* (1945).[6] In September 1942 Dandridge married Harold Nicholas (of the Nicholas Brothers) in Nevada, and one year later, their daughter Harolyn was born with a brain abnormality.[7]

It was during the 1950s that Dandridge further expanded her acting career by landing more prominent roles in films, appearing in *Tarzan's Peril* (1951), *The Harlem Globetrotters* (1951, costarring with William Brown), *Bright Road* (1953, costarring with Harry Belafonte), *Remains to Be Seen* (1953), *Carmen Jones* (1954, costarring with Harry Belafonte), *Island in the Sun* (1957, costarring with Harry Belafonte, James Mason, and John Justin), *The Decks Ran Red* (1958), *Tamango* (1958, costarring with Curt Jurgens), and *Porgy and Bess* (1959, costarring with Sidney Poitier, Sammy Davis Jr., and Brock Peters). For her performance in *Porgy and Bess* she received the Hollywood Foreign Press Association Golden Globe

Award as best actress in a musical.[8] Celebrating this upcoming star, the black press frequently covered Dandridge's roles in these films. On her role in *Tarzan's Peril,* one reporter wrote: "Dandridge . . . looks as seductive in a sarong as the other Dorothy, the Lamour."[9] Dandridge also won considerable acclaim for her acting skills, becoming the first African American actress to be nominated for an Academy Award for best actress for her role in *Carmen Jones.* While this period proved to be successful for Dandridge's career, she endured a number of personal failures, not the least of which was her divorce from Harold Nicholas that became final in 1951. Eight years later, on June 23, 1959, she married Jack Denison (a white restaurant owner); they were divorced in 1962.

Despite Dandridge's unparalleled success as an actress, by the 1960s she found it difficult to work as an actress, appearing in only one more major film, *Malaga* (1960). Reports circulated that Dandridge suffered from bouts of depression, and on September 10, 1965, she died from an overdose of antidepressants.[10]

CREATION OF A DARK STAR

Reflecting upon her star status, one newspaper writer described Dandridge, enmeshed in the Hollywood world of glamour and glitter, as a "movie star" adorned in furs who posed for photographers while sitting on a canvas chair with her name emblazoned across the back. In the fan magazines of the time, she was touted as the "curvaceous Miss Dandridge," the "seductive Miss Dandridge," and the "Sepia Beauty" of the American screen.[11]

Hollywood (with the black press in compliance) constructed Dandridge primarily as the dark star who would elicit the male gaze—more specifically, the white male gaze. She was made beautiful (by Eurocentric standards), rendered sexually desirable (through her posture, demeanor, and dress), and promoted as a star. In publicity materials and in the roles to which she was assigned, she was often cast as the romantic lead opposite a male costar. Because of her blackness and her beauty, Dandridge became Hollywood's dark star and her body became the site through which spectators were allowed to explore their own racial and sexual fantasies.

But because only white actresses could overtly embody desirability in accordance with the norms and values of white society, Hollywood manipulated Dandridge's skin color, making it a signifier of her racial construction. When producers cast her as an African American, they darkened her skin, but when they cast her in the role of a native West Indian or Polynesian, they lightened her skin color to make her acceptable to white audiences. Such rendering of Dandridge reveals how Hollywood marketed her. Her objectification is apparent even in the promotion of her films. The publicity materials, both visual and written, emphasized her physical beauty and sexual appeal, though not to the same extent as they did for white screen actresses. As Rippy points out, "the promotional image that the studio circulated for Dandridge's most widely publicized film, *Carmen Jones,* depicts her posed as Carmen, standing with hands on hips, legs spread, head tossed back in an atmosphere of assertive availability."[12] Thus, while the studio constructed Dandridge as an object of the male gaze by manipulating her sexuality, it also rendered her as a racial Other by controlling perceptions of her race. It made her both desirable and undesirable at the same time—a paradox that problematizes both her on-screen and her off-screen images.

In this chapter, I examine how Dandridge came to internalize Hollywood's mediated construction of her and how the cinema industry (both American and European) victimized her in several ways. First, it objectified her in both her starring roles on screen and in her private off-screen life, influencing her life to become a mirror image of her screen portrayals. Second, the industry victimized Dandridge by altering her racial construction—obfuscating her identity by diluting her blackness so that she represented a wide variety of ethnicities. Third, the industry victimized Dandridge both *externally,* by thwarting her career, and *internally,* by colluding in her self-induced victimization, culminating in her death, which remains shrouded in mystery.

It is of historic interest to note that despite her racial construction, Dandridge, as commodified by the predominantly white cinema industry, bears a striking resemblance to Marilyn Monroe. Monroe's stardom and subsequent career-shattering experiences parallel Dandridge's. Both demonstrate how Hollywood exploited its female stars and perpetuated their exploitation of themselves. My examination of Dandridge's sexual and racial construction, and the appropriation of her death, demonstrates how her on-screen and off-screen lives increasingly intertwined and led toward self-destruction. Dandridge's demise as a star can be seen as the result of her own inability to prevent an industry-created reel image from consuming her real self-image. This examination addresses to what extent she viewed her struggle as personal or political and poses several questions that may not be answerable. Was she attempting to dismantle the proscriptive social norms that barred black-white marriages? The larger question is whether she was obsessed with having a white spouse because of the larger sociopolitical implications that interracial marriages held for many African Americans, that is, that taking a white spouse was somehow a disavowal of one's blackness and a way to ingratiate oneself within white American society. Did Dandridge see herself as symbolically achieving integration in a society plagued by racial division, or had she so thoroughly internalized her exploitation by white males that she identified with her oppressors in order to empower herself? The more she attempted to free herself from the cinema industry's construction of her, the more enveloped she became by the image she was attempting to escape.

DANDRIDGE BECOMES AN OBJECT OF DESIRE

Like most female stars of the 1950s and 1960s, Dandridge's existence, both on and off screen, was anchored in serving as an object of male desire. As a product of the time, she could not escape the codes of conduct imposed on all women, but her race posed an additional burden. Men far too often defined women's existence and validated their importance, rewarding those who made themselves desirable. Like other women, Dandridge was influenced by this dominant discourse, which indoctrinated women and reflected the masculine privilege inscribed in American culture. The cinema industry cast Dandridge in roles that made her a signifier of male desire; simultaneously, the industry rendered her desirable to her male costars (many of whom were white) and also fashioned her into an object of desire for spectators.

Laura Mulvey's assertion that the spectator identifies with the male costar raises questions about how the male costar and the audience lay claim to the black female body.[13] In the case of Dandridge, her sexuality and sensuality, her makeup, her bodily adornments, her natural attributes, and her European features commodified her body and made it the property (through the male's desiring gaze) of white males in particular and spectators in general. It was a vicarious ownership not without historical precedent in society at large. Through the assertion of masculine privilege, the black female was denied control over her own body. Moreover, in the process of losing her claim to her own body, she was also rendered important only *because* of her body. What distinguishes Dandridge from many other black female stars of this period is that she became one of the first black actresses to assume costarring roles opposite leading white males.

For Dandridge, the fictive victimization she experienced on screen became reality in her off-screen life. Her body was converted into a site of contestation both on screen (with her male costars) and off screen (with her real-life lovers). The real person (Dandridge) increasingly became a reflection of the reel image (Dandridge the star). Because Dandridge did internalize her screen representations—becoming the tragic figure that she so often represented on screen—she perfectly illustrates Lacan's theory that for film actors the screen becomes a mirror image of the off-screen self and is central to their ego formation as the two become intertwined in the construction of identity.[14] As Dandridge internalized this mediated image of herself, she became a spectator of her own on-screen image. This intertwining of the reel and the real is readily evident in the early 1950s.

With the beginning of the 1950s, Dandridge's screen acting career took a new direction. Formerly cast in minor roles and usually as a maid,[15] she was now given roles that portrayed her more and more as a sex symbol. This new direction in her career transformed her from the white woman's Other to the white/black male's Other. As she became more sexualized, one form of subordination replaced another. In her first such appearance as this transformed image, she was cast in a major role as the wife of a professional basketball player in *The Harlem Globetrotters* (1951). In the film she portrays an innocent and dedicated wife, Ann Carpenter, who "stands by her man" (played by real-life athlete Bill Brown) even after he has lost his status.[16] This particular role, however, minimizes Dandridge's sexuality and maximizes her domesticity, as evidenced by her dress, style, and submissive demeanor. Although she is portrayed as attractive, innocent, supportive, and appealing as a faithful wife, visually she is not made too sexually appealing. Like most films of the 1950s, *The Harlem Globetrotters* reflects the dominant patriarchal focus on marriage as women's proper place. Dandridge's character demonstrates wifely virtues—nurturing and supporting her spouse at the expense of her own needs. Although relegated to the background of the film, Dandridge proved she had acting talent.

The film's plot revolves around a man's abandonment of a teaching career to pursue and fulfill his dream of becoming a professional basketball player; his failure is attributed to his own self-aggrandizement. His attempt to resolve his internal conflict by abandoning his job as a college instructor to become a professional basketball player is not without racial and political implications for African American men, even today. His decision to change professions reflects the instability and displacement of black males within a larger sociopolitical context. Dandridge's role, which is peripheral to the film's main plot, reveals how women, in this instance black women, become the property of men and merely serve to embellish male careers and status.

That in this film Dandridge is depicted as a married woman who is provided for by her husband conceivably reflects her desire to be a married woman in her off-screen life, especially when we consider the cultural value assigned to marriage at this time. Her failed marriage to Harold Nicholas, a professional dancer, officially ended in divorce in the same year that *The Harlem Globetrotters* (1951) was released.[17] In her marriage to Nicholas, she attempted to live out the fantasy of an ideal marriage, dedicating herself to the institution of marriage and neglecting the development of her own career. It seems that she was deluded by film representations of ideal but unrealistic portrayals of love and marriage. Yet Dandridge recognized that her marriage to Nicholas, who was attempting to advance his own career as a dancer, was in direct contrast to what she desired and to the screen ideal portrayed in *The Harlem Globetrotters,* on which she was working as her marriage reached its end. After a brief hiatus following her troubled marriage, Dandridge had returned to acting because of her desire to resurrect an acting career, provide for her disabled daughter, and recover from the psychological trauma of her failed marriage. Her role in *The Harlem Globetrotters* began to infiltrate her off-screen life and increased her desire for an ideal marriage, such as the one the film fabricated, that escaped her in real life. It is conceivable that because of her desire for an ideal marriage, Dandridge began an endless pursuit of marriage.

As the black male's on-screen Other, Dandridge was able to resolve the problems of a woman whose existence was totally defined by men.

Off-screen, however, the role was less easily played in her own marriage, a marriage that seemed doomed to failure from the beginning. In fact, Dandridge admitted that their difficulties commenced even on their wedding night, when a sexually inexperienced Dandridge resisted her husband, a much more experienced sex partner. Their marriage quickly deteriorated, complicated by a series of events that included Nicholas's absence when she gave birth to their only child, his numerous affairs, and his increasing absence from home.[18]

Nicholas—who clearly regarded the development of his career as primary and his marriage as secondary—shared some similarities with Dandridge's spouse in *The Harlem Globetrotters* in that both were handsome, both were attempting to elevate their own careers, and both relegated women in their lives to the background. Dandridge recognized that the black male's Other was not the position to which she should be relegated. The real-life compromises required were far greater than her real-life expectations—expectations that were in direct opposition to those she had fabricated for the reel-life role. Although Dandridge was able to reconcile herself to the dissolution of her marriage, she was unable to relinquish her desire to be married. "Down deep," Dandridge later admitted, "there was the only thing I wanted: marriage, but marriage to the right man."[19] As she realized that her screen image as the devoted wife was an image that escaped her, her off-screen life became increasingly dissimilar from the role she had popularized.

In *The Harlem Globetrotters* Dandridge demonstrated that she was sexually desiring and desirable. Although she was not overtly constructed on the basis of her sexuality, her sex appeal was undeniably apparent. This led Hollywood to begin to capitalize on her overwhelming sexual appeal and ultimately to define her almost exclusively by this sexuality. Two years after *The Harlem Globetrotters,* she was cast in *Bright Road* (1953, alternately titled *See How They Run*) and the next year in *Carmen Jones* (1954).

ON WITH THE REEL-REAL SHOW

The African American press expressed surprise that Dandridge had landed the role of a country schoolmarm (Jane Richards) in *Bright Road,*[20] but it was impressed with the exposure to this range of her talent as an actress. Because her earlier musical career had established her as a "sexy, satiny" nightclub singer, her casting in this demure role may have seemed inconsistent with the black press's expectations and with Hollywood's new desire to exploit her sexuality. By casting Dandridge in *Bright Road,* Hollywood was retreating from its capitalization on her sexuality, which suggests that at this point in her career, the studio bosses considered her a character actress as opposed to a major screen star commodified primarily because of her sexuality. One review of Dandridge revealed, "Dorothy Dandridge as the inexperienced school teacher is sensitive, beautiful, a bit too tense all the way through, but a joy to behold."[21] In *Bright Road* she was subtly constructed as sexually desiring and desirable, even when it interfered with the film's narrative, but she was not totally defined by her sexuality. Because the filmmakers refused to relinquish entirely her image as sexually alluring, they could not avoid presenting Dandridge as an object of the male gaze and, in this instance, of her male costar, Harry Belafonte.

Dandridge would, however, assume the full-fledged image of sex symbol and full-fledged star status the next year in *Carmen Jones.* As Carmen, Dandridge was overtly endowed with sexuality, while Belafonte, as Joe, was emasculated and rendered virtually devoid of sexual urges, thus reflecting how Hollywood typically deformed black male sexuality on screen while portraying black women as exuding overwhelming sexuality, particularly in the presence of black men. James Baldwin noted at the time that "Belafonte [as Joe] is really not allowed to do anything more than walk around looking like a spaniel: his sexuality is really taken as given because Miss Dandridge wants him. It does not, otherwise, exist and he is not destroyed by his own sexual aggressiveness, which he is not allowed to have, but by the sexual aggressiveness of the girl."[22] Echoing Baldwin's position, other scholars contend that on-screen black males often have their sexuality denied, subverted, or repressed because of their historical image as threatening and dangerous. This is not to deny, of course, that the filmmakers subverted black males in many other ways, especially racially, by constantly presenting their blackness as a problem to themselves or by using them as vehicles against which to juxtapose dominant norms of masculinity. In part, because of the hegemonic discourse from which these representations evolved, black male sexuality was virtually always distorted and reconfigured as something different from white masculinity.

It seems clear that when 1950s Hollywood portrayed blacks as sexual beings, one character's sexuality, usually the man's, was often compromised at the expense of another, perhaps because black male sexuality was historically viewed by white society as dangerous or threatening. Both black men and women were disempowered and rendered non-threatening through the subversion of their sexuality by the social, political, and economic discourse that was subtly inscribed in their screen representations.

In *Carmen Jones*, Dandridge's sexuality is portrayed as uncontainable. One critic observed that Dandridge was a "slinky, hip-swinging, main-drag beauty with a slangy, come-hither way with men."[23] Portraying the black female as sexually promiscuous, while the black male is shown as emasculated, may have been Hollywood's way of inscribing its own sexual and racial anxieties and desires onto black bodies. The film, perhaps reflecting contemporaneous society, asserts that liberal access to the black woman's body is expected and even justified by her perceived rampant sexuality, while black male subordination is reified through the denial of his sexuality. Moreover, in this film, Joe is denied not only his own sexuality but also his claim to the black woman's body. The audience claims Carmen's body, a technique Hollywood frequently exploited to endow Dandridge's sexuality with mass appeal. Laura Mulvey asserts that in many films the female protagonist not only becomes the property of her male costar but also of the spectator, through the spectator's identification with him.[24] For *Carmen*, I submit that the spectator supersedes and replaces the costar in claiming the alluring female body as the male's property. This construction of Dandridge's sexuality earned her a lasting reputation for being able to "set male hormones sizzling."[25]

During the filming of *Bright Road* and *Carmen Jones*, Dandridge's on-screen portrayals again were mirrored in her off-screen life. Dandridge, Belafonte's Other on screen, became Belafonte's Other in real life. A romance developed between the two actors shortly after they first met. Dandridge attested to their mutual attraction, revealing in her autobiography that "We liked each other on sight and were destined to become theatrically and personally involved thereafter."[26] Dandridge launched an ill-fated romance with Belafonte, one that ended much as their screen romance does in *Carmen Jones*. In the film, Dandridge is the independent woman who refuses to succumb to the control of men and is perceived to use her sexuality to dominate black men. Off screen this role became far too real in her romantic relationship with Belafonte.

For both Belafonte and Dandridge, their real-life romance was closely intertwined with their failed romance on-screen. In the film, Joe accuses Carmen of emasculating him. Belafonte replicates this stance in his relationship with Dandridge. According to Dandridge, "Harry felt I castrated him, and he frequently used the term. He didn't feel safe with me, and decided I was too much to cope with, too independent, too dominant a personality.... He liked beauty in a woman, and he even liked intelligent women, but he needed someone who would not take the spotlight away from him."[27]

That the black male is emasculated both on and off screen has larger sociopolitical implications for considering the extent to which Hollywood's representations of reality mirrored the hegemonic discourse of American society. More important, the black male's emasculation becomes indicative of the way black males are restricted in and controlled by a society built on white male privilege, which is carried over into screen representations. Making Carmen/Dandridge responsible for the emasculation of the black male in this film places the onus on the black female, absolves whites (male-dominated Hollywood), and illustrates how both black men and women are manipulated in the service of the larger sociopolitical discourse.

Dandridge herself never resolved the psychological problems that stemmed from her romance with Belafonte. A tragic figure on screen (strangled to death by Joe in *Carmen Jones*), she became even more tragic off screen following her professional and personal relationship with Belafonte, pursuing futile and vacuous relationships with primarily white males and experiencing bouts of depression. While Mulvey argues that in films of this period the male protagonist controls the female image and has power over her, this is not always the case when the characters are black. In *Carmen Jones,* both the leading characters are disempowered because of their blackness, and the female suffers doubly by having her sexuality inscribed as promiscuity. Although the word "promiscuous" does not accurately describe Dandridge's interpersonal relationships after her affair with Belafonte, she did engage in a series of unsuccessful romances, many of them with white men. She was still obsessed with becoming a married woman, but despite her overpowering desire this goal still eluded her.

Dandridge's failures during this period of her life were, again, linked to the exploitation of her race and sexuality—attributes she could not escape and that fueled the conflict between her on-screen and off-screen personae. She failed to win the Oscar for her role in *Carmen Jones* and failed to marry her costar, Belafonte. Nevertheless, she became the first African American to be nominated for an Oscar for best actress, an award that she lost to white actress Grace Kelly, who won for her role in *The Country Girl* (1954). Dandridge's inability to win the Oscar can be partially attributed to the symbolic construction of whiteness commodified by Kelly and appropriated by Hollywood. The blonde Kelly embodied whiteness and, because she was born to a wealthy family, signified propriety and respectability—attributes that were in direct contrast to blackness as well as to Dandridge's blackness.[28] Dandridge, in spite of *Carmen Jones,* never totally embodied desirability to the extent that leading white actresses did. Her obvious talent notwithstanding, her failure to win the Oscar suggested that she would never escape the stigma of Otherness inflicted upon her because of her blackness. Dandridge was always relegated to the status of Hollywood's dark star. Nonetheless, Dandridge increasingly contested this imposed Otherness in her on- and off-screen lives. In her life off screen, this contestation became psychologically destructive as she, to use her term, "hurled" herself into the arms of a succession of white men in search of an ideal marriage. These men, however, indulged their fantasies with her but were prohibited by the dominant racial hierarchies from marrying her.

INTERRACIAL ROMANCES: ON AND OFF SCREEN

Commenting on her affair with Belafonte, Dandridge observed in her autobiography that the failure of this relationship extended to the relationships she subsequently developed with other men: "When I look at Harry in retrospect I realize that I was rejected. I tell this story of my rejection by Harry because in the next ten years I was to be pursued by many men, mostly Caucasians, and I was destined to be rejected—for marriage anyway—by all of them."[29] Rejected and dejected during the period following her romance with Belafonte, Dandridge nevertheless continued to perfect her acting talent and to make a name for herself in the cinema world. Despite her attempts to escape Hollywood's racialized and sexualized construction of her, she became even more imprisoned by this image. This is apparent in the roles she was offered and accepted. For example, when Dandridge and Belafonte returned to the screen as costars in *Island in the Sun* (1957), they were portrayed as estranged lovers, both seeking white mates. Their characters' preference for interracial relationships and rejection of black love suggest that they found something inherently satisfying about attracting the attention of whites. That whiteness is considered desirable while blackness is considered undesirable is reflected in their characters' implicit desire to escape blackness and, thereby, to reject themselves.

Black movie characters seeking white mates can be interpreted as a Hollywood-mediated construction designed to reassure the white patriarchy that its position of power is safe. On the other hand, it is conceivable that even alluding to interracial relationships in cinema allowed spectators to imaginatively transcend their racial differences and cross the boundaries of race through identification with these characters. From time to time Hollywood toyed with interracial relationships (e.g., *Imitation of Life* [1959], *The World, the Flesh, and the Devil* [1959], *Kings Go Forth* [1958], *Night of the Quarter Moon* [1959], etc.) as a way to influence the sociopolitical discourse during a turbulent period of racial strife and unrest. Racial tolerance is not promoted exclusively by devaluing blackness nor by exclusively featuring black men and women with an unceasing desire to seek whiteness. In *Island in the Sun,* it appears that the black characters are seeking white mates for the purpose of achieving whiteness, while whites are seldom shown seeking black partners to achieve blackness.

For example, in this film, the two black characters abandon each other and engage in what Lacan refers to as the desire to become the Other.[30] In this instance, the identity of the self is inextricably related to one's vision of the Other. Margot Seaton (Dandridge) is attracted to Denis Archer (played by white actor John Justin), while David Boyeur (Belafonte) pursues Mavis (played by white actress Joan Fontaine). Joan Collins also appears in the film as a woman who falls in love with a descendant of British aristocracy. According to Marguerite Rippy, it is Collins who becomes the parallel to Dandridge in the film since it is feared that her unborn child might possess "black blood." Rippy contends that "In *Island in the Sun,*

Joan Collins fulfills the role of the woman who appears alternately black or white, depending upon context. Zanuck, the director, contrasts Collins's ability to simulate blackness while remaining ultimately 'white' with Dandridge's blackness. The discourse surrounding Dandridge's character, Margot Seaton, correlates Dandridge's body with authentic exoticism in contrast to Collins's mimicry of exoticism."[31] Archer falls in love with Seaton, who is portrayed as a sexually passionate and enticing woman. In one scene, she dances in a halter top and skirt split high on her thigh; the Caribbean drums beat faster and faster as she dances beneath a metal bar that is gradually lowered to test her limbo skill. Susan Courtney, affirming Seaton's sexuality, adds that "Dandridge's Margot Seaton limbos in a bikini top and sarong, fully reclines on her lover's bed in the middle of the day for us to view (with him) from head to toe, and regularly bursts forth in low-cut dresses of bright yellow, orange, and red."[32] Courtney continues that "Margot [is] visibly circulated at parties as a prized erotic object of black and white male looks."[33] At the end of the film, Archer takes her to England, where she becomes the black wife of a white Englishman.[34] Margot's life with her white husband is never shown in the film, and in her real life, Dandridge did not attain the role of "happy" wife to a white spouse.

By contrast, Boyeur, although attracted to the white woman, Mavis, spurns her advances, declaring that "whereas a white man with a colored wife would only excite interest and envy, a white girl with a Negro husband would mean snubs and misery."[35] Moreover, Mark Reid contends that Belafonte could not visibly display his sexuality in this role because of the threat that black male sexuality posed.[36] The two relationships represent the intersection of race and gender in the cinema of the period. Boyeur's response to such a relationship is more complex and interesting than Margot's because he expresses sympathy for the white female, but his concern that society would ostracize her for choosing a black mate is problematic since it implies that he is denying his own condition as a black male who could expect to be similarly rejected by society at large. Even more disturbing than this denial is the assumption that a black female/white male pairing is more acceptable because it is consistent with historical expectations of the white male laying claim to the black female's body. His statement both accepts and perpetuates such views. Of course, here again his response is a Hollywood-constructed response, a reflection of how Hollywood replicates dominant views of race and racial attitudes and projects them onto black bodies transfigured for white audiences.

In addition to the interracial relationships, *Island in the Sun* is intriguing because it attempts to examine the issue of "whites" who are problematized by their "mixed blood." (The attempt compounds the problem because during this period in the United States, any person with known black ancestry was considered black, not white; the film conveniently reconciles the problem.) Jocelyn (Joan Collins), the daughter of the aristocratic Fleury family, is impregnated by a young English Lord, Euan Templeton (Stephen Boyd). Because a local news reporter reveals that her family is tainted with "mixed blood," Jocelyn's impending marriage is endangered. Fearing that her child will not be able to take Templeton's place in the British aristocracy, she initially declines the marriage offer, declaring that it is inconceivable that a "black man" will ever sit in the House of Lords. But her fears are allayed when her father reassures her that his mother was three-fourths white and that she herself possesses only one-sixteenth "colored blood." Her child, therefore, is bound to be white. Further, Jocelyn's mother reveals privately that her husband is not Jocelyn's biological father, thus eliminating any chance that she is tainted with "black blood." The episode illustrates how Hollywood resolves the dilemma of miscegenation.

The issue of "mixed blood" that thickens the film's interracial themes is subordinated to a murder mystery. The mystery, which involves Jocelyn's brother, Maxwell Fleury (James Mason), adds suspense and another dimension to the question of "mixed blood." Courtney suggests that at the film's "center is a murder plot that derives from Maxwell's paranoid sense of having lost hold of the cultural privileges he expects: the native population of his Caribbean island is on the verge of self-governance; the plantation he has inherited is literally rotting away . . . and he fears that neither his father nor his wife is granting him the phallic recognition he deserves."[37] Maxwell murders a man he believes is having an affair with his wife. He gradually reveals himself to the police and hints at suicide. The two relationships involving Dandridge's and Belafonte's characters are thus dually juxtaposed: the secrecy surrounding the murder is mirrored by the secrecy that surrounds the Fleury family's racial background. If we read Maxwell's attempted suicide as a solution to the issue of miscegenation, the film seems to suggest that death is an appropriate response for those, like Maxwell, who are problematized by "mixed blood" (an offshoot of the tragic mulatto syndrome). It is noteworthy in this regard that Boyeur, the black labor leader, ends his affair with his white lover and that Seaton, although she marries her white lover, is forced to leave the island. Maxwell's implied suicide can be seen as a third indicator of the futility associated with interracial relationships such as the respective ones associated with Belafonte and Dandridge.

Because *Island in the Sun* ventures into the uncharted film territory of interracial relationships during a period when most whites considered such subjects taboo, the film elicited strong public responses. For example, in Baton Rouge, a radio station was prohibited from even mentioning the film on the air.[38] By comparison, the African American press, more sophisticated about racial realities, responded casually, simply complaining that while Hollywood was displaying its liberalism in presenting an interracial romance on screen, it unfortunately had not allowed the couples to kiss. The black press was further troubled by the fact that more physical expression had been afforded in the romance between Dot and Justin (the black female and white male) than in the romance between David and Mavis (the black male and white female). The *Chicago Defender* suggested that the decision to develop the black female/white male affair more fully while treating the white female/black male affair only superficially implied that the filmmakers saw black female sexuality as equated with darkness, which made the portrayal of the black female as sexually promiscuous acceptable.[39] This position is supported by Freud's dark continent trope as explained by Mary Ann Doane, who refers to Freud's implication that the black female became inextricably linked to black sexuality.[40] In *Island in the Sun,* the black female is objectified by the white male gaze, an observation that Donald Bogle confirms when observing that "She's beautiful to watch, a fragile goddess whom the audience cannot help being drawn to."[41] This acceptance contrasts directly with the film's attitude toward the African American male, whose feared masculinity must be denied, repressed, or subverted, as Belafonte's was in this film. Consistent with this stance, Margot diverts the black male gaze.

As she was increasingly sexualized and objectified, Dandridge's screen life continued to be mirrored in her real life. The interracial relationships she experienced in her private life were no less problematic than those she constructed on screen. Following her failed relationship with Belafonte, she increasingly sought the company of white males. Aware that her romances with white men were futile, she nonetheless continued to attract and be attracted to men unwilling to commit themselves to her. She appeared to be as involved as the Hollywood executives in constructing her star image and consequently moved farther and farther away from the reality that these relationships were doomed to failure because of the racial politics of the era. As she struggled to distinguish between her off-screen and on-screen selves, the two became more confused. Her inner conflict even infected her screen representations. According to Bogle, Dandridge's personal conflicts and vulnerability were glaringly apparent, particularly in *Island in the Sun,* in which she seemed misplaced.[42] She appeared to be masquerading as a mediated construction of herself and, because of her inability to avoid being attracted to white males who were unwilling to make a commitment, she became consumed by her own futile behavior.

According to Marguerite Rippy, "At an informal Actors Laboratory gathering in 1948, Dandridge danced with actor Anthony Quinn, unwittingly sparking a media controversy. Columnists Hedda Hopper and Jim Henaghan censured Dandridge's dance as an interracial dancing scandal, and [then] the black press and Hollywood Democratic Committee responded in defense of the Lab's activities."[43] Dandridge was well aware that such public behavior between blacks and whites would not only garner attention but might invite ostracism in the industry. That she engaged in such public behavior suggests that she was attempting to attract attention—even if the attention was negative—for the purpose of elevating her career, even though she understood that crossing these racial boundaries could result in hurting a black actor's career.

In 1948 Dandridge was still married to her black husband, Harold Nicholas, and her dance with Quinn could have been for both of them no more than an innocent transgression of social codes. Yet the white press, and ostensibly its audience, perhaps read romance but definitely read sex into this social act. As innocent as this particular dance might have been, it nevertheless was a precursor to Dandridge's subsequent obsession with establishing romantic relationships with white men. As Dandridge internalized her screen roles, she began to acknowledge her off-screen fascination with attracting the attentions of white males. Increasingly aware that she had been rendered an Other in both her public and private lives, she found the fascination that she held for white males more enslaving, and she became less and less able to distinguish between the real and the reel. Though she was partner in several interracial relationships during the 1950s, her quest for a happy marriage to a white male was never realized.

Among her white suitors were Harding Allbrite, who spurned her marriage proposals and chose a wealthy white woman for his wife, and Peter Lawford, who, although strongly attracted to Dandridge, made it very clear that their relationship would "come to no serious conclusion."[44] According to James Spada's biography of Lawford, the actor was not even willing to risk public embarrassment by openly displaying his affection for Dandridge. A friend told Spada that "Peter didn't have the courage to take Dorothy Dandridge to parties. He'd have me pick her up and I'd walk into the party with her; then she'd hook up with Peter."[45] That the white male was prohibited from publicly acknowledging a black female lover further nuances the trope of darkness and masculine privilege; the white male must do so without exposing himself to public scrutiny. Moreover, as a black woman, Dandridge participated in her own subordination by conceding to such treatment, attesting to her inability to control her own obsession.

Elmer Tyner, a married white hotel owner, was infatuated with Dandridge and offered her a building if she would make herself available to him. His behavior reflects the assumption by some white males that black bodies can be bought, sold, and bartered by them as inscribed in white masculine privilege—an arrangement not so different from slavery. The idea that black women are expendable and marketable commodities is perhaps even more disturbing. This relationship was further complicated by the fact that Dandridge was also involved with Tyner's son. She revealed that "George [the son] told me that he was in love with me, but he couldn't come up with any kind of proposal, not even keeping me in a suite somewhere; and there was nary a word about marriage. For a time I found myself warding off the foam of the older man and trying to figure out what the son was up to and what he wanted."[46]

During the filming of *Bright Road*, Dandridge had an off-screen romance with Jerry Mayer, Louis B. Mayer's nephew. This relationship again hinted at the white masculine privilege that not only allowed white males to claim black women's bodies but also to exercise their claims at will, both on and off screen. The relationship between Mayer and Dandridge ended when she decided that he was not the marrying kind.[47]

Having futile affairs such as these made Dandridge question her relationships with white men. She eventually realized that her fascination had become an obsession, but her psychological insecurity made it impossible for her to get off this self-destructive path. For Dandridge, it was no longer a matter of being able to attract attention; she now desired to openly contest the socially imposed codes that prevented white men from marrying black women. Dandridge's behavior forces one to question whether she viewed her struggle to pursue these relationships as personal or political. To what extent was she attempting to challenge social norms regarding interracial relationships? More specifically, was she obsessed with having a white spouse because of the alleged social and economic advantages that such a marriage might provide, and if she succeeded in her pursuit, would that imply that she was denying her blackness? Most of all, did Dandridge view her behavior as indicating that racial integration could be ultimately achieved in a racially divided society, or was she so exploited by white males that she then identified with the oppressor in an effort to escape her blackness? While these questions cannot be adequately answered in this examination, they certainly speak to the ongoing internal contradictions with which she seemed to be afflicted.

Unfortunately, Dandridge did not overcome her obsessive desire to marry a white man of status. During the filming of *Carmen Jones,* she became romantically involved with the film's producer, Otto Preminger, who convinced her that producers and stars should develop "a coupling until the picture ended . . . if star and director know each other heart and soul—and the rest—the spark of it all might well leap into the beauty of the film."[48] Preminger is symbolic of the white masculine privilege because of his on-screen and off-screen power over Dandridge. Because Preminger was so privileged, Dandridge's quest for what white maleness represented would somehow be psychologically justified if, through identification with him, she felt empowered herself.

Dandridge's futile relationships with white males, both on and off screen, raise a question of whether she was in search of a "father" figure rather than "lover." Dandridge's parents were divorced when she was very young, and she had only infrequent contact with her father. According to Dandridge, her father was the son of a white British gentleman and a woman of African descent, a scenario strikingly similar to that of her character in *Island in the Sun*.[49] If Dandridge's father was a mulatto, then it is plausible that her infatuation with white males represented a search for the whiteness in her father's ancestry as well as a way of filling the void left by her father's absence. Since both a father and white males symbolized power and control, they may have substituted for each other in her emotional life. In her autobiography she mentioned that she saw an aunt who joined the family after the divorce as a substitute father figure. Later, males similarly might have served as paternal surrogates. One man in particular, Otto Preminger, certainly fit the father image because of his age, his dominant personality, and his position of power. In her autobiography, Dandridge even described feeling at the time of her involvement with Preminger that "I had a daddy now."[50]

Their romance ended when Dandridge became pregnant with Preminger's child and made it known that she desired to have his child. He resisted and, Dandridge wrote later, "For me, it was the clue that I was out."[51] The end of their affair was signaled by a reported abortion that, according to Bogle, some argue occurred and that others deny.[52]

While Dandridge acknowledged that the relationship with Preminger had ended, she did not then come to terms with her quest for whiteness or her fascination with being objectified by white males. Rather, she embarked on yet another futile romance—a romance that may have begun before her involvement with Preminger. This time it was with Juan Martinez, a wealthy South American tycoon who was willing to accept Dandridge as his concubine but declared that he could not marry her because she was not a Catholic. So, again, Dandridge was rendered unmarriageable, this time ostensibly by religion, which invites speculation about whether Martinez would really have married her had she been Catholic. The breakup of their relationship sent Dandridge into a deep depression and she was diagnosed as suicidal.[53] Although Martinez himself was not unambiguously white, for Dandridge he was symbolic of whiteness and, therefore, she surmised that she could not be publicly acknowledged by the institution of marriage. Moreover, Dandridge's psychological response to this failed relationship certainly suggests that she was responding not necessarily to this particular rejection but, in the words of Fanon, to a "collective catharsis" of rejection by white males who signified power, privilege, and authority.[54]

For Dandridge, this failed relationship represented a clashing of two personas, Dandridge's reel persona and Dandridge's real persona, who were struggling to retain their own identities while becoming increasingly alike. Unable to resolve this conflict, she developed a physiological response to her psychological dilemma, and her health began to decline. She developed a fever, and because of her inability to sleep a physician gave her narcotics.[55] But most of all, she was afflicted with another case of rejection. Dandridge reports that "It was the realization that I had been psychologically raped by one of the worst human types that made me want to kill myself, and now I searched for the swiftest and easiest means to bring this about. By the time I arrived in Los Angeles the idea of self-destruction was a permanent part of my psyche."[56] In fact, Bogle reports that she had attempted suicide on several occasions with an overdose of sleeping pills and was forced to have her stomach pumped.[57] He notes that "Dorothy remained in therapy with the psychologist John Berman. . . . She talked to Berman about her family, her romantic disaster in South America."[58]

What had begun in the 1940s as a burning desire to be married evolved in the 1950s into an obsession to be married to a white man. Summing up her encounters with white males, she stated in her autobiography: "So many men think there is nothing sweeter than having a brown boff on the side, under wraps, taken in the dark or kept behind the scenes."[59] Yet being "a brown boff on the side" was not her ultimate desire. Recalling her thoughts during this obsessive period in her life, she admitted, "I must *marry* a white man. In my romantic little brain I visualized someone rich, famous, handsome, charming—and he might even love me for my color."[60]

The immediate question that rises is why she felt she must *marry* a white man. Lena Horne pointed out more than once that her marriage to a white man was a career move, made for the power and privilege such a marriage would bring. Yet a career move—the power and privilege she would garner—seemed not to be Dandridge's motivation, nor was her personal taste in men nor her flaunting of social and racial codes and norms. Dandridge's obsession with white men and her insatiable desire to be *married* to one suggest she was driven by issues much broader and deeper. Though a definitive answer to the "why" is probably not possible, there are plausible reasons for her obsession, chief among which is her obsession with whiteness (the term's abstractness notwithstanding). Richard Dyer contends that whiteness can essentially be interpreted as both everything and nothing, an interpretation that Dandridge came to terms with in her own life and used as the title of her autobiography.[61] Because whiteness is a trope that has been created to exacerbate racial difference, and because it is inscribed as a signifier of power and privilege, it becomes all-encompassing and, in Dyer's words, erroneously symbolizes "everything." At the same time, because it is a social construct with no validity other than what whites have inscribed on it, it may represent "nothing." When we consider that the very existence of the trope is dependent upon blackness, then Dandridge's quest for whiteness, or for the power and privilege inscribed on it, becomes even more futile. In titling her autobiography *Everything and Nothing,* Dandridge may have been attempting to reflect her own plight as an African American actress who made it in the white entertainment world—gaining "everything"—but confronted by the harsh reality that what she had acquired was essentially "nothing." But what Dandridge seems not to have recognized was that this title was not exclusively a reflection of her own plight (nor even that of all successful black American entertainers) but is also, and more important, a statement that whiteness itself was, indeed, everything and nothing. Dandridge internalized her rejection, and because she was unable to place the blame for this rejection on those who were responsible for it, and force them to contend with their own racial and sexual attitudes, she ultimately became more problematized. Her pursuit of abstract whiteness, though localized in white males, helped precipitate her demise.

FROM THE REAL TO THE REEL AND BACK AGAIN

During the late 1950s, Hollywood film companies, as well as European film companies, continued to position Dandridge as an object of desire. By then, Dandridge was not only represented as a tragic figure, she literally had become the tragic figure whose on-screen image was fetishized by white males. These men viewed her body voyeuristically as the site on which to explore their own sexual fantasies and racial anxieties but never as a woman with whom they expected to have a serious relationship, either off screen or on screen.

In *The Decks Ran Red* (1958), *Tamango* (1958), and *Malaga* (1960, also known as *Moment of Danger*), Dandridge was cast as a tragic female who finds herself in the arms of white men, often in unsuccessful relationships. She is a tragic female in these films because she is constructed as a woman who is infused with moral weaknesses (specifically, her promiscuity) and psychological maladjustments (specifically, her attraction to white men) and who lacks control over the events that shape her life and lead to her demise. From this perspective, her on-screen characters accurately mirror her life during the previous decade.

In *The Decks Ran Red*, Dandridge's character is the only female on a battered freighter where a mutiny is staged, a situation in itself open to sexual interpretation.[62] The implication is that the white males on the ship are empowered to claim the black female even at the expense of her mate, her black Polynesian husband, who is rendered insignificant, unimportant, and desexualized. In the role of Mahia, the black Polynesian wife of a cook (Joel Fluellen), she is taken hostage because of her "exotic beauty." Wearing a tight-fitting dress with a revealing neckline, Mahia is constantly undressed by the eyes of the white men, and she returns their desiring gaze, targeting especially the ship's captain. Mahia's sexuality is heightened to hypersexuality by the implication that her desiring gaze attracts the attention of not only one particular male but multiple males simultaneously—her husband (because he is her spouse), the white ship captain, and one of the white mutineers. And, of course, she becomes the object of the gaze for spectators. These gazes render Mahia sexually desirable and though she plays a Polynesian in the film, she was well-known to audiences by 1960 as a black actress. Regardless of her race, she is not white and thus is projected and perceived as the racial female Other who is subject to the whims and desires of white males, who make her sexually promiscuous. This implication is also a subtle attempt to justify a white male's attempt to rape her, which is alluded to but not dramatized in the film.

Mahia uses her sexuality to disarm a mutineer by lowering one shoulder of her blouse to lure him closer, then removing his gun and shooting him. The gun may be a signifier of the phallus, since the film alludes to the exploitation of her sexuality without actually depicting it. The inscription of white masculine privilege on her body is signaled by her need to exploit her own sexuality to defend herself; her body becomes her only weapon and her only defense against white male assaults. Her sexuality is thus equated with violence. That the racial Other's sexuality becomes coterminous with violence certainly raises the issue of rape. The scene in which a white male rapes Mahia is subtly implied, rather than dramatized, and no doubt in the mind of American spectators invokes the historical victimization of black women during slavery, when a white man could rape a black woman with social and legal impunity. This referential context is projected onto the film and thus normalizes the audience's pre-existing expectations about this form of interracial sex. Moreover, the black female body is intruded upon through violence, a privilege associated with whiteness and indicative of power. Such power, of course, is denied to blackness, so that when it is associated with blackness it is no longer regarded as power but as violence. This symbolic reconstruction of rape reaffirms for white masculine privilege that violence is inextricably linked with blackness and black sexuality. Slavery as a referential context not only helps account for Mahia's desiring gaze and her implied rape but also for the emasculation of her husband. Seen from the purview of slavery and its aftermath, she, a black female, is the seductress for white males and therefore responsible for her own rape as well as for her husband's demise. In fact, when her husband is murdered, Mahia is presented as expressing little grief and seems preoccupied with the mutineers. She is thus used as a vehicle to render the black male insignificant, although his insignificance is apparent from the beginning of the film.

Of this film and Dandridge's performance, one review claimed that

> Dorothy was no great shake in *Decks* for the simple reason that her style was cramped, so to speak. When the picture appeared in Europe under another name Miss Dandridge was terrific.
>
> Hollywood wanted the picture but not on the same mixing scale. So it did something about the screenplay and that something took all the salt out of the Dandridge performance.... It was what Hollywood did to her part of the picture in the cutting room that nixed any and all possible chances of her being awarded a "best" for her part in *The Decks Ran Red*.[63]

Bogle, commenting on the film's racial and sexual politics, reports that writer/director Andrew Stone titillated the audience by hinting at interracial romance.

> Yet he [Stone] upheld prevailing attitudes by making sure that Dandridge's character Mahia never actually ends up with any of the men on board.... While she flirts with the captain, she does not fall into his arms at the film's finale. In one crucial scene, White actor Stuart Whitman also

grabbed her in his arms and, forcing himself upon her, kissed her. Though
Whitman's kiss was more that of a man violating rather than romancing
her, it still marked Hollywood's first interracial kiss.[64]

Despite the implication of Dandridge's role, the interracial affair hinted
at in *The Decks Ran Red* (the desiring gazes between Mahia and the
ship's captain) reflected the troubles she endured in her off-screen life.
For example, in her posthumously published autobiography, Dandridge
acknowledged her status as the elicitor of the white male gaze: "America
was not geared to make [a black woman] into a Liz Taylor, a Monroe, a
Gardner. . . . My sex symbolism was as a wanton, a prostitute, not as a
woman seeking love and a husband, the same as other women."[65] Rippy
adds that "Whereas the white woman (Monroe) becomes an idealized,
inaccessible, sublime object of desire, the body of the black woman is
perceived as the accessible, material means of attaining carnal satisfac-
tion."[66] Her hypersexuality and, in consequence, her husband's emasculation in *The Decks Ran Red* demonstrate how the cinema industry used
black bodies to affirm the power and privilege of white males. Dandridge
clearly understood that she was the racial Other in the cinema world, a
status the patriarchal cinema industry conferred on her and over which
she had little control.

She was next cast in another film that hinted at an interracial affair:
Tamango (1959), especially the unexpurgated European version (often
spelled *Tomango*). Actually, *Tamango*, when released in the United States,
was similar to *The Decks Ran Red* in that both films focused on ships at
sea with Dandridge centered as the object of the gaze. However, they differ in that *The Decks Ran Red* explored a mutiny that occurs at sea, while
Tamango explored black slaves who attempt to overthrow a Dutch slave
ship during the middle passage while en route to Cuba. One principal
difference between the films is that in *Tamango* the "dark" characters
are blacks, not Polynesians. According to the *Chicago Defender*, in the
U.S. version of this film Dandridge's white male costar, Curt Jurgens (the
ship's captain), "makes only an eye-casting move toward Dandridge."[67]
Nonetheless, in both the European and American versions, Dandridge's
character attracts the attention of white males and becomes an object of
their desiring gaze, a role that she had come to expect. In this film Dandridge becomes an even more egregious solicitor of multiple gazes (from
the white captain, the first mate, and the black leader of the slave revolt)

than she had in *The Decks Ran Red,* and thus she continues to be rendered as sexually promiscuous.

In the U.S. version of *Tamango,* Dandridge's role is defined solely by her sexuality. And although in *The Decks Ran Red* she is depicted as a wife (a role that at least held the possibility for her to be presented as something other than a sex object), in *Tamango* she is cast as the concubine of a white slave ship captain, a role that automatically renders her a sex object. As a *Chicago Defender* critic wrote, "Hollywood makes plain [its] attempt to indicate [that these attractions are] more lust than love."[68]

The continuing control of the image of Dandridge as an object of desire and an object of the male gaze is unambiguously present in *Tamango,* a film in which U.S. slavery is the historical setting rather than a referential context. In this film she plays the mistress of a white slave trader (Curt Jurgens) who promises to free her in exchange for sexual favors. In one scene, she struggles to escape from the embrace of a white male who refers to her scornfully as "white man's trash." The implication is clear: because of her blackness she deserves to be regarded as "trash" and as a white man's property. Yet although she again emerges as the sexually promiscuous black female, this time she is allowed to defend herself and resists the white captain, even if only by giving him a verbal lashing: "I hate you . . . I have always hated you . . . I hate that bed."

The captain, unable to believe that he is losing control over the object of his desire, sends Dandridge's character below deck to join the rest of the slaves. Hoping that she will accept her subordinate position and return to him so that he can again claim her body, he delays execution of a group of rebellious slaves. But when Dandridge's character refuses to return and instead joins the slave revolt, he acknowledges the power the slaves are attempting to exert over him. He is only temporarily devoid of power, though; when he regains control, he orders the murder of the slaves, Dandridge's character included.

Even though her revolt adds dimension to her screen character, her persona remains that of a tragic figure in that her moral weakness and psychological maladjustment prevent her from controlling the events that shape her fate. First, she is internally conflicted with respect to her allegiance to the black revolters and her identity as the captain's concubine. Second, she is pursued by white men who have no interest in her other than to exploit her sexuality. Third, when she joins the slaves she is aware that she is ordering her own demise because all of them will be killed. Fourth, her relationship with the black leader of the slave revolt is short-lived because the revolters will succumb to white male power (again, she is a character unfulfilled in love). Yet although she remains a tragic figure, she is also a complex heroine who recognizes that her fate as a concubine is no different from that of the other slaves. The film's ending is tragic: The white slave traders survive and the black slaves do not. It was an ending Dandridge would internalize and project onto her personal life.

Dandridge's hypersexualized image in *Tamango* became the inevitable target of press reports. Even the *Chicago Defender* could not avoid noticing the flagrant display of her sexuality, which violated Hollywood's censorship policies about both interracial romances and sexually explicit scenes.[69] The *Defender*'s expression of surprise at Hollywood's lax enforcement of its own code and its rendering of Dandridge's sexuality made Dandridge herself appear personally promiscuous. Bogle reports that the European version of this film (produced in France) contained even more explicit love scenes and was banned by the French government.[70] The film's blatant sexual content, as well as its presentation of an interracial affair, reportedly prevented the film's producers from arranging for its release through a major distributor; it was finally released through an independent distributor.[71]

The film created even worse difficulties for Dandridge, whose reputation became permanently associated with sexual promiscuity. Increasingly disillusioned with such portrayals, she began to engage on screen in what bell hooks refers to as the "oppositional gaze."[72] Although unable to prevent her on-screen subjugation and commodification by Hollywood, she did retain the power to project the "oppositional gaze" in defiance of the exploitation she endured. This is exemplified in *Tamango* when Dandridge challenges the white ship captain; not only does she retaliate verbally but she also projects a fiercely confrontational gaze at him as she denounces the exploitation she has endured.

Unable to escape the disaster that seemed to be enveloping her (on screen and off screen), Dandridge was typecast in two more hopeless roles, one of which was in the film *Malaga* (1960). Dandridge is centered as the romantic attraction in a narrative that focuses on two male crooks planning a crime. As in other roles, she is an exotic beauty whose ethnic identity remains obscure, and the two white men find her sexual appeal irresistible. As so often before, she is portrayed as sexually promiscuous because she elicits the gaze of multiple males. In this film, eliciting the gaze of white males who are involved in crime suggests also that blackness is itself somehow inseparable from criminality. Early in the film Dandridge's character aligns herself with one of the criminals but then becomes the romantic partner of the other after her original lover deceives both of them.

According to Bogle, *Malaga* was a problematic film for the producers, who were undecided about how to characterize its romantic relationships. Their uncertainty about creating acceptable on-screen interracial relationships is apparent in reports that the film's script changed so often during production that the plot became incoherent.[73] In her autobiography, Dandridge reported on the cinema industry's apprehensions about the interracial relationships:

> Now there were close-ups, and audiences would see a unique love scene. Above me was a white man, passionate, trembling—Trevor Howard, my costar. His face, truly an Englishman's face, was close to mine.... Close by the camera eye pointed. Trevor bent over me, his lips only a few inches from mine. I folded my arms around him and drew him close. The camera would show my fingers clutching into his back. Another instant and there would have been a bit of motion picture history—a white man kissing the lips of a Negro woman, on the screen for the first time.
>
> Suddenly, the director's voice rang out. "Cut."[74]

Thus, the behavior of African American stars was circumscribed on screen just as it was off screen. Whatever character she played, she was the dark star, a star prevented by the larger sociopolitical context from publicly displaying her affections for a white man—lest such behavior disrupt and challenge the racial hierarchy created to define identities and delegate power. To allow whites and blacks to engage in mutual attraction was to disempower white males and empower blacks.

Even though she was not empowered by her screen roles, Dandridge's star status did give her some power, though that power was vitiated by her screen image. She was celebrated by the African American community and was one of the first African American entertainers allowed to perform at white hotels and nightclubs. Because she opened doors that had traditionally been closed, she was warmly embraced by African Americans and became a symbol of black advancement.

The limits of this power were in evidence when *Confidential* magazine ran an article titled "What Dorothy Dandridge Did in the Woods," which functioned as a real-life representation of Dandridge as sexually promiscuous. So, off screen as well as on screen, social codes were in place to prohibit any public display of affection between a white man and a black woman. When such did occur, as *Confidential* alleged with Dandridge, many considered it lewd behavior, wanton sex rather than romance, and placed the onus on the black woman. Embedded in the title of *Confidential*'s article was the implication that Dandridge was both promiscuous and unsophisticated in her sexual encounters. bell hooks reports that "when a newspaper reported that she had slept with more than a thousand men, she threatened to sue and received a public retraction."[75] Specifically the *Washington Afro-American* reported that

> A white bandleader named Daniel Terry was identified Wednesday as the man with whom Dorothy Dandridge allegedly shared intimacies in a woods near Lake Tahoe, Nevada, sometime prior to May 1957. . . . The story appeared in the [*Confidential*] Magazine's May 1957 issue. . . . According to the piece, the then unidentified male suggested to Miss Dandridge that they go for a ride, which they did; the singer disclosed how she would love to take a walk in the woods, which they did; Dorothy then expressed a fondness for "sitting on grassy plots" and they did.
>   The revelation then purportedly revealed how Miss Dandridge and her escort took their "cue from the birds and bees to do what comes naturally."[76]

The magazine's treatment of her demonstrates that the equation of blackness with illicit and immoral behavior reverberated through the press and was not confined to the film lot.[77] By this time, however, Dandridge had gained some control over her reality. She became the first celebrity to sue *Confidential* for damages for depicting her in an illicit affair and received an out-of-court settlement of $10,000, a large award for that time.[78] Dandridge was applauded by members of the black press for taking such action and for protecting her reputation as an actress. Ralph Matthews in an editorial commended her action by stating: "If through her stand, Dorothy helps to put the quietus on this periodical and send its editors to jail, she will have performed a distinct service to the colored performer at large because, whether you know it or not, *Confidential Magazine* was the worst enemy that the colored performer had in America."[79]

This incident indicates that Dandridge was well aware that she was being maligned in the press and becoming identified with the mediated construction produced by the cinema industry. Moreover, her response indicates that she was trying and beginning to take control of her own life. Although disempowered on screen, she sought to preserve her reputation off screen. Unfortunately, her obsessive desire for a white mate did not diminish, and the amount of power she wieled as a consequence of her star status was not enough to negate the industry's control over her public image.

At the end of *Malaga,* Dandridge's character is left alone as her criminal lover turns himself into authorities, and she promises they will be reunited when he is released from jail, implying that if white males are her goal, she will pursue them no matter what the cost. More disturbing yet is the possibility that her on-screen character is particularly attracted to white males even if they are criminals. Of this film, Bogle observes that "Throughout, Dandridge is lovely but looks lost, at times strained and disoriented, and unfocused."[80] His description suggests that as Dandridge's private life unraveled, her personal conflicts became more visible on screen. He notes that toward the end of her career, "Dandridge didn't seem to be in her movies: that glazed look on her face indicated she was somewhere else."[81] It seems that by this time in her career, Dandridge produces an oppositional gaze by diverting the look that has been projected onto her, refusing to take her marginalized roles seriously.

Bogle's latter observation is an astute one. Dandridge admitted that during the filming of *Tamango,* she was distracted by the planning of her wedding to Jack Denison, a white restaurant owner. At first she refused to finish the picture, but finally she postponed the wedding to complete it. Of all her romances, the interracial marriage to Denison was the most destructive. She stated, "Hellbent on marrying a white man, I don't know what I wanted to prove. If it was respectability or wealth I was after, there was a question whether Jack at any time filled that bill."[82] Later in life, she was more forthright about her self-destructive quest: "Some people kill themselves with drink, others with overdoses, some with a gun; a few hurl themselves in front of trains or autos. I hurled myself in front of another white man."[83] Acknowledging her self-destructive behavior, Dandridge at this late stage in her career realized that, try as she might, she was no longer able to control either the mediated image being constructed for her or its effect on her private life. The marriage ended when Dandridge discovered that Denison had married her only for her money. Thus, the exploitation by men to which she was subjected in *Tamango* and that led to her character's literal death was duplicated in the figurative death Dandridge suffered, as she described it in the quotation above, in her real-life marriage to Denison.

After receiving her divorce, Dandridge faced foreclosure of her home, bankruptcy, several lawsuits, and depression. Acquiring the object of her desire in marrying Denison—a white man—left Dandridge financially and psychologically drained. The sad ending for her character in *The Decks Ran Red*, *Tamango*, and *Malaga*, respectively, reflects to some extent Dandridge's own life situation: she was abandoned by a series of white males. In addition, her screen image in these films as a promiscuous woman was transferred to her personal life.

PORGY AND BESS: DANDRIDGE'S MIMICRY OF THE SELF

In *Porgy and Bess* (1959), a film that mirrored her off-screen self-destructive behavior, Dandridge's character makes an inappropriate choice regarding men. She abandons a nurturing and supportive Porgy (Sidney Poitier) for the wayward and streetwise Sportin' Life (Sammy Davis Jr.).[84] Again, Dandridge is cast as a tragic figure. As Bess, she is consumed by black rather than white males. Three men compete for her attention and admiration and ultimately cause her death. Bess is introduced as the lover of Crown (Brock Peters), who gambles with the locals of Catfish Row, intimidates his peers, and commits murder and rape. Bess flees the violent Crown into the arms of Porgy, a sweet, well-meaning character whose masculinity is called into question because he is crippled. Later, Bess is lured away to the big city by Sportin' Life, who, hoping to exploit her beauty, uses drugs to persuade her to leave Catfish Row.[85]

Bess becomes a tragic figure not only because she is victimized by black males but also because she is exploited for her sexuality. Her sexual appeal is evident in her dress and body movements. She flaunts her charms in a low-cut blouse, tight-fitting skirt split to the upper thigh, a wide-brimmed hat, black stockings (where she stashes her cash), and high-heeled shoes. Even the colors of her clothing—red and pink—are reminiscent of those worn in the earlier *Carmen Jones.* She elicits the gaze of males as she swings her hips and swaggers through the streets of Catfish Row to intrude on a male crap game. As the only woman present interested in gambling, a male-dominated activity, she enhances her status as a woman associated with the underworld. Thus, she is not only hypersexualized but also equated with immoral behavior of other kinds. A signifier of sexuality and immorality, her construction gives legitimacy (if ever appropriate) to her rape by Crown, a rape that is not actually seen in the film. Although Dandridge's body is not violated by white males in this film, white male spectators can vicariously participate in the rape through identification with the black screen character.

Mark Reid notes that "Black sexuality (as in *Carmen Jones* and *Porgy and Bess*) that was limited to the 'primitive' black community or to alleged rapes by black men could be psychically sanctioned by whites if the assaults resulted in a threatened racial lynching of an innocent black man."[86] The rape scene occurs when Bess, returning from a church picnic, is accosted by Crown. She attempts to flee his embrace but he pursues her relentlessly. When Crown catches her, he pins her arms behind her back and proceeds to kiss her. She succumbs to the kiss, implying that she consents to intercourse, but then, struggling to free herself, cries out "Take your hands off me," the same words she utters in *Tamango* when she resists the embrace of the white slave ship captain. Jacquie Jones links this violence with sexuality, asserting that "the sex act itself . . . is manifested through the violent action of the film."[87] So while the rape is not actually seen, it is signified in the violence inflicted by Crown onto Bess. In both *Carmen Jones* and *Porgy and Bess,* a black female's exploitation by the male appears to be justified by her overdetermined sexuality.

Bess's resistance to the black male in *Porgy and Bess* points to events in Dandridge's private life. Otto Preminger claimed that Dandridge consciously resisted playing scenes with the black men in the cast. According to Preminger,

> One night after we had spent the day rehearsing the scene in which Crown, played by Brock Peters, rapes Bess, Dorothy Dandridge called me.
> "Otto," she said, sounding very upset, "you must recast him. I can't stand that man."
> "Dorothy, are you out of your mind? You're not casting the film, I am. I think Brock Peters will be very good in the part. I know he's not ready

yet, but you're not perfect either in everything you're doing." She got more upset. She kept saying she couldn't work with him. "When he puts his hands on me I can't bear it," she cried hysterically. It went on for about fifteen minutes, at the end of which she exclaimed, "And—and—and he's so black!"

I calmed her down and Peters continued in the part, but her tortured "he's so black" revealed to me the tragedy of Dorothy Dandridge. She was divorced from a black man who had fathered her retarded child. From then on she avoided black men. For her love affairs she always chose white men.[88]

One might conclude that Dandridge's resistance to Peters reflected her increasing dislike and fear of black males induced by black males (Nicholas and Belafonte in particular) who failed her in her private life, and that this dislike and fear could explain her desire for the white males in her life. The plausibility of this conclusion loses force when one considers that the white males in her life also failed her.

Whatever the primary cause, Dandridge's growing distrust of males and her psychological debilitation become more understandable when we consider the treatment she endured during the production of *Porgy and Bess*, this time from the white male director. Sidney Poitier was shocked at the treatment Dandridge endured at the hands of Preminger during the film's production.

Otto Preminger jumped on Dorothy Dandridge in a shocking and totally unexpected way. She had done something that wasn't quite the way he wanted it. . . . She hadn't proceeded very far before he exploded again. "No, no, no—what's the matter with you? You can't even do a simple thing like that? That's stupid, what you're doing—you don't have any intelligence at all. What kind of dumb way for a girl to behave! You don't even know who Bess is. You call yourself an actress—you get paid to perform, not to do stupid things." . . . Nobody went to Dorothy's defense. The rationale was, since he was not abusing her physically, since his attacks remained verbal, no matter how brutal, it was still an "artistic dispute" between the director and his actress.[89]

Poitier continues:

There she was, that delicately beautiful woman whose appearance suggested many more things than her personality could deliver, stripped naked. Unable to call on the strength of character that her elegant carriage implied; unable to summon up that survival sense essential to the secure person she wanted people to think she was; unable to strike back, because her defense mechanism was that of the prey, and the predator had selected her, staked her out, marked her for the kill, then struck without warning.[90]

The on-set problems that occurred during the production of this picture bring to the fore Dandridge's resistance to black males and maybe even her own psychosis. They also illuminate her deteriorating relationship with Preminger, with whom she had ended her affair and with whom she might have been mutually at odds, and they pinpoint Poitier's recognition of Dandridge's defenselessness as well as the exploitation that black actors endured in the industry. For Poitier, the fact that black actors were subjected to verbal abuse during production was compounded by the fact that they were assuming stereotypical roles on screen—especially during a period when blacks were attempting to achieve equal rights off screen. In fact, many blacks objected to a revival of *Porgy and Bess* in view of the progress blacks were attempting to make socially and politically. This was further exacerbated by the controversy in the black press that began when black actor Leigh Whipper proclaimed that Preminger had made a racial slur to an unidentified black actress, while actors Sammy Davis Jr. and Pearl Bailey defended Preminger.[91] Yet the victimization Dandridge endured on screen, where she was victimized by black males, was echoed in real life by her exploitation and castigation by the white male, Preminger.

Throughout her career, Dandridge appears to have lived a mirror image of her screen roles in her real-life romances. In fact, by the end of her life, it was clear that Dandridge's greatest role was as herself—a dark screen star created by Hollywood and exploited by an industry that had no place for a talented African American actress. The self and Other merged as Hollywood's mediated construction of Dandridge finally became inseparable from her own self-image.

BLACK: TO BE OR NOT TO BE

At the same time Hollywood was constructing its dark star to make her attractive to mass audiences, and more specifically white audiences, it was also positioning her as a racial Other. Yet this Otherness was conceived of in a way that at times minimized and at other times completely erased her blackness. Richard Dyer contends that female stars constructed by the cinema industry have to convey a quality of desirability (that is, the subject of male desire rather than the object of male desire) that implies not only a set of character traits but also a social position. According to Dyer, the social position usually equates such desirability with white womanhood and, even more specifically, with a woman who is not only white but also blonde.[92] Arguably, because "blondeness" is more closely associated with whiteness than "brunetteness," the blonde white woman is the epitome of whiteness. Since the black woman is far removed from whiteness and blondeness, she can never [aspire to] epitomize desirability and thus remains the *object* rather than the *subject* of male desire. Like Marilyn Monroe, a white screen star created by Hollywood to signify desirability, Dandridge could become a star, but, unlike Monroe, she could never become desirable.[93] Still, by obfuscating Dandridge's blackness or racial identity, white Hollywood could at least hint at her desirability while she remained veiled in her blackness.

In fact, to approximate Dandridge as a desired subject, Hollywood more often than not distorted her actual racial identity. On screen, Bogle contends, "The studios were eager to emphasize the more Caucasian aspects of [Horne and Dandridge's] looks in order to insure their appeal to the mass White audience."[94] According to Marguerite Rippy, "As her performances increasingly catered to white male audiences, directors who paired her with white leading men attempted to distance their films from the racial controversy raging in American culture by recontextualizing Dandridge as anything but African-American."[95]

In some films, the studios distorted Dandridge's actual racial identity in order to suggest a wide range of races, ethnicities, and nationalities other than African American. For example, in *The Decks Ran Red* she was cast as a Polynesian woman, in *Malaga* she was cast as a woman of color of European descent with an Italian name (Gianna), and in *Island in the Sun* she portrayed a Jamaican girl. At times the studios found it necessary to alter her skin tone to achieve the appearance of a race, ethnicity, or nationality other than African American. In *Tamango*, she was so heavily made up that the person/actress Dorothy Dandridge was barely recognizable.[96]

Dandridge attributed her casting in a variety of ethnic character types to the paucity of screen roles for African Americans. She was allowed to play Egyptians, Indians, or Mexicans on the screen and had little control over her racial construction.[97] Even though she may have preferred to be cast as an African American, the scarcity of such roles in Hollywood meant that she could either accept what was available or relinquish her career. Whatever her role, Dandridge had to contend with the fact that Hollywood deliberately altered her racial identity to appropriate her screen persona as their dark star.

Homi K. Bhabha argues that skin is a powerful signifier of cultural and racial difference because it is the most visible fetish in a range of social, political, and historical discourses.[98] Dandridge's skin color could be manipulated to represent a variety of ethnicities that are coded with an endless variety of meanings. In her autobiography, Dandridge reports that a screenwriter once told her that her skin was "neuter" and represented all the skin colorings of the world. He said "It is chameleon, it changes in each swath of light, ranging from white to dark by the instant. It is buff color, it is East Indian soft, it is South American blend, it can be Israeli, Gypsy, Egyptian, Latin."[99] Her skin was even regarded as making people "goosey."[100] Most of all, Dandridge's skin color made it possible for Hollywood to alter her racial identity so she could represent a wide range of ethnicities and become the site for spectators to explore and contest their own racial identities. Moreover, the extent to which Dandridge internalized the subversion of her own identity might help to explain the psychological problems she suffered while constantly facing the struggle between self and Other.

A few times the studios cast Dandridge as an African American mulatto, a construction that allowed white spectators to dilute her blackness and to enhance her whiteness, thus making her more acceptable to those who might be offended by what they perceived as blackness and allowing white male spectators to vicariously explore their own racial and sexual fantasies. Unlike Fredi Washington (and her character Peola in *Imitation of Life*), Dorothy Dandridge was not a white mulatto. She, like Lena Horne and Hazel Scott, was a bright mulatto—a person with what would be considered clearly discernible European physical features but one whose skin tone was not fair enough to be mistaken, under normal circumstances, for a white person's.

In her autobiography, Dandridge attempted to rationalize her "white" or European appearance to African Americans by asserting that it made her acceptable to white audiences in much the same way as Lena Horne was. As Dandridge saw it, because of their white features she and Horne paved the way for integration, since white audiences were more willing at first to accept blacks who looked more like themselves.[101] She was correct in her latter assessment, which is largely why Hollywood commodified her, Horne, and others like them; yet she remained appealing to black audiences as well. From the perspective of white privilege in the cinema industry and in society at large, Dandridge, though a mulatto, was still considered a black Other, though to whites a less objectionable Other than a black with a much darker hue would be. According to Bogle, "neither Lena Horne nor Dorothy Dandridge, despite their talents, would have made the cultural impact that they did if their looks had not suggested—at the very least—that they were racially mixed."[102]

Such subversion of Dandridge's racial identity was facilitated by her unusual coloration, which often provoked commentary. In fact, the author of one profile of Dandridge noted that she is best remembered for her skin color. She was described as

> a beautiful woman whose skin excited men and made them strange. She was a woman of color and sometimes the color was tawny, and sometimes it was caramel, and sometimes it was the particular brown you might have made by stirring butter into molasses and warming them over a flame—it was famous, this color, the color of Dorothy Dandridge's skin.[103]

Because of Dandridge's unusual coloring, and because she represented a variety of ethnicities on the screen, her ability to transcend her own racial identity sheds light on the notion of "passing." Dandridge internalized the representation of the "tragic mulatto" stereotype promoted in literature and cinema. Because this character type was so often transfigured onto her on-screen image, Dandridge was led to ask herself, "What was I? That outdated 'tragic mulatto' of earlier fiction? Oddly enough, there remains some validity in this concept, in a society not yet integrated. I wasn't fully accepted in either world, black or white. I was too light to satisfy Negroes, not light enough to secure screen work, the roles, the marriage status available to a white woman."[104]

When we couple her appearance with her real-life tragic circumstances, she comes to personify the mulatto figure. On screen, Bogle contends, "The studios were eager to emphasize the more Caucasian aspects of [Horne and Dandridge's] looks in order to insure their appeal to the mass White audience."[105] That she enacted a tragic figure on screen is further seen in *Tamango*, where Dandridge's character is split between her loyalty to the African slaves who planned the revolt and to the white ship's captain. She internalized what W. E. B. Du Bois referred to as a double consciousness, in that she viewed the world through two lenses, one white and one black. It was her "black blood" that allowed her to empathize with the black slaves, while it was her "white blood" that gave her the opportunity (and greater freedom) of serving as the captain's mistress. The tragic mulatto configuration is similarly inscribed in her role in *Carmen Jones*, in which she is both dangerous and desirable, the subtle implication being that her black side represents danger while her white side represents desirability. Dandridge's characters in both *Tamango* and in *Carmen Jones* are murdered by their lovers at the end of the films, and thus both films manage to convey the tragedy of the mulatto without explicitly alluding to the racial confusion that causes this conflict.

Appropriated on-screen as the tragic mulatto, Dandridge privately admitted to the racial confusion she often experienced in internalizing this mediated image.

> Contradictory currents flow inside me; they often go in opposite directions at the same time. If you have a part of white America in your soul, and a part of black America in your spirit, and they are pulling against each other, your values, if any clear ones exist to begin with, can get lost or unsettled. Add to that, if you take a girl like me, intended by our environment to be a housemaid, then make a star out of her, don't look for simplicity of personality—look for complexity.[106]

So Dandridge, who became the black (but also often mulatto) tragic figure that white Hollywood had fabricated, was aware of her obsession and her inability to control it. Moreover, she understood that by participating in this mediated image of herself, she would eventually become that image, the boundary between the self and the Other growing ever more indistinct.

For many mulattoes, passing calls for a denial of their blackness. While Dandridge was evidently internally conflicted with respect to her identity, there is no evidence that she was in denial about her blackness. Even though she contended that if she had looked like Betty Grable she could have captured the world, she was always appropriated as the Other.

This contradictory positioning of Dandridge seems to suggest that she was personally conflicted, even though publicly she was well aware that she was a woman of African American descent. In her relationships with white males, she seemed to be acting out the tragic mulatto stereotype, but in her professional performances she presented herself as an African American entertainer who sought to please audiences with her identity and talent.

Though Dandridge was a bright mulatto, in some films the studios did not want her to appear to audiences as anything other than an African American. When she was cast as an African American (with attendant assumptions and connotations), she sometimes was forced to appear on the screen as much darker than she was in real life to avoid any chance that white spectators would mistake her for a white woman. For example, during the shooting of *Bright Road,* producers decided that Dandridge photographed too light and looked Hispanic on screen, so the makeup department darkened her skin to make her readily recognizable as an African American.[107] Dandridge endured what James Snead refers to as "marking," having her racial identity altered so that she appeared identifiably black, a device employed to clearly demarcate the division between white and black.[108] By rendering Dandridge identifiably black, filmmakers could ensure that spectators would make no mistakes about the transfiguring assumptions connoted by the projection of blackness onto the female body.

Though the studios had their ulterior motives for making Dandridge appear identifiably black on screen, Dandridge herself embraced her African American identity off screen, her obsession with white men notwithstanding. As a woman well aware of her black identity and the political and social plight of African Americans, Dandridge challenged discriminatory practices. At the Chase Hotel in St. Louis, for example, she negotiated with the hotel's owner to allow members of the NAACP to have access to the facility to attend her performance. Dandridge was also concerned that African American audiences were often denied access to her performances because they were too expensive.[109] She acknowledged that as an African American performer she felt compelled to present the race at its best, even though that sometimes meant appearing in arenas not open to most blacks, where her own behavior would be used to judge all African Americans. Dandridge declared that "wherever I went and sang, I brought the white–non-white question with me; and somehow, through my appearance and manner and my singing style, it was easier for thousands of whites to 'meet the Negro.'"[110] It is clear that Dandridge was not, at least publicly, an African American in conflict with her blackness. She revealed that she had turned down roles she thought might injure the image of African Americans. Making such choices, she acknowledged, added enormous stress to the dilemma of being a black actress in white Hollywood. Thus Dandridge's public persona expressed a secure ethnic identity and identification with the struggles faced by African Americans. In her private persona, as I have argued above, she was being consumed by the ambiguous racial identity that white Hollywood had created for her.

DANDRIDGE VICTIMIZES HERSELF AND APPROPRIATES HER OWN DEATH

The death of Dorothy Dandridge is shrouded in mystery. This mystery is further problematized by the way she participated in, invited, and prophesied her own death. She seems to have virtually willed herself to die through her constant preoccupation with death. She recognized, as quoted earlier, her self-destructive tendencies: "Some people kill themselves with drink, others with overdoses, some with a gun; a few hurl themselves in front of trains or autos, I hurled myself in front of another white man."[111] The self-appropriation of her death surfaces throughout Dandridge's autobiography, as she sees in each new failure a death threat. According to her sister-in-law, Gerry Branton, the birth of Dandridge's daughter was the turning point: "After that, everything was self-destructive. If there were two choices to be made, she would make the most destructive."[112] If, as I have argued, Dandridge's on-screen construction as a tragic mulatto caused her to internalize this image of herself, an image that created "anxiety and desire," it is certainly conceivable that she developed a fascination with her own tragic end.[113]

She made frequent references to her death. Bogle notes that Dandridge's suicidal behavior began early in her career as her marriage to Harold Nicholas unraveled. For example, when Dandridge performed in Sweden, her sister-in-law had her rushed to the hospital where her stomach was pumped because of a drug overdose. While Dandridge attempted to dismiss the incident, according to Bogle "it was clearly a suicide attempt; as such, it was partly crying out for help, and being a performer, it may have been partly using dramatic effects in hopes of saving the marriage. . . . She made another suicide attempt when the tour took the group to Switzerland not long afterwards."[114] As another example, when some of her friends discouraged her from writing her autobiography, she concluded that they considered her life unworthy of being documented. "There was only one decision I could make," she responded. "I must either kill myself if I was that unworthy, or die of attrition then and there— simply will myself to death, which I felt like doing—or tell my story. Let outsiders decide whether my life, my work, my motherhood, my quest for security, my friendships were so reprehensible, so poor a human story."[115] Though Dandridge managed to begin working on her autobiography, she suffered from severe bouts of depression. Her state of mind prior to her death may well have signified an internal struggle. For Dandridge, this struggle ended in death; her conscious and unconscious engaged in endless battles. The use of phrases such as "kill myself" and "will myself to death" demonstrate her fascination with her own death and support the argument that Dandridge's early death was prefigured in her films.

Four months prior to her death she wrote her will, which was later reprinted in the *New York Times*:

> In the case of death—to whomever [sic] discovers it—don't remove anything I have on—scarf, gown, or other. . . . Cremate me right away—if I have anything, money, furniture give to my mother Ruby Dandridge. She will know what to do. Dorothy Dandridge.[116]

Making a will does not necessarily imply that she believed her death to be imminent, but it does serve as another piece of evidence pointing to her impending death. Even though most screen stars make a will once they achieve a certain level of success, Dandridge's self-destructive behavior and continual references to death suggest that the will prophesied her death, invited it, or expressed a wish for it.

Dandridge was found dead in her apartment on September 8, 1965. Reports conflated and complicated her already internally contradicted personae. Conflicting reports circulated that an injury, or murder, or suicide by drug overdose were responsible for her death. The coroner's office released a preliminary report suggesting that Dandridge had broken a bone in her foot and that fragments of the bone had infiltrated her bloodstream and may have caused her death. Dandridge supposedly sustained this injury in a Hollywood gym five days prior to her death.[117] On November 17, 1965, one month after her death, Los Angeles County's chief medical examiner reported that an exhaustive toxicological analysis provided by the Armed Forces Institute of Pathology identified acute drug intoxication resulting from the ingestion of the antidepressant Trofranil (the brand name of imipramine hydrochloride) as the cause of Dandridge's death. Later reports revealed that Trofranil does not induce sleep or forgetfulness, and so was unlikely to have caused accidental death. Rumors that Dandridge was murdered circulated among her friends, who refused to believe that she had committed suicide. Her former singing coach and pianist, Eddie Beale, believed that although a state of deep depression some three years earlier made suicide a possibility then, her subsequent recovery made it unlikely in 1965. At the time of her death, he said, Dandridge had apparently recovered and was planning to revive her faltering career.[118]

The cause of Dandridge's death was never convincingly resolved. A memorial service commemorated her life and work as one of America's leading African American screen actresses. Peter Lawford, who was scheduled to speak at the memorial service, canceled at the last minute. Harold Nicholas, one of her ex-husbands, reportedly kissed a white rose he laid on her casket. There is no mention that Jack Denison attended the service. A final tribute to Dandridge was paid in 1984 when she received her star in the pavement on Hollywood Boulevard.[119]

CONCLUSION

The virtual exclusion of black women from most mainstream film histories, especially ones that cover the pre-1960s period, has been acknowledged by a number of scholars. For example, Ruth Elizabeth Burks (1996), in her discussion of contemporary filmic representations, points to the glaring absence of the black woman. While she focuses on a specific film, her observations are germane to black women in the white Hollywood film industry since its beginning, and particularly to the pre-1960s era. Burks contends that "The current critical practice of bypassing analyses of black female representations in commercial Hollywood cinema . . . has created a new problematic . . . [that] fails to address the fact that a plethora of both male and female African Americans—not to mention most Americans—still shape their perceptions of themselves as well as others by what they see on Hollywood's silver screen."[1] Burks's proposition then speaks to two important points: the invisibility of the black actress in cinematic representation, and the influence that both this absence, and the problematic representations associated with black actresses, are likely have on spectators. She therefore foregrounds four important issues that emanate from this present study of black actresses in the early period of cinema: (1) invisibility/visibility of the black actress; (2) the construction of black stardom as embodied in the early black actress's screen image; (3) the spectator's identification with the black character/actress; and (4) the implications these screen representations of black cinema actresses likely have for subsequent screen representations.

INVISIBILITY/VISIBILITY

One of the purposes of my study is to address some of the key issues that Burks articulates—specifically, to address the invisibility of the black actress in the pre-1960s—by filling the void that exists in the literature. My interrogation of the racial and sexual spaces in which representative black actresses were situated in films prior to the 1960s is intended to speak for the larger group of black actresses during this period, as well as to suggest ways in which black Otherness was scripted in Hollywood films well after the period I study. While the roles of "maids" and "mammies" assigned to black actresses might have diminished (although it did not disappear) with the escalation of the civil rights and women rights movements in the 1960s, other roles that signified black female Otherness in Hollywood films rose to the fore, particularly ones that scripted the black female as a hypersexualized sex object (sometimes with violent tendencies).

As this study posits, black cinema actresses before the 1960s assumed minimal roles and in many instances were even partially erased. Although they occupied the space of the invisible, most used this disadvantaged position to render themselves visible. A black actress made herself visible through her exceptional talent, through her insistent desire to pursue her acting career, through the way she embellished the on-screen characterizations of white stars, through the resistance that she exhibited to inequitable treatment, and through her unceasing desire to have her voice heard. Black actresses' portrayals were also vital and central to the construction of blackness and black stardom: as they attempted to render themselves visible, they simultaneously participated to some extent in the history and development of these more general constructs. This study, therefore, can be interpreted as one that sheds light on how black stardom was constructed.

CONSTRUCTING BLACK STARDOM

There seems to be considerable agreement among film scholars concerning the almost insurmountable problems faced by black actors and actresses in the first half of the twentieth century in constructing stardom. This investigation of nine black actresses, who within the black community were coded or marked as black stars, is further testament to the fact that these women became symbolic of a unique stardom influenced by their race and gender. In fact, because of their race and gender, they were constructed as "dark" stars (as the chapter on Dorothy Dandridge discusses) who were forever bound to assume a contentious relationship with the industry. The women discussed, then, contribute to the discourse on black stars and stardom—a stardom that would forever be problematized.

It is through this discourse that we can begin to formulate a star discourse for *contemporary* black actresses. Arthur Knight suggests that despite the film industry's exploitation of black stars, the strategic insertion of black actresses (and actors) into Hollywood productions facilitated the construction of black stars and stardom.[2] Adding to these views, Richard Dyer proclaims that "The star phenomenon consists of everything that is publicly available about stars. A film star's image is not just his or her films, but the promotion of those films and of the star through pin-ups, public appearance, studio hand-outs and so on, as well as interviews, biographies and coverage in the press of the star's doings and 'private life.'"[3] In the case of the black actresses examined in this study it is evident that a variety of sources participated in constructing their stardom—the black press, advertisements, biographies, etc. Yet unlike the white screen star, they were not necessarily elevated on the same scale as white stars by the mainstream cinema industry. Rarely could they expect to have a film constructed around them; instead they were merely players in an already constructed story. But because of their involvement in the industry they were derivations of stars in their own right; they were "dark" stars but stars nonetheless. Most important in Dyer's critique is his assertion that a factor in constructing stardom is the extent to which the star participates in the construction of the image—an image that frequently reflected the sometimes contentious relationship the screen star established with the industry. Lena Horne and Hazel Scott became derivations of stars whose images were always associated with resistance because of the political stance they assumed in defiance of the exploitation they endured and the hypersexualization that became synonymous with their screen images. In comparison, Hattie McDaniel's star profile evolved from one who, while placating the industry for the role, subverted the racial inscriptions associated with the role, yet internalized these inscriptions off the screen. The construction of the star image varied from star to star as each brought her own personality and negotiated politics to the arena. Despite how they were similar to or different from each other, these black actresses all demonstrate how a star profile was constructed for each in view of Hollywood's alienation and exploitation. It is these star profiles that garnered identification from spectators and that would have implications for a later generation of actresses.

SPECTATORS' IDENTIFICATION WITH THE BLACK CHARACTER/ACTRESS

Jacqueline Stewart argues that "Characters such as Pauline Breedlove in Toni Morrison's *The Bluest Eye* (1970) and Bigger Thomas in Richard Wright's *Native Son* (1940) exemplify unsophisticated Black spectators who uncritically enjoy Hollywood cinema despite the film's illusionist incongruity with the 'realities' of their Black lives."[4] If we consider that black spectators migrated to the cinema in urban areas to view these representations and in some instances identified with the characters—characters far removed from themselves—then it is certainly plausible that white spectators might have been equally attracted to the black characters (e.g., Mammy in *Gone with the Wind*, 1939) portrayed by the black screen actress. And when we couple this identification with the dependence that existed between the black Other as a shadow of the white self, then the significance of the black actress in Hollywood is made all the more important, both for the characters with whom the black actress was paired on screen, and the off-screen white and black spectators identifying with the on-screen character. Thus, the black actress's role and significance to the cinema industry, despite the demeaning quality of the roles, speaks to the unending appeal and significance that the black actress may have provided to Hollywood cinema. My discussion of the contributions of these nine black women gives credence to this position while pointing to their undeniable appeal, and it speaks to the implications that these women likely had for a later generation of actresses.

IMPLICATIONS FOR CONTEMPORARY REPRESENTATIONS

As my study asserts, the 1960s marks a period of definite changes in the position blacks and women occupied in American society. Some of these changes began to be reflected more fully in Hollywood movies produced after about 1960. Dorothy Dandridge, whose screen career was on an upward swing before her untimely death in 1965, was Hollywood's first "real" female "dark" star. Dandridge was a transitional figure in commercial Hollywood cinema in that she was the first in a series of female "dark" stars who were to follow. While Hollywood elevated Dandridge to the status of star, the construction of Hollywood stars—black or otherwise— did not change significantly after the 1960s. Hollywood continued to exploit actresses—blacks, whites, and others—for their beauty and sexual appeal. Like their predecessors, black females who had become popular as entertainers (especially singers) were recruited as actresses, a practice that continues. Unlike their pre-1960 predecessors in the industry, many were assigned dramatic acting roles and many of these roles were not as subservients (one prominent example is Diana Ross in *Lady Sings the Blues*, 1972). Nevertheless, in many instances an older set of caricatured roles was merely replaced by a new set of caricatures, for example, prostitutes and "angry black women" succeeding maids and "mammies."

One significant change in the status of black actresses in Hollywood after about 1960 was that many more black actresses moved out of the space of the invisible and became "stars" based on their acting talent rather than primarily on their appeal to males' desiring sexual gaze. Ruby Dee and Cicely Tyson are among the black actresses of the late 1960s and 1970s who belong to this post-1960 group. Not only did black actresses move from the margin to the center, but some were even elevated to star status in much the same manner as was Dandridge in an earlier period. This was the case with Whoopi Goldberg, a comedienne turned actress, whose performance in *The Color Purple* (1985) and later in *Ghost* (1990) elevated her to the award-winning category. This move from the margin to the center also extended to black women who became producers and directors (Julie Dash, Kasi Lemmons, etc.) and black writers (such as Terry McMillan, Zora Neale Hurston, and Toni Morrison), whose writings were transformed on screen and allowed black actresses such as Angela Bassett, Loretta Devine, Whitney Houston, Halle Berry, and Lela Rochon to be centered on screen. Another significant change after the 1960s was that the mainstream media and mainstream histories and critiques gave more extended coverage to a larger group of African American actresses than they previously had. Black actresses such as Jada

Pinkett, Queen Latifah, Vivica A. Fox, Alfre Woodard, and others could now expect to be covered by a wide range of media showcasing their talent. When Halle Berry garnered an Academy Award for best actress for her role in *Monster's Ball* (2001), she could expect to be extensively covered by the mainstream press as well as the black press. Despite the many changes that have been made—on screen and in mainstream histories and critiques—the black actress before the 1960s remains relegated to the background (at best), and it has been the intent of this study to address this issue through an examination of nine representative black actresses of the pre-1960 era.

NOTES

Introduction

1. Allmendinger, "The Plow and the Pen," 545; Bowser, Gaines, and Musser, eds., *Oscar Micheaux and His Circle*, xvii.

2. Regester, "Sylvia as a Wilting Flower and Lucy as a Broken Blossom," unpublished paper, February 2009.

3. Jung, *Psychology and Religion*, 1–39.

4. Eva Jessye, "The Truth About *Hallelujah*," *Baltimore Afro-American*, August 2, 1930, 8.

5. Butterfly McQueen's outspokenness halted her career and kept her from achieving the same level of success as McDaniel or some of the other actresses included in this study.

6. Morrison, *Beloved*, 190.

1. Madame Sul-Te-Wan

1. Ellison, *Invisible Man*, 3.

2. Ibid., 439.

3. For her date of birth, I rely on Madame Sul-Te-Wan's death certificate issued by the Department of Health Services, State of California.

4. Gloria J. Gibson-Hudson reports that her mother was named Cleo de Londa (see Gibson-Hudson, "Sul-Te-Wan, Madame," 486). Sul-Te-Wan's death certificate indicates that her mother was Mary Kennedy.

5. "Strange Ethiopian Artist Wins Struggle in Hollywood," in George P. Johnson Film Collection, Department of Special Collections, University of California, Los Angeles.

6. See Beverly J. Robinson, "Sul-Te-Wan, Madame," 1129.

7. "First Negro Movie Actress—Madame Sul-Te-Wan Dies at 85," in George P. Johnson Film Collection, Department of Special Collections, University of California, Los Angeles.

8. Ibid.

334 · NOTES TO PAGES 20–24

9. See Beverly J. Robinson, "Sul-Te-Wan, Madame," 1129.

10. Beasley, *Negro Trailblazers*, 239; Beverly J. Robinson, "Sul-Te-Wan, Madame," 1130.

11. Beasley, *Negro Trailblazers*, 239.

12. Ibid.

13. Gibson-Hudson, "Sul-Te-Wan, Madame," 486; Beverly J. Robinson, "Sul-Te-Wan, Madame," 1130.

14. Beverly J. Robinson, "Sul-Te-Wan, Madame," 1130; Beasley, *Negro Trailblazers*, 240.

15. Beasley, *Negro Trailblazers*, 240.

16. Raymond Lee, "A Walk in the Silents," 20. This resource was provided by the Academy of Motion Picture Arts and Sciences, Margaret Herrick Library, South LaCienega Boulevard, Beverly Hills, California.

17. Ibid.

18. Ibid.

19. Ibid.

20. "First Negro Movie Actress—Madame Sul-Te-Wan Dies at 85," in George P. Johnson Film Collection.

21. Lee, "A Walk in the Silents," 23.

22. Snead, *White Screens, Black Images,* 4–5.

23. "Mme. Sul-Te-Wan Lands *Buccaneer* Role," [date not legible] in George P. Johnson Film Collection.

24. "Stroke Fatal to Sul-Te-Wan, Funeral Friday," in George P. Johnson Film Collection; "Madam Wan Still a Brilliant Star," *Baltimore Afro-American,* May 10, 1941, 14.

25. Lee, "A Walk in the Silents," 22.

26. Bogle, *Bright Boulevards,* 12–14.

27. Gibson-Hudson, "Sul-Te-Wan, Madame," 486.

28. "First Negro Movie Actress Madame Sul-Te-Wan, Dies at 85," in George P. Johnson Film Collection.

29. A partial list of Sul-Te-Wan's films were taken from Slide, *Kindergarten of the Movies,* 159; see also *New York Times Film Reviews, 1913–1968,* 4776; Nash and Ross, eds., *Motion Picture Guide Index,* vol. 12, I-2777; Hanson and Gevinson, eds., *American Film Institute Catalog Feature Films, 1931–1940,* 678; Internet Movie Database, www.imdb.com; "Sul-Te-Wan Body to Lie in State," in George P. Johnson Film Collection; "Mme. Sul-Te-Wan Lands *Buccaneer* Role," in George P. Johnson Film Collection; Beasley, *Negro Trailblazers,* 241; and Beverly J. Robinson, "Sul-Te-Wan, Madame," 1132.

30. "First Negro Movie Actress Madame Sul-Te-Wan, Dies at 85," in George P. Johnson Film Collection; Hazel La Marre, "Rites Set," in George P. Johnson Film Collection.

31. "Stroke Fatal to Sul-Te-Wan, Funeral Friday," in George P. Johnson Film Collection; "Sul-Te-Wan Body to Lie in State," in George P. Johnson Film Collection. This report notes that funeral services for Sul-Te-Wan were held in the Little Chapel of the Valhalla Cemetery in North Hollywood. Rev. Maurice Dawkins of the People's Independent Congregation officiated.

32. "200 Attend Banquet for Oldest Negro Actress," in George P. Johnson Film Collection.

33. Beasley, *Negro Trailblazers,* 240.

34. Film Index International, British Film Institute 1993–1995 (Chadwyck-Healey, France S.A.), CD-ROM; Silva, *Focus on The Birth of a Nation,* 45; Stokes, *D. W. Griffith's The Birth of a Nation,* 87.

35. Lee, "A Walk in the Silents," 22.

36. Guerrero, *Framing Blackness,* 12.

37. Ibid., 14.

38. See Cripps, "The Reaction of the Negro to the Motion Picture *Birth of a Nation,*" 114–124.

39. Beasley, *Negro Trailblazers,* 240–241.

40. Ibid.

41. Bogle, "Black Beginnings: From *Uncle Tom's Cabin* to *The Birth of a Nation,*" 23.

42. Beasley, *Negro Trailblazers,* 241.

43. Hanson and Gevinson, "*The Children Pay,*" *American Film Institute Catalog, 1911–1920,* vol. F1, 139.

44. Ibid., 883.

45. Young, *Fear of the Dark,* 32.

46. Mourdant Hall, "The Screen: The Shy Bachelor—*The Narrow Street,*" *New York Times,* January 5, 1925, in *The New York Times Film Reviews, 1913–1931,* vol. 1, 229.

47. "*In Old Chicago,*" *Variety,* January 5, 1938, in *Variety Film Reviews, 1938–1942,* vol. 6.

48. "*Kentucky* Is Feature at the Lincoln," *Baltimore Afro-American,* February 25, 1939, 11, and "*Kentucky,*" *Variety,* December 21, 1938 in *Variety Film Reviews, 1938–1942,* vol. 6.

49. Crowther, Review of *Maryland, New York Times,* July 13, 1940, in *The New York Times Film Reviews, 1939–1948,* vol. 3, 1720–1721.

50. "*Gunga Din* Role," *Baltimore Afro-American,* July 16, 1938, 11.

51. "Strange Ethiopian Artist Wins Struggle in Hollywood," in George P. Johnson Film Collection.

52. Ibid.

53. Ibid.

54. Hanson and Gevinson, "*Hoodoo Ann,*" in *American Film Institute Catalog, 1911–1920,* vol. F1, 423.

55. Ibid.

56. Morrison, *Playing in the Dark,* 33.

57. Beverly J. Robinson, "Sul-Te-Wan, Madame," 1132.

58. Mordaunt Hall, Review of *Heaven on Earth,* in *New York Times Film Reviews, 1913–1931,* vol. 1, 782.

59. Morrison, *Playing in the Dark,* ix.

60. Mordaunt Hall, Review of *Heaven on Earth,* in *New York Times Film Reviews, 1913–1931,* vol. 1, 782.

61. Ibid.

62. "*Heaven on Earth,*" *Variety,* December 22, 1931, in *Variety Film Reviews, 1930–1933,* vol. 4.

63. Internet Movie Database, www.imdb.com.

64. See Regester, "The Cinematic Representation of Race in *The Birth of a Nation:* A Black Horror Film," 164–182.

65. Wartenberg, "Humanizing the Beast: *King Kong* and the Representation of Black Male Sexuality," 166.

66. Ibid., 167.

67. Snead, *White Screens, Black Images*, 24.

68. Wartenberg, "Humanizing the Beast: *King Kong* and the Representation of Black Male Sexuality," 164.

69. Gaines, *Fire and Desire*, 170.

70. Wartenberg, "Humanizing the Beast: *King Kong* and the Representation of Black Male Sexuality,"158.

71. Sennwald, "The Screen: *Black Moon*," in *New York Times Film Reviews, 1932–1938*, vol. 2, 1074.

72. "*Black Moon*," *Variety*, July 3, 1934, in *Variety Film Reviews, 1934–1937*, vol. 5.

73. Bishop W. J. Walls, "'Salem Maid' Not So Hot, Says Bishop," *New York Amsterdam News*, March 13, 1937, 10. Sul-Te-Wan's association with evil continued in her roles in *King of the Zombies* (1941) and *Revenge of the Zombies* (1943).

74. Ibid.

75. "*Maid of Salem*," *Variety*, March 10, 1937, in *Variety Film Reviews, 1934–1937*, vol. 5.

76. "Madam Sul-Te-Wan To Portray Witch," *Baltimore Afro-American*, February 26, 1938, 10. Harry Levette also notes that Sul-Te-Wan nearly stole a scene from Claudette Colbert in this film. See Harry Levette, "Thru Hollywood," *Chicago Defender*, February 12, 1938, city edition, 12.

77. Koszarski, *The Man You Loved to Hate*, 208. Koszarski provides a photo of Sul-Te-Wan along with Gloria Swanson as Kelly (212). See also Film Index International, British Film Institute, 1993–1994, CD-ROM.

78. Ibid.

79. Stanfield, "An Excursion in the Lower Depths," 96.

80. Sennwald, "A Woman Bandit: *Ladies They Talk About*," review of *Ladies They Talk About*, *New York Times*, February 25, 1933, in *The New York Times Film Reviews*, vol. 2, 912–913.

81. Ibid.

82. Cripps, *Slow Fade to Black*, 282.

83. Ibid.

84. Internet Movie Database, "*Sullivan's Travels*," www.imdb.com. This source identifies Sul-Te-Wan as the church harmonium player.

85. Ellison, *Invisible Man*, 3.

86. Ibid., 3–4.

87. Snead, *White Screens, Black Images*, 6–7.

88. Silva, *Focus on The Birth of a Nation*, 106; "Up From Depths," June 25, 1915 in *Variety Film Reviews, 1907–1920*, vol. 1; and "*Intolerance*," *Variety*, September 8, 1916, *Variety Film Reviews, 1907–1920*, vol. 1.

89. Hanson and Gevinson, "*Intolerance*," in *American Film Institute Catalog, 1911–1920*, vol. F1, 458–459.

90. "*Intolerance*," *Variety*, September 8, 1916, *Variety Film Reviews, 1907–1920*, vol. 1; "Sul-Te-Wan Body To Lie In State" in George P. Johnson Film Collection.

91. Mordaunt Hall, "The Screen: The Shy Bachelor—*The Narrow Street*," in *New York Times Film Reviews, 1913–1931*, vol. 1, 229.

92. "*Uncle Tom's Cabin*," November 9, 1927, *Variety Film Reviews, 1926–1929*, vol. 3; "Madam Sul-Te-Wan Is Signed by Columbia," *Pittsburgh Courier*, January 15, 1927, section

2, 2; "Oldest Actress Signed by Columbia," *Baltimore Afro-American*, January 15, 1927, 9; and "The Screen: Simon Legree and His Slaves—*Uncle Tom's Cabin*," in *New York Times Film Reviews, 1913–1931*, vol. 1, 396.

93. "Strange Ethiopian Artist Wins Struggle In Hollywood" in George P. Johnson Film Collection; "*Thunderbolt*," June 26, 1929, *Variety*, in *Variety Film Reviews, 1926–1929*, vol. 3.

94. Wallace, "The Good Lynching and *The Birth of a Nation*," 87.

95. Ellison, *Invisible Man*, 3.

96. Morrison, *Playing in the Dark*, 9.

97. Spillers, "Notes on an Alternative Model—Neither/Nor," 183.

98. Morrison, *Playing in the Dark*, 10.

99. See Bhabha, "The Other Question," 312–331. Homi K. Bhabha ascertains that "colonial discourse produces the colonized as a social reality which is at once an 'other' and yet entirely knowable and visible" (316). Of even greater importance is Bhabha's claim that the invisible is both visible and invisible.

100. Trinh, *When the Moon Waxes Red*, 187.

101. Ibid.

102. Gaines, *Fire and Desire*, 190.

103. Bogle, *Bright Boulevards*, 360.

2. Nina Mae McKinney

1. This information was taken from several sources, including "Nina Mae McKinney: 'The Screen's First Black Love Goddess'," *Pittsburgh Courier*, June 26, 1999, B3; http://proquest.umi.com/; "McKinney, Nina Mae" (1909–1967), Screenonline, British Film Institute, www.screenonline.org.uk/people. It is of note that her birth date is listed as 1909 yet her death certificate indicates her date of birth as 1913 (death certificate for Nina Mae McKinney, City of New York, Vital Records; Pettus, "Lancaster's Celebrated Film Star"; "Nina Mae McKinney—Actress," South Carolina African American History, www.scafricanamericanhistory.com/currenthonoree/; Ruby Berkley Goodwin, "From Blackbird Chorine to Talkie Star," *Pittsburgh Courier*, 8 June 1929, illustrated feature section 2, 1; "Nina Mae McKinney's Life Highly Romantic," *Chicago Defender*, February 8, 1930, national edition, 7; Frank W. Johnson, "McKinney, Nina Mae," 342–343; Warren, "Nina Mae McKinney," 707–708; Kathleen Thompson, "McKinney, Nina Mae," 772–773; and "Nina Mae McKinney, Nora Holt at Party," *Chicago Defender*, November 22, 1930, city edition, 13. This later report indicates that her mother was named Mrs. Georgia Maynard.

2. *Hallelujah*'s cast members included Daniel L. Haynes (Zekial "Zeke" Johnson), Nina Mae McKinney (Chick), William Fountaine (Hot Shot), Harry Gray (Pappy "Parson" Johnson), Fanny Belle DeKnight (Mammy Johnson), Everett McGarrity (Spunk Johnson), Victoria Spivey (Missy Rose), Milton Dickerson (Johnson child), Robert Couch (Johnson child), Walter Tait (Johnson child), Dixie Jubilee Singers, Matthew "Stymie" Beard (child), Evelyn Pope Burwell (singer), Eddie Conners (singer), William Allen Garrison (Heavy), and Sam McDaniel (brother of Hattie McDaniel) (Adam). Original music was provided by Irving Berlin with songs "Waiting at the End of the Road" and "Swanee Shuffle." Non-original music was provided by Stephen Foster ("Old Folks at Home—Swanee River"), W. C. Handy ("St. Louis Blues"), and Richard Wagner ("Bridal Chorus—Here Comes the Bride"). Henry Thacker Burleigh (uncredited) served as musi-

338 · NOTES TO PAGES 42–47

cal arranger for "Go Down Moses, Let My People Go" and "Swing Low, Sweet Chariot." Eva Jessye (uncredited) served as musical director. *Hallelujah*, Internet Movie Database, www.imdb.com.

3. "All Color'd Cast for *Hallelujah*," *Baltimore Afro-American*, October 13, 1928, 8.

4. "Charming Harlem Dancing Girls in Race for Vidor Lead Film Role," *Pittsburgh Courier*, October 13, 1928, section 1, 9.

5. Waters and Samuels, *His Eye Is On the Sparrow*, 198. According to Waters, "The talent man King Vidor sent East to wave gold bags at me was stalled on the job by colored theatrical people unfriendly to me. He reported that he was unable to find me. But I never was so small and inconspicuous that picture people can't locate me, particularly when the price is right."

6. Chappy Gardner, "Along the Rialto: Honey Brown Returning," *Pittsburgh Courier*, January 5, 1929, section 3, 1.

7. "Honey Smiles Over Reports of Her Death," *Chicago Defender*, September 21, 1929, national edition, 7.

8. Ibid.

9. "When Nina Mae Left Lew Leslie," *New York Amsterdam News*, February 13, 1929, 7.

10. Ruby Berkley Goodwin, "From Blackbird Chorine to Talkie Star," *Pittsburgh Courier*, June 8, 1929, illustrated feature section 2, 1.

11. Bogle, *Bright Boulevards*, 177. Bogle reports that Ruby Berkley Goodwin is an African American reporter.

12. Ruby Berkley Goodwin, "From Blackbird Chorine to Talkie Star," *Pittsburgh Courier*, June 8, 1929, illustrated feature section 2, 1.

13. Ibid.

14. Durgnat and Simmon, *King Vidor, American*, 106.

15. "Hallelujah," *Variety*, August 28, 1929, *Variety Film Reviews, 1926–1929*, vol. 3; see also Sampson, *Blacks in Black and White*, 315.

16. Bogle, *Toms, Coons, Mulattoes, Mammies, & Bucks*, 31.

17. Lesage, "Artful Racism, Artful Rape," 250.

18. Doane, *Femmes Fatales*, 213.

19. Some of her moves evoke images of Josephine Baker, an erotic and exotic black dancer, who took Paris by storm in the 1920s. McKinney may well have been inspired by national figures such as Baker, who was adept at introducing complexity into the deceptively simple act of dancing. McKinney once confessed, "The phenomenal success of Florence Mills [a singer and dancer who performed on stage in Europe and the United States in the early 1900s with Bert Williams and Noble Sissle] and Josephine Baker stimulated me. I longed to hold a place in the hearts of the world as they did." Ruby Berkley Goodwin, "From Blackbird Chorine to Talkie Star," *Pittsburgh Courier*, June 8, 1929, illustrated feature section 2, 1.

20. See Howard, "Hallelujah," 441–451, for a discussion of how music functions in the film as an extension of black sexuality and religion.

21. Gilman, "Black Bodies, White Bodies," 228. Gilman notes that "The association of the black with concupiscence reaches back into the Middle Ages. . . . By the eighteenth century, the sexuality of the black, both male and female, becomes an icon for deviant sexuality in general."

22. *Hallelujah* conflates African Americans' bodies, emotions, and souls, deliberately subverting the sexuality and the religious experience of blacks. For whites, viewing the film allows them to vicariously experience these emotions while remaining disengaged from blacks and blackness. According to Richard Dyer, it is such representations that reaffirm how whites view blacks and blackness. He declares, "The idea that non-whites are more natural than whites also comes to suggest that they have more 'life.' . . . 'Life' here tends to mean the body, the emotions, sensuality and spirituality; it is usually explicitly counterposed to the mind and the intellect, with the implication that white people's over-investment in the cerebral is cutting them off from life and leading them to crush the life out of others and out of nature itself" ("White," 56).

23. Bogle, *Blacks in American Films and Television*, 102.

24. At other points in the film when he is desirous of Missy Rose, he pants deeply and stares fixedly at the woman's body. Also, Zeke recognizes his weakness and his predisposition to sin, even though he is continually haunted by the deceits and distractions of the devil (embodied by Chick).

25. Durgnat and Simmon, *King Vidor, American*, 107.

26. Young, *Fear of the Dark*, 106. McKinney's light complexion was visibly darkened for the screen, as is apparent in a still photo taken during filming. The filmmakers created a calculated racial construct, not wanting to give the impression that she could be white (white females were denied access to black men), but at the same time conveying mulatto status in order to enhance her hypersexualized appeal. Despite how McKinney was photographed for publicity purposes, on screen she personified the mulatto.

27. hooks, *Black Looks*, 72.

28. Durgnat and Simmon, *King Vidor, American*, 106.

29. Ibid.

30. Ibid., 103.

31. Ibid., 101.

32. hooks, *Black Looks*, 67.

33. Cripps, *Slow Fade to Black*, 250.

34. "King Vidor Exposed," *Pittsburgh Courier*, July 26, 1930, in the Tuskegee Institute News Clipping File, 1899–1966.

35. Bogle, *Bright Boulevards*, 93. He suggests that on the film's final night of shooting, black actors were invited to the Beverly Hills family home of Pepi Lederer, niece to white actress Marion Davies, mistress to William Randolph Hearst. McKinney, along with black actors, visited the home and partied for some three days before neighbors complained about the presence of blacks in the neighborhood.

36. "*Hallelujah* to Have Double Opener in N.Y.," *Chicago Defender*, August 17, 1929, city edition, section 1, 9. For further discussion of the film, see Weisenfeld, *Hollywood Be Thy Name* ("'Taint What You Was, It's What You Is Today").

37. Ibid.

38. "'Jim-Crow' Alleged At *Hallelujah* Premier[e]," *New York Amsterdam News*, August 28, 1929, 1; and "Jim-Crow Charges Hit *Hallelujah* in Court Actions," *New York Amsterdam News*, August 28, 1929, final extra–Atlantic City edition, 1.

39. Ibid.

40. "Protest Film Showing," *Chicago Defender*, August 31, 1929, city edition, section 1, 9.

41. "Reported Wed," *Chicago Defender,* August 31, 1929, city edition, section 1, 8.

42. Ibid.

43. "No Wedding Bells, Says Nina Mae," *New York Amsterdam News,* February 12, 1930, 8.

44. "White Movie Stars Praise Nina Mae McKinney's Works," *Chicago Defender,* November 2, 1929, city edition, 12.

45. Harry Levette, "Indian Maharajah at Feet of Nina Mae," *Baltimore Afro-American,* November 16, 1929, 9.

46. "The Original Nina Mae," *Baltimore Afro-American,* January 18, 1930, 8.

47. "Nina Mae McKinney Is Big Hit at Lafayette," *Pittsburgh Courier,* February 8, 1930, 16.

48. "Nina Mae McKinney's Life Highly Romantic," *Chicago Defender,* February 8, 1930, national edition, 7. This association to white actress Clara Bow may have been spawned by *Variety*'s review of McKinney that stated, "Perhaps the best way of describing Nina Mae is that she comes closest to being the Clara Bow of her race, so far seen on the screen." "Hallelujah," *Variety,* August 8, 1929, in *Variety Film Reviews, 1926–1929,* vol. 3.

49. William T. Smith, "City Thrilled as Nina Arrives on the Century," *Chicago Defender,* March 29, 1930, city edition, 11.

50. "Nina Mae McKinney Breaks Met's Attendance Records," *Chicago Defender,* April 5, 1930, city edition, 11.

51. "Nina Mae Will Wear Gorgeous Clothes; Called 'Best-Dressed,'" *Pittsburgh Courier,* April 12, 1930, section 1, 7.

52. Floyd G. Snelson Jr., "Harlem Limited Broadway Bound No. 10—Nina Mae McKinney," *Pittsburgh Courier,* December 13, 1930, section 2, 8.

53. "Nina Mae McKinney Libeled in Nasty Magazine Article: Film Star Suing Movie Magazine For Damages," *Baltimore Afro-American,* April 5, 1930, 4.

54. Ibid.

55. "'Nina Cried for an Hour,' Says Mother Anent Elizabeth Goldberg's Alleged Interview in *Motion Picture Classic,*" *Pittsburgh Courier,* April 19, 1930, section 2, 6.

56. "Nina Mae Loses Out in Movies," *Chicago Defender,* May 31, 1930, city edition, 10.

57. "Nina Mae McKinney Still under Long Term Contract," *Chicago Defender,* August 9, 1930, city edition, 9.

58. "Nina Mae McKinney, Famous Talkie Star to Appear Here in Person April 18," *Pittsburgh Courier,* April 5, 1930, section 1, 7.

59. Ralph Chilton, "Helen Kane, Jack Oakie and Nina Mae McKinney at Met," *Chicago Defender,* August 16, 1930, city edition, 10. Internet Movie Database lists the year for *Manhattan Serenade* as 1929, www.imdb.com.

60. "*Hallelujah* Star Weds Prize Fighter," *Baltimore Afro-American,* August 9, 1930, 9.

61. "Scandal Rumors Stir Hollywood," *Chicago Defender,* September 6, 1930, city edition, 8.

62. "Did Vivacious Nina Cast a Spell to Win Boy Hubby?" *Baltimore Afro-American,* November 8, 1930, 9. The press referred to Douglas Daniels as Master Daniels.

63. "Nee McKinney Takes Daniels as Best Title," *Chicago Defender,* November 1, 1930, city edition, 9.

64. "Married in Haste: Honeymoon in Court," *Baltimore Afro-American,* November 8, 1930, 1.

65. "Husband Can't Keep Up With Nina Mae McKinney," *Philadelphia Tribune,* November 13, 1930, 15.

66. "Nina Mae Seeks Annulment of Marriage," *Baltimore Afro-American,* November 29, 1930, 1.

67. Ibid.

68. Bessye J. Bearden, "Miss M'Kinney Bids America Fond Farewell: To Star in Comedy at Paris," *Chicago Defender,* December 13, 1930, city edition, 7.

69. Floyd G. Snelson Jr., "Harlem Limited Broadway Bound No. 10—Nina Mae McKinney," *Pittsburgh Courier,* December 13, 1930, section 2, 8.

70. Ibid.

71. Edward G. Perry, "Manhattan Madness," *Baltimore Afro-American,* December 13, 1930, 8.

72. Bessye J. Bearden, "Miss M'Kinney Bids America Fond Farewell: To Star in Comedy at Paris," *Chicago Defender,* December 13, 1930, city edition, 7; Floyd G. Snelson Jr., "Nina Mae Leaves U.S. for Tour of Europe," *Baltimore Afro-American,* December 13, 1930, 9.

73. Floyd Snelson, "Nina Mae Signs to Make Film in Africa," *Baltimore Afro-American,* January 24, 1931, 8. The unnamed production possibly referred to *Sanders of the River* (1935) in which she costarred with Paul Robeson.

74. Bogle, *Toms, Coons, Mulattoes, Mammies, & Bucks,* 33.

75. Ralph Matthews, "Does Vivacious Motion Picture Queen Hold Important Angle in Backstage Romance? What Will Happen When Franc [McLennon] Meets Nina Mae in Paris?" *Baltimore Afro-American,* January 17, 1931, 9. This report spells Douglass (Daniels) with a double "s."

76. Ibid. For further information regarding the Whitman Sisters, see Sampson, *Blacks in Black and White.*

77. McKinney's attraction to these men remains unclear since so little information is available on her relationships with them.

78. "N. McKinney, Ill, Boards Ship for U.S.," *Chicago Defender,* March 7, 1931, city edition, 8; Bessye Bearden, "Nina M. M'Kinney Arrives to Visit Her Sick Father," *Chicago Defender,* March 28, 1931, city edition, 8; and Floyd G. Snelson Jr., "Nina Mae Irked By Accounts of Many Loves," *Baltimore Afro-American,* March 28, 1931, 9.

79. Ibid.

80. Floyd G. Snelson Jr., "Nina Mae Irked By Accounts of Many Loves," *Baltimore Afro-American,* March 28, 1931, 9.

81. Ibid.

82. "Going Backstage With the Scribe: Inside Info," *Chicago Defender,* March 28, 1931, city edition, 8.

83. "Nina Mae M'Kinney and Earl Hines for the Regal Stage; Norma Shearer On Screen," *Chicago Defender,* May 23, 1931, city edition, 10.

84. "Anent McKinney," *Chicago Defender,* June 6, 1931, national edition, 5.

85. "D. C. Forgets to Clap; Nina Tells 'Em So," *Chicago Defender,* November 21, 1931, city edition, 9.

86. "Nina Mae McKinney Reported Married," *Chicago Defender,* December 19, 1931, city edition, 1; "Nina Mae McKinney Wins Race Against Time: Opens On Schedule in London; Critics Praise Art," *Pittsburgh Courier,* May 9, 1936, section 2, 7. According to a

source on black women in British cinema, McKinney's "stormy marriage to Jimmy (a.k.a. Jimmie) Monroe ended in divorce (a few years later he wed Billie Holiday)." Stephen Bourne, "Secrets and Lies," *Pride*, July 1997, 114. Ernest Erskine directed my attention to this source.

87. *Safe in Hell* (1931), Internet Movie Database, www.imdb.com.

88. Cripps, *Slow Fade to Black*, 272.

89. "Nina Mae McKinney on Met's Screen Saturday: Her Effort in *Safe in Hell* Draws Praise," *Chicago Defender*, January 30, 1932, city edition, 6.

90. Hilda See, "Nina Mae Is Quite An Artist In New Film: Her Work Gets Applause Even from a Critic," *Chicago Defender*, January 16, 1932, city edition, 7. It is noteworthy that prior to her appearance in the film, reports circulated that she lost the part to black actress Reverdia Woods. McKinney publicly corrected this erroneous report. Harry Levette, "Nina Mae M'Kinney Out and Reverdia Woods in *Safe in Hell* on Warner Brothers Lot," *Chicago Defender*, July 11, 1931, city edition, 9; Floyd G. Snelson Jr., "Nina Mae Not Out of Picture," *Baltimore Afro-American*, July 18, 1931, 17.

91. Advertisement for Golden Brown Skin Ointment, *Baltimore Afro-American*, February 27, 1932, 8.

92. Everett, *Returning the Gaze*, 166.

93. "Nina Mae Has Learned What Stage Wants," *Chicago Defender*, February 13, 1932, city edition, 6.

94. Bogle, *Bright Boulevards*, 93; Cripps, *Slow Fade to Black*, 234.

95. Sampson, *Blacks in Black and White*, 417.

96. "Shorts: *Pie, Pie, Blackbird*," *Motion Picture Herald*, June 25, 1932, 29.

97. "Reviews of Short Subjects: *Pie, Pie, Blackbird*," *Film Daily*, June 11, 1932, 17; "Nina Mae to Make Another Star Picture," *Chicago Defender*, August 6, 1932, city edition, 7.

98. "Nina, Be Good!" *Pittsburgh Courier*, October 22, 1932, 2.

99. "Ready for London Triumph," *Chicago Defender*, March 4, 1933, city edition, 8; "Nina Mae Captivates 'Show Spots' of Europe with Fine Screen, Stage Performances," *Pittsburgh Courier*, [date not legible], in the Tuskegee Institute News Clipping File, 1899–1966.

100. "Ready for London Triumph," *Chicago Defender*, March 4, 1933, city edition, 8.

101. "London Dubious of Nina Mae," *Baltimore Afro-American*, March 11, 1933, 18.

102. "Nina Mae To Remain Over Pond; Shines," *Chicago Defender*, March 11, 1933, city edition, 9.

103. "Going Backstage with the Scribe," *Chicago Defender*, May 27, 1933, city edition, 8.

104. "Nina McKinney's Mother Ill; Star Is Asked Home," *Chicago Defender*, May 12, 1934, city edition, 9. In this report, McKinney's mother is referred to as Mrs. James Ervin, indicating that her mother may have married for a third time, or this could be an erroneous report since later reports identify her mother as Georgia McKinney Maynor.

105. "Nina Mae McKinney, Eubie Blake's Orchestra Coming to Granada Screen," *Pittsburgh Courier*, July 14, 1934, section 2, 8.

106. "Nina McKinney Is In Another London Movie," *Chicago Defender*, August 4, 1934, city edition, 6.

107. "Nina Mae In Bad for Her Snubbing Act," *Chicago Defender*, November 3, 1934, city edition, 8.

108. "Nina Mae to Play in Robeson, Rogers Film: Fox Studio To Demand Her Return for Berth In Film," *Chicago Defender,* December 8, 1934, city edition, 7; *Steamboat Round the Bend* (1935), Internet Movie Database, www.imdb.com.

109. Advertisement for *Life Is Real, Los Angeles Sentinel,* April 16, 1936, 4.

110. Ted Yates, "Nina Mae in Debut: Star of *Hallelujah* Now Has Her Own Swing Band," *Chicago Defender* [date not legible], in the Tuskegee Institute News Clipping File, 1899–1966.

111. Ibid.

112. "Robeson-McKinney Film Booked for Broadway," *Pittsburgh Courier,* January 5, 1935, section 2, 8.

113. That Bosambo practices polygamy and that Lord Sandy is critical of this practice reflect how Western culture is juxtaposed to non-Western culture and is indicative of how colonialism is inscribed in the film.

114. Sennwald, Review of *Sanders of the River, New York Times,* June 27, 1935, in *The New York Times Film Reviews* vol. 2, 1932–1938, 1187.

115. Billy Rowe, "Nina Mae McKinney Back To Broadway In Pictures," *Chicago Defender,* July 6, 1935, city edition, 8.

116. "Robeson, McKinney Film Wins Award," *Baltimore Afro-American,* January 11, 1936, 11.

117. Ibid.

118. Bogle, *Bright Boulevards,* 93.

119. Bernice Patton, "Nina Mae M'Kinney To Return to Hollywood: Pretty Star Is Signed By M-G-M," *Pittsburgh Courier,* January 26, 1935, section 2, 8.

120. "Joe Louis Fight and Nina McKinney at Opera House," *New York Amsterdam News,* April 20, 1935, 10; "Nina Mae Wins Honors in N.Y.," *Chicago Defender,* April 27, 1935, city edition, 8.

121. Allan McMillan, "Nina Mae McKinney Tops List of Greats on Bill," *Chicago Defender,* July 27, 1935, city edition, 9.

122. Bogle, *Bright Boulevards,* 93.

123. Ted Yates, "Nina Mae Tires of Playing 'Hell-Cat' Roles, Now She's A Lady in Revue," *Baltimore Afro-American,* September 7, 1935, 9.

124. Ibid.

125. "East Raves Over 'New' Nina Mae McKinney: Says Star is Tops in Acting and Clothes in Cotton Club," *Chicago Defender,* September 14, 1935, city edition, 9.

126. "Nina Mae and Hudgins Star in Show," *Chicago Defender,* December 7, 1935, city edition, 13.

127. Florence M. Collins, "Nina Mae Is Jittery over Operation," *Baltimore Afro-American,* March 21, 1936, 1; "Sails Saturday," *Chicago Defender,* March 21, 1936, city edition, 5.

128. "Europe Thinks Nina Mae Is Tops On Stage: Star is Greeted by Throngs as She Reaches Edinburgh," *Chicago Defender,* May 2, 1936, city edition, 9.

129. Cripps, *Slow Fade to Black,* 234, 355.

130. Sampson, *Blacks in Black and White,* 357.

131. "Shorts: *The Black Network," Film Daily,* April 1, 1936, 4.

132. "Rapidly Recovering in Australia," *Chicago Defender,* January 8, 1937, national edition, 19; Besik Blukess, "Nina Mae McKinney Undergoes Two Operations in Australia," *Chicago Defender,* December 25, 1937, city edition, 8.

133. "Nina Mae Ill; Ralph Cooper's Film Delayed," *Baltimore Afro-American,* January 22, 1938, 10.

134. Stephen Bourne, "Secrets and Lies," *Pride,* July 1997, 114–115.

135. Robert G. Law, "Nina Mae McKinney Seeks Divorce in British Courts From Her Hubby," *Chicago Defender,* May 1, 1937, national edition, 13.

136. James Monroe, "'Nina Mae Left Me' Writes James Monroe," *Chicago Defender,* May 1, 1937, national edition, 13.

137. "Nina Mae Eyes New Romance in East," *Pittsburgh Courier,* May 14, 1938, 1.

138. Ibid.

139. "'I Will Definitely Not Play Maid Roles Any Longer,' Vows Nina Mae McKinney," *Chicago Defender,* April 9, 1938, national edition, 18.

140. "Nina Danced with Dr. Buckner Only," *Baltimore Afro-American,* May 14, 1938, 12.

141. "Nina Mae Signs for Movie Role," *Chicago Defender,* July 30, 1938, city edition, 9. Henry Sampson identifies *St. Louis Gal* in *Blacks in Black and White,* 614.

142. Bob Hayes, "Nina Mae McKinney Guest at '65' Club," *Chicago Defender,* September 3, 1938, city edition, 9.

143. Lawrence LaMar, "Actress Says Ralph Cooper Attacked Her," *New York Amsterdam News,* October 8, 1938, in the Tuskegee Institute News Clipping File, 1899–1966.

144. Ibid. McKinney allegedly altered the story.

145. "Bodyguards to Protect Nina Mae From Gangsters," *Los Angeles Sentinel,* December 22, 1938, 8.

146. *Gang Smashers* (1938), Internet Movie Database, www.imdb.com.

147. "Nina Mae to Lead Orchestra," *Baltimore Afro-American,* November 25, 1939, 14.

148. Ted Yates, "Nina Mae in Debut: Star of *Hallelujah* Now Has Her Own Swing Band," *Chicago Defender,* December 23, 1939, national edition, 21; "Nina Mae's Band Clicks in Dixieland," *Chicago Defender,* January 13, 1940, national edition, 21; and "A Pretty Girl and a New Serenader," *Baltimore Afro-American,* January 13, 1940, 13.

149. "Wanted Coffee, Is Given Beating," *Pittsburgh Courier,* January 13, 1940, 1; "Nina Mae Slugged in Florida," *Washington Afro-American,* January 13, 1940, 2.

150. "Nina Mae McKinney Is Starred in *Straight to Heaven* at Regent," [date not legible], in the Tuskegee Institute News Clipping File, 1899–1966.

151. "McKinney Film Best Shown Yet," *New York Amsterdam News,* November 18, 1939, 21.

152. "Nina Mae Returns as 'Good Neighbor' Star," *Baltimore Afro-American,* September 13, 1941, 14.

153. Ralph Matthews, "*Tan Manhattan,*" *Washington Afro-American,* January 16, 1941, 10.

154. *The Devil's Daughter* (1939), Internet Movie Database, www.imdb.com.

155. "Midnight Show at the Met Features Nina Mae McKinney," *Chicago Defender,* March 20, 1943, city edition, 11. Although *The Devil's Daughter* was made in 1939, the film was not widely covered by the black press until 1943.

156. L. Mason, "Only the Film Fails to Please in Midnight Show," *Chicago Defender,* April 3, 1943, city edition, 13.

157. "Nina M. McKinney Weds in Baltimore," *Baltimore Afro-American,* June 5, 1943, 10.

158. E. B. Rea, "Encores and Echoes," *Baltimore Afro-American*, July 1, 1944, 8. She assumed maid's roles in *The Power of the Whistle* (1945, as Flotilda, Constantina's maid) and *Night Train to Memphis* (1946, as an unnamed maid), Internet Movie Database, www .imdb.com.

159. "New Nina Mae McKinney," *Baltimore Afro-American*, July 1, 1944, 8.

160. Lawrence F. LaMar, "*Dark Waters*, Her Latest Film Proves Nina Mae McKinney Has It," *Chicago Defender*, November 18, 1944, city edition, 10.

161. "Lengthen Role in Film for Nina Mae McKinney," *Chicago Defender*, June 10, 1944, city edition, 11.

162. "*Pinky*: Story on Girl Who Passes Will be Most Debated Film of Year," *Ebony*, September 1949, 23; "Nina Called 'Hussy,' Sues for $700,000," *Chicago Defender*, October 22, 1949, city edition, 1.

163. "Elopes," *Pittsburgh Courier*, April 23, 1949, 1.

164. "Nina in *Canyon*," *Chicago Defender*, June 4, 1949, city edition, 35.

165. "Nina Mae McKinney to Star in 'Rain,'" *New York Amsterdam News*, August 4, 1951, 28.

166. Bogle, *Bright Boulevards*, 93–95.

167. "Nina Mae McKinney—Dead," *New York Amsterdam News*, May 13, 1967, 1.

168. Death certificate for Nina Mae McKinney, City of New York, Vital Records.

169. Bogle, *Bright Boulevards*, 95.

3. Louise Beavers

1. Death certificate for Louise Ellen Beavers, State of California, Department of Health Services. It is of note that some sources have given other dates for her birth. For example, Warren, "Louise Beavers," 75, and Sarah P. Morris, "Beavers, Louise," 104, report that she was born March 8, 1908.

2. "New Contract Establishes Louise Beavers Movie Star: First Member of Race to Gain High Standing in Film World," *Chicago Defender*, November 7, 1936, city edition, 8; James E. Hill, "Cincinnati-Born Louise Beavers Never Had First Lesson in Acting," *Pittsburgh Courier*, January 15, 1938, 21; and Al Monroe, "Swinging the News," *Chicago Defender*, July 29, 1944, national edition, 6.

3. Warren, "Louise Beavers," 75. However, the *Baltimore Afro-American* reports that Beavers finished high school in 1918. Matthews, "Looking at the Stars: Pete Beavers, The Pancake Queen," *Baltimore Afro-American*, January 26, 1935, 9.

4. Faye A. Chadwell, "Beavers, Louise," 43.

5. Warren, "Louise Beavers," 75, and Ralph Matthews, "Looking at the Stars: Pete Beavers, The Pancake Queen," *Baltimore Afro-American*, January 26, 1935, 9.

6. Louise Beavers, "My Biggest Break," *Negro Digest*, December 1949, 22.

7. Ibid. For additional information on Charles Butler's role as a casting agent in Hollywood, see Regester, "African American Extras in Hollywood during the 1920s and 1930s," 95–115.

8. Beavers, "My Biggest Break," 22.

9. Ralph Matthews, "Looking at the Stars: Pete Beavers, The Pancake Queen," *Baltimore Afro-American*, January 26, 1935, 9.

10. Beavers, "My Biggest Break," 22.

11. Louis Lautier, "Louise Beavers Wouldn't Use Epithet in *Imitation of Life*," *Baltimore Afro-American*, March 2, 1935, 9. An additional source reveals that although Beavers did not assume the role for which she auditioned, she did appear in *Uncle Tom's Cabin* as a cook ("Louise Beavers Believes Talkie Roles Misunderstood," *Baltimore Afro-American*, February 23, 1935, 14). She is listed among the cast members according to the Internet Movie Database, www.imdb.com.

12. "Louise Beavers Secured Film Role Through Luck," *Chicago Defender*, January 5, 1935, national edition, 8.

13. James E. Hill, "Cincinnati-Born Louise Beavers Never Had First Lesson in Acting," *Pittsburgh Courier*, January 15, 1938, 21.

14. "Louise Beavers Secured Film Role Through Luck," *Chicago Defender*, January 5, 1935, national edition, 8.

15. "Double Trouble for La Beavers," *Baltimore Afro-American*, April 1, 1944, 6; Lillian Johnson, "Louise Beavers Almost Turned the Movies Down," *Baltimore Afro-American*, January 15, 1938, 11.

16. "Bob Clark, Louise Beavers's ex-Mate, Weds Young Dancer," *Baltimore Afro-American*, August 23, 1947, 6.

17. Ethel Payne, "Louise Beavers, Film Star Turns to Broadway Next," *Chicago Defender*, March 19, 1955, city edition, 17; death certificate for Louise Ellen Beavers, State of California, Department of Health Services.

18. Warren, "Louise Beavers," 76–77.

19. Ibid.; "Louise Beavers on SAG Board," *Pittsburgh Courier*, October 6, 1945, 17.

20. Ethel Payne, "Louise Beavers, Film Star Turns to Broadway Next," *Chicago Defender*, March 19, 1955, city edition, 17.

21. Death certificate for Louise Ellen Beavers, State of California, Department of Health Services.

22. *Coquette* was adapted to the screen from a stage play about a woman who commits suicide upon learning that she is pregnant by her fiancé, who has been murdered by her father. Mary Pickford won an Oscar for best actress in 1929 for her performance in this film. *Films in Review* 48, no. 1–2 (January–February 1997): 61.

23. Bhabha, "The Other Question," 312.

24. Bogle, *Brown Sugar*, 73.

25. Dyer, "White," 54.

26. Bhabha, "The Other Question," 313.

27. Mulvey, "Visual Pleasure and Narrative Cinema," 22.

28. Linda Williams, *Playing the Race Card*, 210–212; Dyer, "White," 54–55; and Williamson, "How Black Was Rhett Butler?" 97–105.

29. Lesage, "Artful Racism, Artful Rape," 244–252.

30. Bogle, *Blacks in American Films and Television*, 358.

31. Lillian Johnson, "Louise Beavers Almost Turned the Movies Down," *Baltimore Afro-American*, January 15, 1938, 11.

32. Mulvey, *Fetishism and Curiosity*, 44–45.

33. Dyer, *Heavenly Bodies*, 14.

34. Robertson, *Guilty Pleasures*, 32.

35. See Doane, *Femmes Fatales*, 7–32.

36. Haskell, *From Reverence to Rape*, 116.

37. Modleski, *Feminism Without Women*, 132. See also Judith Butler, *Gender Trouble*, 43–57.

38. Modleski, *Feminism Without Women*, 133.

39. As Pearl helps a woman who has attempted suicide to dress (associating the black with the body), she comments, "I wouldn't want no policeman to catch me without a petticoat." These remarks by the black maid demonstrate how sexuality becomes linked to blackness.

40. Robertson, *Guilty Pleasures*, 36.

41. See Richard Dyer's critique of Marilyn Monroe in Dyer, *Heavenly Bodies*, 42–50.

42. See hooks, "The Oppositional Gaze," 288–302.

43. Beavers similarly assumes an assertive role in *Bullets or Ballots* (1936), a gangster drama in which she plays a Harlem racketeer. In this instance, although she is not a subservient and is glamorized, she is also linked to the underworld in a role that is no more redeeming. She attempts to dominate white gangsters, and even has her bodyguard "rough them up" to re-assert her authority and maintain control of Harlem's rackets.

44. "Louise Beavers Gets Big Role in New Flicker," *Chicago Defender,* August 16, 1941, city edition, 10.

45. Anna Everett provides a comprehensive discussion of *Imitation of Life* and its reception in the African American press. Most notable is the controversy that erupted between Sterling Brown, a professor at Howard University, and Fannie Hurst, the author of the novel upon which the film was based. See Everett, *Returning the Gaze.* Their dispute was reprinted in *Opportunity* magazine in April 1935. See Sterling A. Brown, "*Imitation of Life:* Once a Pancake," *Opportunity,* March 1935, 87–88; Fannie Hurst, "Letter to the Editor," *Opportunity,* April 1935, 121; and Sterling A. Brown, "Letter to the Editor," *Opportunity,* April 1935, 121–122.

46. Sterling A. Brown, "*Imitation of Life:* Once a Pancake," *Opportunity,* March 1935, 88.

47. Baker, "When Lindbergh Sleeps with Bessie Smith," 86. See Berlant's chapter, "National Brands, National Body," 107–144, on the commodification of the female body in both versions of this film.

48. Jeremy Butler, "*Imitation of Life* (1934–1959)," 292.

49. Flitterman-Lewis, "Imitation(s) of Life," 326.

50. Gaines, *Fire and Desire*, 194.

51. Ibid.

52. Courtney, "Picturizing Race," 2, www.genders.org/g27.

53. Ibid., 7.

54. E. Washington Rhodes, "Greatest Condemnation of Prejudice in America Seen in *Imitation of Life*," *Philadelphia Tribune*, February 14, 1935.

55. Flitterman-Lewis, "Imitation(s) of Life," 335.

56. Spillers, "Notes on an Alternative Model—Neither/Nor," 165–187.

57. E. Washington Rhodes, "Greatest Condemnation of Prejudice in America Seen in *Imitation of Life*," *Philadelphia Tribune*, February 14, 1935.

58. Chauncey Townsend, "Out of the Kitchen," *The Crisis*, January 1935, 15.

59. "Showmen's Reviews: *Imitation of Life*," *Motion Picture Herald*, December 1, 1934, 39.

60. "*Imitation of Life*," *Variety*, November 27, 1934, *Variety Film Reviews, 1934–1937*, vol. 5.

61. "Cinema: *Imitation of Life*," *Time*, December 3, 1934, 47.

62. Camera Eye, "Screenings," *Negro Liberator*, December 22, 1934, 5.

63. Chappy Gardner, "Beavers Has Lost Screen Award," *Pittsburgh Courier*, March 9, 1935, section 2, 9.

64. Jimmie Fidler, "Should Louise Beavers Win Academy Award for Best Performance of Year?" *Washington Afro-American*, February 23, 1935, 4.

65. *California Graphic*, February 1935. Cited in "Color Bars Louise Beavers," *Pittsburgh Courier*, March 2, 1935, Section 2, 8.

66. Advertisement for *Good Sam*, *Chicago Defender*, October 2, 1948, city edition, 16.

67. Everett, *Returning the Gaze*, 210.

68. Ibid., 213.

69. Chauncey Townsend, "Out of the Kitchen," *The Crisis*, January 1935, 15.

70. Fay Jackson, "Louise Beavers, Overnight Star, Snubs Colored Reporters," *Baltimore Afro-American*, December 22, 1934, 8.

71. Ibid.

72. Harry Levette, "Your Hollywood Correspondent Reports a Bit," *Chicago Defender*, January 19, 1935, national edition, 8.

73. Ibid.

74. Ibid.

75. Roi Ottley, "Louise Beavers Strongly Defends 'Aunt Jemima' Roles Given Her," *New York Amsterdam News*, February 20, 1937, 8.

76. James H. Purdy Jr., "Star Gets Cold Reception," *Chicago Defender*, June 18, 1938, national edition, 18.

77. Ibid.

78. "Louise Beavers Clicks in Texas," *Chicago Defender*, July 16, 1938, national edition, 19.

79. "What's Wrong with This Portrayal?" *Baltimore Afro-American*, October 10, 1942, 10.

80. Lawrence LaMar, "Louise Beavers Retired From Film Actors Nominating Committee List," *Baltimore Afro-American*, October 8, 1949, 8.

81. Everett, *Returning the Gaze*, 218.

82. Harry Levette, "*Imitation of Life* Is Possible Best Seller," *Chicago Defender*, December 15, 1934, national edition, 9.

83. Ibid. It is of note that during production Dorothy Black, who plays the part of the young Peola, was reluctant to tell Beavers, as Delilah, that she didn't want her because she was black. The director had to coax Black into making this comment, which was consistent with the script, by agreeing to pay her five dollars. See Louis Lautier, "Louise Beavers Wouldn't Use Epithet in *Imitation of Life*," *Baltimore Afro-American*, March 2, 1935, 9.

84. Louis Lautier, "Louise Beavers Wouldn't Use Epithet in *Imitation of Life*," *Baltimore Afro-American*, March 2, 1935, 9.

85. "Louise Beavers Believes Talkie Roles Misunderstood," *Baltimore Afro-American*, February 23, 1935, 14.

86. Roi Ottley, "Louise Beavers Strongly Defends 'Aunt Jemima' Roles Given Her," *New York Amsterdam News*, February 20, 1937, 8.

87. Ibid.

88. Ibid.

89. Bogle, *Blacks in American Film and Television*, 359.

90. Lula Jones Garrett, "Nothing Delilah-Like in Real Louise Beavers," *Baltimore Afro-American*, May 18, 1935, 9.

91. "Louise Beavers Sees Race Studios," *Chicago Defender*, January 16, 1937, national edition, 25.

92. "Screen Stars Go 400 Miles for a Soldiers' Party," *Chicago Defender*, May 20, 1944, national edition, 8.

93. "Popular Character: Louise Beavers Here Again at Loew Houses," *New York Amsterdam News*, September 21, 1935, 10.

94. Ibid.

95. Lula Jones Garrett, "Nothing Delilah-Like in Real Louise Beavers," *Baltimore Afro-American*, May 18, 1935, 7.

96. "Suit Won By Louise Beavers," *Pittsburgh Courier*, May 1, 1937, 18.

97. Chauncey Townsend, "Out of the Kitchen," *The Crisis*, January 1935, 15.

98. Rob Roy, "Stepin Fetchit and Louise Beavers Here: Star of *Imitation of Life* Says Career First; Then Wed," *Chicago Defender*, February 16, 1935, national edition, 8.

99. Ethel Payne, "Louise Beavers, Film Star Turns to Broadway Next," *Chicago Defender*, March 19, 1955, city edition, 17.

100. Ibid.

101. Peter Filene, historian, suggested that most African Americans supported Republican candidates until the 1960s.

102. "Popular Character Artist At Local Theatre: Louise Beavers Here Again at Loew Houses," *New York Amsterdam News*, September 21, 1935, 7.

103. Lawrence LaMar, "This Is Hollywood," *Chicago Defender*, October 25, 1947, city edition, 30.

104. "Stage Shorts," *Baltimore Afro-American*, August 1, 1936, 10.

105. "Substitute for Hands of Beavers," *Baltimore Afro-American*, July 6, 1940, 13.

106. "Louise Beavers," *Baltimore Afro-American*, May 18, 1935, 7.

4. Fredi Washington

1. Everett, *Returning the Gaze*, 222.

2. Bogle, *Blacks in American Films and Television*, 478.

3. Fredi Washington, "Biographical Notes," Fredi Washington Papers (hereafter FWP); Etheridge, "Fredi Washington," 1212. Washington's first name is spelled differently depending on the source.

4. Bogle, *Bright Boulevards*, 130.

5. Norma Jean Darden, "Oh, Sister! Fredi and Isabel Washington Relive '30s Razzmatazz," *Essence*, September 1978, 99.

6. Washington, "Biographical Notes," FWP; Norma Jean Darden, "Oh, Sister! Fredi and Isabel Washington Relive '30s Razzmatazz," *Essence*, September 1978, 99.

7. Norma Jean Darden, "Oh, Sister! Fredi and Isabel Washington Relive '30s Razzmatazz," *Essence*, September 1978, 105.

8. Etheridge, "Fredi Washington," 105.

9. Norma Jean Darden, "Oh, Sister! Fredi and Isabel Washington Relive '30s Razzmatazz," *Essence,* September 1978, 105. Elida Webb's name is spelled Alida Webb in other sources.

10. Ibid. Washington reports that she was a chorus dancer with *Shuffle Along* at the Club Alabam between 1922 and 1926 (Washington, "Biographical Notes," FWP).

11. "Paul Robeson Stars," *Chicago Defender,* September 4, 1926, national edition, section 1, 6.

12. Norma Jean Darden, "Oh, Sister! Fredi and Isabel Washington Relive '30s Razzmatazz," *Essence,* September 1978, 105; Washington, "Biographical Notes," FWP.

13. Washington, "Biographical Notes," FWP. Washington notes that in France she performed at La Boule, St. Raphael, and Brise La Bain.

14. Henry Sampson reports that Washington was cast in *Square Joe* (1922), produced by the Colored Feature Photoplay Company. See Sampson, *Blacks in Black and White,* 618. Donald Bogle claims that Washington was romantically involved with Duke Ellington, an affair that started during the production of *Black and Tan.* Bogle further suggests that Washington's marriage to Lawrence Brown, a band member with Duke Ellington's band, was an attempt by Washington to remain close to Ellington. See Bogle, *Bright Boulevards,* 133.

15. Etheridge, "Fredi Washington," 1212; Washington, "Biographical Notes," FWP; and Bogle, *Brown Sugar,* 79.

16. Louis Lautier, "Courier Critic Pre-Views *One Mile From Heaven,*" *Pittsburgh Courier,* August 28, 1937, 20. This source reports, "The story describes a colored seamstress, who is rearing a white child. Quite accidentally, the child becomes an object of curiosity when three male newspaper reporters play a trick on a girl who is assigned to cover the courts. One of them telephones her to go to a lot at 112 South Maple Street where she will find a body. . . . Miss Fredie Washington gives a fine performance as Flora Jackson. She is perhaps at her best in the juvenile court scene when she is striving to keep the child."

17. Washington, "Biographical Notes," FWP, and Etheridge, "Fredi Washington," 1213.

18. Isabel Washington's name is spelled differently in various sources.

19. Washington, "Biographical Notes," FWP.

20. Washington, "Biographical Notes," FWP, and Etheridge, "Fredi Washington," 1213.

21. Ibid.

22. According to Martin Duberman, *Black Boy* was designed to parallel the life of prizefighter Jack Johnson. See Duberman, *Paul Robeson,* 103.

23. "*Black Boy* Has Opening," *Baltimore Afro-American,* October 9, 1926, 19. Robeson, like Washington, could not escape being racialized and sexualized on the stage. Even the name of his character, "Black Boy," was embedded with racial and political implications.

24. Gilliam, *Paul Robeson,* 48.

25. "*Black Boy,*" *Chicago Defender,* October 30, 1926, city edition, 8.

26. E. B. Taylor, "Women Who Have Known Adventure: True Stories of Famed Women You Ought to Know," *Baltimore Afro-American,* September 30, 1933, 13.

27. Young, *Fear of the Dark,* 94–95.

28. Snead, "Spectatorship and Capture in *King Kong,*" 28.

29. Bowser and Spence, *Writing Himself into History,* 164.

30. Duberman, *Paul Robeson*, 601.

31. Fay Jackson, "Hollywood Star Dust," *Baltimore Afro-American*, January 19, 1935, 8.

32. Ralph Matthews, "Looking at the Stars: Peola Off-Stage." *Baltimore Afro-American*, November 16, 1935, 8. Sheila Rule reports that when Washington performed with Duke Ellington's band during its southern tour, she entered a segregated ice cream store and purchased ice cream for band members. Whites assumed that she was white and characterized her as a "nigger-lover." See Sheila Rule, "Fredi Washington, 90, Actress; Broke Ground for Black Artists," *New York Times*, June 30, 1994, D21.

33. Young, *Fear of the Dark*, 95.

34. "The New York Show World," *Pittsburgh Courier*, October 16, 1926, 10.

35. Cripps, *Slow Fade to Black*, 207.

36. Bessye Bearden, "Fredi Washington Weds Duke's Trombonist: Stage's Prettiest Star Signs a Mate," *Chicago Defender*, August 19, 1933, city edition, 7.

37. Bogle, *Brown Sugar*, 76.

38. Charles Petioni, "Letter Box: Protests Picture," *New York Amsterdam News*, September 27, 1933, 9.

39. Several works have explored this notion of whites who masquerade as black, including Toni Morrison, *Playing in the Dark*; Rogin, "Democracy and Burnt Cork," 1–34; and Lott, "Love and Theft," 38–62.

40. Young, *Fear of the Dark*, 94.

41. Snead, "Spectatorship and Capture in *King Kong*," 28.

42. Courtney, *Hollywood Fantasies of Miscegenation*, 171.

43. Bogle, *Bright Boulevards*, 129.

44. Ibid.

45. Fred Daniels, "Fredye Washington May Talk Herself out of the Movies," *Chicago Defender*, April 21, 1934, city edition, 9.

46. Ibid.

47. Everett, *Returning the Gaze*, 222.

48. Rob Roy, "City Still Raves over *Imitation of Life*: Popularity Also Includes Fredi Washington in Wave," *Chicago Defender*, February 23, 1935, national edition, 9. Bogle reports that Washington was allowed a script change (which was rare for an unknown actress in this period), was given the amount of money desired, and even consulted with an attorney before finally signing her contract with Universal Studios. See Bogle, *Bright Boulevards*, 134–135.

49. Doane, *Femmes Fatales*, 233.

50. Hurst, "Zora Hurston: A Personality Sketch," 173.

51. Hardy and Thomas, "Listening to Race," 426.

52. Courtney, *Hollywood Fantasies of Miscegenation*, 164.

53. Ibid., 164–165.

54. Dyer, "White," 48, 54–55.

55. Valerie Smith, "Reading the Intersection of Race and Gender in Narratives of Passing," 46.

56. There are at least suggestions of homosexuality and incest in this film (Delilah rubbing Bea's tired feet, and the mother and daughter dancing). Although this deserves mention, it is not the focus of the present investigation.

57. Young, *Fear of the Dark,* 93.

58. Lacan, *Ecrits,* 5.

59. Fanon, *Black Skin, White Masks,* 45.

60. hooks, "The Oppositional Gaze," 288–302.

61. Bhaba, "The Other Question," 325.

62. "On the Current Screen: *Imitation of Life," Literary Digest* 118 (December 8, 1934): 31.

63. *"Imitation of Life," Variety,* November 27, 1934, 15, in *Variety Film Reviews, 1934–1937,* vol. 5.

64. Everett, "I Want the Same Things Other People Enjoy," 47.

65. Fay Jackson, "Fredi Washington Hits New Note in *Imitations," New York Amsterdam News,* December 15, 1934, 10.

66. Conrad, "American Viewpoint: To Pass or Not To Pass?" in FWP; "'Part in *Imitation* Is Not Real Me,' Says Fredi," *Chicago Defender,* January 19, 1935, national edition, 9.

67. L. Herbert Henegan, *"Imitation of Life* White Folks Play Says Film Star," *Baltimore Afro-American,* February 9, 1935, 1.

68. Sterling A. Brown, "Letter to the Editor," *Opportunity,* April 1935, 122.

69. Fay Jackson, "Hollywood Is the Bunk to New York Stage-Star Who Won't 'Pass' to Attain Success: Says Only Hope For Our Artists Is In New York," *Baltimore Afro-American,* April 21, 1934, 8.

70. Ibid.

71. "'Part In *Imitation* Is Not Real Me,' Says Fredi," *Chicago Defender,* January 19, 1935, national edition, 9.

72. Ibid.

73. Ralph Matthews, "Looking at the Stars: Peola Off-Stage," *Baltimore Afro-American,* November 16, 1935, 8.

74. Ibid.

75. Earl Conrad, "American Viewpoint: To Pass or Not To Pass?" *Chicago Defender,* June 16 [year illegible], weekly magazine, in FWP.

76. "'Part In *Imitation* Is Not Real Me,' Says Fredi," *Chicago Defender,* January 19, 1935, national edition, 9.

77. Ibid.

78. "No Imitation: Fredi Washington," *Chicago Defender,* January 19, 1935, national edition, 9. See caption underneath photo.

79. "Going Backstage With the Scribe," *Chicago Defender,* January 19, 1935, national edition, 8.

80. Rob Roy, "City Still Raves over *Imitation of Life:* Popularity Also Includes Fredi Washington in Wave," *Chicago Defender,* February 23, 1935, national edition, 9.

81. "Armband Feb. 11 Wear Your Black," *Baltimore Afro-American,* February 12, 1938, 13.

82. "She is Frail Ingénue by Night, A Forthright Crusader by Day," *New York Herald Tribune,* March 5, 1939, Schomburg Clipping File for Research in Black Culture of the New York Public Library [microfiche] (Cambridge/Alexandria: Chadwyck-Healey, 1986).

83. See Hamilton, *Adam Clayton Powell Jr.,* 84.

84. "Fredi Washington Prevents Picketing: D.C. Fight Off After She and Johnson Plead," *Baltimore Afro-American,* February 3, 1940, 14.

85. Ibid.

86. Fredi Washington, "Headlines—Footlights: Apollo Comedy Bad for Race," *People's Voice*, July 31, 1943, in FWP. See writings by Washington in Lant and Periz, *Red Velvet Seat: Women's Writings on the First Fifty Years of Cinema.*

87. Ibid.

88. Fredi Washington, "Headlines—Footlights: Tim Moore Replies," *People's Voice*, August 7, 1943, in FWP.

89. Ibid.

90. Ibid.

91. Fredi Washington, "Headlines—Footlights," *People's Voice*, February 5, 1944, 22, in FWP.

92. Ibid.

93. Ibid.

94. Leon Hardwick, "Headlines—Footlights," *People's Voice*, February 12, 1944, 30, in FWP.

95. Cripps, *Making Movies Black*, 102–125.

96. Fredi Washington, "Headlines—Footlights," *People's Voice*, April 29, 1944, in FWP.

97. Ibid.

98. Fredi Washington, "Headlines—Footlights," *People's Voice*, August 5, 1944, 22, in FWP.

99. Cripps, *Slow Fade to Black*, 288.

100. Fredi Washington, "Letter to Mr. Darr Smith, *L.A. Daily News*," August 2, 1949, in FWP.

101. Fredi Washington, "Fredi Says," *People's Voice*, September 6, 1947, in FWP.

102. Major Robinson, "Film Role for Harlem Scribe: Fredi Washington Takes Screen Test," *Chicago Defender*, March 22, 1947, city edition, 26.

103. "Sorry, Wrong Number," *Baltimore Afro-American*, February 5, 1949, 7.

5. Hattie McDaniel

1. Carlton Jackson, *Hattie*, 4–7. Jill Watts reports that McDaniel was born June 10, 1893 (see Watts, *Hattie McDaniel*, 17). Yet McDaniel's death certificate indicates that she was born June 10, 1895 (death certificate for Hattie McDaniel, Department of Health Services, State of California). Note that Watts's biography was published after this chapter was originally conceived. Therefore, Jackson's biography was my primary source for information about McDaniel's background.

2. Carlton Jackson, *Hattie*, 7–11.

3. Ibid., 12–15.

4. Ibid., 16–20.

5. Carlton Jackson, 22; Thomas, *International Dictionary of Films & Filmmakers*, 656; Internet Movie Database, www.imdb.com; and Watts, *Hattie McDaniel*, 283–286.

6. Watts reports that McDaniel appeared in *The Impatient Maiden* (1932), in which audiences heard her speak her first lines on film (Watts, *Hattie McDaniel*, 90). Other roles in 1933 included *Hello, Sister* and *Goodbye Love*, according to Internet Movie Database, www.imdb.com.

7. Other films in which McDaniel appeared include *Lost in Stratosphere* (1934), *Little Men* (1934), *Babbitt* (1934), *Imitation of Life* (1934), *Flirtation* (1934), *Fate's Fathead* (1934), and *King Kelly of the USA* (1934). McDaniel reportedly appears in the funeral scene of *Imitation of Life*. See Thomas, *International Dictionary of Films & Filmmakers*, 656; Carlton Jackson, *Hattie*, 22–54; Internet Movie Database, www.imdb.com; and Watts, *Hattie McDaniel*, 283–286.

8. Carlton Jackson, *Hattie*, 30.

9. Ibid., 25.

10. Thomas, *International Dictionary of Films & Filmmakers: Actors and Actresses*, 656; Carlton Jackson, *Hattie*, 55–95; Internet Movie Database, www.imdb.com; and Watts, *Hattie McDaniel*, 283–286.

11. Carlton Jackson, *Hattie*, 95–101.

12. Ibid., 75 and 132. Donald Bogle reports that McDaniel married Larry C. Williams in 1947 (*Bright Boulevards*, 268), but Carlton Jackson notes that this marriage occurred in 1949. Jill Watts reports that McDaniel was involved in two early marriages, one to Howard Hickman in 1911 and another to Nym Lankfard prior to 1922 (Watts, *Hattie McDaniel*, 37, 55).

13. Carlton Jackson, *Hattie*, 152–153, 158–159; Warren, "Hattie McDaniel: Hi-Hat-Hattie," 704.

14. Wallace, "Race, Gender and Psychoanalysis in Forties Film," 264.

15. "Best of the Year: She's On the Ballot," *Baltimore Afro-American*, March 2, 1940, 14.

16. "McDaniel Award Shows Temper of Modern Times," *New York Amsterdam News*, March 23, 1940, 20.

17. Bogle, *Blacks in American Film Films and Television*, 417.

18. "Hattie McDaniel Wins Academy Award: Actress Called 'Darling' of Motion Picture Arts Banquet," *Baltimore Afro-American*, March 9, 1940, 14.

19. Ibid.

20. "Hattie McDaniel Receives Academy Award as 'Best Supporting Actress of 1939' For Portrayal of 'Mammy' in *Gone with the Wind* Epic," *Philadelphia Tribune*, March 7, 1940, 14.

21. Ibid.

22. Mae Tinee, "It's True! *Gone with the Wind* Has Everything," *Chicago Tribune*, January 26, 1940, 17. It is of note that McDaniel is frequently referred to with an "s" attached to her last name, but the correct spelling of her last name does not include an "s."

23. Muse, "Hattie McDaniels First of Race to Win Movie Award," *Chicago Defender*, March 9, 1940, national edition, 21.

24. Ibid.

25. Ibid.

26. Dalton Trumbo, "Blackface, Hollywood Style," *The Crisis*, December 1943, 366–367. Hattie McDaniel appeared on the front cover of *The Crisis* 47, April 1940.

27. Wiley, *Inside Oscar*, 100.

28. Ibid.

29. John C. Mosher, "The Current Cinema: Riotously with the Throng," *New Yorker*, December 30, 1939, 47.

30. Nugent, "The Screen in Review: *Gone with the Wind*," *New York Times*, December 20, 1939, in *The New York Times Film Reviews, 1939–1948*, vol. 3, 1661–1662.

31. "Entertainment: *Gone with the Wind*," *Newsweek,* December 25, 1939, 28.

32. "Hollywood Comes of Age," *Theatre Arts* 24, no. 2 (February 1940): 126–129.

33. Franz Hoellering, "Films," *The Nation,* December 30, 1939, 740.

34. Al Monroe, "*Gone with the Wind* Has Too Many Insults," *Chicago Defender,* January 6, 1940, national edition, 21.

35. Dan Burley, "*Gone with the Wind*—Subtle Propaganda of Anti-Negro Film Told By Reviewer," *New York Amsterdam News,* January 6, 1940, 16.

36. "Hattie McDaniel Clicks in *Gone with the Wind;* A Critic Gets the Boot," *Philadelphia Tribune,* December 28, 1939, 14. Jimmie Fidler's name is spelled differently in various sources.

37. "*Gone with the Wind* Had Outstanding Players," *Washington Afro-American,* April 6, 1940, 15.

38. Harry B. Webber, "*Gone with the Wind* Has Some Good Points," *Baltimore Afro-American,* January 20, 1940, 13.

39. Lillian Johnson, "Light and Shadow," *Baltimore Afro-American,* March 23, 1940, 13.

40. Al Monroe, "*Gone with the Wind* Has Too Many Insults," *Chicago Defender,* January 6, 1940, national edition, 21.

41. "Broadway Is Killing the Negro!" *New York Amsterdam News,* February 17, 1940, 20.

42. Ross Hawkins, "At Odds With Editorial on *Gone with the Wind,*" *New York Amsterdam News,* March 30, 1940, 12.

43. William L. Patterson, "*Gone with the Wind:* Lies About the Civil War," *Chicago Defender,* January 6, 1940, national edition, 15.

44. "*Gone with the Wind,*" *Chicago Defender,* January 6, 1940, city edition, 14.

45. Oscar Polk, "Oscar Polk Defends *Gone with the Wind,*" *Chicago Defender,* April 8, 1939, city edition, 10.

46. "Mammies in Films OK'd," *New York Amsterdam News,* May 20, 1939, 21.

47. Ibid.

48. Ibid.

49. Ibid.

50. Ibid.

51. Earl Morris, "Race Actors Flayed for *Gone with the Wind* Parts," *Chicago Defender,* February 11, 1939, national edition, 19.

52. Benjamin Davis, "*Gone with the Wind* Is Insidious Propaganda Says Daily Associate Editor," *New York Age,* January 6, 1940, 4.

53. William L. Patterson, "*Gone with the Wind:* Lies About the Civil War," *Chicago Defender,* January 6, 1940, national edition, 15.

54. "*Gone with the Wind,*" *Chicago Defender,* January 6, 1940, city edition, 14.

55. Burley, "*Gone with the Wind,*" 16.

56. "Fight Showing of *Gone with the Wind:* Baptists Join War on Dixie Picture," *Chicago Defender,* September 16, 1939, national edition, 20.

57. "Threaten Boycott: Alliance Protests *Gone with the Wind* Production," *New York Amsterdam News,* March 11, 1939, 16; "Harlem to Protest Film, *Gone with the Wind,*" *Chicago Defender,* January 6, 1940, national edition, 2.

58. William Gaulden, "*Gone with the Wind* Vicious," *New York Amsterdam News,* January 13, 1940, 14.

356 · NOTES TO PAGES 150–162

59. "Chicagoans Picket *Gone with the Wind:* More Than 100 Urge Boycott of Epic Film," *Chicago Defender,* February 3, 1940, national edition, 9.

60. "Student Pickets Tackle *Gone with the Wind,*" *Washington Afro-American,* March 9, 1940, 16.

61. St. John, "It Ain't Fittin'," 135.

62. Linda Williams, *Playing the Race Card,* 212.

63. Hale, *Making Whiteness,* 112–113.

64. Ibid., 113

65. Vera and Gordon, *Screen Saviors,* 101.

66. Spillers, "Notes on an Alternative Model—Neither/Nor," 165–187.

67. Fanon, *Black Skin, White Masks,* 70.

68. Taylor, *Scarlett's Women,* 172.

69. Doane, "The 'Woman's Film,'" 288.

70. Williamson, "How Black Was Rhett Butler?" 87–107.

71. Linda Williams, *Playing the Race Card,* 212.

72. Taylor, *Scarlett's Women,* 173.

73. Al Monroe, "*Gone With the Wind* Has Too Many Insults," *Chicago Defender,* January 6, 1940, national edition, 21.

74. hooks, "The Oppositional Gaze," 288–302.

75. Mulvey, "Visual Pleasure and Narrative Cinema," 28. This essay was originally published in *Screen,* Winter 1975–6, 119–30.

76. Carby, *Reconstructing Womanhood.*

77. William L. Patterson, "*Gone with the Wind:* Lies About the Civil War," *Chicago Defender,* January 6, 1940, national edition, 15.

78. "Mammies in Films OK'd," *New York Amsterdam News,* May 20, 1939, 21.

79. hooks, "Choosing the Margin as a Space of Radical Openness," 36, 15–23; hooks, "The Oppositional Gaze," 288–302.

80. Carl Lawrence, "No Romance For Me Says Miss McDaniels," *New York Amsterdam News,* June 8, 1940, 3.

81. Ibid.

82. "This Is Hattie," *Baltimore Afro-American,* March 9, 1940, 14.

83. "A $7.00 Hattie: That Is Salary Star of *Gone with the Wind* Once Received," *Chicago Defender,* May 18, 1940, national edition, 21.

84. Hilda See, "Hattie McDaniel Weds: Star Elopes For Her Third Trip To Altar," *Chicago Defender,* March 29, 1941, city edition, 12.

85. Lawrence LaMar, "Hattie McDaniel Seeking Divorce," *Baltimore Afro-American,* August 18, 1945, 10.

86. Ibid.

87. Leon Hardwick and Harry Levette, "Thru Hollywood," *Chicago Defender,* June 10, 1944, national edition, 8.

88. E. B. Rea, "Encores and Echoes," *Baltimore Afro-American,* December 16, 1944, 6; "Hattie M'Daniel Wins Divorce," *Washington Afro-American,* December 29, 1945, 17.

89. "Hattie M'Daniel Wins Divorce," *Washington Afro-American,* December 29, 1945, 17.

90. "Encores," *Baltimore Afro-American,* December 16, 1944, 6.

91. "Star of Wind to Adopt Child," *Baltimore Afro-American,* April 19, 1941, 14.

92. Carlton Jackson, *Hattie,* 89.

93. "Hattie McDaniel," *Washington Afro-American,* January 16, 1943, 17.

94. J. Robert Smith, "Miss McDaniel Accused of Using Offensive Epithet," *Washington Afro-American,* April 29, 1944, 14.

95. "Hattie McDaniel's Film Is Barred," *Baltimore Afro-American,* June 30, 1945, 2.

96. Ibid.

97. Lawrence LaMar, "Hattie McDaniel Gets Big Role in *George Washington Slept Here,*" *Chicago Defender,* April 18, 1942, city edition, 11.

98. "Hattie in Spotlight," *Baltimore Afro-American,* October 30, 1943, 8.

99. Harry Levette, "High School Show Causes Near Riot: Hattie Again," *Chicago Defender,* January 18, 1941, national edition, 21. McDaniel's reputation as a scene stealer is affirmed by Judith Mayne, who suggests that Bette Davis was so fearful that McDaniel would take the spotlight away from her in *The Great Lie,* where McDaniel was cast as a maid, that she had her scenes cut. See Mayne, *Cinema and Spectatorship,* 139.

100. "Her Man Did Wrong," *New York Amsterdam News,* October 28, 1950, 1; Allan McMillan, "Allan's Alley: Private Papers of a Cub Reporter," *New York Amsterdam News,* October 21, 1950, Brooklyn section, 26.

101. "Hattie McDaniel Divorcing Mate of Five Months," *Pittsburgh Courier,* November 5, 1949, 1.

102. Carlton Jackson, *Hattie,* 146.

103. "Egg Fry," *Time,* December 1, 1947, 102.

104. Delores Calvin, "Established Actress: Hattie McDaniel 'Top Cheese' on CBS Show," *Baltimore Afro-American,* January 14, 1950, 8.

105. Harry Levette, "High School Show Causes Near Riot: Hattie Again," *Chicago Defender,* January 18, 1941, national edition, 21.

106. Carlton Jackson, *Hattie,* 153.

107. Betty Granger, "Noted Actress Dies: Hattie McDaniel in Life Role At Pinnacle of Movie Stardom," *New York Amsterdam News,* November 1, 1952, 32; Chester Washington, "Film Stars Laud Life of Actress," *Pittsburgh Courier,* November 8, 1952, 1; and "Lowly Debut Salary Mounted to Five-Figure Weekly Take Home Pay," *Chicago Defender,* November 8, 1952, national edition, 22.

108. "Milestones," *Time,* November 3, 1952, 98.

109. "Transition: Died," *Newsweek,* November 3, 1952, 71.

110. Dwyer, "Celebrating Black Gay and Lesbian History: Hattie McDaniel," *Vanguard,* February 8, 1991, 7, Part II. In the Academy of Motion Pictures Arts and Sciences, Margaret Herrick Library, Beverly Hills, California.

111. Carlton Jackson, *Hattie,* 134.

112. Ibid., 158–159; George P. Johnson Film Collection. According to a report titled "Thousands Attend Last Rites for Hattie McDaniel," it was revealed that "Nearly 3,000 mourners including many Hollywood movie stars, paid last respects to Hattie McDaniel.... Miss McDaniel who was 54, died of cancer in nearby San Fernando Valley, Calif. After the ceremonies at Peoples Independent Church of Christ, 125 limousines formed a procession to follow the body to Rosedale Cemetery. Representing the movie industry, screen and radio actor Edward Arnold read the eulogy. Hattie had a green casket carried in a green Cadillac hearse" (George P. Johnson Film Collection). Those in attendance included Louise Beavers, Lena Horne, Clarence Muse, Lillian Randolph, Ruby and Dorothy Dandridge,

Bill Walker, and Les Hite, among others. See Chester Washington, "Film Stars Laud Life of Actress," *Pittsburgh Courier,* November 8, 1952, 1.

6. Lena Horne

1. J. Robert Smith, "Miss McDaniel Accused of Using Offensive Epithet," *Washington Afro-American,* April 29, 1944, 14.
2. Muller and Richardson, *Lacan and Language,* 281.
3. Stanfield, "An Excursion into the Lower Depths," 90.
4. Rothe, "Horne, Lena," 310; Moritz, "Horne, Lena," 194–198; and Kathleen Thompson, "Horne, Lena," 580.
5. Ibid.
6. Rothe, "Horne, Lena," 311.
7. Ibid.; Kathleen Thompson, "Horne, Lena," 581–582.
8. Kathleen Thompson, "Horne, Lena," 196; Thomas, *International Dictionary of Films & Filmmakers,* 474.
9. Moritz, "Horne, Lena," *Current Biography Yearbook 1985,* 197.
10. Ibid.
11. Ibid.
12. Ibid.; Kathleen Thompson, "Horne, Lena," 583–584.
13. Eonline Internet Source, www.eonline.com/Facts/people.
14. "Leana Horne Leads Sissle's Band and Sings With It Too," *Chicago Defender,* June 20, 1936, national edition, 11.
15. Bogle, *Toms, Coons, Mulattoes, Mammies, & Bucks,* 127.
16. Advertisement for Dr. Fred Palmer's skin whitener ointment, *Pittsburgh Courier,* May 16, 1936, section 1, 5.
17. Harry Levette, "Thru Hollywood," *Chicago Defender,* February 19, 1938, national edition, 19.
18. Knight, "Star Dances," 402–403.
19. "Leana Horne Joins White Orchestra," *Chicago Defender,* January 4, 1941, city edition, 10. Horne also is covered in "Joins White Band: Miss Leana Horne," *Chicago Defender,* January 4, 1941, city edition, 1.
20. Doane, *Femmes Fatales,* 209–248.
21. Maurice Dancer, "Lena Horne and Charlie Barnet to Exchange Guest Appearances," *Chicago Defender,* April 26, 1941, national edition, 21.
22. Arstein and Moss, *In Person: Lena Horne,* 165.
23. Knight, "Star Dances," 405.
24. "Helena Horne a Busy Chirper," *Baltimore Afro-American,* August 30, 1941, 13; "Horne, Barnet on Lend-Lease Basis," *Pittsburgh Courier,* April 26, 1941, 20.
25. Leonard G. Feather, "Lena Horne, Golden Gate Boys Rock Historic Carnegie Hall with Swing," *Pittsburgh Courier,* May 3, 1941, 21.
26. "Lena Horne Leaves," *Pittsburgh Courier,* October 25, 1941, 21; "Horne, Barnet on Lend-Lease Basis," *Pittsburgh Courier,* April 26, 1941, 20; "Lena Takes Time Off As Charlie Barnett and Band Go South," *Pittsburgh Courier,* February 8, 1941, 21; and Bessie M. Gant, "Lena Horne Likes Seafood, So Bess Dedicates a Salad," *Pittsburgh Courier,* February 7, 1942, 9.

27. Buckley, *The Hornes,* 154.

28. Ibid.

29. Lindsay Patterson, *Black Films and Film-makers,* 141–142.

30. Ibid., 142.

31. "Romantic Lena Horne: Studio Decides Only Such Parts Are To Be Given Beauteous Star," *Chicago Defender,* January 23, 1943, national edition, 19.

32. Knight, "Star Dances," 404; Wallace, "Race, Gender and Psychoanalysis in Forties Film," 265.

33. Buckley, *The Hornes,* 165.

34. Ibid., 154.

35. Lawrence LaMar, "Lena Horn[e] Gets Long Contract with Metro Goldwyn Pictures," *Chicago Defender,* March 14, 1942, national edition, 20.

36. Bill Chase, "Meet Lena Horne, the 'New Type' Sepia Movie Star," *New York Amsterdam News,* June 20, 1942, 16.

37. Bessie M. Gant, "Bess' Secrets," *Pittsburgh Courier,* February 7, 1942, 9.

38. Al Monroe, "Lena Horne, Bill Robinson To Entertain Europe AEF," *Chicago Defender,* January 16, 1943, city edition, 1.

39. Lindsay Patterson, *Black Films and Film-makers,* 143.

40. Bill Chase, "Meet Lena Horne, the 'New Type' Sepia Movie Star," *New York Amsterdam News,* June 20, 1942, 16.

41. Lindsay Patterson, *Black Films and Film-makers,* 143–144.

42. Dyer, *Heavenly Bodies,* 40.

43. Philip Carter, "Lena Horne Fresh Copy for Scribes," *Baltimore Afro-American,* November 21, 1942, 10.

44. "The Screen," *New York Times,* May 28, 1943, in *The New York Film Reviews, 1939–1948,* vol. 3, 1939.

45. Rob Roy, "Critic Says Hollywood Caters to South in Pictures: Even Lena Horne Gets Red Light, He Writes," *Chicago Defender,* June 26, 1943, national edition, 10.

46. Lindsay Patterson, *Black Films and Film-makers,* 149–150.

47. "*Cabin in the Sky* Jinx to Three of Its Stars," *Baltimore Afro-American,* October 31, 1942, 10.

48. "Term *Cabin* Film Downright Criminal," *Baltimore Afro-American,* March 13, 1943, 10.

49. "*Cabin in the Sky,*" *Time,* April 12, 1943, 96.

50. Manny Farber, "The Great White Way," *The New Republic,* July 5, 1943, 20.

51. E. B. Rea, "Encore and Echoes," *Baltimore Afro-American,* June 19, 1943, 8.

52. Cripps, *Making Movies Black,* 83.

53. Lawrence LaMar, "Brand Story of *Stormy Weather* Re-Take As False: Picture Receives OK from Studio Officials," *Chicago Defender,* April 3, 1943, national edition, 19. This rumor, however, was denied. See "*Stormy Weather* Viewed as Box Office Hit by Fox's Studio," *Baltimore Afro-American,* April 10, 1943, 8.

54. Lawrence LaMar, "Brand Story of *Stormy Weather* Re-Take As False: Picture Receives OK from Studio Officials," *Chicago Defender,* April 3, 1943, national edition, 19.

55. Buckley, *The Hornes,* 174.

56. "Even Studio Officials Hep to Jive Spilled All Over Studio," *Chicago Defender,* March 13, 1943, national edition, 18.

57. "Cinema: The New Pictures: *Stormy Weather*," *Time,* July 12, 1943, 96.

58. Harry Levette, "Say! Bill Is No 'Thomas': Coast Scribe Praises Film and Our Bojangles In Midst of 'Bombs,'" *Chicago Defender,* March 13, 1943, national edition, 19.

59. Harry Levette, "Thru Hollywood," *Chicago Defender,* February 20, 1943, national edition, 19; "Says Studio Wants Crude, Corny Themes," *Baltimore Afro-American,* February 13, 1943, 8; and "Hollywood Laughs at 'Scandal' but Frowns on Girls' Giggles," *Chicago Defender,* February 27, 1943, national edition, 12.

60. "Lena's Salary Revealed; Studio Gets Most of It," *Baltimore Afro-American,* July 10, 1943, 8.

61. "*Stormy Weather,*" *Variety,* June 2, 1943, in *Variety Film Reviews,* vol. 7.

62. Thomas Pryor, "The Screen: Stormy Weather," *New York Times,* July 22, 1943, in *The New York Film Reviews,* 1939–1948, vol. 3.

63. Aaron Davis, "Hear Problems Slow Work on Film *Stormy Weather:* Everybody Wants To Star Before Lights They Say," *Chicago Defender,* February 6, 1943, national edition, 18; "*Stormy Weather* Has Merit Even If Carelessly Screened," *Chicago Defender,* July 24, 1943, city edition, 12.

64. Noble, *The Negro in Films,* 205.

65. Cripps, *Making Movies Black,* 80.

66. Bogle, *Toms, Coons, Mulattoes, Mammies, & Bucks,* 127.

67. Knight, "Star Dances," 405.

68. Ibid.

69. "Lena Horne and Berry Brothers Cast in Movie," *Pittsburgh Courier,* April 18, 1942, 21.

70. Buckley, *The Hornes,* 159.

71. "*Colliers* Says of Lena Horne, But, You Guess, Just What Pal," *Chicago Defender,* June 26, 1943, national edition, 10.

72. Ibid.

73. Ibid.

74. "Music," *Newsweek,* January 4, 1943, 65.

75. Philip Hartung, "Shadows but No Substance," *The Commonweal,* September 25, 1942, 544.

76. Bill Chase, "Meet Lena Horne, the 'New Type' Sepia Movie Star," *New York Amsterdam News,* June 20, 1942, 16.

77. "A Plea by NAACP May Get Race Movie Lift," *Chicago Defender,* August 8, 1942, national edition, 12.

78. Buckley, *The Hornes,* 154.

79. Knight, "Star Dances," 405–406.

80. "Native Son Author Has A New Show," *Chicago Defender,* February 6, 1943, city edition, 12.

81. "Music," *Newsweek,* January 4, 1943, 65.

82. Ibid.

83. "Lena Horne Still Idol," *Pittsburgh Courier,* July 3, 1943, 20; "Lena Horne Packing Bags for Trip East," *Chicago Defender,* October 2, 1943, national edition, 19.

84. Ibid.

85. "Simpkins, Two Others Are Signed by MGM," *Pittsburgh Courier,* August 21, 1943, 20.

86. Dyer, *Heavenly Bodies*, 15.

87. "Cinema: The New Pictures-*I Dood It*," *Time*, November 29, 1943, 92.

88. Philip Hartung, "The Screen: Belonging," *The Commonweal*, January 30, 1953, 424.

89. "MGM Features Lena and Hazel Scott in All Colored Sequence," *New York Amsterdam News*, June 12, 1943, 17.

90. Diawara, "Black Spectatorship," 217.

91. Knight, "Star Dances," 405.

92. "Lena Horne Stars in Summer Films," *New York Amsterdam News*, February 26, 1944, 3-B; Internet Movie Database, www.imdb.com.

93. "Lena Makes the Regal Feature of This Week Groovy," *Chicago Defender*, May 6, 1944, city edition, 9.

94. Abramson, "Lena Horne," 147.

95. Buckley, *The Hornes*, 163–164.

96. "Lena 'Clipped' By Memphis Censor," *Pittsburgh Courier*, January 15, 1949, 1.

97. "Horne and Rochester to Feature New Film," *Chicago Defender*, August 21, 1943, national edition, 18.

98. Advertisement for *Broadway Rhythm*, *Chicago Defender*, July 15, 1944, city edition, 9.

99. "Hollywood in the Dark," *Baltimore Afro-American*, August 5, 1944, 8.

100. "Sweetie Inks for 'Fleshie': Says Lena Under-cast," *Baltimore Afro-American*, July 8, 1944, 8.

101. Buckley, *The Hornes*, 191.

102. "Singing Sensation in *Two Sisters and a Sailor*," *Baltimore Afro-American*, February 12, 1944, 8.

103. Ibid.; "A Star and a Starlett Hit the News in Pictures," *Chicago Defender*, May 13, 1944, national edition, 8.

104. Leon Hardwick, "Lena Horne, Three Others Given Awards for Work in Hit Films," *Chicago Defender*, May 6, 1944, national edition, 8.

105. "Lena Horne Between Devil and Deep Blue, Says Writer," *Baltimore Afro-American*, June 10, 1944, 8.

106. "Lena Horne Begins a New Movie," *Ebony*, March 1946, 20. The caption reads "Lena's big ambition is to quit singing, be an actress."

107. "Lena Horne's Life Story on *Democracy—USA*," *Chicago Defender*, November 23, 1946, city edition, 1.

108. Buckley, *The Hornes*, 191.

109. Harry Levette, "Lena Cast in *Follies* Film," *Baltimore Afro-American*, July 15, 1944, 8.

110. Dyer, *Heavenly Bodies*, 138.

111. Ibid., 168–170.

112. Dyer, "A Star Is Born and the Construction of Authenticity," 139.

113. Harry Levette, "Lena Would Marry Again If the Right Man Came Along," *Baltimore Afro-American*, August 5, 1944, 8.

114. "Lena Horne Stars in Regals Picture," *Chicago Defender*, August 3, 1946, city edition, 23.

115. "Binford Snips Lena's Scene from *Follies*," *Baltimore Afro-American*, March 23, 1946, 14.

116. "MGM Cuts Lena Horne–Avon Long Number out of *Ziegfeld Follies,*" *Baltimore Afro-American,* June 9, 1945, 8.

117. Cripps, *Making Movies Black,* 261.

118. Buckley, *The Hornes,* 195.

119. "Lena Horne in Regal's Film Starting Friday," *Chicago Defender,* April 26, 1947, city edition, 30.

120. "Lena Horne Begins a New Movie," *Ebony,* March 1946, 20.

121. Ibid., 14.

122. Ibid., 20.

123. "Lena 'Clipped' by Memphis Censor Board," *Pittsburgh Courier,* January 15, 1949, 1.

124. E. B. Rea, "Encores and Echoes," *Baltimore Afro-American,* September 6, 1947, 6.

125. John M. Lee, "Is Lena Horne Fading as Box Office Attraction?" *Baltimore Afro-American,* August 17, 1946, 6.

126. Ibid.

127. Ibid.

128. Ibid.

129. "Lena Horne Set for Theatre Tour," *Baltimore Afro-American,* November 2, 1946, 6.

130. Rosa R. Riley, "This Is Hollywood," *Chicago Defender,* April 19, 1947, national edition, 18.

131. Knight, "Star Dances," 404.

132. "Music: Lena in Paris," *Time,* December 8, 1947, 68.

133. Rudolph Dunbar, "Lena Horne Fascinates London Hordes; Basks in Their Admiration and Adulation," *Baltimore Afro-American,* December 20, 1947, 6.

134. Ibid.

135. "Music: Lena in Paris," *Time,* December 8, 1947, 68.

136. Delores Calvin, "Lena Can't Dance, But She's Great in Musical: Has No Gorgeous Gams But Beauty," *Baltimore Afro-American,* January 15, 1949, 7.

137. Ibid.

138. Lena Horne, "My Life Story," *Negro Digest,* July 1949, 12.

139. Arstein and Moss, *In Person: Lena Horne,* 228–229.

140. "Lena Clipped by Memphis Censor," *Pittsburgh Courier,* January 15, 1949, 1.

141. Lawrence LaMar, "La Horne in Running in Filmland's Oscar," *New York Amsterdam News,* February 12, 1949, 25.

142. Lillian Scott, "Fans, Not Lena Horne, Credit Star with 'Entirely New' Singing Style," *Chicago Defender,* July 31, 1948, city edition, 27.

143. Barry Ulanov, "How Lena Learned to Sing," *Negro Digest,* December 1947, 30.

144. Lydia T. Brown, "Lena Tells Why She Tried to Break Contract with Studio," *Baltimore Afro-American,* February 7, 1948, 9.

145. "Lena," *Chicago Defender,* April 23, 1949, city edition, 40.

146. J. C. Tachella, "Patrons Prefer Pictures with White Cast, Lena Horne Thinks," *Chicago Defender,* July 29, 1950, city edition, 30.

147. Dyer, *Heavenly Bodies,* 15.

148. Essie Mae Seabron, "Lena Horne's Nude 'Body' Put in Mothballs by MGM; Read On," *Baltimore Afro-American,* May 20, 1950, 8; Essie Mae Seabron, "Horne's Body Shipped: Is Lena Through at MGM?" *Chicago Defender,* May 13, 1950, national edition, 21.

149. "Dots, Dashes and Little Flashes: Hill in Hollywood," *Pittsburgh Courier,* June 5, 1949, 20.

150. Alice Dunnigan, "La Horne Gets Riled over MGM Brush-off in D.C.," *Pittsburgh Courier,* January 29, 1949, 7.

151. David Hanna, "Beautiful But Not Dumb," *Negro Digest,* September 1944, 18.

152. Herbert Feinstein, "Lena Horne Speaks Freely on Race, Marriage, Stage," *Ebony,* May 1963, 64.

153. Allen Cowser, "Letters: Lena Horne in *Show Boat,*" *Ebony,* August 1951, 11.

154. Hans Massaquoi, "Ebony Interview with Lena Horne," *Ebony,* May 1980, 42.

155. Buckley, *The Hornes,* 197.

156. Ibid.

157. Gerald Clarke, "Theater: *Stormy Weather* on Broadway," *Time,* May 25, 1981, 96.

158. Knight, "Star Dances," 406.

159. "The Private Life of Lena Horne," *Ebony,* September 1953, 67–69.

160. S. W. Garlington, "Pointed Points: Is Lena Wrecking Her Future?" *New York Amsterdam News,* November 12, 1949, 2.

161. Ralph Matthews, "Who Worries about Race when Dan Cupid Strikes?" *Baltimore Afro-American,* November 26, 1949, 7. The fact that Horne's mother was involved in an interracial marriage with a white Cuban as she launched a second marriage made Lena's marriage even more acceptable. *Ebony,* October 1950, 36.

162. Gerald Clarke, "Theater: *Stormy Weather* on Broadway," *Time,* May 25, 1981, 96.

163. hooks, "The Oppositional Gaze," 288–302.

164. Alfred E. Smith, "Lena Horne Quits USO Tour in Row over Army Jim Crow," *Chicago Defender,* January 6, 1945, national edition, 1.

165. Ibid.

166. Ibid.; "War Dept. Awaits Probe of Camp JC Against Lena Horne," *Baltimore Afro-American,* January 20, 1945, 8.

167. Al Monroe, "Swinging the News," *Chicago Defender,* May 31, 1947, national edition, 10.

168. "Lena Horne Hit by L.A. Home Ban," *Chicago Defender,* May 24, 1947, city edition, 2; Barry Ulanov, "How Lena Learned to Sing," *Negro Digest,* December 1947, 29.

169. Barry Ulanov, "How Lena Learned to Sing," *Negro Digest,* December 1947, 29.

170. "Barred," *New York Amsterdam News,* September 24, 1949, 1.

171. Alfred Duckett, "Fabulous Lena Horne Rivals That 'Tree Growing in Brooklyn' Says Scribe Who Saw Her Blossom Out," *Chicago Defender,* August 28, 1954, national edition, 7. Horne's activism continued into the 1960s, "when a white restaurant patron loudly and repeatedly referred to her with that ugly six-letter epithet too many people carelessly utter, she let go with several ash trays in his direction." In "Miss Lena Horne," *Washington Afro-American,* February 20, 1960, 4.

172. Cliff MacKay, "News in Tabloid," *Baltimore Afro-American,* October 1, 1949, 5.

173. "La Horne Proud of Films About Negroes," *New York Amsterdam News,* April 16, 1949, Brooklyn section, B-2, 17.

174. Alvin Moses, "Lena Horne Swats Radio's Jim Crow," *Chicago Defender,* September 20, 1947, city edition, 18.

175. "La Horne Quits Cast of Backward Musical," *New York Amsterdam News,* September 15, 1945, 1-A.

176. Cripps, *Making Movies Black,* 187.

177. "Guild Seeks to Eliminate Lena Horne or 'Dis and Dat' from *St. Louis Woman,*" *Chicago Defender,* September 8, 1945, city edition, 21. The same article also appeared in the national edition but on a different page.

178. Leon Hardwick, "Lena Definitely Out of *St. Louis Woman,*" *Washington Afro-American,* September 29, 1945, 20.

179. "Lena Horne Joins NAACP," *Pittsburgh Courier,* July 31, 1943, 20.

180. *The Crisis,* December 1949, 392; *The Crisis,* March 1953, 171; *The Crisis,* May 1956, 260; and *The Crisis* 52, May 1945, 138. Megan Williams has examined Horne's long-term relationship with *The Crisis* as Horne symbolized the black middle class. See Megan Williams, "*The Crisis* Cover Girl," 200–218.

181. "Lena Horne Joins Notables Backing FDR's Re-Election," *Chicago Defender,* October 21, 1944, national edition, 1.

182. "Lena Horne," *Chicago Defender,* July 12, 1947, national edition, 19. Horne appears in a photograph with a caption that notes her contribution to this program.

183. "Screen Guild Elects Lena to Its Exec. Board," *New York Amsterdam News,* September 30, 1944, 7-B.

184. "Lena Horne Takes Office," *Chicago Defender,* March 9, 1946, city edition, 27; Leon Hardwick, "Personalities of Radio, Screen, Studios Honored," *Baltimore Afro-American,* June 2, 1945, 10.

185. "Radio Guild Names Officers: Lena Horne Among New Stars Chosen," *Chicago Defender,* February 9, 1946, city edition, 27.

186. "Harlem Dope," *Chicago Defender,* March 13, 1948, city edition, 27.

187. "Lena Horne Quotes AFRO in Address to 25,000," *Baltimore Afro-American,* September 20, 1947, 7. Horne's activism is solidified when she narrates a Cuban documentary by Santiago Alvarez on the civil rights movement in the United States and sings her famous song, "Now," which was banned in the United States in the 1960s. Horne's activism is discussed by Dreher, *Dancing on the White Page,* 29–59. See also Regester, "Hazel Scott and Lena Horne," 81–95.

188. "Lena Horne Tells How Robeson Changed Her," *Baltimore Afro-American,* October 11, 1947, 6.

189. Buckley, *The Hornes,* 220.

190. "Lee and Lena Horne Deny Red Charge," *Chicago Defender,* June 18, 1949, national edition, 1.

191. Buckley, *The Hornes,* 220.

192. Ibid., 221.

193. Ibid., 221–222.

194. Harry Levette, "Gossip of the Film Lots," *Baltimore Afro-American,* April 8, 1950, 8.

195. "Fans Wonder If Graciousness, Not Membership, Tagged Lena As 'Red,'" *Chicago Defender,* May 5, 1951, national edition, 32.

196. Abramson, "Lena Horne," 148.

197. "Fans Wonder if Graciousness, Not Membership, Tagged Lena as 'Red,'" *Chicago Defender,* May 5, 1951, national edition, 32.

7. Hazel Scott

1. Diawara, "Black Spectatorship," 211.

2. Wallace, "Race, Gender and Psychoanalysis in Forties Film," 265.

3. Salem, "Scott, Hazel," 444; MacFarlane, "Scott, Hazel," 1019; and Louie Robinson, "Hazel Scott Comes Home to the 'Action,'" *Ebony*, March 1968, 104. According to Robinson, Thomas Scott spoke seventeen Chinese dialects, was considered a black nationalist, and was a supporter of Marcus Garvey. It is not certain that he taught at Fisk University; according to Karen Chilton's biography of Scott, which was not available when this chapter was developed, that report may have been part of Hazel Scott's promotional campaign.

4. Michael Carter, "She Makes the Wounded Wiggle," *Negro Digest*, April 1945, 67–68; MacFarlane, "Scott, Hazel"; "Bye-Bye Boogie: Hazel Scott Leaves Night Clubs and Moves to Concert Stage," *Ebony*, November 1945, 32.

5. Salem, "Scott, Hazel," 444–445; MacFarlane, "Scott, Hazel," 1019; Hazel Scott Powell, "I Found God in Show Business," *Ebony*, May 1956, 41.

6. Hazel Scott Powell, "I Found God in Show Business," 42.

7. MacFarlane, "Scott, Hazel," 1019.

8. "Bye-Bye Boogie: Hazel Scott Leaves Night Clubs and Moves to Concert Stage," *Ebony*, November 1945, 34.

9. Ibid.

10. MacFarlane, "Scott, Hazel," 1019.

11. Michael Carter, "She Makes the Wounded Wiggle," *Negro Digest*, April 1945, 67.

12. Lerone Bennett Jr., "Adam Clayton Powell: Enigma on Capitol Hill," *Ebony*, June 1963, 25–42.

13. "Hazel Gets TV Show," *Chicago Defender*, February 11, 1950, national edition, 36.

14. E. A. Wiggins, "Hazel Scott Triumphs in Paris, France Debut," *Chicago Defender*, April 13, 1957, national edition, 9; Roberta Brandes Gratz, "Closeup: After the Blue Jeans" [date not legible], Schomburg News Clipping File.

15. E. A. Wiggins, "What Goes In Paris," *Chicago Defender*, August 16, 1958, national edition, 19.

16. Hazel Scott, "The Truth About Me," *Ebony*, September 1960, 139.

17. Bogle, *Brown Sugar*, 106.

18. Hazel Scott, "The Truth About Me," *Ebony*, September 1960, 139; Louie Robinson, "Hazel Scott Comes Home to the 'Action,'" *Ebony*, March 1968, 96–97.

19. MacFarlane, "Scott, Hazel," 1019; Hazel Scott, "The Truth About Me," *Ebony*, September 1960, 144. See Karen Chilton, *Hazel Scott*.

20. Stanfield, "An Excursion into the Lower Depths," 92.

21. Ibid.

22. Ibid.

23. Stuart Hall, "The Whites of Their Eyes," 40.

24. Ibid., 40–41.

25. Wallace, "Race, Gender and Psychoanalysis in Forties Film," 265.

26. Bobo, *Black Women as Cultural Readers*, 50.

27. Ibid., 36.

28. "Hazel Scott and Lena Horne Have Parallel Careers on Road to Fame," *Baltimore Afro-American*, January 16, 1943, 8.

29. Bogle, *Bright Boulevards*, 239.

30. Bill Chase, "All Ears," *New York Amsterdam News*, August 1, 1942, 8.

31. Cripps, *Making Movies Black,* 95.

32. "She Made Jive Respectable: Condensed from *Time,*" *Negro Digest,* November 1942, 8.

33. Michael Carter, "She Makes the Wounded Wiggle," *Negro Digest,* April 1945, 68.

34. Bogle, *Bright Boulevards,* 239.

35. E. B. Rea, "Encores and Echoes," *Baltimore Afro-American,* May 1, 1943, 8.

36. Lamparski, *Whatever Became Of?* 156.

37. "Why Dusky Hazel Scott Sings in the Movies," *Baltimore Afro-American,* August 29, 1942, 10.

38. Negra, *Off-White Hollywood,* 39.

39. "Why Dusky Hazel Scott Sings in the Movies," *Baltimore Afro-American,* August 29, 1942, 10.

40. "White Press Please Copy," *Baltimore Afro-American,* August 29, 1942, 10.

41. Ibid.

42. Bill Chase, "All Ears," *New York Amsterdam News,* August 1, 1942, 8.

43. "Hazel Scott Featured in New Mae West Film," *New York Amsterdam News,* February 20, 1943, 15.

44. "Hazel Scott," *New York Amsterdam News,* March 11, 1944, 10-A.

45. Michael Carter, "She Makes the Wounded Wiggle," *Negro Digest,* April 1945, 69.

46. Lamparski, *Whatever Became Of?* 157.

47. Another commanding black presence in her life was her husband, U.S. congressman Adam Clayton Powell Jr., one of the most powerful African American politicians of the twentieth century.

48. Cripps, *Making Movies Black,* 96.

49. Buckley, *The Hornes,* 185.

50. Don Seymour, "Scott, Horne Deny Hairpulling Story," *Baltimore Afro-American,* November 6, 1943, 8.

51. "Hazel Scott's Next Film Is *I Dood It,*" *Chicago Defender,* May 15, 1943, national edition.

52. "MGM Features Lena Horne: *I Dood It* Picture Adds All-Negro Part," *New York Amsterdam News,* June 12, 1943, 17.

53. Ibid.; Internet Movie Database, www.imdb.com. The *New York Amsterdam News* reports that Vivian Dandridge appeared in the film, yet Internet Movie Database reveals that Ruby Dandridge was cast in the film. See "MGM Features Lena Horne: *I Dood It* Picture Adds All-Negro Part," *New York Amsterdam News,* June 12, 1943, 17.

54. Buckley, *The Hornes,* 185.

55. "Wows Filmland," *Chicago Defender,* June 26, 1943, national edition, 10; "Harlem-Broadway-Hollywood: N.Y.'s Piano Darling Goes Hollywood," *New York Amsterdam News,* June 19, 1943, 16.

56. Lawrence LaMar, "Writer Fears Hazel Scott Has Become 'Hollywood,' One Writes," *Chicago Defender,* July 31, 1943, national edition, 18.

57. Ibid.

58. "Lena to Do Boogie Step in New Film," *Baltimore Afro-American,* July 31, 1943, 8.

59. Stuart Hall, "The Whites of Their Eyes," 40–42.

60. "Lena to Do Boogie Step in New Film," *Baltimore Afro-American,* July 31, 1943, 8.

61. "Hazel Scott Back Again at 'Uptown,'" *New York Amsterdam News*, August 14, 1943, 17.

62. Bogle, *Bright Boulevards*, 244.

63. Ibid.

64. Cripps, *Making Movies Black*, 96–97.

65. "Hazel Signed as Gershwin's Inspiration in *Rhapsody*," *Baltimore Afro-American*, September 18, 1943, 8.

66. Phil Carter, "Hazel Scott Is Queen Once More in Warner's *Rhapsody in Blue*," *Chicago Defender*, September 1, 1945, national edition, 21.

67. "Bye-Bye Boogie: Hazel Scott Leaves Night Clubs and Moves to Concert Stage," *Ebony*, November 1945, 35.

68. David Platt, "Hazel Scott's Role in Film Heavily Chopped in Memphis," *Daily Worker*, February 3, 1946, in Schomburg Clipping File.

69. "Bye-Bye Boogie: Hazel Scott Leaves Night Clubs and Moves to Concert Stage," *Ebony*, November 1945, 34.

70. Bogle, *Blacks in American Film and Television*, 464.

71. Ibid.

72. Bogle, *Brown Sugar*, 106.

73. Phil Carter, "Hazel Scott Is Queen Once More in Warner's *Rhapsody in Blue*," *Chicago Defender*, September 1, 1945, national edition, 14.

74. "Four Pictures $4,000 a Week," *Baltimore Afro-American*, December 4, 1943, 10.

75. Dyer, "White," 54.

76. Wiggins, "What Goes On In Paris," 19.

77. Hazel Scott, "The Truth About Me," *Ebony*, September 1960, 142–143.

78. "N.Y.'s Cafe Society Uptown Built for, Around Hazel Scott," *Baltimore Afro-American*, December 30, 1944, 5.

79. Earl Wilson, "Keeping Abreast of Hazel: Condensed from *New York Post*," *Negro Digest*, January 1944, 44.

80. Diawara, "Black Spectatorship," 214–219.

81. Ibid., 219.

82. "Four Pictures $4,000 a Week," *Baltimore Afro-American*, December 4, 1943, 10.

83. Earl Wilson, "Keeping Abreast of Hazel: Condensed from *New York Post*," *Negro Digest*, January 1944, 44.

84. Ibid., 43–44.

85. Elizabeth Hawes, "Elizabeth Hawes Applauds This Torch Singer's Clothes," Schomburg News Clipping File.

86. Earl Wilson, "Keeping Abreast of Hazel: Condensed from *New York Post*," *Negro Digest*, January 1944, 44.

87. Ibid., 44.

88. Ibid.

89. "Bye-Bye Boogie: Hazel Scott Leaves Night Clubs and Moves to Concert Stage," *Ebony*, November 1945, 32.

90. Bobo, *Black Women as Cultural Readers*, 46.

91. Adam Clayton Powell Jr., *Adam by Adam*, 225.

92. "Hazel Upholds Boogie-Woogie," *Baltimore Afro-American*, January 29, 1944, 8.

93. Ibid.

94. "Is It True What They Say?" *Baltimore Afro-American*, November 25, 1944, 15; "Rev. Powell, Wife Split: Hazel Scott Admits She's 'Other' Woman—Singer Says She Wants to Marry Pastor," *Chicago Defender*, November 25, 1944, city edition, 1.

95. "Opinion: The Adam Powell's Wash (Soiled) Linen," *Baltimore Afro-American*, December 2, 1944, 4; "Mrs. Powell Defiant: Refuses to Give Up Church Parsonage," *Baltimore Afro-American*, December 2, 1944, 1; and "Mrs. Powell's Separation Suit Settled: Divorce Action May Follow," *Baltimore Afro-American*, December 9, 1944, 1.

96. "Rumors of Powell Settlement Persist," *Baltimore Afro-American*, December 23, 1944, 3.

97. "Hazel Scott Ill," *Chicago Defender*, July 21, 1945, city edition, 20; "Cong. Powell and Hazel Scott to Wed August 1," *Chicago Defender*, July 28, 1945, city edition, 12.

98. Earl Conrad, "Congressman Powell, Hazel Scott, Marry," *Chicago Defender*, August 4, 1945, city edition, 1.

99. Ibid., 2

100. "Bye-Bye Boogie: Hazel Scott Leaves Night Clubs and Moves to Concert Stage," *Ebony*, November 1945, 32.

101. "The Powell's," *Ebony*, May 1946, 36.

102. "Bye-Bye Boogie: Hazel Scott Leaves Night Clubs and Moves to Concert Stage," *Ebony*, November 1945, 32.

103. Lamparski, *Whatever Became Of?* 156.

104. "Holtz Guilty of Bad Taste," *New York Amsterdam News*, October 11, 1941, 19.

105. "N.Y. Café Stars Swing Music for British Aid," *Baltimore Afro-American*, May 31, 1941, 13; "Hazel Scott Appears on Giant Bond Rally," *Pittsburgh Courier*, July 10, 1943, 20.

106. Tucker, *Swing Shift*, 240.

107. "Bye-Bye Boogie: Hazel Scott Leaves Night Clubs and Moves to Concert Stage," *Ebony*, November 1945, 32.

108. Venice Spraggs, "Rep. Powell Protests DAR Ban on Hazel Scott in D.C.," *Chicago Defender*, October 6, 1945, city edition, 1.

109. Venice Spraggs, "President Truman Raps DAR Ban on Hazel Scott," *Chicago Defender*, October 20, 1945, city edition, 1.

110. Ibid.

111. Ibid.

112. Ed Lee Webster, "Here Is the Inside Story of the DAR: Sidelights," *Baltimore Afro-American*, October 27, 1945, 5.

113. Ibid.

114. "Hazel Scott Agrees to Play for Lily-White D.C. Press Club," *Chicago Defender*, November 10, 1945, city edition, 15.

115. Venice Spraggs, "Hazel Scott Won't Play for Lily-White Press Club," *Chicago Defender*, November 17, 1945, city edition, 15.

116. "Hazel Scott to Tour Nation in Fight Against Jim Crow," *Chicago Defender*, December 1, 1945, city edition, 3.

117. Ibid.

118. Ibid.

119. Delores Calvin, "Here Are Some Things to Remember about Stars of the Year Just Ended," *Chicago Defender*, January 5, 1946, national edition, 12.

120. "Discrimination Challenged by Hazel Scott," *Los Angeles Sentinel,* February 28, 1946, 18.

121. "Hazel Scott Balks at University of Texas Jim Crow," *Baltimore Afro-American,* November 27, 1948, 6.

122. Michael Carter, "She Makes the Wounded Wiggle," *Negro Digest,* April 1945, 69.

123. "Hazel Scott Balks at University of Texas Jim Crow," *Baltimore Afro-American,* November 27, 1948, 6.

124. "Marian Anderson, Hazel Scott Split on Jim Crow Issue," *Chicago Defender,* March 19, 1949, national edition, 16.

125. "No Pot for Miss Scott in Pasco," *Chicago Defender,* February 19, 1949, city edition, 31.

126. "Hazel Scott Sues Café for $50,000," *Baltimore Afro-American,* February 26, 1949, 7.

127. "Hazel Scott," *Chicago Defender,* April 22, 1950, city edition, 1.

128. "Hazel Scott Nets $120,000 on Tour," *Pittsburgh Courier,* February 12, 1949, 20.

129. Adam Clayton Powell Jr., "My Life with Hazel Scott," *Ebony,* January 1949, 42–50.

130. Edith P. Smith, "Letters and Pictures: The Powells," *Ebony,* March 1949, 4.

131. Adam Clayton Powell Jr., "My Life with Hazel Scott," *Ebony,* January 1949, 48.

132. "Barred Again," *Pittsburgh Courier,* May 21, 1949, 4.

133. "Scott Concert Tickets Are Now on Sale," *Daily Tarheel,* March 4, 1950, 1.

134. "Scott Concert Is Scheduled Again Tonight," *Daily Tarheel,* March 23, 1950, 1.

135. "Only Students Are Given Scott Seats," *Daily Tarheel,* March 24, 1950, 1.

136. Ibid.

137. Wink Locklair, "Great Scott! They Said," *Daily Tarheel,* March 24, 1950, 2.

138. John L. Poindexter Jr., "Letters to the Ed: Scott Concert," *Daily Tarheel,* March 25, 1950, 2.

139. Roberta Brandes Gratz, "Closeup: After the Blue Jeans" [date not legible], Schomburg News Clipping File.

140. "Hazel Gets TV Show," *Chicago Defender,* February 11, 1950, city edition, 36.

141. Bogle, *Brown Sugar,* 106.

142. "Scott, Robeson, Others Declared Un-American," *Baltimore Afro-American,* September 27, 1947, 6.

143. American Business Consultants, *Red Channels: The Report of Communist Influence in Radio and Television,* 129–30.

144. Louis Lautier, "Hazel Scott Joins Parade before House Group's Mourners' Bench," *Baltimore Afro-American,* September 23, 1950, 3.

145. Testimony of Hazel Scott Powell, hearing before the House Un-American Activities Committee, House of Representatives, Eighty-First Congress Second Session, September 22, 1950, 3615.

146. Ibid., 3612.

147. Ibid., 3623.

148. Lamparski, *Whatever Became Of?* 157.

149. "Hazel Scott's Taxes Settled," *Washington Afro-American,* February 13, 1954, 18.

150. Louie Robinson, "Hazel Scott Comes Home to the 'Action,'" *Ebony,* March 1968, 102.

151. Ibid., 100–102.

152. Hazel Scott, "The Truth About Me," *Ebony*, September 1960, 139.

153. Lamparski, *Whatever Became Of?* 157.

154. Diawara, "Black Spectatorship," 213.

8. Ethel Waters

1. Lindsay Patterson, *Black Films and Film-makers,* 149–150.

2. "Ethel Waters," *Current Biography* 1951, 645; Fitch, "Waters, Ethel," 549–550; Vick, "Ethel Waters," 1225–1226; "Closeup of Ethel Waters Comedienne," *Baltimore Afro-American,* March 6, 1926, 6; Waters and Samuels, *His Eye Is On the Sparrow,* 48–49; and Leo J. Trese, "Book Review: *His Eye Is On the Sparrow,*" *The Commonweal,* April 6, 1951, 652. These sources provide conflicting reports on Waters's year of birth.

3. "Ethel Waters," *Current Biography* 1951, 645; Fitch, "Waters, Ethel," 549–550; Vick, "Ethel Waters," 1236–1238; Bogle, *Blacks in American Film and Television,* 479; Geraldyn Dismond, "Through the Lorgnette of Geraldyn Dismond: Ethel Waters," *Pittsburgh Courier,* September 17, 1927, section 2, 1; and Waters and Samuels, *His Eye Is On the Sparrow,* 141–142, 197. Waters was considered for a part in *Hallelujah* (1929), reported in "Ethel Waters Has Tries For Talkies," *Baltimore Afro-American,* September 1, 1928, 8.

4. Rothe, "Ethel Waters," 645; Internet Movie Database, www.imdb.com; Ethel Waters, "The Men in My Life," *Ebony,* January 1952, 26–34.

5. Rothe, "Ethel Waters," 646; Vick, "Ethel Waters," 1225–1226; and Harry Levette, "Sheds Tears For Waters: Saw Her As Oscar Winner," *Chicago Defender,* April 8, 1950, national edition, 34.

6. Bogle, *Bright Boulevards,* 309; Rothe, "Ethel Waters," 646; Vick, "Ethel Waters," 1225–1226; and Internet Movie Database, www.imdb.com.

7. Vick, "Ethel Waters," 1228–1229.

8. Waters and Samuels, *His Eye Is On the Sparrow,* 263.

9. "*The Member of the Wedding,*" *Ebony,* December 1952, 47.

10. Waters and Samuels, *His Eye Is On the Sparrow,* 274.

11. Linda Williams, *Playing the Race Card,* 203.

12. Young, *Fear of the Dark,* 44. John Henry (Brandon DeWilde) is another youngster whose sexuality is ambiguous. We are aware that he is male because of his name, but he also is feminized in appearance and engages in the "feminine" behavior of playing with dolls and parading in Berenice's high-heeled shoes.

13. Waters and Samuels, *His Eye Is On the Sparrow,* 201.

14. Ibid.

15. Gill, *No Surrender!* 68.

16. Hurston, *Dust Tracks on a Road,* 200. Thanks to Keith Mitchell for bringing my attention to Hurston's critique of Waters.

17. Ibid., 68.

18. Waters and Samuels, *His Eye Is On the Sparrow,* 260.

19. Harry Levette, "Ethel Can Recoup Loss by Giving up Car and Home to Secretary," *Baltimore Afro-American,* September 4, 1943, 8.

20. Feeling isolated after Berenice's departure (Berenice leaves for the afternoon after being picked up by T. T.), Frankie persuades John Henry (her alter ego) to spend the night with her. He eventually accedes to her wishes after playing games with her in much the

same manner that she had played games with him. As the two are united, the night air is filled with the sounds of the black trumpeter's jazz rhythms; when the music comes to an abrupt halt, John Henry assumes (based primarily on Brown's race) that the trumpeter has been apprehended by police. Jazz has historically been linked to sexuality; here the sexuality Frankie seeks is awakened after her exposure to the jazz rhythms.

21. Lindsay Patterson, *Black Films and Film-makers*, 149–150.

22. "South Demands Ethel Waters Quit the Radio," *Chicago Defender*, February 17, 1934, national edition, 5.

23. Ralph Matthews, "Show Stealing Cause of Broadway Feud," *Baltimore Afro-American*, February 1, 1936, 10.

24. Ibid.

25. "Ethel Waters' 'Special Midnight Show For Colored' Boycotted in Kansas City: Race Patrons Refuse to Pay 50 Cents To See Show Whites Saw For A Quarter," *Chicago Defender*, March 6, 1937, city edition, 13.

26. "DAR Hall Denied for Armstrong Concert: Ethel Waters and Hall Johnson Also Feel Sting," *Baltimore Afro-American*, August 16, 1947, 6.

27. Waters and Samuels, *His Eye Is On the Sparrow*, 98.

28. Ibid., 93.

29. Ibid.

30. Gill, *No Surrender!* 71.

31. Waters and Samuels, *His Eye Is On the Sparrow*, 274.

32. Ibid., 57.

33. Ibid., 58.

34. When her cat is lost, Frankie appropriates her newly assumed femininity: She contacts the police and instructs them to notify her, the newly renamed F. Jasmine Addams, when they find the cat.

35. Ethel Waters, "The Men in My Life," *Ebony*, January 1952, 24–38. Waters revealed in this article that African American boxer Jack Johnson was attracted to her, but according to her autobiography, their relationship was purely platonic.

36. Ibid., 35.

37. Ibid., 34.

38. Ibid.

39. Waters and Samuels, *His Eye Is On the Sparrow*, 220.

40. Ibid., 259.

41. "Ethel Waters Captivates City in *Africana*: Possesses World of Charm," *Pittsburgh Courier*, January 28, 1928, section 2, 2.

42. Philip Hartung, "The Screen: Belonging," *The Commonweal*, January 30, 1953, 424; "Cinema: The New Pictures," *Time*, December 29, 1952, 64.

43. Waters and Samuels, *His Eye Is On the Sparrow*, 13.

44. Ibid., 263.

45. Ethel Waters, "The Men in My Life," *Ebony*, January 1952, 28.

46. Waters and Samuels, *His Eye Is On the Sparrow*, 263.

47. Doane, *Femme Fatales*, 153. This quote is in reference to another film but is applicable to *The Member of the Wedding*.

48. Young, *Fear of the Dark*, 61.

49. Muller and Richardson, *Lacan and Language*, 340, 326–327.

50. Ibid., 344.

51. Judith Butler, *Gender Trouble*, 16–34.

52. Gilman, "Black Bodies, White Bodies," 228.

53. Doane, *Femme Fatales*, 210. Frantz Fanon also alludes to the association of blackness with sexuality: "If one wants to understand the racial situation psychoanalytically . . . considerable importance must be given to sexual phenomena. . . . [When one thinks] of the Negro, one thinks of sex" (Fanon, *Black Skin, White Masks*, 160).

54. Gilman, "Black Bodies, White Bodies," 257.

55. Fanon, *Black Skin, White Masks*, 129.

56. Silverman, *The Acoustic Mirror*, 80.

57. Gilman, "Black Bodies, White Bodies," 237.

58. Ibid., 253.

59. Ibid., 237.

60. Doane, *Femme Fatales*, 25.

61. Fanon, *Black Skin, White Masks*, 191.

62. Alfred Lewis Levitt, "Author Scores Film Roles Given Negroes: Cites Waters' Part As Racial Slight," *New York Amsterdam News*, April 4, 1953, 14.

63. Ibid.

64. Morrison, *Playing in the Dark*, 37.

65. Dyer, "White," 54.

66. Bogle, *Bright Boulevards*, 84.

67. "Ethel Waters Refuses Salary Cut; Quits Performance Cold," *Chicago Defender*, April 8, 1933, city edition, 9.

68. "Vendome Offers *On With the Show* with Ethel Waters," *Chicago Defender*, November 2, 1929, city edition, 13.

69. Ibid.

70. Ralph Matthews, "Looking at the Stars: An Open Letter to Miss Ethel Waters, Letter Dated: 5 April 1934," *Baltimore Afro-American*, April 14, 1934, 20.

71. Ibid.

72. Hilda See, "Ethel Waters in Picture at Vendome With Tate's Band," *Chicago Defender*, January 13, 1934, city edition, 8.

73. "Ethel Waters a Hit in Movie Short," *Washington Afro-American*, October 28, 1933, 21.

74. Sampson, *Blacks in Black and White*, 232.

75. "Ethel Waters Coming to the Harlem," *Baltimore Afro-American*, March 24, 1934, 9.

76. "Ethel Waters in Picture *Gift of Gab* at the Met," *Chicago Defender*, December 22, 1934, city edition, 6.

77. "Ethel (Stormy Weather) Waters Storms Hollywood," *Baltimore Afro-American*, October 10, 1942, 10.

78. Philip Carter, "Role of Domestic Servant in Films Raised to New Dignity," *Baltimore Afro-American*, November 14, 1942, 10.

79. Cripps, *Making Movies Black*, 55.

80. Cripps, *Slow Fade to Black*, 384.

81. Cripps, *Making Movies Black*, 75.

82. Waters and Samuels, *His Eye Is On the Sparrow*, 257.

83. Ibid.

84. Snead, "Spectatorship and Capture in *King Kong*," 28–29.

85. Robert Pollak, "More Orchids for Star of *Cabin in the Sky*," *Baltimore Afro-American*, May 17, 1941, 14.

86. Waters and Samuels, *His Eye Is On the Sparrow*, 258.

87. Ibid., 261.

88. Cripps, *Slow Fade to Black*, 257.

89. Knight, *Disintegrating the Musical*, 151.

90. Massood, *Black City Cinema*, 33.

91. Ibid., 37.

92. Wallace, *Dark Designs & Visual Culture*, 481.

93. Knight, *Disintegrating the Musical*, 154.

94. Ibid., 154–155.

95. Al Monroe, "Speaking of Stage's Best Just Name Miss Ethel Waters—Period," *Chicago Defender*, April 14, 1945, national edition, 17.

96. Hilda See, "Critic Finds Ethel Waters' Style A 'Natural' Employed by Many Stars," *Chicago Defender*, June 14, 1947, national edition, 18.

97. Waters and Samuels, *His Eye Is On the Sparrow*, 272.

98. According to Cindy Patton, "The film did not recognize the racism in Tom's willingness to not see Pinky as Black; instead, it was Pinky's assertion of a racial identity she could not see that breached their relationship. Thus, the internal discourse about prejudice operated as a relay between Pinky's attempt to produce herself as race and Tom's refusal to read her" (Cindy Patton, "White Racism/Black Signs," 75).

99. Courtney, *Hollywood Fantasies of Miscegenation*, 171.

100. Kydd, "The Ineffaceable Curse of Cain," 113.

101. Regester, "Miss Em's Voyeuristic Gaze of *Pinky*," 70. See this essay for further discussion of the argument that the film is really about white desire for blackness and that Miss Em is desirous of blackness and vicariously experiences blackness through her association with the mulatto character Pinky, as the two become mirror images of each other.

102. Ibid., 76.

103. Ibid., 70. For alternative readings of *Pinky*, see Petty, "Passing for Horror: Race, Fear, and Elia Kazan's *Pinky*," *Genders* Issue 40 (2004), www.genders.org/recent.html.

104. Harry Levette, "Sheds Tears For Waters: Saw Her As Oscar Winner," *Chicago Defender*, April 8, 1950, national edition, 34.

105. "Cinema: The New Pictures," *Time*, October 10, 1949, 98.

106. Robert Hatch, "Film Review: *Pinky*," *The New Republic*, October 3, 1949, 23.

107. Walter White, "Regrets He Has No Words of Praise for *Pinky*," *Chicago Defender*, October 29, 1949, national edition, 7.

108. "*Pinky*: Story on Girl Who Passes Will Be Most Debated Film of Year," *Ebony*, September 1949, 23.

109. Regester, "Miss Em's Voyeuristic Gaze of *Pinky*," 82.

110. "*The Heart Is a Rebel*," Internet Movie Database, www.imdb.com.

111. Gill, *No Surrender!* 71.

9. Dorothy Dandridge

1. Rippy, "Commodity, Tragedy, Desire," 178.

2. Bogle, *Dorothy Dandridge*, 2–42; Freydberg, "Dandridge, Dorothy," 137.

374 · NOTES TO PAGES 284-292

3. "DC Likes Them: The Dandridge Sisters," *Baltimore Afro-American*, April 15, 1939, 10.

4. Bogle, *Dorothy Dandridge*, 34–46; "We Passed Twelve Subs Coming Back From Europe," *Baltimore Afro-American*, September 23, 1939, 1.

5. Donald Bogle, *Dorothy Dandridge*, 77.

6. Ibid., 585–587.

7. Bogle, *Dorothy Dandridge*, 99, 104, 112; Bogle, *Bright Boulevards*, 296.

8. Freydberg, "Dandridge, Dorothy," 587–588.

9. Harry Levette, "Dot Lamour Has Rival in Saronged Dot Dandridge," *Baltimore Afro-American*, December 2, 1950, 8.

10. "Dorothy Dandridge Found Dead at Her Apartment in Hollywood," *The New York Times*, September 9, 1965, 41; "Dandridge Estate $2," *The New York Times*, November 7, 1965, 59; "Dorothy Dandridge Died of Pill Dosage, Coroner Now Says," *The New York Times*, November 18, 1965, 58; Freydberg, "Dandridge, Dorothy," 138; and Bogle, *Dorothy Dandridge*, 589, 176, 177.

11. Cynthia Gorney, "The Fragile Flame of Dorothy Dandridge: Remembering the Shattered Life of a Beautiful 1950s Movie Star," *Washington Post*, February 9, 1988, E1.

12. Rippy, "Commodity, Tragedy, Desire," 183.

13. Mulvey, "Visual Pleasure and Narrative Cinema," 27. According to Mulvey, the female protagonist, when paired with a male costar with whom she is romantically involved, is rendered as a signifier of male desire not only to her male costar but to the audience as well. It is Mulvey's contention that as the female protagonist becomes the property of her male costar, she also becomes the possession of the audience because of the audience's identification with the male star.

14. Muller and Richardson, *Lacan and Language*, 29–34.

15. Isadora Smith, "Democratic Movies Can Make Money At Nation's Box Office," *Pittsburgh Courier*, February 13, 1943, 20. This source reports on Dandridge's maid role, noting that "In *Lucky Jordan*, starring Alan Ladd, Paramount got an idea for what should be done by casting Dorothy Dandridge, as a maid. The picture presented her with dignity. She looked beautiful, spoke well and flitted across the screen proudly." An additional report reveals, "Miss Dandridge, who plays the role of the Negro maid, Thalia, a confidante of Miss Carroll in *Bahama Passage*, is not yet 20 years of age, but already she has proved her worth and apparently has a dazzling future. . . . She was selected by Producer-Director Edward H. Griffith for *Bahama Passage* after several of the actresses had been tried out, and won because of her beauty and talent" ("Dorothy Dandridge Stars in Paramount Picture and Ellington-Anderson Stage Show 'Jump for Joy,'" *Pittsburgh Courier*, August 9, 1941, 20).

16. Bogle, *Dorothy Dandridge*, 185.

17. Ibid., 104, 176, 177. Bogle reports that Dandridge and Harold Nicholas were married September 6, 1942, and were divorced September 29, 1950—a divorce that became official in October 1951.

18. Dandridge and Conrad, *Everything and Nothing*, 62–66.

19. Ibid., 126.

20. "*See How They Run*: Hollywood's First Dramatic Movie With All-Negro Cast Proves One Of Its Finest," *Ebony*, April 1953, 45.

21. "*Bright Road* Shows Negro in True Light," *New York Amsterdam News*, March 28, 1953, 27.

22. Baldwin, "On the Horizon," 77. See also Herman Gray's essay on constructions of black masculinity and visual culture ("Black Masculinity and Visual Culture," 401–405) and Guerrero, "The Black Man On Our Screens," 395–400.

23. Crowther, "Screen in Review: *Carmen Jones*," *New York Times*, October 29, 1954, 27. In *The New York Times Film Reviews, 1949–1958*, vol. 4, 2821.

24. Mulvey, "Visual Pleasure and Narrative Cinema," 27.

25. Louie Robinson, "Dorothy Dandridge: Hollywood's Tragic Enigma," *Ebony*, March 1966, 75.

26. Dandridge and Conrad, *Everything and Nothing*, 90.

27. Ibid., 93.

28. Cynthia Gorney, "The Fragile Flame of Dorothy Dandridge: Remembering the Shattered Life of a Beautiful 1950s Movie Star," *Washington Post*, February 9, 1988, E1. See also Harris, "The Building of Popular Images." Harris argues that Kelly was constructed as refined, genteel, elegant, reserved, and poised while Marilyn Monroe was constructed as a signifier of male desire, the ideal, attainable playmate.

29. Dandridge and Conrad, *Everything and Nothing*, 94.

30. Muller and Richardson, *Lacan and Language*, 281.

31. Rippy, "Commodity, Tragedy, Desire," 194.

32. Courtney, *Hollywood Fantasies of Miscegenation*, 212.

33. Ibid., 213.

34. Edward Scobie, "Finds *Island in the Sun* Not Dimmed by Bias: Two Interracial 'Romances' Help Make Pix Unique," *Chicago Defender*, February 9, 1957, national edition, 8.

35. Ibid.

36. Reid, *Redefining Black Film*, 53.

37. Courtney, *Hollywood Fantasies of Miscegenation*, 203.

38. "Nation Awaits Film *Island in the Sun*: Harry Belafonte and Dandridge Film Is Reason," *Chicago Defender*, May 4, 1957, national edition, 8. In his uncomplimentary review of the film, Philip Roth wrote, "As portrayed by Dorothy Dandridge, the clerk is dark and hip-swinging, but amazingly devoid of any of the characteristics we normally associate with human behavior" (Philip Roth, "Movies: 'I Am Black But O My Soul . . . ,'" *The New Republic*, July 29, 1957, 21). Jamaica's governor, Sir Hugh Foot, was similarly offended by the film: "In any country where there are people of different colours, the colour question is important. . . . But the striking fact about the West Indies is not that West Indians are obsessed by colour; the most striking fact of all is that they are not" (in Wilbert E. Hamming, "Jamaica's Governor Explains Why Pix *Island in the Sun* Was Banned," *Chicago Defender*, August 24, 1957, national edition, 19). The film was also banned from exhibition in Memphis (Hilda See, "Finds Dixie States 'Incorporating' *Island in the Sun, Edge of the City*: However, Tennessee Censors Rule Both Pics Out of Bounds." *Chicago Defender*, July 20, 1957, national edition, 19). According to the *New York Amsterdam News*, "In South Carolina a legislator has proposed a measure to fine any operator showing *Island in the Sun* because it includes an interracial 'romance' between Belafonte and Miss Fontaine. In Greensboro, N.C., theatre officials haven't decided whether or not they'll show the picture and the decision may rest with North Carolina theatres, Inc., in Charlotte" (Jesse H. Walker, "Theatricals," *New York Amsterdam News*, June 1, 1957, 16).

39. "Eartha Kitt, Dandridge Almost Crossed Line," *Chicago Defender*, April 11, 1959, national edition, 19.

40. Doane, *Femmes Fatales*, 209-248.

41. Bogle, *Blacks in American Films and Television*, 121.

42. Ibid.

43. Rippy, "Commodity, Tragedy, Desire," 152-157.

44. Dandridge and Conrad, *Everything and Nothing*, 94-114; Spada, *Peter Lawford*, 138.

45. Spada, *Peter Lawford*, 138.

46. Dandridge and Conrad, *Everything and Nothing*, 118.

47. Ibid., 129-131. Gerald Mayer responded to the account of their relationship given in Hilton Als's review of Bogle's Dandridge biography. He contends that "I never discussed marriage, for a number of reasons, among them that my career was just starting and I couldn't think ahead to marriage, and that I was rooted in Hollywood, while she spent her life touring. It was for these reasons that our relationship lasted only slightly more than a year" (Gerald Mayer, "The Mail: Dorothy Dandridge," *The New Yorker*, September 22, 1997, 26).

48. Dandridge and Conrad, *Everything and Nothing*, 172.

49. Ibid., 14-16.

50. Ibid., 183.

51. Ibid., 192.

52. Bogle, *Dorothy Dandridge*, 377-378.

53. Dandridge and Conrad, *Everything and Nothing*, 158-159.

54. Fanon, *Black Skin, White Masks*, 145.

55. Dandridge and Conrad, *Everything and Nothing*, 152-154.

56. Ibid., 159.

57. Bogle, *Dorothy Dandridge*, 143.

58. Ibid., 259.

59. Dandridge and Conrad, *Everything and Nothing*, 115.

60. Ibid., 132.

61. Dyer, "White," 45.

62. It is noteworthy that an advertisement for this film reads, "Dorothy Dandridge the only woman on board with a love-starved crew!" *Chicago Defender*, October 25, 1958, city edition, 14.

63. "Interracial Romances May Void Several 'Oscar' Hopes," *Chicago Defender*, January 10, 1959, national edition, 18.

64. Bogle, *Dorothy Dandridge*, 404.

65. Dandridge and Conrad, *Everything and Nothing*, 196.

66. Rippy, "Commodity, Tragedy, Desire," 201.

67. "Eartha Kitt, Dandridge, Almost Crossed Line," *Chicago Defender*, April 11, 1959, national edition, 19.

68. Ibid.

69. "U.S. May See Uncut, Original Version of Dandridge's *Deck*," *Chicago Defender*, July 25, 1959, national edition, 18.

70. Bogle, *Blacks in American Films and Television*, 213. One report reveals that the film "was banned by the French government in Algiers on the grounds 'it's exciting to rebellion'" ("Dandridge Film Banned by French in Algiers," Schomburg Clipping File, Schomburg Center for Research in Black Culture). The film was also believed to "incite to ... riot" ("Dorothy Dandridge To Incite Film Riot," Schomburg Clipping File).

71. Louie Robinson, "Dorothy Dandridge: Hollywood's Tragic Enigma," *Ebony*, March 1966, 75.

72. hooks, "The Oppositional Gaze," 289.

73. Bogle, *Blacks in American Films and Television*, 144. Bogle reports that the film was released in Europe in 1960 but in the United States in 1962. Bogle, *Dorothy Dandridge*, 444.

74. Dandridge and Conrad, *Everything and Nothing*, 202–203.

75. hooks, *Reel to Real*, 13.

76. "Name Bandsman As Dandridge's Man in the Woods," *Washington Afro-American*, August 24, 1957, 1.

77. Dandridge was not alone in being exploited by such cinema tabloids. When she went to court, she was accompanied by white actress Maureen O'Hara, who was also challenging a story that appeared in *Confidential* magazine that charged that she had engaged in "torrid-lovemaking in Grauman's Chinese Theater" (see "'Preposterous,' says Dottie," *Washington Afro-American*, September 7, 1957, 1). Even black male actors Billy Daniels and Herb Jeffries were the targets of similar scandalous reports (see "Name Bandsman As Dandridge's Man in the Woods," *Washington Afro-American*, August 24, 1957, 1).

78. Louie Robinson, "The Private World of Dorothy Dandridge," *Ebony*, June 1962, 120. The case is disclosed in more detail in Florabel Muir and Theo Wilson, "Birds and Bees Didn't Tell on Dot—He Did," *Daily News*, August 22, 1957. Schomburg Clipping File.

79. Ralph Matthews, "Thinking Out Loud," *Washington Afro-American*, September 17, 1957, 4.

80. Bogle, *Blacks in American Films and Television*, 144.

81. Ibid., 213.

82. Dandridge and Conrad, *Everything and Nothing*, 204.

83. Ibid., 196.

84. It is important to note that Poitier was reluctant to accept this role because of its personification of a black stereotype and the resulting controversy it provoked during a critical moment of the civil rights movement. See Bogle, *Dorothy Dandridge*, 397–398.

85. Donald Bogle notes that Davis in playing this role described the character as "slick and devilishly sexy but [doing so] with the greatest of ease; [really] came across like a shrimp trying to act like a big fish" (*Toms, Coons, Mulattoes, Mammies, & Bucks*, 214).

86. Reid, *Redefining Black Film*, 53.

87. Jones, "The Construction of Black Sexuality," 251.

88. Preminger, *Preminger: An Autobiography*, 138.

89. Poitier, *Sidney Poitier: This Life*, 221. Donald Bogle's biography of Dandridge relates in extensive detail her experiences during the production. It is noteworthy that the film was castigated by some members of the African American community. For example, Lorraine Hansberry, the author of *A Raisin in the Sun*, denounced the film: "We object to roles which consistently depict our women as wicked and our men as weak. We do not want to see six-foot Sidney Poitier on his knees crying for a slit-skirted wench who did him wrong. We do not want the wench to be beautiful Dorothy Dandridge who sniffs 'happy dust' and drinks liquor from a bottle at the rim of an alley crap game" (Era Bell Thompson, "Why Negroes Don't Like *Porgy and Bess*," *Ebony*, October 1959, 54). Another reviewer harshly criticized Dandridge's performance: "But she not only can't act. She cannot conceive a woman's role. There were only two scenes in the entire picture which Miss Dandridge can claim as her

own" (Almena Lomax, "*Porgy and Bess* Called 'Unforgettable Document,' Stars 'Saga of Negro Survival,'" Schomburg Clipping File).

90. Poitier, *Sidney Poitier: This Life,* 222.

91. Chester Washington, "*Porgy-Bess* Starts Rolling As Verbal Feud Smolders," *Pittsburgh Courier,* August 23, 1958, 22; Lawrence LaMar, "Stars Look Other Way As Whipper 'Lashes' New Director for *Porgy,*" *Chicago Defender,* August 23, 1958, city edition, 16; Chester Washington, "Sammy Davis, Pearl Bailey, Defend New *Porgy* Director," *Pittsburgh Courier,* August 16, 1958, 22.

92. Dyer, *Heavenly Bodies,* 42.

93. Ibid.

94. Bogle, *Dorothy Dandridge,* 123.

95. Rippy, "Commodity, Tragedy, Desire," 191.

96. Bogle, *Blacks in American Films and Television,* 213.

97. Louie Robinson, "The Private World of Dorothy Dandridge," *Ebony,* June 1962, 120.

98. Bhabha, "The Other Question," 324.

99. Dandridge and Conrad, *Everything and Nothing,* 218.

100. Cynthia Gorney, "The Fragile Flame of Dorothy Dandridge: Remembering the Shattered Life of a Beautiful 1950s Movie Star," *Washington Post,* February 9, 1988, E1.

101. Dandridge and Conrad, *Everything and Nothing,* 89.

102. Bogle, *Dorothy Dandridge,* 122–123.

103. Cynthia Gorney, "The Fragile Flame of Dorothy Dandridge: Remembering the Shattered Life of a Beautiful 1950s Movie Star," *Washington Post,* February 9, 1988, E1.

104. Dandridge and Conrad, *Everything and Nothing,* 164–165.

105. Bogle, *Dorothy Dandridge,* 123.

106. Dandridge and Conrad, *Everything and Nothing,* 219.

107. "*See How They Run,*" *Ebony,* April 1953, 45.

108. Snead, *White Screens, Black Images,* 5–6.

109. Luix Virgil Overbea, "Dandridge Seeking More Negro Fans," *New York Amsterdam News,* October 24, 1953, 28.

110. Dandridge and Conrad, *Everything and Nothing,* 107.

111. Ibid., 196.

112. Cynthia Gorney, "The Fragile Flame of Dorothy Dandridge: Remembering the Shattered Life of a Beautiful 1950s Movie Star," *Washington Post,* February 9, 1988, E2.

113. Rippy, "Commodity, Tragedy, Desire," 204.

114. Bogle, *Dorothy Dandridge,* 143.

115. Dandridge and Conrad, *Everything and Nothing,* 226.

116. "44-Word Handwritten Will of Miss Dandridge Filed," *The New York Times,* October 12, 1965, 58.

117. "A Fracture Fatal to Miss Dandridge," *The New York Times,* September 11, 1965, 27; Louie Robinson, "Dorothy Dandridge: Hollywood's Tragic Enigma," *Ebony,* March 1966, 80.

118. Louie Robinson, "Dorothy Dandridge: Hollywood's Tragic Enigma," *Ebony,* March 1966, 72.

119. Cynthia Gorney, "The Fragile Flame of Dorothy Dandridge: Remembering the Shattered Life of a Beautiful 1950s Movie Star," *Washington Post,* February 9, 1988, E3. See also Bogle, *Dorothy Dandridge,* 553.

Conclusion

1. Burks, "Imitations of Invisibility," 25. See Jane Gaines's discussion of the absence of black women in feminist theory in "White Privilege and Looking Relations," 12–27.

2. Knight, "Star Dances" 406.

3. Dyer, *Heavenly Bodies,* 2–3.

4. Stewart, *Migrating to the Movies,* 96.

BIBLIOGRAPHY

Abramson, Dan. "Lena Horne." *Films in Review* 37, no. 3 (March 1986): 147.

Allmendinger, Blake. "The Plow and the Pen: The Pioneering Adventures of Oscar Micheaux." *American Literature* 75 (September 2003): 545–569.

American Business Consultants. *Red Channels: The Report of Communist Influence in Radio and Television.* New York: Publishers of *Counterattack—The Newsletter of Facts to Combat Communism,* June 1950. 129–130.

Arstein, Helen, and Carlton Moss. *In Person: Lena Horne.* New York: Greenberg, 1950.

Baker, Houston A., Jr. "When Lindbergh Sleeps with Bessie Smith: The Writing of Place in Toni Morrison's *Sula*." In *The Difference Within,* ed. Elizabeth Meese and Alice Parker, 85–113. Philadelphia, Pa.: John Benjamins, 1989.

Baldwin, James. "On the Horizon: Life Straight in De Eye." *Commentary* 19 (January 1955): 77.

Beasley, Delilah L. *The Negro Trailblazers of California.* Los Angeles: R and E Research Associates, 1968 [1919].

Berlant, Lauren. "National Brands, National Body: *Imitation of Life*." In *The Female Complaint: The Unfinished Business of Sentimentality in American Culture.* Durham, N.C.: Duke University Press, 2008.

Bernardi, Daniel, ed. *Classic Hollywood, Classic Whiteness.* Minneapolis: University of Minnesota Press, 2001.

Bhaba, Homi K. "The Other Question: The Stereotype and Colonial Discourse." In *The Sexual Subject: A Screen Reader in Sexuality,* 312–329. London: Routledge, 1992. Originally published in *Screen* 24, no. 6 (Winter 1983): 18–36.

Bobo, Jacqueline. *Black Women as Cultural Readers.* New York: Columbia University Press, 1995.

——. *Black Women Film and Video Artists.* London: Routledge, 1998.

Bogle, Donald. "Black Beginnings: From *Uncle Tom's Cabin* to *The Birth of a Nation*." In *Representing Blackness: Issues in Film and Video,* ed. Valerie Smith, 13–24. New Brunswick, N.J.: Rutgers University Press, 1997.

——. *Blacks in American Films and Television: An Illustrated Encyclopedia.* New York: Fireside/Simon & Schuster, 1988.

———. *Bright Boulevards, Bold Dreams: The Story of Black Hollywood.* New York: Ballantine Books, 2005.

———. *Brown Sugar: Eighty Years of America's Black Female Superstars.* New York: Harmony Book, 1980.

———. *Dorothy Dandridge: A Biography.* New York: Amistad, 1997.

———. *Toms, Coons, Mulattoes, Mammies, & Bucks: An Interpretive History of Blacks in American Films.* 4th ed. New York: Continuum, 2001 [1973].

Bowser, Pearl, Jane Gaines, and Charles Musser, eds. *Oscar Micheaux and His Circle: African American Filmmaking and Race Cinema in the Silent Era.* Bloomington: Indiana University Press, 2001.

Bowser, Pearl, and Louise Spence. *Writing Himself into History: Oscar Micheaux, His Silent Films, and His Audiences.* New Brunswick, N.J.: Rutgers University Press, 2000.

Brown, Jayna. *Babylon Girls: Black Women Performers and the Shaping of the Modern.* Durham, N.C.: Duke University Press, 2008.

Buckley, Gail Lumet. *The Hornes: An American Family.* New York: Alfred Knopf, 1986.

Burks, Ruth Elizabeth. "Imitations of Invisibility: Black Women and Contemporary Hollywood Cinema." In *Mediated Messages and African-American Culture: Contemporary Issues,* ed. Venise T. Berry and Carmen L. Manning-Miller, 24–39. Thousand Oaks, Calif.: Sage Publications, 1996.

Butler, Jeremy. "*Imitation of Life* (1934 –1959): Style and the Domestic Melodrama." In *Imitation of Life,* ed. Lucy Fischer, 289–301. New Brunswick, N.J.: Rutgers University Press, 1991.

Butler, Judith. *Gender Trouble: Feminism and the Subversion of Identity.* New York: Routledge, 1990.

Carby, Hazel. *Reconstructing Womanhood: The Emergence of the Afro-American Novelist.* New York: Oxford University Press, 1987.

Chadwell, Faye A. "Beavers, Louise." In *African American Women: A Biographical Dictionary,* ed. Dorothy C. Salem, 43–45. New York: Garland, 1993.

Chilton, Karen. *Hazel Scott: The Pioneering Journey of a Jazz Pianist from Café Society to Hollywood to HUAC.* Ann Arbor: University of Michigan Press, 2008.

Courtney, Susan. *Hollywood Fantasies of Miscegenation: Spectacular Narratives of Gender and Race, 1903–1967.* Princeton, N.J.: Princeton University Press, 2005.

———. "Picturizing Race: Hollywood's Censorship of Miscegenation and Production of Racial Visibility through *Imitation of Life.*" *Genders* 27 (1998): 2. http://www.genders .org/g27.

Cripps, Thomas. *Making Movies Black: The Hollywood Message Movie from World War II to the Civil Rights Era.* New York: Oxford University Press, 1993.

———. "The Reaction of the Negro to the Motion Picture *Birth of a Nation.*" *The Historian* 25 (May 1963): 344–362. In *Focus on The Birth of a Nation,* ed. Fred Silva, 114–124. Englewood Cliffs, N.J.: Prentice-Hall, 1971.

———. *Slow Fade to Black: The Negro in American Film, 1900–1942.* New York: Oxford University Press, 1993 [1977].

Crowther, Bosley. Review of *Maryland. New York Times,* July 13, 1940. In *The New York Times Film Reviews, 1939–1948,* vol. 3, 1729–1721. New York: The New York Times and New Arno Press, 1970.

———. "Screen in Review: *Carmen Jones*." *New York Times*, October 29, 1954, 27. In *The New York Times Film Reviews, 1949–1958,* vol. 4, 2821. New York: The New York Times and Arno Press, 1970.

Dandridge, Dorothy, and Earl Conrad. *Everything and Nothing: The Dorothy Dandridge Tragedy.* New York: Harper Collins, 2000 [1970].

Diawara, Manthia, ed. *Black American Cinema.* New York: Routledge, 1993.

———. "Black Spectatorship: Problems of Identification and Resistance." In *Black American Cinema,* ed. Manthia Diawara, 211–220. New York: Routledge, 1993.

Doane, Mary Ann. *Femmes Fatales: Feminism, Film Theory, Psychoanalysis.* New York: Routledge, 1991.

———. "The 'Woman's Film': Possession and Address." In *Home Is Where the Heart Is: Studies in Melodrama and the Woman's Film,* ed. Christine Gledhill, 283–298. London: British Film Institute, 1987.

Dreher, Kwakiutl L. *Dancing on the White Page: Black Women Entertainers Writing Autobiography.* Albany: State University of New York Press, 2008.

Duberman, Martin. *Paul Robeson: A Biography.* New York: Ballantine Books, 1989.

Dunn, Stephane. *"Baad Bitches" & Sassy Supermamas: Black Power Action Films.* Champaign: University of Illinois Press, 2008.

Durgnat, Raymond, and Scott Simmon. *King Vidor, American.* Berkeley/Los Angeles: University of California Press, 1988.

Dwyer, Sandy. "Celebrating Black Gay and Lesbian History: Hattie McDaniel." *Vanguard,* February 8, 1991, 7. In the Academy of Motion Pictures Arts and Sciences, Margaret Herrick Library, Beverly Hills, California.

Dyer, Richard. *Heavenly Bodies: Film Stars and Society.* New York: Routledge, 2004 [1986].

———. "A Star Is Born and the Construction of Authenticity." In *Stardom: Industry of Desire,* ed. Christine Gledhill, 132–140. London: Routledge, 1991.

———. "White." *Screen,* Autumn 1988, 44–64.

Ellison, Ralph. *Invisible Man.* New York: Random House, 2002 [1952].

Etheridge, Sharynn. "Fredi Washington." In *Notable Black American Women,* ed. Jessie Carney Smith, 1212–1214. Detroit, Mich.: Gale Research, 1992.

Everett, Anna. "'I Want the Same Things Other People Enjoy': The Black Press and the Classic Hollywood Studio System, 1930–40." *Spectator,* Fall/Winter 1996, 40–53.

———. *Returning the Gaze: A Genealogy of Black Film Criticism, 1909–1949.* Durham, N.C.: Duke University Press, 2001.

Fanon, Frantz. *Black Skin, White Masks.* London: Pluto Press, 1986 [1952].

Fischer, Lucy, ed. *Imitation of Life.* New Brunswick, N.J.: Rutgers University Press, 1991.

Fitch, Nancy Elizabeth. "Waters, Ethel." In *African American Women: A Biographical Dictionary,* ed. Dorothy C. Salem, 549–550. New York: Garland Publishing, 1993.

Flitterman-Lewis, Sandy. "Imitation(s) of Life: The Black Woman's Double Determination as Troubling 'Other.'" In *Imitation of Life,* ed. Lucy Fischer, 325–335. New Brunswick, N.J.: Rutgers University Press, 1991.

Fredi Washington Papers on Microfilm, 1925–1979. Cited as FWP.

Freydberg, Elizabeth Hadley. "Dandridge, Dorothy." In *African American Women: A Biographical Dictionary,* ed. Dorothy C. Salem, 137–140. New York: Garland, 1993.

Gaines, Jane. *Fire and Desire: Mixed-Race Movies in the Silent Era.* Chicago: University of Chicago Press, 2001.

———. "White Privilege and Looking Relations—Race and Gender in Feminist Film Theory." *Screen,* Autumn 1988, 12–27.

Gates, Henry Louis, Jr., ed. *Race, Writing, and Difference.* Chicago: University of Chicago Press, 1986.

George P. Johnson Film Collection on Microfilm. Department of Special Collections, University of California, Los Angeles.

Gibson-Hudson, Gloria J. "Sul-Te-Wan, Madame." In *African American Women: A Biographical Dictionary,* ed. Dorothy C. Salem, 485–487. New York: Garland, 1993.

Gill, Glenda E. *No Surrender! No Retreat! African American Pioneer Performers of Twentieth Century American Theater.* New York: St. Martin's Press, 2000.

Gillespie, Michele K., and Randal L. Hall, eds. *Thomas Dixon Jr. and The Birth of Modern America.* Baton Rouge, La.: Louisiana State University Press, 2006.

Gilliam, Dorothy. *Paul Robeson: All-American.* Washington, D.C.: New Republic Book, 1976.

Gilman, Sander L. "Black Bodies, White Bodies: Toward an Iconography of Female Sexuality in Late Nineteenth-Century Art, Medicine, and Literature." In *Race, Writing, and Difference,* ed. Henry Louis Gates, Jr., 223–261. Chicago: University of Chicago Press, 1986.

Gledhill, Christine, ed. *Home Is Where the Heart Is: Studies in Melodrama and the Woman's Film.* London: British Film Institute, 1987.

Gray, Herman. "Black Masculinity and Visual Culture." *Callaloo* 18, no. 2 (1995): 401–405.

Guerrero, Ed. "The Black Man On Our Screens and The Empty Space In Representation." *Callaloo* 18, no. 2 (1995): 395–400.

———. *Framing Blackness: The African American Image in Film.* Philadelphia, Pa.: Temple University Press, 1993.

Hale, Grace Elizabeth. *Making Whiteness: The Culture of Segregation in the South, 1890–1940.* New York: Pantheon Books, 1998.

Hall, Mordaunt. Review of *Heaven on Earth. New York Times,* December 19, 1931. In *The New York Times Film Reviews, 1913–1931,* vol. 1, 782. New York: The New York Times and Arno Press, 1970.

———. "The Screen: The Shy Bachelor—*The Narrow Street.*" *New York Times,* January 5, 1925. In *The New York Times Film Reviews, 1913–1931,* vol. 1, 229. New York: The New York Times and Arno Press, 1970.

Hall, Stuart. "The Whites of Their Eyes: Racist Ideologies and the Media." In *Silver Linings: Some Strategies for the Eighties,* ed. George Bridges and Rosalind Brunt, 28–52. London: Lawrence & Wishart, 1981.

Hamilton, Charles V. *Adam Clayton Powell Jr.: The Political Biography of an American Dilemma.* New York: Atheneum, 1991.

Hanson, Patricia King, and Amy Dunkleberger, eds. *American Film Institute Catalog of Motion Pictures Produced in the United States: Feature Films, 1941–1950.* Berkeley and Los Angeles: University of California Press, 1999.

Hanson, Patricia King, and Alan Gevinson, eds. *The American Film Institute Catalog: Feature Films, 1931–1940.* Berkeley: University of California Press, 1993.

Hardy, Sarah Madsen, and Kelly Thomas. "Listening to Race: Voice, Mixing, and Techno-logical 'Miscegenation' in Early Sound Film." In *Classic Hollywood, Classic Whiteness*, ed. Daniel Bernardi, 415–441. Minneapolis: University of Minnesota Press, 2001.

Harris, Thomas. "The Building of Popular Images: Grace Kelly and Marilyn Monroe." In *Stardom: Industry of Desire*, ed. Christine Gledhill, 40–44. New York: Routledge, 1991.

Haskell, Molly. *From Reverence to Rape: The Treatment of Women in the Movies*, 2nd ed. Chicago: University of Chicago Press, 1987 [1974].

"Heaven on Earth." *Variety*, December 22, 1931. In *Variety Film Reviews, 1930–1933*, vol. 4. New York: Garland Publishing, 1983.

hooks, bell. *Black Looks: Race and Representation*. Boston, Mass.: South End Press, 1992.

———. "Choosing the Margin as a Space of Radical Openness." *Framework* 36 (1989): 15–23.

———. "The Oppositional Gaze: Black Female Spectators." In *Black American Cinema*, ed. Manthia Diawara, 288–302. New York: Routledge, 1993.

———. *Reel to Real: Race, Sex, and Class at the Movies*. New York: Routledge, 1996.

Horne, Lena, and Richard Schickel. "Lena." In *Black Films and Film-makers: A Comprehensive Anthology from Stereotype to Superhero*, ed. Lindsay Patterson, 139–150. New York: Dodd, Mead, and Co., 1975.

Howard, Jessica. "*Hallelujah:* Transformation in Film." *African American Review* 30, no. 3 (1996): 441–451.

Hurst, Fannie. "Zora Hurston: A Personality Sketch." In *Imitation of Life*, ed. Lucy Fischer, 173–176. New Brunswick, N.J.: Rutgers University Press, 1991.

Hurston, Zora Neale. *Dust Tracks on a Road*. New York: Harper Perennial, 1996 [1942].

"In Old Chicago." *Variety*, January 5, 1938. In *Variety Film Reviews, 1938–1942*, vol. 6. New York: Garland Publishing, 1983.

Jackson, Carlton. *Hattie: The Life of Hattie McDaniel*. Lanham, Md.: Madison Books, 1990.

Johnson, Frank W. "McKinney, Nina Mae." In *African American Women: A Biographical Dictionary*, ed. Dorothy C. Salem, 342–343. New York: Garland, 1993.

Jones, Jacquie. "The Construction of Black Sexuality." In *Black American Cinema*, ed. Manthia Diawara, 247–256. New York: Routledge, 1993.

Jules-Rosette, Bennetta. *Josephine Baker in Art and Life*. Champaign: University of Illinois Press, 2007.

Jung, Carl Gustav. *Psychology and Religion*. New Haven, Conn.: Yale University Press, 1963 (1938).

Keeling, Kara. *The Witch's Flight*. Durham, N.C.: Duke University Press, 2007.

Knight, Arthur. *Disintegrating the Musical: Black Performance and American Musical Film*. Durham, N.C.: Duke University Press, 2002.

———. "Star Dances: African-American Constructions of Stardom, 1925–1960." In *Classic Hollywood, Classic Whiteness*, ed. Daniel Bernardi, 386–414. Minneapolis: University of Minnesota Press, 2001.

Koszarski, Richard. *The Man You Loved to Hate: Erich Von Stroheim and Hollywood*. New York: Oxford University Press, 1983.

Kydd, Elspeth. "'The Ineffaceable Curse of Cain': Racial Marking and Embodiment in *Pinky*." *Camera Obscura* 43, no. 15 (2000): 95–119.

Lacan, Jacques. *Ecrits*. New York: W. W. Norton, 1977.

Lamparski, Richard. *Whatever Became Of?* New York: Crown, 1985.

Lant, Antonia, with Ingrid Periz, eds. *Red Velvet Seat: Women's Writings on the First Fifty Years of Cinema.* London: Verso, 2006.

Lee, Raymond. "A Walk in the Silents." *Offbeat* 1, no. 6 [date not legible]: 20. In the Academy of Motion Picture Arts and Sciences, Margaret Herrick Library, Beverly Hills, California.

Lesage, Julia. "Artful Racism, Artful Rape: Griffith's *Broken Blossoms*." In *Home Is Where the Heart Is: Studies in Melodrama and the Woman's Film,* ed. Christine Gledhill, 244–252. London: British Film Institute, 1987.

Lott, Eric. "Love and Theft: 'Racial' Production and the Social Unconscious of Blackface." In *Love and Theft: Blackface Minstrelsy and the American Working Class,* 38–62. New York: Oxford University Press, 1993.

MacFarlane, Fenella. "Scott, Hazel." In *Black Women in America: An Historical Encyclopedia,* vol. 2, ed. Darlene Clark Hine. New York: Carlson, 1993. 1019–1020.

"*Maid of Salem*." *Variety,* March 10, 1937. In *Variety Film Reviews, 1934–1937,* vol. 5. New York: Garland Publishing, 1983.

Margaret Herrick Library. Academy of Motion Pictures Arts and Sciences, Beverly Hills, California

Mask, Mia. *Divas on Screen: Black Women in American Film.* Champaign: University of Illinois Press, 2009.

Massood, Paula. *Black City Cinema: African American Urban Experiences in Film.* Philadelphia, Pa.: Temple University Press, 2003.

Mayne, Judith. *Cinema and Spectatorship.* London: Routledge, 1993.

Meese, Elizabeth, and Alice Parker, eds. *The Difference Within.* Philadelphia: John Benjamins, 1989.

Minh-Ha, Trin T. *Where the Moon Waxes Red: Representation, Gender, and Cultural Politics.* New York: Routledge, 1991.

Modleski, Tania. *Feminisim Without Women: Culture and Criticism in a "Postfeminist" Age.* New York: Routledge, 1991.

Moritz, Charles, ed. "Horne, Lena." In *Current Biography Yearbook 1985.* New York: H. W. Wilson, 1986.

Morris, Sarah P. "Beavers, Louise." In *Black Women in America: An Historical Encyclopedia,* ed. Darlene Clark Hine, 104–105. New York: Carlson, 1993.

Morrison, Toni. *Beloved.* New York: Alfred Knopf, 1987.

———. *Playing in the Dark: Whiteness and the Literary Imagination.* New York: Vintage Books/Random House, 1992.

Morse, Evan. "Ethel Waters." In *Black Women in America: An Historical Encyclopedia,* ed. Darlene Clark Hine, 1236–1238. New York: Carlson, 1993.

Muller, John P., and William J. Richardson. *Lacan and Language: A Reader's Guide to Ecrits.* New York: International Universities Press, 1982.

Mulvey, Laura. *Fetishism and Curiosity.* Bloomington: Indiana University Press, 1996.

———. "Visual Pleasure and Narrative Cinema." In *The Sexual Subject: A Screen Reader in Sexuality,* 22–34. New York: Routledge, 1992. Originally published in *Screen* 16, no. 3 (1975): 6–18.

Nash, Jay Robert, and Stanley Ralph Ross, eds. *The Motion Picture Guide Index,* vol. 12. Chicago: Cinebooks, 1987.

Negra, Diane. *Off-White Hollywood: American Culture and Ethnic Female Stardom.* London and New York: Routledge, 2001.

Noble, Peter. *The Negro in Films.* New York: Arno Press and The New York Times, 1970.

Nugent, Frank S. "The Screen in Review: *Gone with the Wind.*" *New York Times,* December 20, 1939. In *The New York Times Film Reviews, 1939–1948,* vol. 3, 1661–1662. New York: The New York Times and Arno Press, 1970.

Patterson, Lindsay, ed. *Black Films and Film-makers: A Comprehensive Anthology from Stereotype to Superhero.* New York: Dodd, Mead, and Co., 1975.

Patton, Cindy. "White Racism/Black Signs: Censorship and Images of Race Relations." *Journal of Communication* 45, no. 2 (Spring 1995): 65–77.

Pettus, Louise. "Lancaster's Celebrated Film Star." *Sandlapper: The Magazine of South Carolina.* http://www.sandlapper.org/mckinney.htm.

Petty, Miriam J. "Passing for Horror: Race, Fear, and Elia Kazan's *Pinky.*" *Genders* Issue 40 (2004). //www.genders.org/recent.html.

Poitier, Sidney. *Sidney Poitier: This Life.* New York: Alfred Knopf, 1980.

Powell, Adam Clayton, Jr. *Adam by Adam.* New York: Dial Press, 1971.

Preminger, Otto. *Preminger: An Autobiography.* New York: Doubleday, 1977.

Pryor, Thomas. "The Screen: *Stormy Weather.*" *New York Times,* July 22, 1943. In *The New York Film Reviews, 1939–1948,* vol. 3, 1948. New York: New York Times and Arno Press, 1970.

Regester, Charlene. "African American Extras in Hollywood during the 1920s and 1930s." *Film History* 9, no. 1 (1997): 95–115.

———. "The Cinematic Representation of Race in *The Birth of a Nation: A Black Horror Film.*" In *Thomas Dixon Jr. and The Birth of Modern America,* ed. Michele K. Gillespie and Randal L. Hall, 164–182. Baton Rouge, La.: Louisiana State University Press, 2006.

———. "Hazel Scott and Lena Horne: African American Divas, Feminists, and Political Activists." *Popular Culture Review* 7, no. 1 (February 1996): 81–95.

———. "Miss Em's Voyeuristic Gaze of Pinky: White Desire for Blackness." *Popular Culture Review* 14, no. 1 (February 2003): 67–85.

———. "Sylvia as a Wilting Flower and Lucy as a Broken Blossom: Examining the Construction of Black Stardom in Evelyn Preer's Career as Oscar Micheaux's Premiere Black Actress." Unpublished essay, presented at Faded Glory: Oscar Micheaux and the Pre-War Black Independent Cinema, February 6–7, 2009, Columbia University School of the Arts Film Program and Film Society of Lincoln Center, New York.

Reid, Mark. *Redefining Black Film.* Berkeley and Los Angeles: University of California Press, 1993.

Rippy, Marguerite H. "Commodity, Tragedy, Desire: Female Sexuality and Blackness in the Iconography of Dorothy Dandridge." In *Classic Hollywood, Classic Whiteness,* ed. Daniel Bernardi, 178–209. Minneapolis: University of Minnesota Press, 2001.

Robertson, Pamela. *Guilty Pleasures: Feminist Camp from Mae West to Madonna.* Durham, N.C.: Duke University Press, 1996.

Robinson, Beverly J. "Sul-Te-Wan, Madame." In *Black Women in America: An Historical Encyclopedia* vol. 2, ed. Darlene Clark Hine, 1129–1132. New York: Carlson, 1993.

Robinson, Cedric J. *Forgeries of Memory and Meaning: Blacks and the Regimes of Race in American Theater and Film before World War II.* Chapel Hill: University of North Carolina Press, 2007.

Rogin, Michael. "'Democracy and Burnt Cork': The End of Blackface, the Beginning of Civil Rights." *Representations* 46 (Spring 1994): 1–34.

Rothe, Anna, ed. "Horne, Lena." In *Current Biography Yearbook 1944*. New York: H. W. Wilson, 1945.

———. "Ethel Waters." In *Current Biography 1951*. New York: H. W. Wilson, 1945.

Rule, Sheila. "Fredi Washington, 90, Actress; Broke Ground for Black Artists." *New York Times*, June 30, 1994, D 21.

Salem, Dorothy C. "Scott, Hazel." In *African American Women: A Biographical Dictionary*, ed. Dorothy C. Salem, 444–446. New York: Garland, 1993.

Sampson, Henry. *Blacks in Black and White: A Source Book on Black Films*, 2nd ed. Metuchen, N.J.: Scarecrow Press, 1995.

Schomburg Clipping File for Research in Black Culture of the New York Public Library [microfiche]. Cambridge, U.K.: Chadwyck-Healey, 1986.

Scott, Lillian. "Fans, Not Lena Horne, Credit Star with 'Entirely New' Singing Style." *Chicago Defender*, July 31, 1948, city edition, 27.

Sennwald, Andre. "A Woman Bandit: *Ladies They Talk About*." Review of *Ladies They Talk About*. *New York Times*, February 25, 1933. In *The New York Times Film Reviews, 1932–1938*, vol. 2, 912–913. New York: The New York Times and Arno Press, 1970.

———. Review of *Sanders of the River*. *New York Times*, June 27, 1935. In *The New York Times Film Reviews, 1932–1938*, vol. 2, 1187. New York: The New York Times and Arno Press, 1970.

———. "The Screen: *Black Moon*." *New York Times*, June 28, 1934. In *The New York Times Film Reviews, 1932–1938*, vol. 2, 1074. New York: The New York Times and Arno Press, 1970.

Silva, Fred, ed. *Focus on The Birth of a Nation*. Englewood Cliffs, N.J.: Prentice-Hall, 1971.

Silverman, Kaja. *The Acoustic Mirror: The Female Voice in Psychoanalysis and Cinema*. Bloomington: Indiana University Press, 1988.

Slide, Anthony. *The Kindergarten of the Movies: A History of the Fine Arts Company*. Metuchen, N.J.: Scarecrow Press, 1980.

Smith, Valerie, ed. "Reading the Intersection of Race and Gender in Narratives of Passing." *Diacritics* 24, no. 2–3 (Summer–Fall 1994): 43–57.

———. *Representing Blackness: Issues in Film and Video*. New Brunswick, N.J.: Rutgers University Press, 1997.

Snead, James. *White Screens, Black Images: Hollywood From the Dark Side*. Edited by Colin MacCabe and Cornel West. New York: Routledge, 1994.

———. "Spectatorship and Capture in *King Kong*: The Guilty Look." In *Representing Blackness: Issues in Film and Video*, ed. Valerie Smith, 25–45. New Brunswick, N.J.: Rutgers University Press, 1997.

Sotiropoulos, Karen. *Staging Race: Black Performers in Turn of the Century America*. Cambridge, Mass.: Harvard University Press, 2006.

Spada, James. *Peter Lawford: The Man Who Kept Secrets*. New York: Bantam Books, 1991.

Spillers, Hortense J. "Notes on an Alternative Model—Neither/Nor." In *The Difference Within: Feminism and Critical Theory*, ed. Elizabeth Meese and Alice Parker, 165–187. Amsterdam, Neth.: John Benjamins, 1989.

St. John, Maria. "'It Ain't Fittin': Cinematic and Fantasmatic Contours of Mammy in *Gone with the Wind* and Beyond." *Qui Parle* 11, no. 2 (Fall/Winter 1999): 135.

Stanfield, Peter. "An Excursion in the Lower Depths: Hollywood, Urban Primitivism, and *St. Louis Blues*, 1929–1937." *Cinema Journal* 41, no. 2 (Winter 2002): 96.

Stewart, Jacqueline. *Migrating to the Movies: Cinema and Black Urban Modernity.* Berkeley: University of California Press, 2005.

Stokes, Melvyn. *D. W. Griffith's The Birth of a Nation: A History of "The Most Controversial Motion Picture of All Time."* New York: Oxford University Press, 2007.

Taylor, Helen. *Scarlett's Women: Gone with the Wind and Its Female Fans.* New Brunswick, N.J.: Rutgers University Press, 1989.

Testimony of Hazel Scott Powell. Hearing before the House Un-American Activities Committee, House of Representatives, Eighty-First Congress Second Session, September 22, 1950. Washington: U.S. Government Printing Office, 1951.

Thomas, Nicholas. *International Dictionary of Films & Filmmakers: Actors and Actresses,* vol. 3, 2nd ed. Detroit, Mich.: St. James Press, 1990.

Thompson, Kathleen. "Horne, Lena." In *Black Women in America: An Historical Encyclopedia,* vol. 1, ed. Darlene Clark Hine, 580–584. New York: Carlson, 1993.

——. "McKinney, Nina Mae." In *Black Women in America: An Historical Encyclopedia,* vol. 2, ed. Darlene Clark Hine, 772–773. New York: Carlson, 1993.

Tucker, Sherrie. *Swing Shift: "All-Girl" Bands of the 1940s.* Durham, N.C.: Duke University Press, 2000.

Tuskegee Institute News Clipping File, 1899–1966 on Microfilm, Tuskegee Institute, Tuskegee, Ala.

Vera, Hernan, and Andrew M. Gordon. *Screen Saviors: Hollywood Fictions of Whiteness.* Lanham, Md.: Rowman & Littlefield Publishers, 2003.

Vick, Marsha. "Ethel Waters." In *Notable Black American Women,* ed. Jessie Carney Smith, 1225–1226. Detroit, Mich.: Gale Research, 1992.

Wallace, Michele. *Dark Designs & Visual Culture.* Durham, N.C.: Duke University Press, 2004.

——. "The Good Lynching and *The Birth of a Nation:* Discourses and Aesthetics of Jim Crow." *Cinema Journal* 43, no. 1 (Fall 2003): 85–104.

——. "Race, Gender and Psychoanalysis in Forties Film: *Lost Boundaries, Home of the Brave,* and *The Quiet One.*" In *Black American Cinema,* ed. Manthia Diawara, 257–271. New York: Routledge, 1993.

Warren, Nagueyalti. "Hattie McDaniel: Hi-Hat-Hattie." In *Notable Black American Women,* ed. Jessie Carney Smith, 340–342. Detroit, Mich.: Gale Research, 1992.

——. "Nina Mae McKinney." In *Notable Black American Women,* ed. Jessie Carney Smith, 707–708. Detroit, Mich.: Gale Research, 1992.

——. "Louise Beavers." In *Notable Black American Women,* ed. Jessie Carney Smith, 75–77. Detroit, Mich.: Gale Research 1992.

Wartenberg, Thomas E. "Humanizing the Beast: *King Kong* and the Representation of Black Male Sexuality." In *Classic Hollywood, Classic Whiteness,* ed. Daniel Bernardi, 157–177. Minneapolis: University of Minnesota Press, 2001.

Washington, Fredi. "Biographical Notes." Fredi Washington Papers.

Waters, Ethel, and Charles Samuels. *His Eye Is On the Sparrow.* Garden City, N.Y.: Doubleday & Co., 1951.

Watts, Jill. *Hattie McDaniel: Black Ambition, White Hollywood.* New York: Amistad/Harper Collins, 2005.

Weisenfeld, Judith. *Hollywood By Thy Name: African American Religion in American Film, 1929–1949*. Berkeley and Los Angeles: University of California Press, 2007.

Wiley, Mason. *Inside Oscar: The Unofficial History of the Academy Awards*, 4th ed. New York: Ballantine, 1993.

Williams, Linda. *Playing the Race Card: Melodramas of Black and White From Uncle Tom's Cabin to O. J. Simpson*. Princeton, N.J.: Princeton University Press, 2001.

Williams, Megan E. "*The Crisis* Cover Girl: Lena Horne, The NAACP, and Representations of African American Femininity, 1941–1945." *American Periodicals* 16, no. 2 (2006): 200–218.

Williamson, Joel. "How Black Was Rhett Butler?" In *The Evolution of Southern Culture*, ed. Numan V. Bartley, 87–107. Athens: University of Georgia Press, 1988.

Wilson, Earl. "Keeping Abreast of Hazel: Condensed from *New York Post*." *Negro Digest*, January 1944, 44.

Young, Lola. *Fear of the Dark: Race, Gender and Sexuality in the Cinema*. London: Routledge, 1996.

INDEX

Abbott, Robert, 104

Abramson, Dan, 193, 213–214

Academy Award: for Berry, 331; black actresses overlooked for, 10, 15–16, 98; for Goldberg, 330; for McDaniel, 8, 10, 12, 134, 140–143, 161

Academy Award nomination: for Dandridge, 286, 295; for Waters, 247, 280

Affectionately Yours (1941), 134

African American actors. *See specific actors* (e.g., Belafonte, Harry; Robeson, Paul)

African American actresses: invisibility of, 8–9, 19, 34–39, 265–267, 327, 330; visibility of, 19–39, 265–267, 327. *See also specific actresses* (e.g., Dandridge, Dorothy; Waters, Ethel); Other, racial; roles, for African American actresses; shadow, to white actresses

African American audiences, 50, 101, 131

African American press: on Beavers, 15–16, 99–100; on *Broadway Rhythm,* 194–195; on Dandridge, 291–292, 310–312; on *Gone With the Wind,* 149–150; on Horne, 178, 181, 186, 188–189, 196–197, 199, 208; on *I Dood It,* 224; on *Imitation of Life,* 98–101; on *Island in the Sun,* 299; on McDaniel, 139–148, 161–172;

on McKinney, 54–57, 60, 63, 66, 69–70; on *The Member of the Wedding,* 264–265; on Scott, 219, 224–235, 237; on Sul-Te-Wan, 33, 36–38; on *Till the Clouds Roll By,* 201–202; on Washington, 114, 122–123; on Waters, 253–254, 268, 280. *See also* mainstream press

Africana (Broadway show), 246

Akst, Harry, 267

Alice Adams (1935), 134–135

Allbrite, Harding, 301

Allen, Gracie, 235

Allyson, June, 193, 196, 200, 202

Anderson, Eddie "Rochester," 86, 182, 184, 190, 195, 274, *figure 8, figure 9*

Anderson, Louisa Tar, 245

Anderson, Marian, 235, 238

Anderson, Mary, 20

Anderson, Sally, 245

Another Face (1935), 134

Arthur Russell (character), 135

As Thousands Cheer (stage musical), 246

As You Like It (Shakespeare), 145

Astaire, Fred, 197

Astor, Mary, 193

At Home Abroad (1935), 246

Atlantic City (1944), 285

audiences, African American. *See* African American audiences

Charlene Regester is Associate Professor of African and Afro-American Studies at the University of North Carolina Chapel Hill. She co-edits the *Oscar Micheaux Society Newsletter* and serves as an editorial board member of the *Journal of Film and Video*.